T
0-82
MO

Principles and Practices of TEACHING READING

Principles and Practices of TEACHING READING Fourth Edition

ARTHUR W. HEILMAN
Pennsylvania State University

CHARLES E. MERRILL PUBLISHING COMPANY
A Bell & Howell Company
Columbus   Toronto   London   Sydney

Published by
CHARLES E. MERRILL PUBLISHING COMPANY
A Bell & Howell Company
Columbus, Ohio 43216

This book was set in Caledonia.
The Production Editor was Cynthia Donaldson.
The cover was prepared by Will Chenoweth.

International Standard Book Number: 0-675-08537-3

Library of Congress Catalog Card Number: 76-51089

4 5 6 7 8 9 10 / 82 81 80

Printed in the United States of America

Photo Credits

The author and the publisher wish to thank the following individuals and organizations for use of the photographs which illustrate this text. The Charles F. Kettering Foundation photos were taken in conjunction with the Dartmouth College Jersey City Project.

C. F. Kettering Foundation (Weir McBride photographer): pp. 62, 63, 232, 296, 300, 317, 326, 327, 329, 342, 457, 504.

Cincinnati Public Schools: pp. 224, 511.

De Wys, Inc.: p. 469.

Dr. and Mrs. James B. Ebersole: p. 229.

Ford Foundation (Ellen Levine photographer): p. 3.
            (William R. Simmons photographer): p. 239.

H. Armstrong Roberts: p. 179.

National Education Association (Joe Di Dio photographer): pp. 393, 456.
            (Ben Spiegel photographer): p. 520.

Cover photograph courtesy of H. Armstrong Roberts.

All other photographs were taken by William J. Stoll.

To Dorothy

Preface

The fourth edition of *Principles and Practices of Teaching Reading* continues to focus on children as learners who are engaged in the process called *reading*. However, considerable emphasis has been added on the *hidden agenda* which is part of all reading conference and in-service programs; namely, the ubiquitous question, "How do you motivate children to read?"

The question is important because it implies we are doing something in the school which interferes with reading becoming a self-sustaining activity for many pupils. The problem may be the purposes for which reading is used in the school. Is it possible that children are continually asked to read material which they sense can never make a difference in their lives? Do their reading assignments really grab their minds and draw them deeper into reading? Do curricular materials imbue children with a felt need for more reading?

The purpose of the school is twofold: 1) to help children develop and expand concepts; and 2) to help them develop language tools which will make them self-sufficient learners. Schools have overemphasized the teaching of factual concepts to the point where "digging the facts" has become the nemesis of both teachers and learners. On the other hand, reading instruction fails to transmit to children an appreciation of the power, beauty, and precision that can be attained in language usage. Language is the only magic available to the school, and not to use it fully is counter productive. Developing the ability to manipulate language must become the schools' top priority.

Educators must have the vision for schools that Faulkner had for mankind. It is not enough for our schools to *survive*—they must prevail. Facts are transient but the mastery of language insures the validity of

Thomas Paine's observation that every man of learning eventually becomes his own teacher.

Many users of the third edition have offered helpful comments for this revision. Their time and interest is greatly appreciated. Specifically, I want to thank Prof. Florence C. Franmeni and Prof. A. Sterl Artley for their extensive comments, and Miss Ruby Thompson, the senior author of Chapter 11.

I wish to acknowledge the contribution of members of the Editorial Production and Art Staff of Charles E. Merrill Publishing, particularly Cynthia Donaldson, editor, who worked with me on this fourth edition.

Arthur W. Heilman
March, 1977

Contents

Part 2   Beyond Beginning Reading

PART 1

Foundations for Teaching Reading

Chapter 1

Principles of Teaching Reading

The Purpose of the School

"The purpose of the school is to guide students in developing and expanding concepts, along with the tools for doing this." The tools are language and reading.

What Is Reading?

Reading is interacting with language that has been coded into print. The uncontrolled variable is the degree of interaction that is posited. In some cases reading may involve getting the meaning. This is likely to occur only occasionally if one is reading the Bible, tax laws, James Joyce, or even the Constitution of the United States. The fact that experts have never agreed on the definitions of reading is probably not highly significant. Reading is a bit complicated. Terms such as *love, salvation, democracy,* and *intelligence* present much the same problem.

It was once current practice to define intelligence as "something that an intelligence test measures." It would be equally meaning__ (ful-less) to define reading as "what a good reader does when he is reading." Huey was either defining reading or suggesting that we not worry too much about defining it when he wrote

> And so to completely analyze what we do when we read would almost be the acme of a psychologist's achievements, for it would be to describe very many of the most intricate workings of the human mind, as well as to unravel the tangled story of the most remarkable specific performance that civilization has learned in all its history (6).

The question "what is reading" is of little consequence to the man in the street, bookstore proprietor, editor of the local paper, or the community's most successful professional writer. However, one's concept of what reading is would seem to be of considerable importance to the person whose primary task is to teach reading. The following discussion deals with the two facets of reading that teachers must get into proper perspective if they are to guide children's growth in reading. These are

decoding print into sound.

decoding a graphic representative of language into meaning.

Ab se bo sem fleebat is a series of speech sounds frequently heard in English, but to speak the above with any of several intonation patterns would not meet the requirement of language usage. One important criterion of language is missing. There has been no agreement as to the meaning of those speech sounds in the order found here.

"Anyone who can read English can ____ this material"
The word you decide upon can provide insight into your definition of reading.

If *ab se bo sem fleebat* happened to be the graphic representation of an utterance found in the English language, one could not "read" it unless he knew or could discover what spoken words were represented by the graphic symbols. The potential reader might

1. Know each printed word symbol as a sight word.
2. Recognize some words at sight and analyze letter sounds in others until he "hits" upon the pronunciation of each of the printed word symbols.

3. Assign intonation patterns which at least approximate those which would be acceptable in oral English usage.

Would he also, in order to qualify as a reader, have to ascribe particular meanings to each word symbol as well as to the "total word combination?"

A third grader had just been asked to interpret this sentence, " 'I will sample your wares,' said the traveler." Following the child's response, the teacher said in a kindly voice, "John, I believe you read that wrong—the traveler was going to *buy* something from the peddler, not *sell* him something." The point of this illustration is that the teacher had not heard John read the sentence in question, yet she said, "I believe you *read* it wrong."

A further insight might be gained by reference to another sentence in English. "As face answereth face in water, so the heart of man speaketh to man." Many primary-level readers could read aloud (i.e., pronounce) each word in this passage, but many of these same children could not arrive at an understanding of its meaning. (In essence, no further context is needed.) A school curriculum committee examining a science or social science text which contained many concepts at the difficulty level of this example would agree that, "This book is too difficult for third graders to read." Few, if any, critics of this position would counter with "most third graders can recognize the words in this book. I recommend it be adopted."

The following are English sentences. Anyone who reads English will have no trouble with word recognition or intonation:

1. Some squares do not have four sides.
2. Thomas Jefferson was a friend of Tyranny.

These sentences, like all reading situations, demand reader interaction. The person reading "Some squares do not have four sides" might react in any of a number of ways: "This is a misprint—it should say, 'all squares have four sides.' No, maybe that's not the kind of square it means; Michael Philbutt is a square and he doesn't have four sides. No, that's not what it means. Now a square is a plane figure, but it has a front and back, or does it have a back side? That's either five or six sides. What is the author talking about? Well, no matter what he means, I don't see how he can say that some squares do not have four sides. Maybe this is one of those trick statements. I better read another paragraph or two. If that doesn't help, I'll ask someone."

In sentence two, a reader with no background knowledge about Jefferson might reason, "Well, it's good to be apprised of this man's character. I'll be suspicious of everything he says or writes, particularly about government and people's rights." With any degree of historical background, however, one immediately says, "How ridiculous! Who is writing this stuff; where was this book published? I better read a little more, this might be a misprint. Didn't Jefferson say, 'I have sworn eternal hostility to every form of tyranny over the mind of man?' This statement is weird."

While the above discussion has not provided a specific definition of reading, it has attempted to put the two essentials, decoding and arriving at meaning, in proper perspective. Recognizing, or distinguishing between, printed word symbols is an absolutely necessary prerequisite for reading. But the mere pronunciation of words is not reading until this act of recognition evokes meaning(s) which the written words-in-combination carry in oral language usage.

There are simpler concepts as to what the reading process involves. A number of these concepts, however, fail to take into consideration the interdependent relationship between word recognition and word meaning. Teachers of reading, as well as of other school subjects, must understand the complex nature of reading. Accepting a definition which is too simple can easily result in overemphasis on one facet of the learning process.

Teaching reading is undoubtedly as complex as defining it. Today, there is general agreement that reading programs never rise above the quality of the instruction found in them. Teaching must be based on understanding of children as learners, and learning to read must be viewed as a long-term developmental process. These concepts lead logically into a discussion of *principles* of reading instruction.

The principles found in this chapter can be thought of as guidelines that should govern teaching behavior. Principles do not spell out instructional practices that are to be followed, but they can provide the criteria for evaluating practices. It is possible that one could hold to certain principles which would preclude the use of a particular set of materials or methodology. More likely, however, one would adjust or adapt practices in order to make principles and practices compatible. Sound principles of instruction tend to be learner-oriented; therefore, they do not vary from grade level to grade level. They can be applied quite consistently to children who are noticeably different in regard to capacity, interest, and experience.

Principles of teaching reading should evolve from the best knowledge available in the fields of psychology, educational psychology, and curriculum planning, from studies in child growth and development, and from child-guidance and psychological clinics. In formulating these principles, it is necessary to consider all facets of human growth and development, including the intellectual, physiological, and emotional.

Most teachers are familiar with the principles discussed in the following pages. Like scientific laws, the principles of teaching reading are subject to modification or repeal as new data are discovered and new theories erected on the basis of these data. Some readers will undoubtedly feel that one (or more) of the following principles is not absolutely valid. Such questioning is healthy, especially if it stimulates the formulation of rational alternatives. If the following principles are a sound basis for teaching reading at all levels of instruction, there are many practices in our schools which need to be reexamined.

Principles Related to Instruction

Disregarding for the moment the wide range of methods-materials available for teaching reading, *there are some guidelines or principles of instruction that merit teacher attention.*

1. *Reading is a language process. The child being taught to read must understand the relationship between reading and his language.* Much has been written about "what the child brings to school" and that the school must *build on the skills children have acquired.* In the final analysis, the only thing the child brings to school that can transfer to learning to read is the language he uses.

Unfortunately, many of the child's early experiences in beginning reading tend to mask the fact that he is engaged in a language process. He is asked to focus on single words and letters within words. While such analysis is essential, instruction should prevent the new reader from *equating* these skills with reading. One more step is essential: Reading must incorporate the melody of oral language. This leads to the next principle.

2. *During every reading-instruction period, students should read and discuss something that grabs their minds. This can be a brief passage through which children experience the power and beauty of language.* Many children are turned away from reading because of what the school asks them to read. The curriculum and curricular material are fact oriented. Teachers should make sure that each day, students have

an opportunity to manipulate and interpret a bit of nontextbook language. A rule of thumb that might be applied is that a good riddle is worth six facts; two malapropisms equal eight state capitols; and any sentence that is so powerful that "it should be preserved for posterity" more than equals any chapter in any sixth grade textbook.

Reading for meaning is reading.

3 3. *Instruction should lead children to understand that reading must result in meaning.* This principle applies to all stages of reading instruction. It means that reading is more than a mechanical process, even though mechanics are an essential part of the process. It rejects the thesis that beginning reading deals only with mechanics and that *meaning* is an additive to be inserted at some later point on the learning continuum.

If this principle is followed from the start, it mitigates the possibility that children will develop a *set* that reading is saying or sounding out words. For some reason, this particular set resists extinction, and unless children are reading for meaning, they cannot translate print into the language patterns that it represents.

This principle does not imply that some instructional periods cannot focus on isolated skills such as letter-sound relationships. Obviously, all facile readers master such skills, not in lieu of critical reading, but as part of the process.

4 4. *Pupil differences must be a primary consideration in reading instruction.* This implies that instruction cannot be dominated by the grade-level system, promotion practices, or graded instructional materials. It is hypothesized that any classroom will house pupils whose present achievement and instructional needs vary greatly. Identical educational experiences, particularly reading the same material, cannot be equally effective for all. Differentiation of both instruction and free-choice reading will inevitably result in larger pupil differences, which in turn will call for more differentiation.

Culturally different children are now recognized by the school as providing a major challenge in regard to meeting their individual needs. We have known for years that extreme cultural-economic differences exist in our society. Further, we have known that these differences in culture and deficits in standard of living affected school learning. Until recently, however, this knowledge resulted in no significant changes in the curriculum or teaching methods. A school attended exclusively by culturally different black children would confront them with a curriculum that was no different from the one found in a school twenty miles away in the suburbs.

The educational philosophies we verbalized were always adequate to take care of this problem, i.e., "fit the teaching to the child," "meet him where he is," "teach to his needs and interests," "build readiness for learning." Unfortunately, we never implemented this philosophy; however, some of the educational practices which resulted from the new awareness of poverty and the ghetto are discussed in Chapter 11.

5. *Proper reading instruction depends on the diagnosis of each child's weaknesses and needs.* This principle is applicable to ordinary classroom teaching, as well as to remedial reading. Individual diagnosis in reading has somehow become associated more with "retarded" readers and pupils with a clinical history of nonlearning than with ordinary classroom procedure. Diagnosis has become associated too often with cure or remedy rather than with preventing the development of poor reading. In many cases, proper diagnosis will warn a teacher before bad habits or unhealthy emotional reactions cripple a potentially capable reader.

A survey test used as the basis for grouping children into poorest, average, and best categories is not in itself a diagnosis. To know that children A, B, and C are among the poorest in the class and that they are reading at least a year below their grade level tells us nothing about what it is that inhibits their reading progress. Nor does such a test tell us what aspect of reading should be attacked first in order to improve the child's reading. To determine that a child is reading below what might be expected is not diagnosis. It is an invitation to diagnosis.

6. *The best diagnosis is useless unless it is used as a blueprint for instruction.* Diagnosis itself has no salutary effect on the performance of

the child tested. If diagnosis alone had salutary effects, it would be possible to raise a child's level of performance indefinitely by more and more diagnosis. It may be noted that extensive testing and metal filing cabinets full of individual folders do not necessarily make a better school. Testing in many American schools has become an end in itself. When test results are not used for instructional purposes, the educational objectives of the testing program are defeated.

There is no area of the curriculum in American schools more ideally suited to constant diagnosis than reading in the elementary and intermediate grades. The good teacher knows this and proceeds with continuous diagnosis of the children in her room. She knows that numerous factors inhibit progress in reading during this period. Any skill not mastered or only partially mastered may be instrumental in producing other reading problems. A teacher's manual or curriculum guide can point out a logical sequence for introducing skills and tasks, but it offers no help in determining what in the sequence has been learned. The manual or guide is like an artist's conception of the total edifice before it is constructed. Intelligent instruction must be based on accurate information regarding children's present accomplishments and weaknesses. In this sense, a thorough diagnosis is a blueprint for instruction.

7. *Any given technique, practice, or procedure is likely to work better with some children than with others. Hence, the teacher of reading must have a variety of approaches.* Virtually every method and procedure described in the vast literature on reading is reported to have been successful with some children and unsuccessful with others. Therefore, creativity and versatility are basic requirements for successful teaching. If a teacher begins to take sides in methodological squabbles, or if she begins to crystalize her ideas on an either/or basis, she is likely to be less receptive to other points of view and approaches which may be helpful to her teaching.

Authorities in the field of reading are in general agreement that "there is no one best method of teaching." The evidence indicates that one method is not necessarily superior to another. Regardless of the efficiency of a given method of teaching reading, it will produce its share of problem cases and impaired readers if used exclusively. If there are significant individual differences in the way children learn to read, it follows that different approaches are advisable. Unfortunately, children do not have identifiable characteristics which make it possible to know at a glance which approach will yield the highest return in learning. For this reason, flexibility, ingenuity, and creativity are essential to successful teaching, particularly for teaching reading.

When a teacher becomes enamored of one method to the exclusion of others, she shuts out the possibility of adjusting this method to individual pupil needs. Although such a teacher may be highly successful in teaching some of her pupils, she will inevitably produce a number of frustrated, unhappy misfits in the educational arena. If she is authoritarian and presses hard, some of her pupils will develop behaviors which result in such labels as *bad, dull, dreamers, lazy,* and *antisocial.* These behaviors, instead of being interpreted as the logical psychological outcome of failure, frustration, and tension evolving from the reading situation, become in turn the explanations of why the child failed in reading.

8. *Early in the learning process the child must acquire ways of gaining independence in identifying words whose meanings are known to him but which are unknown to him as sight words.* Pronouncing words is not reading, but sounding out words not known as sight words is essential in independent reading. The more widely a child reads, the less likely it is that he will know as a sight word every word he meets. Hence, developing independence in reading depends on acquiring methods of unlocking the pronunciation of words. The clues used in identifying words, discussed in later chapters, include unique configuration of words, structural analysis (prefixes, suffixes), context clues, and phonic analysis. Phonics is undoubtedly the most important of the word analysis skills.

The Cooperative Reading Studies (2, 5) reported data on a number of methodological issues. In many instances the data failed to reveal any clear cut superiority for particular instructional procedures and materials. However, in regard to the efficacy of teaching letter-sound relationships, the findings were remarkably uniform. Programs of instruction which featured systematic phonics instruction resulted in consistently superior pupil reading achievement when compared with programs which did not.

The principle just discussed is not in conflict with our previous statement that the child must see reading as a meaning-making process. To read for meaning, one must be able to recognize printed word forms. Those words which are not instantly recognized must be analyzed by associating printed letters with speech sounds.

9. *Learning to read is a long-term developmental process extending over a period of years.* This principle rests on two premises. First, every aspect of the instructional program is related to the ultimate goal of producing efficient readers. This is particularly important in light of the many recent "newer approaches" to beginning reading instruction. What is done during this period influences the child's concept as

to what constitutes reading. In other words, beginning reading instruction can inculcate any one of a number of pupil *sets*.

The second premise is that the child's early attitude toward reading is important from the educational standpoint. It can influence a student's reading habits for life. Nothing should be permitted to happen in beginning instruction which impairs later development of efficient reading.

There are several approaches to beginning reading which may result in a "fast start" or relatively high achievement at the end of a year of intensive instruction. The materials used stress analysis of letter sounds and, in the opinion of some observers, fail to achieve a balanced program. The overemphasis on analysis permits rapid initial growth, but carries with it the potential of producing readers who overlearn this specific technique. Some pupils will tend to overrely on analysis to the detriment of smooth facile reading.

The question which teachers must answer is, "Do higher reading achievement scores at the end of grade one establish the procedures and materials used as the best approach to *beginning reading instruction?*" If principle nine is accepted as valid, the question cannot be answered on the basis of the short-term achievement.

10. *The concept of readiness should be extended upward to all grades.* Few teachers maintain that readiness applies more to one level of education than to another. Nevertheless, in the area of reading, there seems to be a preference for associating readiness with beginning or first-grade reading. This is the level at which we have "readiness tests," and much of the literature on readiness is concerned with the beginning reader. Even though readiness has been achieved at one level of experience, it does not necessarily follow that readiness is retained at a higher level of experience. There should be as much concern with readiness at the third-, fourth-, or sixth-grade levels as there is at the first-grade level.

A good start is an important factor in the learning process. But a good start is not always half the race because reading is a continuous developmental process. What is learned today is the foundation for what is learned tomorrow. A smooth, unfaltering first step is not a guarantee that succeeding steps will be equally smooth. For example, some children display no complications in learning until they are asked to sound out a number of words not known at sight. At this point they encounter difficulties, the degree of which could not have been predicted on the basis of readiness tests administered in the first grade. Even so, some of these failures stem from nonreadiness for the experience.

11. *Emphasis should be on prevention rather than cure. Reading problems should be detected early and corrected before they deteriorate into failure-frustration-reaction cases.* However excellent the instruction in our schools, some children will not profit as much as others. The early detection of impairments and immediate attention to them are cornerstones of effective reading instruction. Although this may be obvious, the emphasis in our schools is still on cure, not prevention.

//

12. *No child should be expected or forced to attempt to read material which at the moment he is incapable of reading.* Although applied here specifically to reading, this principle has a much wider application in our schools. All curriculum study and the placing of learning tasks at different points on the educational continuum are related to this principle. The principle should be followed in all areas of child growth and development—physical, social, emotional, intellectual. The principle amounts to a rejection of the myth that "the child is a miniature adult." We know that he is not. Today, informed teachers and parents expect the average child of six years to have developed social and emotional responses only to a level of maturity commensurate with his experience.

/2

This principle is also related to the fact that different children develop at different rates and that the growth pattern of an individual child is not uniform. The data from which we derive norms or averages of physical, emotional, social, and intellectual growth warn us that there are differences in rates of development. The principle does not imply that children should avoid difficult tasks or that a child should be able to read a passage perfectly before he attempts to read it. It does imply that we cannot expect a child to perform up to a given standard when at the moment he is incapable of such performance. To do this is to expect the impossible.

The following episode, although it illustrates the point under discussion, is not advanced as being representative of teacher practice. Arrangements were made in an elementary school for thorough testing of a number of pupils who were not making expected academic progress. One fourth-grade boy could read successfully no higher than primer level. The counselor inquired of the boy's teacher what reading program he was following. The teacher explained that for a while she had the boy attempt to read third-grade materials. Failing in these, he was given second-grade materials with no better success. Since the boy read these materials no better than he read the fourth-grade texts, the teacher concluded that he might as well read the fourth-grade books. Even teachers who would not endorse this solution may occasionally expect a child to do what he cannot do at the moment. Untold numbers of pupils face such a situation, and probably more instances occur because of lack of reading ability than for all other reasons combined.

A given child may have average or superior overall ability but currently may be below grade norm in his reading. With proper guidance, he may later master the reading process commensurate with his ability. Each child is entitled to the best guidance available. It is not conducive to social, emotional, or educational growth to subject a child to failure experiences because he is physically present in a classroom where arbitrary achievement goals have been set.

13. *A child capable of advancing to a higher level of reading should not be prevented from doing so.* This principle warns against instruction becoming a prisoner of graded materials. In the upper primary and intermediate levels, a child may be able to move through graded materials at a much faster pace than does the average reader. He may also have less need for and less interest in these materials. This child should be encouraged to move at his own pace and select materials of his own choosing.

Locating supplementary reading materials can be a joint teacher-pupil effort.

14. *Learning to read is a complicated process, one sensitive to a variety* */4*
of pressures. Too much pressure or the wrong kind of pressure may
result in nonlearning. A fact that attests to the complexity of the reading process is that authorities have never agreed on one definition of
reading. There are, however, many statements about the complexity
of reading on which experts would agree. Reading is a language function. It is the manipulation of symbolic materials. Psychologists and
other observers of human behavior tell us that the symbolic process is
sensitive to many pressures. Language is the most sensitive indicator
of personal or emotional maladjustment. Yet, in no area of learning in
our schools is greater pressure brought to bear on the pupil than in
the area of reading. This is partly due to the high value which our
society places on education and to the recognition that education is
based on reading skill.

Often the school and the home present a united front in exerting
overt and subtle pressures on the child (7). Reading is the first school
task in which the child is deliberately or inadvertently compared with
others in his peer group. It is the first task in which he must compete.
How he fares in this competition has a tremendous impact on his ego,
his concept of himself, and the attitudes of his peers toward him. But,
most important, this is the first school activity in which his performance
has a direct impact on his parents' egos. Parents may sense that their
anxiety is not an intelligent or mature response. Insofar as the average
parents can be coldly analytical of their motivation and involvement
in their child's nonsuccess in reading, they know their feelings are
never far below the surface. These feelings of disappointment are perceived by the child as a judgment that he does not measure up to parents' expectations.

15. *Children should not be in the classroom if they have emotional* */5*
problems sufficiently serious to make them uneducable at the moment
or if they interfere with or disrupt the learning process. Physical dis-
turbances such as a slight temperature, an inflamed throat, an ab-
scessed tooth, or a skin blemish are cause for removing a child from
the classroom. Many schools require that children not come to school
until inoculated against certain diseases; other schools strongly urge
these precautions. These measures seem natural and logical today. The
suggestion that serious emotional problems be corrected before a child
can attend school will probably be scoffed at—today. Tomorrow the
concept of emotional health will be as readily accepted as the concept
of physical health. Just as the practice of "beating the devil" out of the
"obsessed" came to an end, so we will stop trying to beat learning into
a child who is at the moment uneducable.

The reason for emphasizing emotional health in a book on reading is that our entire educational structure is based on the ability to read. One of the principles stated earlier was that a child should not be expected to do something he cannot do. When a child is uneducable because of serious emotional involvements and we persist in drilling him on sight words which he cannot learn, we are violating this earlier principle. Unless the classroom teacher can overcome the barrier to learning, the uneducable child should leave the classroom while being treated and return when he is educable. The vast majority of youngsters with emotional problems can be helped with personal and environmental therapy. If the emotional problem is not severe, it is possible for some children to continue in school while receiving outside treatment; in some cases the treatment can take place concurrently with regular learning in the classroom. In the latter situation, the teacher is a key factor.

16. *Reading instruction should be thought of as an organized, systematic, growth-producing activity.* If any combination of strictly environmental factors will, in the absence of systematic instruction, produce optimum growth in reading, then instruction per se is superfluous. Sound instruction will start from the premise that the classroom environment is an integral part of instruction. The presence of adequate reading materials and the evolvement of a desirable classroom organization are prerequisites for good instruction. The absence of these precludes effective instruction, but their presence does not assure it.

17. *The adoption of certain instructional materials inevitably has an impact and influence on a school's instructional philosophy.* How reading should be taught has for many decades been the most widely debated topic in American education. Always, the major concern and emphasis has been on beginning reading instruction. In recent years this debate has been intensified.

It is interesting to note that for years our schools used basal reader materials almost exclusively. All such materials provided an instructional program covering the entire elementary school period. In contrast, the past fifteen years have seen many materials and methodologies introduced which focus only on beginning reading.

The materials available for beginning reading instruction reflect different philosophies which in large measure determine initial instructional strategies. The major differences in materials can be traced to the way the following pedagogical issues are treated.

1. The way initial reading-vocabulary is controlled.
2. The amount of phonics (letter-sound relationships) taught.

3. The emphasis on *meaning* in beginning instruction.
4. The degree to which various facets of the total language-arts program are integrated, specifically the emphasis on children's writing.
5. The temporary use of respellings or alphabet modifications.
6. "Content" of materials. (This, of course, is determined by prior decisions made in regard to items 1, 2, 3 above.)

Sound principles provide a "floor"
for instructional endeavors.

SUMMARY

Principles and practices should be compatible. It is logical that a book on teaching reading should open with a statement of the principles upon which good teaching is based. Principles should evolve ahead of practices so that teacher and school practices can be evaluated in light of these principles. The view accepted here is that the principles formulated above are sound and that teachers who find them so should follow them in teaching reading.

In recent times, reading instruction has been subject to considerable criticism. One response to this has been the emergence of many new (or modified) instructional materials, hailed by their producers as instructional breakthroughs. Another response—made by many schools —was to accept any new material at its advertised face value and hope that a panacea had been found. Reading instruction seems particularly susceptible to overenthusiasm for whatever bears the "new" label. Soon interest wanes, and aproaches heralded as breakthroughs are deserted for some other new approach in which interest builds to a peak and then recedes (16).

During periods of ferment, it is easy to lose sight of fundamental principles of instruction. Much time and energy can be spent in climbing on and off so-called "instructional bandwagons." Occasionally, a "new emphasis" in instruction emerges which has some excellent features but which may neglect certain essentials while overemphasizing others. Sound principles of instruction apply with equal validity to any instructional approach and to all levels of instruction.

YOUR POINT OF VIEW?

The problems following each chapter are not intended primarily to test recall of material presented. The problems may serve as a basis for class discussion or, in some instances, library research papers.

Respond to the following problems:

1. Assume you are the director of a five-year state project, the aim of which is to reduce by 60 percent the number of children experiencing reading difficulties. You have adequate financial resources to do what you want to do. What would you propose doing?
2. In your opinion, which one of the principles discussed in this chapter is the most important for improving reading instruction? Provide a rationale for your choice.
3. Assume that you are assigned the task of improving the teaching of reading in your state and that you can eliminate or modify *one* school practice which is now prevalent. What would be your recommendation? Why?
4. What would you have to add to the following statement to make it consistent with your definition of *the purpose of the school?*

    "The purpose and function of the school is to help the child develop and expand concepts, and to help him develop the language tools which will permit him to do this independently."

Defend or attack the following statements:

A. When a school system makes provisions for remedial reading instruction, it is likely that this instruction will follow sounder principles of teaching than does the regular instructional program.
B. America's free public education system is the world's foremost example of "socialized education."

C. One's definition of reading would, in the final analysis, have little impact on practices followed in teaching the reading process.

BIBLIOGRAPHY

1. Allen, James E., Jr., "The Right to Read—Target for the 70's," *Elementary English* (April 1970): 487–92.
2. Bond, Guy L. and Dykstra, Robert, "The Cooperative Research Program in First-Grade Reading Instruction," *Reading Research Quarterly* (Summer 1967): 5–142.
3. Cutts, Warren G., ed., *Teaching Young Children to Read.* Washington, D.C.: U.S. Office of Education, Bulletin No. 19, 1964.
4. Dale, R. R., "Anxiety about School among First-Year Grammar School Pupils, and Its Relation to Occupational Class and Co-Education," *British Journal of Educational Psychology* (February 1969): 18–26.
5. Dykstra, Robert, "Summary of Second-Grade Phase of the Cooperative Research Program in Primary Reading Instruction," *Reading Research Quarterly* (Fall 1968): 49–70.
6. Huey, Edmund Burke, *The Psychology and Pedagogy of Reading.* Cambridge, Mass: M.I.T. Press, 1968.
7. Ilg, Frances L. and Ames, Louise Bates, *School Readiness.* New York: Harper and Row, 1965.
8. Levin, Harry and Williams, Joanna P., *Basic Studies on Reading.* New York: Basic Books Inc., 1970.
9. Sartain, Harry W. and Stanton, Paul E., *Modular Preparation for Teaching Reading.* Newark, Del.: International Reading Association, 1974.
10. Schreiner, Robert and Tanner, Lina R., "What History Says about Teaching Reading," *Reading Teacher* 29 (February 1976): 468–73.
11. Rogers, Carl R., *Freedom to Learn.* Columbus, O.: Charles E. Merrill Publishing Co., 1969.
12. Rutherford, William L., "Five Steps to Effective Reading Instruction," *The Reading Teacher* (February 1971): 416–21.
13. Singer, Harry, "Research That Should Have Made a Difference," *Elementary English* (January 1970): 27–34.
14. Singer, Harry and Ruddell, Robert B., ed., *Theoretical Models and Processes of Reading,* second edition. Newark, Del.: International Reading Association, 1976.
15. Smith, Frank, *Understanding Reading.* New York: Holt, Rinehart and Winston, Inc., 1971.

16. Smith, Nila Banton, *American Reading Instruction*. Newark, Del.: International Reading Association, 1965.

17. Smith, Richard; Otto, Wayne; and Harty, Kathleen, "Elementary Teacher's Preferences for Pre-Service and In-Service Training in the Teaching of Reading," *Journal of Educational Research* (July–August 1970): 445–49.

18. U.S. Office of Education, *Do Teachers Make a Difference?* Washington, D.C., 1970.

Chapter **2**

Assessing and Developing Reading Readiness

The Concept of Readiness

Readiness is a factor at all reading levels, but here we will focus on readiness for beginning reading instruction. All children have been getting ready for reading throughout their preschool careers—some much more so than others—but entrance into first grade is not necessarily based on readiness for what will transpire there.

Several school-community practices militate against an ideal match up between pupil and school activities. The first of these is the legal requirement that all children begin formal education on the basis of chronological age. While this practice has some virtue from the standpoint of administration, it has little relationship to learning the complicated process of reading. Many children are absorbed into a school environment that resembles an assembly line. Each child is expected to move a specified distance along an instructional continuum within a specified time. However, some children are simply not ready to move at this predetermined rate.

A second factor is the *value* that the society has placed on *learning to read*. Our society decrees that every child must learn to read and that she must make a certain amount of progress in the first calendar year of formal instruction.

A third factor is traceable to materials and methodology. These may differ a bit from district to district, but within a given classroom the materials and methodology are rather fixed. Usually, practices found within this classroom seem to indicate a philosophy that children are interchangeable units. Each child is expected to profit equally with all others from whatever goes on in that classroom.

In summary, the above practices and expectations negate what we purport to know about individual differences. When our overt behaviors refute a principle which we allege to hold with conviction, then lip service to that principle must be intensified. Thus, given the conditions that children start school on the basis of chronological age, that reading *is* the curriculum, that all children must learn how to read because they are in school, and that they must learn with the materials and methodology adopted locally, concern for reading readiness is understandably intensified.

For several decades the term reading readiness has been used as if it had some universally accepted meaning. Recently, certain ambiguities in this concept have been discussed. MacGinitie points out that the question, "Is the child ready to read?" is poorly phrased on at least two counts. First, it ignores that learning to read is a long-term process, not a fixed point on a continuum. "Reading is a process that takes some time for any person at any age. Part way through the process, the child becomes ready to profit from experience he would have found meaningless at the beginning" (29). Secondly, he raises the question as to how readiness scores can predict reading achievement when actual methodology and instruction have not been specified.

In general, the readiness period is viewed as an attempt to synthesize new experiences with the previous experiences that children have had. These previous experiences, or the lack of them, are extremely important, since they determine to a large degree the kind and the amount of experience that is still needed and which the school must provide prior to formal instruction in reading. How accurately the teacher discerns what is still needed and how successful he is in filling these needs may well be the most important factor in determining each child's later success or failure in reading.

A good readiness program would include activities for individual pupils which lead to their later maximum success in reading. It is not aimed at removing individual differences among pupils, but at seeing that each child has experiences which will remove blocks to learning. It can be thought of as a filling-in and smoothing-out process.

Thus, it would be difficult to defend a readiness program that involved all children doing the same things for equal periods of time. Such a program would ignore the known facts about individual differences and would negate any instructional cues that might be disclosed by readiness tests. On the other hand, it must be kept in mind that there are many activities which can involve all children.

A good readiness program achieves a high degree of flexibility. In practice, however, some first-grade teachers follow a schedule of a given number of weeks of readiness activities followed by instruction in reading. At this point, responses to instruction tend to separate children into groups in which they might be labeled *unready, partially ready*, and *ready*.

When a readiness program is determined primarily by a calendar, the unready are likely to suffer at about the same intensity levels as if readiness had been totally ignored. In dealing with the unready, teachers face very difficult decisions. Both the school and the community operate from the premise that since children are in school, they must be ready for what the school has planned—in grade one this is the learning of reading. Ironically, teachers frequently rationalize some of their practices on the grounds that "parents insist that their children start reading" or that "the school administration expects it." This is another example of teacher knowledge being ahead of practice. If teachers are professionally qualified, it is essential that they work toward achieving conditions in which it will not be necessary for them to sacrifice their professional integrity and their pupils' psychological well-being because of pressures from the community.

Hopefully, the preceding discussion will not lead the reader to infer that the readiness period is a waiting period. It is educational malpractice to force children to come to school and then require them to wait for the unfolding of some maturational milestone. Flexibility does not imply *laissez faire;* it includes structure and a deliberately planned program. At least in theory, it weighs both the school's goals for the child and the child's capabilities and needs in relation to these goals.

Readiness and Reading: Not a Dichotomy

A misconception that might arise is that there are a number of readiness activities that are distinct from other activities that are labeled *beginning reading instruction*. The literature on the teaching of reading has developed in such a way that differences seem to be as real as they are apparent. One's belief in the concept of readiness need not be weakened by the perception that readiness activities blend, almost imperceptibly, into beginning reading instruction.

For example, a good first-grade teacher may honestly believe that he doesn't use a readiness program or teach readiness activities. The odds are, however, that he will also go on record that he "moves along with reading at a pace the children can follow." If he were observed by individuals who strongly believe in "readiness activities," they might well agree that his readiness program is the best in the district.

For a concrete example, assume you see a film clip of a group being taught the visual pattern *M* and the association of this letter symbol with the initial sound heard in the words *Mike* and *Mary*. Could you say with assurance that you are observing a readiness activity or reading instruction? Some teachers use this technique the first day of school and again (or a variation of it) in December and February. Teachers in higher grades should also use it with any child who has not mastered this letter-sound relationship.

Some instructional materials have designated certain tasks as *prereading* activities, and this term is widely accepted as a synonym for readiness activities. Providing practice in discriminating rhyming elements in words is one excellent and widely used prereading activity. However, work with rhyming elements will be used again and again throughout the period in which letter-sound relationships are taught and not just at the prereading level.

Factors Associated with Readiness for Reading

Numerous factors have been studied in relation to their impact on learning to read. Since reading is a very complicated process, it is very difficult either to establish precise relationships or to completely rule out certain factors as being of no importance. The following discussion will be limited to only a few factors whose importance in learning to read has been widely accepted.

**Mental Age:
The Intelligence Factor**

During the 1930s and 1940s, the importance of mental age appeared to be settled once and for all. A most interesting phenomenon of this period was the almost universal acceptance that children should have attained a mental age (M.A.) of 6–5 (years and months) before they were instructed in reading. This concept was based on the report and conclusions of one study published in 1931 by Morphett and Washburne (30).

They reported data for 141 first-grade children who were given an intelligence test at the beginning of the school year and tested on reading achievement in February. The subjects were then divided into nine groups on the basis of mental age. The lowest range was 4–5 to 4–11, the highest 8–6 to 9–0 (these figures represent years and months of mental age). Of approximately 100 children who had attained an M.A. of 6–6 or higher, 78 percent made satisfactory progress in general reading, and 87 percent made satisfactory progress in sight words. Of a group of twenty children whose M.A. ranged from 6–0 to 6–5, 52 percent made satisfactory progress in reading and 41 percent in sight words. Children below this range in M.A. showed little success in reading achievement.

In a follow-up study, Washburne (41) reported on a group of twenty-five pupils who were delayed in beginning reading instruction until the middle of second grade. Their reading achievement was compared with a number of control pupils who began reading at the usual time in first grade. By the end of the third grade, the experimental group had caught up with the controls; by the end of the fourth grade, they had surpassed them; and at the end of seventh grade, they were approximately one year ahead of the controls in reading. Unfortunately, the original experimental group of twenty-five had been reduced to approximately half that number by the end of the experiment, and drawing conclusions on such a small sample is precarious. In addition, there were, according to the author, important variables which could not be controlled.

During the 1950s and 1960s, the criterion of 6–6 years of mental age for beginning reading instruction was the most prominent finding in reading research. This criterion persisted despite that fact that the study suggesting it was never replicated. Another interesting phenomenon is that during the same decade, Gates published a study (next paragraph) containing data which was contradictory to that of Morphett and Washburne. Recently, Durkin* has suggested that the unquestioning attitude toward the 6–6 years mental age concept was perhaps due to the fact it was in harmony with popular beliefs at the time.

Gates (14) unequivocally challenged the contention that research data have established a "critical point" on the M.A. continuum below which reading cannot be mastered. He stated, "The fact remains . . . that it has by no means been proved as yet that a mental age of six and a half years is a proper minimum to prescribe for learning to read by all school methods or organizations or *all* types of teaching skills and procedures." In a study of four different first-grade classes, Gates reports the correlation between M.A. and reading achievement as .62, .55, .44, and .34. He maintained that much of the discrepancy between these figures was actually accounted for by the instructional procedures found in the classrooms and that good instruction results in a higher correlation between pupil M.A. and success in reading.

MacGinitie (29) supports Gates's position in his statement, "it is hazardous to interpret the findings of readiness studies when the teaching method and materials are not specified, particularly when the sample is small." An analysis of the data from the First Grade Studies led Bond and Dykstra (8) to conclude that teaching is probably the most important variable in determining beginning reading achievement.

The objective in discussing mental age was not to minimize its importance in learning to read, but rather to place it in its proper perspective. The data available attest to the importance of M.A., but at the same time do not establish a particular point on the mental-age continuum as the point below which children will not achieve success in reading. To claim that 6–6 mental age is such a point implies that all children with this M.A. are alike and ignores the fact that all teachers, teaching methods, and programs are not comparable.

Other investigations attest to the importance of factors such as prereading activities, methodology, and readiness programs in determining how well children learn to read. One such study, carried on in first grade, reports that some children with an M.A. of 5–6 who previously had no specific readiness program did not achieve up to grade norms in reading, while a group with M.A.'s of 5–0 who previously had an

---

* Dolores Durkin, "What Does Research Say about the Time to Begin Reading Instruction?" *Journal of Educational Research* 64 (October 1970): 51–56.

extensive twelve-week readiness program did achieve up to national norms. Furthermore, a number of children who did poorly on readiness tests, and for whom prognosis in reading achievement was poor, achieved up to grade norm following specific readiness instruction.*

Preschool Experience and Informational Background

Preschool experience and informational background have been studied to determine their relationship to reading readiness. In one study, scores made by first-grade children on a readiness test correlated .49 with later achievement in reading. However, when only the scores of those children who had attended kindergarten were treated separately, the correlation between the two measures was .68 (26). After studying a group of children who had kindergarten experience and a group which had no such experience, Pratt (34) questioned the validity of using the same reading readiness tests and applying the same assumptions to both groups.

In a study designed to show the relationship between children's informational background and progress in reading, first-grade children were tested on vocabulary, picture completion, and previous experience. On the basis of data secured, children were divided into "rich background" and "meager background" groups. Reading readiness tests were administered to all children at the beginning of first grade. Reading achievement tests were administered to first graders in January and again in December of their second year. The rich background group was superior on both readiness tests and later reading achievement, although there was no significant difference between the groups in mental age (22).

Both the school and society have recently focused attention on the preschool experiences of children who are economically deprived or whose cultural background and language patterns differ significantly from that of middle class or *mainstream* children. The reason for the concern stems from the fact that many children who come from culturally different backgrounds exhibit difficulty in adjusting to a curriculum that was developed without regard for their previous experience.

---

* R. W. Edmiston and Bessie Peyton, "Improving First Grade Achievement by Readiness Instruction," *School and Society* LXXI (April 1950).

In theory, our educational philosophy is that the school will adjust to the child's needs and "meet her where she is" with regard to what to teach. However, in actual practice, the schools frequently expect the child to "adjust" to a curriculum that is quite foreign to her present needs and past experiences. As children fail to learn under these circumstances, the school consciously or unconsciously places the blame on the learner. Instead of making necessary adjustments in methodology and content, many schools gradually abdicate their role as educational institutions and function as "holding actions" for meeting the legal age requirements for keeping a child in school. The problem of culturally different children is discussed in detail in Chapter 11.

Auditory Discrimination

Some studies indicate that impaired readers lack skill in the discrimination of speech sounds. Durrell and Murphy (9) state, "Although there are many factors which combine to determine the child's success in learning to read, it is apparent that his ability to notice the separate sounds in spoken words is a highly important one." The authors indicate that most children who are referred for clinical help in reading because they have not achieved beyond the first-grade level are unable to discriminate among speech sounds in words. Tests usually reveal that the problem of these children is not a hearing loss, but an inability to discriminate among minute differences in speech sounds.

Hildreth asserts that the rapid noting of auditory clues results in more efficient reading (20). Betts stresses a substantial relationship between a child's inability to name the letters and impaired reading (6). He adds that this does not imply that rote memorization of the alphabet is desirable. Walter B. Barbe and others identified the types of reading difficulties found among eighty remedial readers receiving help at a reading clinic. More than forty different problems were noted and tabulated. The weakness showing the highest incidence was sound of letters not known (found in 95 percent of cases at the primary and 62 percent at the intermediate age levels).

Other studies suggest the importance of the ability to synthesize or fuse phonetic elements of words. Hester (19), reporting data gathered on approximately two hundred children admitted to a reading laboratory, states that blending of consonant sounds was particularly difficult for these children. Another study of over one hundred remedial readers (retarded two years or more on the basis of M.A.) indicated that these impaired readers were below average on auditory memory span as measured by specific subtests on the *Stanford Binet* (36).

A series of studies conducted at Boston University which tested over fifteen hundred first-grade children led Durrell to conclude that "most reading difficulties can be prevented by an instructional program which provides early instruction in letter names and sounds, followed by applied phonics and accompanied by suitable practice in meaningful sight vocabulary and aids to attentive silent reading."*

Rudisill (37) reports data from a study which compared achievement of children who participated in a planned program emphasizing letter-sound relationships, with the achievement of a matched group which did not receive this instruction. At the end of eight months, the experimental group had mean reading achievement and spelling scores which were superior to the mean scores of the control group at the end of sixteen months.

Visual Factors

The bulk of all visual work in reading is at close range. The stimulus is about fourteen inches from the eyes. The retinas of both eyes reflect the image seen, in this case, word symbols. For proper vision, the tiny images on both retinas must be perfectly synchronized or "fused." If fusion does not take place, the image will be blurred or, in extreme cases, two distinct images will appear. When the stimulus is near the eyes, as in reading a book, the eyes must converge slightly. This convergence is accomplished by muscles in each eye. Any muscular imbalance between the eyes can result in the lack of fusion described above.

Other muscles operate to put pressure on the lens of the eye, which is capable of changing its shape (degree of convexity). This adjustment is essential in order to compensate for differences in the reflected light rays striking the two eyes. The muscular action determining the degree of convexity of the lens is called *accommodation*.

Ruling out the more serious visual defects which prevent the child from seeing printed word symbols, it is difficult, on the basis of published research, to come to a conclusion regarding the precise rela-

---

* Donald D. Durrell, ed., "Success in First Grade Reading," Boston University, *Journal of Education* (February 1958).

tionship between visual problems and reading deficiency. A number of authorities have suggested deferring the teaching of reading past the age at which it is currently begun. In discussing the relationship between poor vision and reading problems among children between six and eight, one might conclude from research that the problem stems from a lack of maturation, or slow development of good binocular vision, rather than from actual visual defects. This point of view finds support among investigators in the area of child development who are not primarily concerned with reading behavior.

More recently, Eames (13) has conducted research which he interprets as refuting the "claims that children's eyes are too immature for them to start reading safely at the usual ages of school entrance. Children five years of age were found to have *more* accommodative power than at any subsequent age." Poor visual acuity (near vision) was not found to be a significant factor which would interfere with the child's reading of the usual textbook material.

One of the most common visual problems found among children beginning school is farsightedness (hyperopia). A child with this problem may see quite adequately and pass a far-vision test, such as the Snellen, or be able to read an experience chart at the front of the room, and still be poorly equipped visually to deal with material in a book twelve to fourteen inches from her eyes. Any test of vision which purports to have a relationship to actual reading must include a test of near vision. The farsighted child may be able to compensate by straining eye muscles for short periods of time to correct some refractional problem, but she cannot do this for any great duration without causing strain and fatigue. If the teacher can detect the visually immature child, he may be able to protect her from too much close work.

There are a number of studies which have attempted to establish the relationship between visual discrimination and achievement in reading. Goins (15) reports a study of first-grade children designed to determine: (1) the relationship between visual perception and reading ability, and (2) whether training in rapid recognition of digits and geometric and abstract figures would aid children in beginning reading achievement. A visual perception test consisting of fourteen subtests was designed. It included no verbal or reading content, such as letters or words, but did include numerous items of matching pictures and geometrical figures, completion of geometric designs which had a part missing, finding a reversed picture in a series otherwise identical, and a test of closure in which incomplete pictures were the stimulus and the child identified what was represented by the incomplete drawing.

The total scores of first-grade pupils on the visual discrimination test showed a correlation of .49 with reading achievement at the end of grade one. Certain of the visual discrimination subtests showed considerable value in predicting first-grade reading achievement. Further, certain of the subtests indicated that among first-grade children, poor and good readers appear to be "different types of perceivers." This was particularly true of the ability to achieve "closure" and to keep in mind a particular configuration. The hypothesis was advanced that children who are widely different in these skills possibly should be taught reading by different methods in grade one.

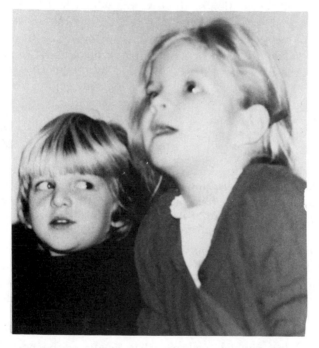

If you can "name it," that means you can distinguish it from others similar to it!

It was found that training with the tachistoscope (flashing digits and figures on a screen for extremely brief exposures) was helpful with good readers in improving their visual perception of such forms, but that this type of training resulted in no appreciable improvement in reading achievement (15). Barrett (5) found that visual discrimination factors, namely, the ability to name letters and numbers, was the best single predictor of reading achievement at the end of grade one. However, he cautions that the predictive precision of these factors does not warrant their being used exclusively to predict first-grade achievement.

Barrett (5) summarized the research which focused on the relationship between visual discrimination measures administered prior to reading instruction and reading achievement at the end of grade one. He reports that studies show that matching letters and matching whole words have about the same predictive value. However, children's ability to name letters has a higher predictive value than the ability to match letter or word forms. Shea tested beginning first graders on visual discrimination-memory of word forms. At mid-year, the subjects were tested on recognition of those words which had been presented thus far in their basal program. The author reported relatively high relationships between scores on these two measures, with the highest predictive value occurring among pupils who scored in the lowest quartile on the mid-year test.*

Modality
Strengths

Recent discussion has focused on the desirability of determining whether a child learns better through exposure to visual- or auditory-oriented instruction (44). One theory being that instruction should be geared to the child's strength, Wepman (42) reported that the ability to discriminate speech sounds is influenced by maturational factors and that frequently this skill is not achieved until the child reaches eight years of age. He reported a positive relationship between poor auditory discrimination and poor reading achievement. Wepman suggested that in cases where there are marked differences in visual and auditory discrimination, beginning reading instruction should emphasize the modality in which the learner has developed the most efficiency.

Bateman† separated first graders into two groups, *auditory* and *visual*, on the basis of their scores on selected subtests of *The Illinois Test of Linguistic Ability*. The group that scored highest on the auditory factor were taught by a method that emphasized phonics. The group selected for visual instruction were taught with materials which

* Carol Ann Shea, "Visual Discrimination of Words and Reading Readiness," *The Reading Teacher* (January 1968): 361–67.

† Barbara Bateman, "The Efficacy of an Auditory and a Visual Method of First Grade Reading Instruction with Auditory and Visual Learners," *Perception and Reading*, Proceedings, International Reading Association 12, part 4, 1968, pp. 105–12.

stressed learning sight words and included a minimum amount of phonics instruction. The auditory group scored significantly higher on reading achievement at the end of grade one than did the visual group.

In evaluating this data, one must keep in mind that in a large number of studies, the subjects were not selected on the criterion noted above. Instructional programs, which included systematic phonics, resulted in reading achievement that was significantly higher than that reported for programs which included little or no systematic phonics instruction. In regard to modality based instruction, there are several unsettled issues: First, how much of a discrepancy in visual-auditory perception must be present for the difference to be considered significant. Second, in the case of children who are not learning disability cases, would teaching to the weaker modality be as advantageous as teaching to the stronger one? Finally, can children become independent readers without developing *both* visual and auditory discrimination skills?

Assessing Readiness
for Reading

Since there are noticeable differences among children who enter first grade, it is rightly assumed that some of these differences have considerable effect on their learning to read. Hundreds of studies have attempted to pinpoint "which differences" have the most impact on learning to read. Some of the factors studied include chronological age, mental age, knowledge of letter names, language facility, knowledge of word meanings, and the ability to make visual discriminations (between letters, words, geometric figures, etc.), follow directions, make auditory discrimination of speech sounds within words, and draw the human figure. Subtests found on most readiness tests purport to measure a number of these variables.

Teacher Estimates
of Readiness

A number of studies, Karlin (23), Annesley et al. (1), Koppman and La Pray (25), and Henig (18) report that teacher estimates of pupil success in reading, made without knowledge of readiness scores, correlate with reading achievement at approximately the same level as do the actual test scores. It is interesting to note that an early study (1934) by Lee and Clark (26) reported that only about half of the teachers in that study were as effective in predicting pupil achievement as was a readiness test. This might suggest that, over the years, teachers have become more sensitive to readiness factors. Regardless of teachers' ability to judge readiness, there is little evidence that schools rely on teacher judgment to the exclusion of readiness tests. Results from a national survey (Austin et al.) (2) indicated that approximately 80 percent of responding schools reported using readiness tests for evaluation.

Reading Readiness Tests

These tests are standardized instruments designed to assess the child's ability to profit from formal instruction in reading. They fulfill their purpose insofar as they predict success in learning to read. That is, the score made on the test itself must be indicative of what can be expected in achievement in reading during the first year or two of formal reading instruction. Readiness tests are, as a rule, administered as group tests, though some may contain one or more subtests which must be given individually. Representative test items include

1. *Associating pictured objects with the spoken word for that object.* The child has before him a series of four or five pictures in a line across the page. The pictures might be of a frog, a boat, a shoe, and a turkey. He is asked to "underline (or circle) the shoe."

2. *Visual discrimination.* Four or five similar objects are shown. One is already circled or checked. One other picture in the row is exactly like this one. The child is to mark the identical picture. Variations of this test include the recognition of one or more digits or letters which are identical to the stimulus at the beginning of the line.

3. *Sentence comprehension.* The child must grasp the meaning of an entire sentence. Before him are pictures of a calendar, clock, lawnmower, and thermometer. "Mark the one which tells us the time."

4. *Drawing a human figure.* In a space provided in the test booklet, the child is asked to draw a person.

5. *Ability to count and to write numbers.* A series of identical objects are shown, and the child is told to mark the second, fourth, or fifth object from the left.

   To test his ability to recognize digits, he is told to underline or put an *x* on a certain digit in a series.

6. *Word recognition.* A common object (doll, house, barn, cow, man, etc.) is pictured. Three or four words, including the symbol for the picture, are shown, and the child is to mark the word represented by the picture.

7. *Copying a model.* A series of geometric figures and capital letters serve as models. The child is to duplicate the stimulus.

8. *Auditory discrimination.* On a group test this might consist of a series of pictures placed horizontally across the page. At the left of each series is a stimulus picture. The child marks each object in the series whose name begins with the same initial sound as the name of the stimulus. If the first picture is that of a dog, for example, it might be followed by illustrations of a doll, a cow, a door, and a ball. Another test situation would be marking each picture whose name rhymes with the name of the stimulus picture.

How and *what* the school teaches
makes auditory discrimination a
prerequisite for learning.

Readiness tests vary as to the types of skills tested. Some of the older tests lack provision for measuring auditory discrimination, but most of the more recently published ones include such a subtest. In general, norms are based on total scores which determine pupil placement in categories such as superior, above average, average, or poor. Since the chief objective of readiness tests is prediction of success in learning to read, it is hoped that the test will separate the ready from the nonready and that, when first-grade pupils are thus identified, the school will adjust the curriculum accordingly. This brings us to the question of just how accurately reading readiness tests predict success in beginning reading.

Predictive Value of Readiness Tests

During the past forty years, hundreds of studies involving the use of readiness tests have been reported. Any attempt to distill and interpret this large amount of data is complicated by a number of factors. Few studies are actually comparable, since different studies used different population samples, measured the impact of different variables, controlled some variables and ignored others, and used different tests, statistical treatments, and limits of significance.

In addition, test items on readiness tests may purport to measure a particular skill which is generally viewed as an absolute necessity for learning to read. (Examples might be visual- and auditory-discrimination skills.) However, even though test items focus on a particular skill, they may call for responses that do not parallel the actual tasks children perform in reading. Insignificant correlations have been reported between two subtests (from different tests) which were designed to measure the same readiness factor.

Dykstra (10) studied the relationship between auditory discrimination and reading achievement. His pretest battery consisted of seven subtests from several different readiness tests. Two subtests measured auditory discrimination of speech sounds. One of these subtests, "Making Auditory Discriminations" (*Harrison-Stroud Readiness Test*), required children to draw a line from a stimulus picture to another picture whose naming word began with the same initial sound as the stimulus picture. This subtest made the highest contribution to prediction of reading achievement at the end of grade one.

Another subtest, "Auditory Discrimination of Beginning Sounds" (*Murphy-Durrell Readiness Test*), required pupils to place an *x* on a given picture if the name of that picture began with the same sound as a stimulus word pronounced by the examiner. This subtest failed to contribute significantly to any predictive multiple regression equation. Dykstra commented, "Furthermore the correlation between these two tests was only .30, a very insignificant relationship in light of the similarity of the task the two tests were designed to measure" (11).

MacGinitie (29) has identified two popular approaches used to establish the relationship between particular readiness skills and reading achievement. One is to measure children with a readiness test prior to reading instruction. The scores on a reading test administered at the end of grade one are correlated with the scores on the readiness measure. The predictive values of the various readiness subtests can then be charted. The second approach is to identify *good* and *poor* readers after a period of instruction and then test both groups on certain readiness variables believed to be related to reading. If poor readers have low scores and good readers have high scores on subtest *X*, causal relationships are frequently inferred. As noted earlier, MacGinitie suggests that generalizing from any particular study must be limited because the *method of teaching* has traditionally been ignored in both of these approaches.

Despite these and other methodological problems, the research data show a rather remarkable internal consistency. If summary statements relative to the predictive value of readiness tests had been made at the close of each of the past four decades, they would be very much alike. On the whole, readiness scores alone lack precision in predicting reading achievement for individual pupils. In general, though, the experimental data indicate a positive relationship between scores on readiness tests and success in beginning reading. Referring to relationships found between readiness test scores and reading achievement, Dykstra writes, "predictive validity correlation coefficients are in general quite consistent. Most of the relationships can be found in the range .40 to .60 with a few extremes on either end" (11).

Subtest versus Battery

Most reading readiness tests consist of six or seven subtests, and scores from the entire battery are usually used for predicting reading achievement. In recent years, due to the availability of computers and more sophisticated statistical techniques, more attention has been paid to the relative predictive value of each subtest in a total battery. Data from a number of studies present evidence that scores from a single subtest will often predict reading achievement as accurately as does the entire test. Linehan (27), Barrett (5), and Dykstra (11) report studies in which children's knowledge of letter names was the best predictor of later success in reading. This finding was supported by an analysis of data from the *Cooperative First Grade* (8) and *Second Grade* (12) *Studies*.

Thus, experimental data suggest that readiness tests, intelligence tests, and teacher evaluations appear to be about equally effective in predicting success in beginning reading. This does not imply that readiness tests have little value to teachers, but it does suggest that educators should not project into these tests a degree of predictive infallibility which they do not possess. It appears that some readiness tests "overrate" children in regard to reading readiness. It is possible that some of the tasks on such tests are more closely related to the child's previous experiences than to what she will actually encounter in beginning reading.

It must be kept in mind that readiness tests measure only selected factors which are believed to be related to reading. There are many other factors which affect learning to read, such as the instruction the child receives, her attitude toward her teacher and toward reading, her reaction to varying degrees of success and failure, her home stability, and the like. This points up the need for intelligent use of readiness test results. The purpose of administering such tests is not to get a score for each child or to rank or compare children in the group, but rather to secure data for planning experiences which will promote successful learning.

In fact, unless the teacher is alert, actual scores may divert attention from child behavior which merits close scrutiny. This tendency is particularly marked when the administration of tests has become an end in itself. When this occurs, the inevitable result is that many trees become obscured by the forest. If teachers would analyze readiness tests results, and if they could adjust their teaching to each child's needs, numerous reading problems might be averted.

Developing
Readiness Skills

One of the major tasks of the school is to provide children with experiences which will make them good readers when formal reading instruction begins. The major skills involved are visual-auditory discrimination; the major process involved is language. To complicate matters, reading is not carried out by specialized reading organs, and reading cannot be isolated from other growth processes. Thus, in the readiness period and in all later development, factors such as social-emotional adjustment, ability to work in groups, ability to work independently, self-concept, interest and motivational level will impinge on learning.

Developing
Visual Discrimination

By the time she comes to school, a child has had thousands of experiences in seeing and noting likenesses and differences. She has developed the ability to make fairly high-order visual discriminations, in many cases based on relatively small clues. At the age of three years she was able to identify and claim her tricycle from a group of three-wheelers, even though she was not able to tell us the exact criteria she used in this identification. All we do know is that it was a visual discrimination. Later, two coins much the same size but bearing different symbols will not confuse her. The pictured head of a man or woman no larger than a postage stamp will contain enough visual clues for correct identification. Common trademarks are correctly identified on the basis of size, color, and configuration. A pack of playing cards can be sorted correctly as to suit on the basis of visual perception.

The child's need to make fine visual discriminations is self-evident since the symbols which must be read are visual stimuli. Even a cursory examination of words is sufficient to establish that many of them look very much alike. A child who cannot differentiate between the various words in a passage cannot possibly get meaning from that passage. The widely accepted definition that "reading is getting meaning from printed symbols" does, to some degree, slight the sensory skills which are absolutely essential before reading can become "getting the meaning."

Maturation cannot be hastened, but visual discrimination can be sharpened through experience and practice. The school must provide as much of this experience as is needed, and different children will need different amounts. Fortunately, there are many ready-made exercises which the teacher can use. Reading readiness books provide practice in developing the ability to make finer and finer discriminations.

Both reading readiness tests and workbooks can aid the teacher in evaluating the child's progress, provided they are used with diagnosis in mind.

For the child who needs more practice than is provided in these activities, a number of teacher-made exercises can be developed. Such exercises take time to build; therefore, they should be duplicated in quantities and used from year to year. They never become outdated with one class use. One thorough preparation will provide for many pupils who need this particular type of experience.

A few examples of visual discrimination exercises follow. Each example could be developed by the teacher into a full page of work.

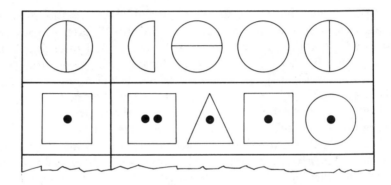

Figure 1

Underline the figure that is exactly
like the sample at the left.

6	9	6	8
5	6	7	5

Figure 2

Underline the number that is exactly
like the one at the left.

Teaching Letter Recognition

Reference has been made to studies which report that the ability to recognize letter forms is the best single predictor of reading achievement at the end of grade one. Further, the ability to discriminate between letter forms is essential for instruction in phonics. If a child cannot discriminate visually between *b* and *p* or *l* and *t*, she will be confused when instructed to associate a particular sound with these letter forms. A few illustrative approaches for teaching and reviewing letter recognition are provided.

After a few letter forms have been taught at the chalkboard or with flashcards, children may be provided with two or more letter-cards. One letter such as ⟦a⟧ ⟦e⟧ ⟦b⟧ is printed on both sides of a card. The group is then invited to "hold up the letter *e*," then *a*, *b*, etc. As the children's responses are observed, the teacher notes diagnostic clues which become the basis for smaller group or individual practice. Other letter-word recognition exercises follow.

M	N	W	M	Z	U
WHO	HOW	WON	WHO	WAH	

Figure 3

Underline the letter or word that is
exactly like the one at the left.

Recognizing Words

The objective of the various experiences in the visual readiness program is to prepare the child for making very fine visual discriminations between words which look very much alike. It is as easy for a person who reads to see the difference between *cat* and *dog* as it is for the six-year-old to see the difference between *a* cat and *a* dog. Yet, the child beginning to read must very rapidly develop the ability to distinguish between hundreds of written word symbols.

Prior to the use of preprimers and long after their introduction, most teachers will provide classroom activities aimed at helping chil-

E - - - - e m a	M	h f m	R	s r n
H	n h m	A	m s a	G	g h f

Figure 4

Match capital and lower case letters.
Connect capital and lower case letter
forms with a line.

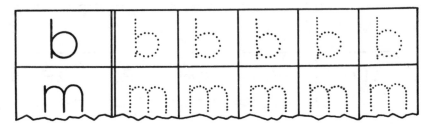

Figure 5

Practice tracing letter forms.

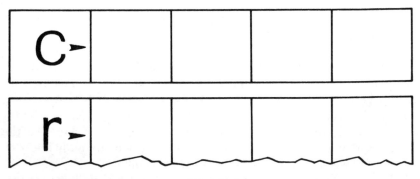

Figure 6

Write letter forms using a visual
model.

shall	Sally	shot	hall	shut
from	frog	flap	fry	free

Figure 7

Underline the beginning of each word
that is exactly like the sample.

hat	hit	hot	cat	has
hill	bell	mill	fill	call
ball	fall	pill	call	halt

Figure 8

Underline the ending of words which
are exactly like the sample.

dren to learn to recognize words. Teachers will employ different methods, but most prefer to teach words related to the child's actual experience. Discussion of the experience method and the use of experience charts is found in Chapter 6. Examples of readiness experience commonly used to help children in word recognition are briefly described here.

1. *Child's name.* Probably the easiest word to teach a child is her own name. She sees her name on her readiness book and on her pictures and drawings which the teacher displays. In addition, there will be many occasions when the teacher will write pupils' names on the board for birthdays, committees, special assignments, and the like. The child will notice similarities between her own name and other pupils' names and will learn a few words in this manner.

a	a small black ant ate it all
l	a small lady led the lads

Figure 9

**Underline each letter in the sentence
which is like the sample at the left.**

2. *Color names.* To teach color names, large circles cut from solid-color construction paper can be placed on the blackboard or a table. Names of colors are printed on white cards. The pupil selects a card, says the word, and places the color name on the proper colored circle.

3. *Matching words, with pictures.* All children in the readiness group are capable of identifying a great number of objects and pictures of objects. Familiar pictures are found, and word names are printed on separate cards: *car, swing, duck, cow, house.* Each child selects a word and places it beneath the proper picture.

4. *Objects in classroom.* A word card is made for familiar objects in the classroom, such as *door, table, window, book, chair.* A child selects a word card, shows it to the group, and touches the object.

5. *Following directions.* Words previously studied can be used in "direction sentences" printed on heavy paper or oaktag. A child selects a sentence, reads it aloud, and does what it suggests: *walk to the door; clap your hands; ask John to stand.*

In any exercise that uses single words as stimuli, the teacher can ask that the word be used in a sentence. As he writes on the board, he pronounces each word and then the whole sentence. Emphasis can be placed on visual clues found in words, on the sentence as a meaning unit, and on left-to-right progression in reading.

Developing
Auditory Discrimination

The major objective of auditory discrimination activities is to help the child become conscious of speech sounds within words. Specifically, she should become able to recognize the same sound at the beginning or end of words, rhyming elements, blended sounds, and the like. The readiness and beginning reading program should provide sufficient experience and drill to assure that every child develops a good foundation in auditory discrimination of speech sounds. Some children will need much more instruction in this area than will others. A few suggestions follow.

Rhyming Element in Words

Prior to each exercise, review the concept of rhyming words and explain the activity.

1. *Number rhymes.* Review the number words from one to ten. Then say, "I will say two words that rhyme. You give me a *number word* that rhymes with these two words."
   a. *Late* and *gate* rhyme with _____. (eight)
   b. *Alive* and *dive* rhyme with _____. (five)
   c. *Sun* and *fun* rhyme with _____. (one)
   e. *Do* and *shoe* rhyme with _____. (two)
   d. *Hen* and *pen* rhyme with _____. (ten)
   f. *Fine* and *mine* rhyme with _____. (nine)
   g. *Store* and *floor* rhyme with _____. (four)
   h. *Free* and *bee* rhyme with _____. (three)
   i. *Sticks* and *mix* rhyme with _____. (six)
   j. *Heaven* and *eleven* rhyme with _____. (seven)

2. *Color-name rhymes.* "Name a color that rhymes with _____."
   a. *Say* and *day* _____ (gray)
   b. *Said* and *Fred* _____ (red)
   c. *Flew* and *chew* _____ (blue)
   d. *Mean* and *seen* _____ (green)
   e. *Mellow* and *Jello* _____ (yellow)
   f. *Down* and *frown* _____ (brown)
   g. *Fan* and *man* _____ (tan)
   h. *Tack* and *shack* _____ (black)
   i. *Wink* and *drink* _____ (pink)
   j. *Night* and *sight* _____ (white)

3. *Animal-name rhymes.* "Name an animal that rhymes with _____."
   now (cow); *cantalope* (antelope); *trunk* (skunk); *box* (fox); *sat* (cat/rat); *deep* (sheep); *coat* (goat); *fog* (dog/frog); *hair* (bear)

4. *Intonation* and *rhyming elements* may be stressed in jingles and rhyming lines. These usually involve longer language units, which also provide experiences for developing *auditory memory*. The example that follows uses number words and calls for children to discriminate the word that is stressed and to complete the statement with a number-word that rhymes with that word.

   a. I saw a number on the *door.*
      The number that I saw was ____ .
   b. The snakes I counted in the *den*
      were more than six—I counted ____
   c. Words like *bee* and *tree* and *see*
      rhyme with good old number ____ .
   d. To keep this rhyming game *alive*
      we have to say the number ____ .*

Drill on Initial Sounds in Words

1. Explain to the children that you will say some words that begin with the same sound. (At this stage the children do not need to identify the *letter* that represents this initial sound.) Children are then to think of and say any word that begins with the same sound as the stimulus words.

   *l*ook, *l*ine, *l*ake
   *b*ird, *b*at, *b*oat
   *m*oney, *m*onkey, *m*an
   etc.

2. *Use of children's names.* "Listen to the sound that begins Mike's name—Mike. Can you think of any other children's first names which begin with this sound?" (*M*ary, *M*ark, *M*arcia.) The beginning sound should be emphasized but not distorted. The names of different children in the class may be used as stimulus words. Several names beginning with the same letter-sound may be written in a column on the board to provide the child with the visual pattern (letter form) that represents the initial sound.

Sue	Cathy	John	Pat	Herman
Sam	Carl	James	Paul	Helen
Sally	Carol	Jerry	Peggy	Harry

---

* Arthur W. Heilman and Ann Holmes, *Smuggling Language into the Teaching of Reading* (Columbus, Ohio: Charles E. Merrill Publishing Company, 1972).

3. *Use of pictures.* Secure a large number of pictures from workbooks, magazines, or catalogues. Select those pictures whose naming words illustrate the sound that is to be taught.

   a. Place several pictures along the chalktray: *b*ird, *t*elevision, *h*ouse. Have volunteers tell which picture name begins with the same sound as stimulus words pronounced orally: *b*oy, *h*at, *t*able.

   b. Select 4 or 5 pictures, all of whose naming words except one begin with the same sound: *b*ird, *b*at, *b*ug, *h*and. A volunteer pronounces all of the picture names that begin with the same sound.

      After letter-sound relationships have been taught, children identify the letter that represents the initial sound: "*b*ird, *b*at and *b*ug all begin with *b*; *h*and begins with *h*."

   c. Place in random order on the chalkboard pictures which have been selected so that several of their naming words begin with the same sound: *h*oe, *f*an, *f*ence, (*t*ub), *h*en, (*t*ire), *f*oot, (*t*eeth), *h*orn. Children arrange the pictures into groups according to the initial sound heard in the picture names.

Final Sounds in Words

The same procedures used for working with initial sounds can be used for teaching discrimination of final sounds in words.

1. Children match or group pictures whose naming words end with the same sound: ne*t*-ba*t*; ma*n*-fa*n*.

2. Pronounce three words, two of which end with the same sound. Pupils repeat the words that end with the same sound: *door*, house, *car*.

3. After letter-sound relationships have been taught, children name or write the letter which represents the final sound heard in picture names or stimulus words spoken orally.

Developing Listening Skills

In developing listening skills, one deals with a much broader area than auditory discrimination of speech sounds. Listening is involved in every facet of the curriculum, and the school is programmed in such a way that children's listening skills must be effective if learning is to take place. Listening is required for following directions, developing and expanding concepts, maintaining discipline, planning curricular activities, and the like. Listening is closely related to many reading behaviors, such as utilizing intonation patterns in reading, developing auditory memory, and processing language presented orally in stories or discussion.

Children differ noticeably in listening ability. Some children come to school with poor listening habits, and others develop inadequate habits early in their school careers. This naturally has an impact on classroom activities and results in impaired learning. For example, the child who does not use the intonation patterns of English speech in her reading will never enjoy reading in English because her habits will interfere with reading for meaning.

Listening involves more than being physically present and immobile while the teacher is speaking. It is just as important to provide experience listening if we want learning to take place as it is to provide experience reading. It is inevitable that there will be a great number of learning activities in the school which depend on listening. These include listening to recordings of stories, poetry, and songs; listening to music and acting out what the music suggests; listening to the teacher read stories; and participating in speaking-listening situations. A few exercises which can be used in prereading as well as at higher levels are briefly described below. These activities involve the child in listening to and interpreting language units ranging from single sentences through paragraphs and stories. The learner is called upon to attend, process, retain, and respond to language stimuli.

Critical listening from which to draw conclusions. Here the teacher reads short, descriptive passages, and the children are asked to identify or draw a picture of what is described. This technique can be tied in with motor coordination and imagination.

1. I grow outdoors.
   I grow tall.
   In summer I am full
   of leaves. Birds sit
   on my branches and sing.
   What am I?
   Draw a picture of me.
2. People live in me.
   I have windows and doors.

I come in many different
sizes and colors.
Draw a picture of me.

The descriptions the teacher reads can vary in length and complexity, depending on the maturity or age level of the group. These exercises can help teachers discover many things about their pupils, such as

1. Which children can listen effectively and which cannot.
2. Which children are self-sufficient and able to work on their own initiative.
3. Which children are dependent and receive clues from others.
4. Information relative to the degree of maturity of each child.
5. Unusual responses which may suggest other problems needing attention.

Story periods. Practically all children can be held spellbound by a good story well told. When the teacher tells or reads stories, he plants the idea in the children's minds that good listening is the key to enjoyment of the story. Equally important is the fact that he can stress a purpose for listening, whether for enjoyment, for information, for answers to specific questions, or for practice in social living.

Following directions. This can be used either as a class exercise, with small groups within a class, or with individual pupils. Several short commands are stated and the child, or the group, is to execute them in the order given. The performance will reveal ability to attend to oral directions and the ability to hold these in memory.

Finishing the story. This provides practice in developing language skills in listening, use of imagination, practice in using language, and expecting logic and meaning from reading. The teacher, while reading a story, interrupts it at a point of high interest and asks the children, "What happens next?"

"Once upon a time Jack went to visit his grandfather and grandmother. They lived on a farm. He went with his father and mother in their car. When they drove up to grandfather's house a big dog rushed out to the car and barked and barked. The boy and his parents had never seen this dog before. Father said ' _____ .' " (Child finishes story.)

A good start is half the race — and
understanding the directions is a
good start.

"Jane and Henry were tired of running and playing. They sat
down on the porch to rest and talk. Jane said, 'Henry, let's ask
mother to make us some lemonade.'

" 'Good,' said Henry, 'cold lemonade; I'm so thirsty I could
drink three glasses.' They started into the house and Henry said:
'Jane, do you think your mother would make enough lemonade so
we could have a lemonade stand and sell lemonade in paper cups?'

"Jane said, '_____.' "

Completing the sentence. This is a variation of the above in which the
child supplies a word which has been omitted. "A big dog came up
to the car and _____ at them." "Jim was tired of running.
He sat down to _____ ." This exercise gives practice in listening and in getting meanings from context.

What word disagrees with the picture? While looking at a picture,
pupils listen to the teacher as he says a series of four words, one of
which could not be logically associated with the picture. Children are
then asked to identify the word which does not belong. This can be a
challenging game, because children must observe closely, listen carefully, and remember the word while other stimuli are presented.

Retelling a story. The teacher reads a story or passage to one group
who then tell the story to children who have not heard it. This experi-

ence motivates children to be good listeners since they must pay attention and comprehend if they are to retell the story successfully.

Emphasizing expression. The teacher reads a sentence or short passage word by word, without inflection, then reads it with good expression. Pupils are lead to see that how a passage is read affects its interpretation.

Silly sayings. Read the following or similar sentences one at a time. After each sentence, call on a volunteer to explain what is wrong with the sentence and how it might be changed to make sense.

1. Mother cooked the corn in an old shoe.
2. The boys played baseball in the sand box.
3. John turned on the radio to watch a program.
4. The elephant drank water through his ear.
5. Mary read the book from back to front.
6. The man went in the jewelry store and ordered breakfast.

Listen and do. Prepare a series of commands or tasks. Explain that you will describe a task and will then call on a volunteer to carry it out. Children must listen carefully since they do not know ahead of time who will be called upon.

1. Repeat this sentence: "George Washington was our first President."
2. Come to the front of the room and roar like a lion.
3. Stand up, turn around completely, sit down.
4. Move like an elephant (rabbit, snake, turtle, etc.).
5. Go to the blackboard, make two marks, then erase one of them.

Whisper a sentence. Whisper a sentence to a child who in turn whispers it to another child, continuing until four or five children have participated. The last child says the sentence aloud. Then determine what changes were made in the message. A number of groups or teams may participate at the same time using the same message.

SUMMARY

Learning to read is an extension of language skills which the child has already developed. Yet reading calls for several skills which are very much different from those previously learned. Specific examples include visual discrimination of letters and word forms, auditory discrimination of speech sounds within words, association of printed letters with the sounds they represent, and the blending of a number of letter sounds to arrive at the pronunciation of words in one's oral vocabulary, but which are not known as sight words. Failure to make adequate progress in these skills will inevitably slow or disrupt the entire developmental process of reading. Despite the importance of these factors, preparing for reading involves many other skills and capacities. Growing into reading is part of the child's total growth pattern. Certainly social-emotional factors are the key to success or failure in beginning reading for some children. These factors are not measured on reading readiness tests, and possibly this may be one reason why the predictive value of these tests is not higher.

The readiness period should not be thought of as ending with a calendar date or dealing with a limited number of specific skills measured by readiness tests. The length of the readiness period should vary for different children, since no predetermined school schedule could possibly fit all children's development. The readiness program does not attempt to remove individual differences among pupils. It does give the school the opportunity to work with children who have deficiencies in skills which are believed to be important to progress in reading. No part of the readiness period should be thought of as a waiting period. Preparing for reading implies activity on the part of the child and a deliberate structuring of experiences on the part of the school.

Concern for a child's readiness to read is highly justifiable. Expecting a child to read before she is ready violates an important principle of teaching reading. The chief aim of the readiness period is to assure that children get off to a good start in learning to read. Experiencing failure in the early stages of learning to read can lead to attitudes which have far-reaching influence on later development.

YOUR POINT OF VIEW?

What is the basis for your agreement or disagreement with each of the following propositions?

1. American schools' emphasis on reading readiness is more apparent than real. The concept of readiness is verbally embraced, but a large number of pupils are subjected to reading instruction before they are ready.

2. The school provides readiness activities in order to assure that all pupils have a common experience background on which to build future instruction.
3. Reading readiness tests could also be defined as intelligence tests.
4. The extent to which pictures are used in beginning reading materials is unsound since some children form the habit of depending on the picture clues rather than mastering sight words.
5. Language usage is the best single indicator of a child's mental ability.
6. Readiness scores of pupils from culturally/economically depressed backgrounds can be expected to be low. The readiness experiences which the school traditionally provides are inappropriate for this group of children.
7. Teaching children to listen is, in general, neglected in the American elementary school.

BIBLIOGRAPHY

1. Annesley, Fred; Odhner, Fred; Madoff, Ellen; and Chansky, Norman, "Identifying the First Grade Underachiever," *Journal of Educational Research* (July–August 1970): 459–62.
2. Austin, Mary C., et al., *The Torch Lighters: Tomorrow's Teachers of Reading.* Cambridge: Harvard University Press, 1961.
3. Bagford, Jack, "Reading Readiness Scores and Success in Reading," *Reading Teacher* (January 1968): 324–28.
4. Barrett, Thomas C., "Visual Discrimination Tasks as Predictors of First Grade Reading Achievement," *Reading Teacher* (January 1965): 276–83.
5. ———," The Relationship between Measures of Pre-Reading Visual Discrimination and First Grade Reading Achievement: A Review of the Literature," *Reading Research Quarterly* (Fall 1965): 51–75.
6. Betts, Emmett Albert, "Reading: Perceptual Learning," *Education* (April–May 1969): 291–97.
7. Bougere, Marguerite Bondy, "Selected Factors in Oral Language Related to First-Grade Reading Achievement," *Reading Research Quarterly* (Fall 1969): 31–58.
8. Bond, Guy L. and Dykstra, Robert, "The Cooperative Research Program in First Grade Reading Instruction," *Reading Research Quarterly* (Summer 1967): 5–142.
9. Durrell, Donald D. and Murphy, Helen A., "The Auditory Discrimination Factor in Reading Readiness and Reading Disability," *Education* (May 1953): 556–60.
10. Dykstra, Robert, "Auditory Discrimination Abilities and Beginning Reading Achievement," *Reading Research Quarterly* (Spring 1966): 5–34.

58 Foundations for Teaching Reading

11. ———, "The Use of Reading Readiness Tests for Prediction and Diagnosis: A Critique," in *The Evaluation of Children's Reading Achievement*, T. C. Barrett, ed. Newark, Del.: International Reading Association, 1967, pp. 35–51.

12. ———, "Summary of Second-Grade Phase of the Cooperative Research Program in Primary Reading Instruction," *Reading Research Quarterly* (Fall 1968): 49–70.

13. Eames, Thomas H., "Physical Factors in Reading," *Reading Teacher* (May 1962): 427–32.

14. Gates, A. I., "The Necessary Mental Age for Beginning Reading," *Elementary School Journal* (March 1937): 497–508.

15. Goins, Jean Turner, *Visual Perceptual Abilities and Early Reading Progress*. Chicago: University of Chicago Press, Supplementary Educational Monographs no. 78, 1958.

16. Hall, Mary Anne, "Prereading Instruction: Teach for the Task," *Reading Teacher* 30 (October 1976): 21–27.

17. Harris, Albert J. and Sipay, Edward R., *How to Increase Reading Ability*, sixth ed. New York: David McKay Co., Inc., 1975. Chapters 2, 3.

18. Henig, Max S., "Predictive Value of a Reading Readiness Test and of Teacher Forecasts," *Elementary School Journal* (September 1949): 41–46.

19. Hester, Kathleen B., "A Study of Phonetic Difficulties in Reading," *Elementary School Journal* (November 1942): 171–73.

20. Hildreth, Gertrude H., "The Role of Pronouncing and Sounding in Learning to Read," *Elementary School Journal* (November 1954): 141–47.

21. Hillerich, Robert L., "Kindergartners Are Ready! Are We?" *Elementary English* (May 1965): 569–74.

22. Hilliard, G. H. and Troxell, Eleanor, "Informational Background as a Factor in the Reading Readiness Program," *Elementary School Journal* (December 1937): 255–63.

23. Karlin, Robert, "The Prediction of Reading Success and Reading Readiness Tests," *Elementary English* (May 1957): 320–22.

24. King, Ethel M., and Muehl, Siegmar, "Different Sensory Cues as Aids in Beginning Reading," *Reading Teacher* (December 1966): 163–68.

25. Koppman, Patricia S. and LaPray, Margaret H., "Teacher Ratings and Pupil Reading Readiness Scores," *Reading Teacher* (April 1969): 603–08.

26. Lee, J. M.; Clark, W. W.; and Lee, D. M., "Measuring Reading Readiness," *Elementary School Journal* (May 1934): 656–66.

27. Linehan, Eleanor B., "Early Instruction in Letter Names and Sounds as Related to Success in Beginning Reading," *Journal of Education* (February 1968): 44–88.

28. Lundsteen, Sara W., "Critical Listening: An Experiment," *Elementary School Journal* (March 1966): 311–16.

29. MacGinitie, Walter H., "Evaluating Readiness for Learning to Read: A Critical Review and Evaluation of Research," *Reading Research Quarterly* (Spring 1969): 396–410.

30. Morphett, Mabel V. and Washburne, Carleton, "When Should Children Begin to Read?" *Elementary School Journal* (March 1931): 496–503.

31. Olson, Arthur, "School Achievement, Reading Ability, and Specific Visual Perception Skills in the Third Grade," *Reading Teacher* 19 (1966): 490–92.

32. Paradis, Edward and Peterson, Joseph, "Readiness Training Implications from Research," *Reading Teacher* 28 (February 1975): 445–48.

33. Pikulski, John J., "Assessment of Pre-Reading Skills: A Review of Frequently Employed Measures," *Reading World* 13 (March 1974): 171–97.

34. Pratt, Willis E., "A Study of the Differences in the Prediction of Reading Success of Kindergarten and Non-Kindergarten Children," *Journal of Educational Research* (March 1949): 525–33.

35. Robeck, Mildred C. and Wilson, John A. R., *Psychology of Reading: Foundations of Instruction.* New York: John Wiley and Sons, Inc., 1974. Chapters 6, 7, 8.

36. Rose, Florence C., "The Occurrence of Short Auditory Memory Span among School Children Referred for Diagnosis of Reading Difficulties," *Journal of Educational Research* (February 1958): 459–64.

37. Rudisill, Mabel, "Sight, Sound, and Meaning in Learning to Read," *Elementary English* (October 1964): 622–30.

38. Stanchfield, Jo M., "Development of Pre-Reading Skills in an Experimental Kindergarten Program," *The Reading Teacher* (May 1971): 699–707.

39. Strag, Gerald A. and Richmond, Bert O., "Auditory Discrimination Techniques for Young Children," *Elementary School Journal* 73 (May 1973): 447–54.

40. Tutolo, Daniel, "Teaching Critical Listening," *Language Arts* 52, (December 1975): 1108–12.

41. Washburne, Carleton, "Individualized Plan of Instruction in Winnetka," *Adjusting Reading Programs to Individuals,* William S. Gray, ed. Chicago: University of Chicago Press, 1941, pp. 90–95.

42. Wepman, Joseph M., "Auditory Discrimination, Speech, and Reading," *Elementary School Journal* (March 1960): 325–33.

43. Witkin, Belle Ruth, "Auditory Perception-Implications for Language Development," *Journal of Research and Development in Education* (Fall 1969): 53–71.

44. Wolpert, Edward M., "Modality and Reading: A Perspective," *The Reading Teacher* (April 1971): 640–43.
45. Zintz, Miles V., *The Reading Process, the Teacher and the Learner,* second ed. Dubuque, Ia: William C. Brown Company, 1975. Chapters 8, 9.

Chapter 3

Moving into Reading: Focus on Learners

Structuring the Climate for Learning

There are many things that can go wrong in reading instruction. Learning to read is a highly complex task and the pressures that have become attached to "learning-to-read" often interfere with mastery of this symbol system. A little failure can create and nourish interferences to learning; thus, it is essential to maintain a classroom climate that arouses and sustains the child's interest in reading.

Fortunately, there are potentially powerful motivators available to every classroom. No child has an innate drive not to learn to read. Most children come to school eager to explore the mysteries of print. Every child has ego needs which for a period of time can be fulfilled in part by success in learning to read. Another exceptionally powerful asset is the fact that reading is a language process and that children love to use and manipulate language. Unfortunately, the magic and power of language is frequently not utilized to its fullest in reading instruction. If reading is divorced from language, then learning to read becomes mechanistic. Interest wanes, and even if learning occurs, it tends to lose some of its self-sustaining ingredients.

Factors within the child—those habits, attitudes and concepts which already exist when the child comes to school—impinge on learning. If the school wishes to teach children to read, these factors cannot be ignored. No teaching materials can, simply because they exist, compensate for or negate feelings of inadequacy, poor self-concept, lack of independence, or variability in rate of learning. Children must learn how to learn as they move through the curriculum the school provides. Teaching consists of more than manipulating instructional materials. This is why we continue to honor the cliche "the teacher is the most important variable in any learning situation." In reality, the learner holds the key to learning. How teachers fare as catalysts is what is measured on achievement tests. The following discussion focuses on a few areas in which teachers must serve as catalysts.

Developing Independent Work Habits

Learning to read is part of the total development of children. The period devoted to beginning reading instruction is not too early to help children develop self-responsibility and a degree of independence in their work habits. While many teachers would agree with this premise, it is possible we have underestimated the relationship between these factors and success or failure in reading.

In any discussion of reading readiness, one invariably meets the term *immaturity*. An immature child has not attained a specific level of behavior associated with his chronological age. Lack of responsibility, or self-dependence, is universally cited as evidence of immaturity. The child of six who has avoided or who has been prevented from developing independence and self-reliance is not likely to become self-reliant and independent in school unless he receives some specific guidance. The point is that immaturity, in the psychological sense, has been learned. The child's behavior may have developed out of the parents' need to keep the child dependent. It should be kept in mind that one of the easiest things to learn in early life is a pattern of abdicating responsibility. The child who learns this pattern has become accustomed to social controls from without. He will naturally find it difficult to develop self-discipline or controls from within. In this connection, Staiger (42) suggests that some children fail to learn to read because they have never had to do anything and, therefore, feel that they do not have to learn to read. Delays, procrastination, and lack of self-responsibility can only increase the difficulty of learning to read. In other situations where this behavior was learned, the parents can eventually make a response which resolves the problem. They can hang up the clothes, pick up the toys, write an excuse for the child when he is tardy, and take him to school in the car if he misses the bus. But learning to read is a task which no parent can perform for the child.

The aim of instruction in beginning reading is to make the child an independent reader. It is here that the child will develop habits of reading and study which will help or hinder him throughout his academic career. Independent work habits and self-responsibility are essential for children in today's schools because of group instruction in which children have to work out their own problems. Grouping practices create a problem since the teacher must divide her time among several different groups, thus leaving the child on his own during a good part of the time devoted to reading instruction.

Training for responsibility begins early and involves guidance from adults. This guidance must take into consideration that children learn self-responsibility only by practicing it. There is no single blueprint of teacher behaviors that would be effective for each child in a class. While expectations for individual children will differ, every child needs consistency from the adult authority.

The child who develops independence and self-discipline in his work habits early in the process of learning to read is not likely to become a severely retarded reader. The child who loses, or never gains, confidence in himself, the child who cannot work alone, complete tasks and, in general, assume some responsibility for learning is not well-prepared to weather a learning crisis. There are a number of ways in which a teacher can help pupils get off to a proper start in developing good work habits.

Give responsibility to all children and not just those who are already confident and at ease. Collecting workbooks or readers, stacking them neatly, cleaning up after art work, arranging chairs after group work, and stopping or beginning a task when requested to do so help develop self-discipline. It should be remembered that children learn best through experience.

Independent readers assume some
responsibility for their own growth.
They develop "self-direction"
habits.

Do not give a child tasks that he does not understand or cannot do. He
will lose interest, procrastinate, daydream, and soon conclude that this
is what one does in school.

Set short-term goals which can be readily achieved. The teacher
should never tell her students that she will look at their work when it
is finished and then fail to do so. The child wants a reward, and the
teacher's approval of the completed task is interpreted as a reward. The
child will then have many experiences of success which he associates
with the reading situation.

It is stated above that children should learn to begin and stop
activities when requested to do so. If a child is engrossed in a task, such
as coloring, printing, or working a page in a readiness book, permitting
him to complete it might be better than interrupting and insisting that
he join a group to do something else. When grouping is flexible and a
good learning climate exists, he will be able to join the group in a few
minutes without disrupting the activity. Furthermore, children have a
relatively short attention span and become tired even of tasks they
enjoy.

If a child works slowly on an activity that the teacher feels should
be completed, she can give a moment's help and then praise the child
for completing the task, thus instilling the idea that this is the standard
of performance which she expects from him. Children's reading behav-

ior should be observed very closely so that no child experiences too much failure and frustration with reading. Children should be praised when they try, even if their accomplishment falls short of arbitrary standards.

Children as Readers

The school cannot undo or revise the experiences a child has had prior to his arriving at school. The fact that children are so different when they come to school makes it imperative that the teacher discover those differences which are important factors in learning to read. Then she must develop a program of teaching which, at its maximum effectiveness, will help each child to grow at a rate commensurate with his ability. The teacher must guard against practices and classroom experiences which may damage the child psychologically and inhibit learning in the future. The discussion which follows attempts to show how differences among pupils are related to instruction.

Scott was a boy of average intelligence who gave the appearance of being shy. He was reluctant to respond in class or to join in the playground activities for fear that he would fail. He would give up easily, make no effort to get help from the teacher when it was needed, and was showing no progress in reading. He was socially immature and inadequate in the group. Within three or four months, he had been generally rejected by the group. While he seemed to accept this on the surface, he nevertheless harbored intense hostility.

He did not manifest this hostility through overt attacks on other children, but through such immature behavior as scribbling on another pupil's drawing, breaking another child's pencil, and putting his own coat on a hallway hook in place of another, which he would then drop on the floor. He displayed a tendency to tattle and call the teacher's attention to other pupils' shortcomings. Whatever form his aggression took, he always seemed to get caught.

Jerry was a boy of above average intelligence and, according to the teacher, just the opposite of Scott. She characterized him as being "pushy" in class, attempting to be the center of everything that went on. He was able to achieve leadership status among the class but still had an insatiable need to be the center of attention and to dominate others. Physically, he was more mature than the other boys and extremely well-coordinated. Because his superiority in things physical was never questioned, he was never a problem as a bully.

Despite high ability, he made a poor adjustment in class. He was unable to work alone or carry any project through to its conclusion. Instead of doing assigned seat work, he would wander around the room in an attempt to get an audience. Jerry and Scott both got off to a very poor start in reading.

Doris, a girl of high average intelligence, was one of the most mature children in the class. Her language facility was above average and, while not the brightest child in the class, she was as well-informed as any. She was accepted by both boys and girls as a leader and yet, did not insist on the leadership role. Her social adjustment was excellent both in and out of class. She enjoyed reading from the start. Making better than expected progress in beginning reading, she continued this same level of performance in the following years.

What were the real differences between these pupils? On the basis of C.A., I.Q., and M.A., they were fairly equal. All came from higher than average socio-economic homes. Each child had been read to a great deal prior to school and since early infancy. Each had many books at home, and each had rich and varied experiences prior to entering school, which included family picnics, rides on trains, long trips by car, eating out with their families, and visits to large cities, farms, zoos, and parks. How did they differ?

Scott was the older of two boys. Both parents set very high standards for him. His parents were perfectionists, and he could never quite measure up to their expectations. He became very aware of this. It was impossible to do anything exactly right. His parents always nagged when he attempted anything, and his withdrawal was a most logical response. This response he soon learned and eventually over-learned. His ego was threatened by this inability to please his parents. When he really did wrong, he was not rejected or severely punished. In fact, he was treated as an individual, for his parents tried to discover "Why did Scott do this?" The closest his psychological needs ever came to being fulfilled was when he was caught in some misbehavior which was a threat to his parents. School simply became a new and different arena, and he used the same weapons and approach, even though, from an adult standpoint, his responses were not the most logical ones available.

Reading became a threat to him very early in school. Like most parents, his were concerned about reading. They wanted him to get a good start. His confidence in himself and in his ability was already undermined, and he started from the premise that he would fail in reading. It is not surprising that with this emotional conflict, he was unable to bring his energies to bear on the reading task. As tension from failure mounted, he used responses which further alienated him from people—his parents, peer group, and teacher. Needing acceptance more than anything else and being denied it, he withdrew from any situation which, in his mind, might further jeopardize his status.

Jerry was the only child of parents who had both finished college, done graduate work, and acquired professional standing. They were quite concerned with status, but unconsciously so. They never verbalized comparisons between Jerry and members of his peer group. In their own minds such invidious comparisons were a sign of immaturity. Yet, their need for Jerry to succeed, to be the best in all types of endeavor, while not perceived by them, was so close to the surface that it was clearly sensed by him. His security became tied up with excelling, with dominating others. Success was the safety region for him. Through it, he could dominate the home; it was the price paid for love, affection, and acceptance. As he grew to school age, most of his endeavors were rewarded by success. He was "superior."

Reading was a different story. He did not start school with a superiority in this skill. He found himself in a group where, in one particular skill, he was only average. He seemed never to be interested in reading. As other pupils' superiority in reading became marked, reading became a threat to him. A frontal attack on the problem was not the solution he chose. He elected to compensate. He withdrew from reading, disrupted class activities, interfered with others' learning, and tried to capture attention and maintain his status in numerous ways.

The needs and motives of the two boys were strikingly similar, as were their attitudes toward reading. Yet, their overt reactions to a frustrating situation were quite different, so much so that the teacher identified the boys as being "just the opposite." Would knowing the background of each boy, as related here, help the teacher in dealing with their reading problems?

Our third case, Doris, was not a reading problem. This girl was a well-adjusted, thoroughly accepted child. She was the youngest of several siblings, adored by her family, but not spoiled. She did not have to compete for affection. An outward appearance of the home lives of all three children appeared to be similar. Yet, only one of the three had found security at home. Could this factor have had an important relationship to reading?

The three children just described were members of the same first-grade class. This class contained over twenty other children, some of whom would merit an equally extensive individual analysis if they were to be understood as beginning readers. Here, only an important fact or two concerning these twenty children will be mentioned; teachers' knowledge or experience will show why these facts are important in beginning reading.

Some of the children were barely old enough to enter school. Others were eight or nine months older. Some had attended kindergarten the previous year; others had not. Three children had attended nursery school since they were three years old. Two of the mothers worked outside the home during those years.

The I.Q.'s of children in this group ranged from 76 to 130. Three children measured 85 or below. Mental age varied as much as 24 months within the group. Education of parents ranged from one year in high school to graduate work in college. Occupation of the parents ranged from manual laborer to physician. Two children had medical records showing excessive illness during childhood. One child wore glasses. Children other than Scott and Jerry had emotional problems.

These and many other factors are definitely related to learning to read and to the differences in reading ability which will inevitably emerge in any first-grade class. Being able to detect differences and understand their significance is an invaluable aid to the teacher as she plans experiences and sets goals for individuals in her group. From the potential learner's position, having a teacher with this ability to detect subtle but important differences is a form of insurance against being pushed too fast, losing self-confidence, and forming an aversion to school and to reading.

Attitudes toward Self and Adjustment

The reaction of the school and the home to reading skill has a very pronounced effect on the beginning reader. Children quickly see the importance which is attached to learning to read. Many beginning readers must fail because success is measured by an arbitrary criterion, grade level achievement. We will look briefly at the way in which attitudes and later behavior are influenced during the beginning reading period.

Among educators, parents, or psychologists, there would be few dissenters to the proposition that "getting the right start" in learning to read is of the greatest importance. For some children who experience difficulty, a poor start is often the key to later reading difficulty as well as a factor in maladjustment. The fact that some children can fail in the beginning stages of reading and still develop into adequate readers and well-adjusted individuals does not in the least militate against the fact that the beginning stage in reading is extremely important. It is during this period that the child develops attitudes toward himself, toward reading, and toward competition. These attitudes, in turn, are related to the motivations which may arouse anti-social behavior.

The child's attitude toward self is influenced by the attitudes of others toward him. There are parental reactions toward him as their child and as a learner, possibly complicated by an unconscious comparison of him with siblings. The teacher, in turn, reacts to the child as a learner, to his home and parents, and to the child as a problem if he develops behavior not condoned by the school. The child senses that his parents and his teacher feel that learning to read is extremely urgent. Pressures from home, school, and self do not always result in learning. There are many activities which may call for intense competition, but in most cases it is optional with the individual whether he elects to compete. In the elementary school, there is no choice of curricula, one including reading and the other not. The curriculum is *based* on reading. The nonreader has no place to hide except behind whatever defenses he can devise. Unfortunately, these are not honored as substitutes for reading by the society in which he lives. Examples of these defenses are

> I'm too dumb to read.
> Don't-care attitude.
> Aggression.
> Withdrawal, daydreaming.
> Compensation.

Self-confidence is very important for the beginning reader. The child who lacks confidence in his own ability is likely to over-react when he encounters difficulty in learning to read. The type of home the child comes from and the relationships he has had with parents or adults will have already affected his confidence before he gets to school. It is the teacher's task to structure school experiences in such a way that the classroom will be an area of safety rather than a threat. This is one of the most difficult tasks confronting the teacher; it is also one of the most important. The task is difficult because the school is only one of several institutions which parcel out failure and success, ego-satisfaction, and frustration. It has no control over the home, neighborhood, or community. Children entering school have patterns of behavior which reflect experiences of rejection, overprotection, success, personal inadequacy, and the like (49).

Today there are few educators who question that these experiences relate to learning. It is true that the school cannot undo the past experiences of each child, nor can it control the present in the community and home. A child may come to school with feelings of inadequacy so strong and so reinforced by his home that the school cannot satisfy his need for attention and acceptance. But the school can, in many cases, compensate to some degree for the unfulfilled needs of children. Even if teachers take the position that their only job is to teach an agreed upon curriculum, they must still understand that they teach the subject matter to potential learners. Factors which diminish this potential among learners are teaching problems.

An alert and observant teacher can see many clues which suggest how a particular child fits in with, or is accepted by, his peer group. Four children are playing in the sand box. Eddie approaches with the intention of joining the group but is met with: "Get away from here!" "You can't play with us." "There's no more room—let us alone." These responses in themselves are not atypical of six-year-olds. What the teacher has to discover is whether this is just a group of "haves" protecting their domain, the sandbox, from a "have not," or whether this is an illustration of the group's rejection of Eddie.

There are two types of behavior, over-shyness and aggression, which pose special problems for the teacher and special threats to the learning situation. These behaviors are vastly different, yet it is safe to conclude that the same drives are often behind these apparent opposites in behavior. The shy child and the aggressive child both desire responses from others. Each has learned the behavior patterns which he uses in an attempt to cope with his environment. Each will also need some help in learning to use behavior that will be likely to lead to group acceptance rather than group rejection.

Attitudes toward Reading

Most first-grade teachers would agree that one of the most important aims of the beginning reading period is to help the child develop a positive attitude toward reading. Failure in reading is likely to produce the opposite attitude. When the school sets an arbitrary goal or level of achievement, namely the reading of first-grade material, the child feels that nonsuccess in achieving this arbitrary standard is failure regardless of promotion policies.

A number of experienced teachers were given a conventional checklist of reading difficulties. This was a one-page list of difficulties which appear frequently among retarded readers. The teachers were asked to select the two problems which they thought would:

> Be present in most remedial reading cases
> Be the most serious problems noted

The majority of teachers gave as their first choice "aversion to reading." If one thought only in terms of the actual mechanics of reading, he might not include aversion as a reading problem. However, it *is* a problem in working with most reading failures. Once a child has developed a dislike for reading, stemming from failure, he is not likely to give up his aversion as a result of persuasion based on the authoritarian statements that reading is fun, pleasant, and important. The child's dislike of reading is a most logical reaction. The fact that the child will be told it is an unfortunate response will have little influence on its removal.

Variability in Learning Rates

Prior to focusing on methods and materials, teachers should be aware of the differences that exist among children in regard to rate of growth in learning to read. Two topics which have received considerable attention are sex differences in learning to read and children who are early readers. Even though all aspects of these phenomena may not be clearly understood at the moment, awareness of the data may provide insights for teachers seeking to understand children as learners.

Sex Differences in Learning to Read

Research data compiled over the past few decades have reported conclusive evidence that girls as a group achieve *significantly higher* in beginning reading than do boys as a group. As one reviews the literature on early achievement in reading, it becomes apparent that sex difference has significance for teachers who are interested in children as readers. The material that follows is advanced as representative of the data available on the topic.

Ayres (5) was one of the first to call attention to sex differences in school achievement. His book *Laggards in Our Schools* does not deal with differences in reading per se. However, he pointed out that 12.8 percent more boys than girls repeated grades; that 17.2 percent more girls than boys completed "common school" (eighth grade); and that there was 13 percent more retardation among boys.

St. John (38) reported no significant difference in the measured intelligence of approximately one thousand pupils in grades one through four, but stated that girls very distinctly excel boys in reading at grade levels one through four. The study covered a four-year period and reported that boys showed 7 percent more repeating of grades or non-promotions than did girls.

Wilson et al. (47) report a study covering three years at Horace Mann School. Boys and girls in first grade showed no differences on mental tests, but the authors state, "the difference between girls and boys in paragraph reading in this grade was statistically reliable." In reading at the second-grade level, "the average of chances was 88 in 100 that the girls would be superior." At the third-grade level, girls surpassed the boys but not significantly. It should be pointed out that the intelligence level of the pupils in this study was considerably above the mean for all children their age.

Alden et al. (1) report data from children in grades two through six who were tested with the *Durrell Sullivan Reading Capacity Test.**
Over six thousand children were tested, and the number of boys who were one or more years retarded in reading was double that of girls in each of the first five grades. Table 1 gives the data on these sex differences.

Table 1

Sex differences between boys and girls
in reading retardation measuring one
year or more retardation.

Grade	Percent Boys Retarded	Percent Girls Retarded
2	9.7	4.2
3	14.7	7.1
4	23.6	12.0
5	25.5	11.6
6	13.7	9.9

One of the most significant studies on sex differences was reported by Stroud and Lindquist (43) in 1942. Over three hundred schools with

* Harcourt Brace and World, Inc., New York.

50,000 pupils were the source of data. The data compiled covered a number of years of testing in the Iowa schools, using the *Iowa Every-Pupil Basic Skills Test*. In this program, grades three through eight are tested on reading comprehension, vocabulary, word study skills, basic language skills, and arithmetic skills. The authors state, "Girls have maintained a consistent, and on the whole, significant superiority over boys in the subjects tested, save in arithmetic, where small insignificant differences favor boys." Table 2 shows the mean difference in reading comprehension scores between boys and girls for grades three through eight. It should be noted that the largest differences occur at grades three and four and decline significantly at grade six.

Table 2

Sex differences in reading comprehension as measured by the *Iowa Every-Pupil Test of Basic Skills*.

Grade	Mean Differences (all favoring girls)	Significance Ratios
3	2.12	2.57
4	2.75	3.38
5	1.29	1.77
6	.30	.39
7	.10	.14
8	.47	.50

Hughes (20) using the total comprehension scores from the *Chicago Reading Tests*, measured reading achievement of boys and girls in grades three through eight. She found that the greatest difference was at grade three where the girls achieved more than a half school year above the boys. This difference favoring girls was significant at the 1 percent level. At grade four the difference favoring girls was significant at only the 5 percent level, while in grades five through eight, girls made higher reading scores than did boys, but the differences were not statistically significant.

Nila (30), during the first weeks of school, tested three hundred first graders on a number of individual and group readiness tests. She reports that on the basis of these test scores, the boys as a group and the girls as a group were equally ready to read. These pupils were tested at the end of the school year for reading achievement. Seventy-two were designated as reading failures; forty-five of the failures, or 63 percent, were boys, and 37 percent were girls.

Gates (16) tested over thirteen thousand children in grades two through eight and compared girls' and boys' mean scores on three reading subtests at each grade level. He states, "In each of the twenty-one comparisons the mean raw score for girls is higher than the mean raw scores for boys, and most of the differences are significant."

Prescott (32) tested over seven thousand boys and seven thousand girls beginning first grade on the *Metropolitan Readiness Test* to determine whether or not this test showed sex differences. He reports that when chronological age is equated, the performance of girls is superior to that of boys (difference favoring girls significant at the 5 percent level). Carroll (10) also found sex differences in reading readiness at the first-grade level. These differences were in favor of girls and were large enough to be statistically significant.

Cooperative USOE Studies

During the school year 1964–65, twenty-seven first-grade reading studies were supported by grants from the U.S. Office of Education. Analyzing the data from these studies, Bond and Dykstra (8) reported that girls rated higher than boys on both readiness measures and reading achievement at the end of grade one. During the following year, fifteen of these studies were continued into grade two. Dykstra (13) reported that girls maintained their superiority in reading achievement at the end of grade two.

Clinical Data

Further data on sex differences in reading are found in reports from clinical sources, such as child-guidance clinics and remedial reading clinics. Rarely do the data from these sources deal primarily with sex differences. As a rule, the titles of reported research do not indicate that sex differences are discussed but, almost without exception, these studies reveal a disproportionate number of referrals of boys as compared with girls and, also, an even more disproportionate percentage of seriously retarded readers among boys. The range of percentages is from approximately 65 percent boys and 35 percent girls to 90 percent boys and 10 percent girls. Monroe (28) reported an exhaustive study of over four hundred children who had been referred to the Chicago Institute for Juvenile Research for various problems, including impaired reading. One group of 155 children was referred specifically for reading problems; in this group 86 percent were boys and 14 percent were girls.

Blanchard (7), in discussing seventy-three consecutive cases seen at the Philadelphia Child Guidance Clinic in which reading was given as one reason for referral or where a reading problem was found to exist, reports that sixty-three of these cases were boys, and ten cases were girls.

Young (50), investigating forty-one cases diagnosed as retarded in reading and referred to the Psycho-Educational Clinic, Harvard University, reports that thirty-seven of the cases were boys and four cases were girls. He further reports that over a period of years, this same ratio held for all children referred who were retarded in reading but had at least average intelligence.

Preston (33) studied the effects of security-insecurity in the home, the school, and the social situation of retarded readers. In a sample of one hundred reading failures possessing normal intelligence and no physical defects, there were seventy-two boys and twenty-eight girls.

Missildine (27), studying the emotional adjustment of thirty retarded readers picked at random from clinic files, reported twenty-five of the thirty were boys. All but two of the children in this study were below ten years of age.

McCollum (22), discussing forty severe reading disability cases referred to a reading clinic during one year, reports that 78 percent were boys. Axline (4) reported a study of thirty-seven second graders selected on the basis of reading retardation or nonreading. Twenty-eight, or 76 percent of the retarded readers, were boys. Vorhaus (46) described 225 reading disability cases seen at the New York University Reading Institute. One hundred seventy-eight, or 80 percent of these cases, were boys. All cases were reported as having average or better intelligence.

Fabian (15) reports on a group of 279 children given diagnostic tests at the Brooklyn Juvenile Guidance Center. Ninety-nine of these children were at least eight years of age, had I.Q.'s of eighty or above, and showed reading achievement at least 25 percent below expectation based on mental age. Of these ninety-nine children, sixty-seven were boys and thirty-two were girls.

Many other clinical and remedial studies, particularly those of a "case study" nature, also report a preponderance of boys as remedial reading cases. However, these reports are not cited here because the number of cases they discuss is too small for evaluation.

Hypotheses as to Causes of Sex Differences in Reading

The data on sex differences in learning to read should not be dismissed as just another educational statistic. If we are interested in children as readers (and learners), then the school must evaluate all practices which might be related to this differential in beginning reading achievement. Today there is growing support for the hypothesis that these differences are probably not entirely traceable to the nervous systems of the learners. The methodological practices and educational climate found in classrooms are also a factor.

Several recent studies have contributed data which suggest that the cultural milieu of the school, *including instruction,* may play a significant role in producing sex differences in early reading performance. The important implication here is that there are variables within the learning environment which, when taken into consideration, tend to enhance the performance of boys. Two such variables are the teacher (her attitude and behavior patterns) and teaching materials.

McNeil and Keislar (23) found kindergarten boys' achievement superior to that of girls when beginning instruction relied exclusively on the use of programmed materials. When this instruction was followed by four months of teacher instruction (all women teachers), girls' achievement was superior to that of boys. The authors state, "The fact that the superiority in reading of boys was not maintained under teacher direction indicates that there are variables within the classroom which militate against the maximum performance of young male learners."

Heilman (18) conducted an intensive in-service program in which participating teachers studied and discussed research data relevant to sex differences in learning to read. These teachers did make a number of classroom and teaching adjustments. Boys taught by these teachers had higher mean scores on each of the subtests of the *Stanford Achievement Test* at the end of grade one than did boys taught by control-teachers in the same community. "In-service training which resulted in teacher awareness of sex differences in learning to read appears to have evoked classroom practices which tended to enhance the performance of boys."

Preston's (34) study of reading achievement of German children reports sex differences favoring boys. In addition, he reports more variability among scores made by girls, which is at variance with most findings of American studies. These data strongly suggest cultural influence as being important factors in learning the reading process.

A number of the hypotheses which have been advanced in an effort to explain why girls have consistently shown superiority over boys in early reading achievement are cited here.

1. *Boys and girls mature at different rates and some phases of growth are closely related to reading.* Since the data are conclusive that girls develop more rapidly than boys, this hypothesis is sometimes seen as

the key to the problem under discussion. In skeletal development, girls as a group are superior to boys throughout the preschool period, and by the age of six years, they are at least a full year ahead of boys. Since boys are less physiologically mature, eye muscles and visual acuity may not be equal to the task of beginning reading, and their attention span may not be developed enough to allow for lengthy concentration on teacher guidance.

A long-term study carried out at the University of Michigan compares the chronological age at which boys and girls begin to read and the "rate of progress" made after each has mastered a certain level of reading ability. The authors report a significant difference favoring girls in the age of learning to read. However, once children achieved a reading age of eighty-four months on the *Gates Primary Reading Test,* no difference between boys' and girls' rate of advancement was found (3).

2. *The school environment and curriculum at the primary level are more frustrating to boys than to girls.* This hypothesis is very closely related to the preceding one. For instance, if boys and girls mature at different rates, it is logical to suppose that participating in the same classroom activity is not the same experience for each group. One group is more mature than the other, but each group is equally expected to do close work, make fine discriminations, sit quietly for extended periods of time, pay attention, cooperate, finish tasks, and inhibit aggression. Many educators think that these are the factors which frustrate boys as a group more than girls.

Robinson (37) is convinced that research supports a hypothesis of sex difference in reading achievement during the first few years of formal schooling, but she states, "At present it is not clear whether just being a girl gives a young child a better chance for early reading success or whether something inherent in the school situation or the social setting militates against the progress of boys." After pointing out that boys as a group produce more remedial reading problems, get lower school marks, have a higher incidence of nonpromotion, and produce more "behavior problems" than do girls as a group, Smith and Jenson (40) conclude, "all these findings emphasize the fact that the school functions less effectively for boys than for girls."

3. *Basal reader materials are less motivating and satisfying to boys than to girls.* This idea is an extension of hypothesis two, since the reading materials are naturally part of the curriculum. The rationale behind this hypothesis is that the rather sterile, repetitious "look, oh look;

This male trio seems to be digging
what's going on in school!

see baby play" vocabulary and the rigid conformist mood, tone, and
atmosphere contained in and conveyed by the preprimers, primers, and
early readers are considerably less challenging to boys than to girls.
It is often alleged that the "content" is a far cry from what the culture
has taught to and expects from boys. Therefore, beginning reading,
which should be an exciting, challenging new adventure, is actually a
dull, regressive sort of experience unless the teacher can project more
excitement into the material.

4. *Most primary teachers are women*. Allen (2) states, "Social environments for males and females are not and never have been the same or
equal," and points out that from this fact may stem differences in interests, values, and achievement. Bell (6) holds that the difference in reading success between boys and girls is related to their emotional relationships with their teachers. It is his opinion that it is easier for girls
to identify with women teachers and that boys are not provided with

enough opportunities for the expression of aggression. The various studies all agree that boys show more aggressive tendencies than do girls. The school frowns on aggressive behavior, and this no doubt influences some teachers to react toward boys in a manner different from that manifested toward girls who, as a group, may have a reputation for being docile, quiet, and cooperative. Terman (44) states that there is ample indication that some sort of "halo" effect operates in the classroom to give girls higher teacher ratings or grades than would be merited on the basis of objective achievement test results. St. John (38) does not question the fact that in grades one through four, girls "distinctly" excel boys in reading and general school achievement, but he states, "They (girls) excel *less* when achievement is measured by standard tests than when it is measured by *teacher marks.*"

5. *Boys are less motivated to learn to read.* This hypothesis is closely related to certain others that have previously been mentioned, but it is advanced often enough in the literature on reading to be considered independently. Nila (30) is of the opinion that girls are more likely to work up to the capacity of their abilities than are boys. She states, "The writer believes that the reason boys and girls who are equally ready to read do not make the same progress lies in the factor of motivation." Wilson et al. (47) state, "It would seem probable that the reasons for more rapid progress by girls are related to learning interests and dispositions, rather than to more subtle sex differences such as mental qualities or characteristics of femininity."

**Early
Readers**

Some children begin mastering the reading process at an early age without the benefit of formal instruction. In our society these early readers are often viewed with fascination and even awe. In his early studies of genius (upper 1 percent of population based on intelligence scores), Lewis M. Terman reported a high incidence of early readers. There are many case studies which report on individual children as early readers. The biographies of a number of famous individuals noted for high achievement in science, art, or literature also report early reading. This data, coupled with certain other case studies of early readers, has tended to associate early reading with genius or very high intellectual ability.

When they make a good start, encourage them to keep moving.

Data from recent studies by Durkin (12) has suggested that genius is not an absolute prerequisite for early reading. One group of forty-nine early readers had a median IQ of 121; and a second group of 156 children attained a median IQ of 133. While the data indicates most early readers in these groups measured relatively high in regard to intelligence, there were others in the group who fell within the average range.

Study of one group of subjects covered a five-year span and provided interesting data on reading achievement for the forty-nine subjects (12). The median grade level achievement for the group at the beginning of grade one was 1.9. A median gain of eighteen months was reported at the end of grade one and a three-month gain was noted over the summer months. Thus, the median reading achievement score for the group at the beginning of grade two was 4.0. The successive median grade level achievements reported were

> End of grade two   4.9 gain of nine months
> End of grade three   5.3 gain of four months
> End of grade four   6.7 gain of fourteen months
> End of grade five   7.6 gain of nine months

The most rapid growth in reading achievement was recorded in grade one. At the end of the fifth grade, the group of early readers had a median reading grade achievement of 7.6, which exceeded the normal expectancy (6.9) by seven months. This was approximately the degree of superiority noted at the beginning of grade one. The data on gains in achievement could likely be interpreted in different ways. Undoubtedly, a study of individual children and an analysis of their progress would provide important clues that are masked by the group median scores presented here.

The Debate on Early Instruction

Paralleling the recent emphasis on moving the teaching of subject matter downward in the grade-level structure, there has been considerable discussion relative to providing formal reading instruction in kindergarten. Each highly publicized account of a child, or small group of children, who acquire some reading ability before entering school is interpreted in some quarters as evidence supporting earlier formal reading instruction.

Questions relative to the teaching of reading in the kindergarten are often posed in such a way as to lead protagonists into defending an either/or position. Polar positions preclude the possibility of arriving at a meaningful consensus. The question "Should reading be taught in the kindergarten?" is not the same as "Should some children be taught reading in the kindergarten?" The former can lead to logical analyses under such diverse titles as *Let's Not Teach Reading in Kindergarten* (25) and *Kindergartners Are Ready! Are We?* (19).

The early reading controversy is rooted in an important educational principle to which lip service is paid by practically all educators. This principle is that "the school is to educate each child up to his maximum ability, taking each child where he is and moving him at his own pace." Speaking of learning the reading process, Newman (29) states, ". . . no child should be denied entré to probably the most important of our school-learned forms of expression if he is at the point in his development when it is opportune for him to take part in this expression himself. . . ."

When relatively few children attended kindergarten, the issue of reading could be safely ignored. With the rapid increase in kindergarten (and even earlier preschool experiences), the problem of "What is the proper curriculum for kindergarten?" becomes a significant educational issue. To attempt to resolve this question by recourse to personal preferences results in a meaningless debate.

It is probable that one's concept of the role of the kindergarten will influence his attitude toward early reading instruction. If the kindergarten is seen as a *preschool* experience, the principle referred to above may be waived. On the other hand, if kindergarten is seen as an integral part of the planned educational sequence rather than as play time or an educational holding action, growth in significant educational processes would be expected.

In much of the discussion of reading instruction in the kindergarten, there is either a tacit or openly expressed fear that if reading is taught, the situation can, and likely will, somehow get out of hand. Past practices in our schools would seem to indicate that such fears are well-founded. Newman (29) presents a rationale which favors reading instruction in the kindergarten, adding the reservation, "but only if the reading activities are taught in such a way as to build enthusiasm for books and reading and the foundation for a lifelong interest in reading for pleasure and inquiry. This is a big 'if. . . .'"

In addition to the problem of what type of reading instruction might be appropriate for kindergarten, there is the question of "instruction for whom?" There is no experimentally established chronological or mental age at which children should begin receiving reading instruction. It is well-established that large numbers of children admitted to first grade on the basis of chronological age, rather than readiness for reading, do experience difficulty in learning. Many of these nonreading pupils react adversely to the pressures which accompany instruction under such conditions. The fear of many educators is expressed in the question, "What is to prevent more of this type of pressure, administered even earlier in the child's educational career, if formal reading instruction is moved into the kindergarten?"

By a process of careful selection of research data, one can build a fairly strong case for earlier reading instruction for *some* children. No manipulation of data will result in a mandate for extending earlier instruction to *all* children.

There is good reason for raising the question of how well the school is equipped for making the proper differentiation of instruction. If we have failed to achieve a workable differentiation at the level at which we now introduce reading instruction, by what educational alchemy can we expect to achieve this goal by making the task much more complicated?

There is a related problem which should be considered. It is unrealistic to devise a new role for the kindergarten without revamping the curriculum and teaching practices of later grades. One of the saddest things that could happen to a community would be to develop an outstanding kindergarten program in which reading is taught to those children who are ready to read and in which the primary grades continued their present traditional grade-level-dominated teaching.

Any gains made in reading would be lost if succeeding grades did not provide a flexible program built on on-going diagnosis of children's present achievement. A breakthrough achieved at any particular level must be accompanied by breakthroughs all along the educational continuum.

It might be argued that the above rationale is extraneous to the question of whether or not reading should be taught in the kindergarten. It should be kept in mind that the points raised are not advanced as arguments *against* the proposition, but rather as an effort to view it in a larger educational context.

"Should reading be taught in the kindergarten?" is the type of question heard too often in education. In essence, this is an abstraction, or even an isolated fragment, of a much more complex question. The larger question should focus on "What are the experiences one would find in an ideal kindergarten?" As a first step in answering this question, one would have to determine the *purpose* of kindergarten.

It would take years of evaluation and reevaluation to cut through the shibboleths developed in the past. Purpose could hardly be divorced from learning and learners. Is kindergarten to be characterized by an informal relaxed approach to growth? Growth in what areas? Is its purpose to take advantage of one of the "golden years" of great potential growth in formal learning? Or is it to "school break" the child and prepare him for the institutionalized environment of the school? Is kindergarten a last fling before institutionalism? Is it to be child-centered? If so, what does this mean? Does the kindergarten have a curriculum? Should much of the present first-grade curriculum be moved down into kindergarten? Should kindergarten be renamed first grade?

Emotions and Learning

The school may take partial credit when children learn at a level approximating their capacity or when they exhibit social and emotional behavior that society recognizes as acceptable and healthy. Yet, few of us like to admit that the schools must also share responsibility for pupil maladjustment. Problems in learning to read do not stem exclusively from methods and teaching materials. While methodology may often be a contributory factor, the human organism is extremely flexible, and it is a proven fact that children can and do learn to read under the most adverse methodological procedures, provided that they are physically and emotionally ready to read. Teaching reading involves helping children face frustration, accept reality, drain off tension, and apply energy to learning tasks.

It is apparent from the literature on emotions and reading that there are two major hypotheses which might account for the interaction between emotions and reading disability.

1. Where emotional behavior and reading problems are found together, the emotional involvement stems from failure, frustration, tension, and pressure connected with the reading problem.

Reading failure⟶Emotional reactions

Here it is implied that the child's emotions become involved in reading through success or failure. While competition may not be new to the child, the type of competition he encounters in the reading situation *is* new to him. Never before has so much been expected from him by his parents and his teacher. Reading ability is very highly prized in our society, and pressures on the child from parents, teachers, and peers all seem to focus on this one front. He has not sensed this type of pressure in his drawing and coloring activities, in rhythm activities, in listening to stories the teacher has read, or in other activities found in the curriculum.

The child's frustrations mount as a result of failure and also as a result of his inability to please the figures of authority—parents and teachers. His attitudes toward himself are influenced by attitudes around him. Feelings of inferiority and personal inadequacy result. When one's ego is threatened, tension and emotional conflict are inevitable. Under these circumstances, the child resorts to some behavior which, irrational as it may appear to adults, seems to the child to be a means of escape from an untenable position.

It is amazing how varied the responses of different children are to frustration and ego-threatening situations. The same classroom stimulus will not produce like responses among different children. The teacher's remark, "now let's open our reading workbooks—we should be on page thirty-nine," may elicit responses varying from elation to nausea among the various pupils in the class. The individual child's past experiences both at home and school, and the impact these experiences have had on the child's attitudes toward himself, toward the teacher, and toward parents and peers, will all determine the response which this stimulus evokes. One child may give the appearance of functional deafness—he didn't hear the request; one may request to leave the room; another child may respond with the ultimate of conformity and open his book to page 39, even though he has never worked successfully on any of the preceding pages or any preceding workbooks.

2. *Unresolved emotional problems, which originally need not have been related to reading, may prevent the child from applying his energies to the learning task. The nonreading behavior is simply a symptom of the emotional problem.*

Unresolved emotional problem——➤Reading problem

When reading problems and emotional involvements are found together, there may also be other factors contributing to the reading problem (i.e., physical factors, educational procedures used, learned responses to frustration).

Several principles of teaching reading discussed in Chapter 1 are related to emotional problems and reading. Unrelenting pressure brought to bear on a child to make him read will not always achieve desirable results.

The Teacher's Role in Dealing with Emotionally Involved Reading Problems

What should the teacher do for children with reading problems who also show evidence that there is an emotional factor involved? Several factors make this question difficult to answer.

1. Some teachers, parents, school boards, and critics of education do not yet admit that in many cases nonlearning and emotional problems are inextricably knit together. Nevertheless, the belief that the schools have a tremendous impact on ego-development, or ego-starvation, of pupils is gaining wider acceptance, and teachers are coming to realize that they are necessarily involved in the process of dealing with social and emotional maladjustments. Yet, there are many critics of American education who think that the school's concern with the social and emotional development of children is a tender-minded, do-gooder escape mechanism, thrown up as a rearguard action by confused teachers engaged in a retreat from teaching.

It must be admitted that some teachers who verbally embrace the principle that the school should be concerned with the pupil's emotional health are hazy as to *why*. "Meeting the child's needs and interests" may have, through constant usage, been reduced to jargon, but it once was meaningful. "Educating the whole child" may share the same present-day reputation, but this, too, once had meaning. Both of these principles involved the recognition that all school experiences are related to learning. The school cannot meet the needs of children if it ignores psychological needs, such as the need for success, self-realization, creativity, and an acceptable concept of self. Failure in school is the most important factor in thwarting the fulfillment of the child's needs.

2. *The teacher's ego needs can contribute to the child's insecurity and pose threats to his adjustment and concept of self.* The fact that some children fail to make progress commensurate with grade-level norms may become a threat to the teacher. This threat is often met with more pressure and sometimes with unconscious hostility.

3. *Another important factor is the conviction on the part of teachers that they are not prepared to deal with emotional problems.* This lack of preparation is undoubtedly the case with some teachers, some parents, some clinicians, and quite a few detention homes. Also, it is probably true that most of the maladjusted are not equipped to help themselves. There are some children who have emotional problems which teachers cannot hope to alleviate, just as there are some pupil maladjustments produced by the school which could have been prevented.

Many teachers do practice a certain amount of therapy, and they rarely see it as something extraneous to the learning situation. It is simply part of the job of guiding the learning activities of children.

To illustrate, an elementary school arranged for a thorough diagnosis of a number of children with severe reading problems. One third grader, Mary, was a nonreader. She had intelligence adequate for learning and was attractive but shy and retiring. When asked about friends, she had only one friend, Miss Blank (her teacher). In answer to other questions, Whom do you like to play with? walk home with? visit? Miss Blank was the only human being mentioned. At noon, this child and teacher were observed in the cafeteria. All the children in the third grade sat around one long table, the teacher at one end. Mary sat next to her and was most possessive. She put her hand in the teacher's, looked at her most of the time, talked to her (not shy here). In fact, before the meal was over, she had managed to slip her chair up very close to the teacher and place her head on the teacher's lap. The teacher stroked her head and shoulder all the while talking to others around her and keeping in touch with all that was going on around the large table. As the group left, Mary and the teacher left hand-in-hand.

Later, Mary's problem was discussed. Her teacher brought up the matter of the child's complete dependence on her and stated that she had to be very careful that Mary's possessiveness did not arouse antagonism among the other children. (There had been absolutely no resentment shown in the cafeteria although this type of behavior was a daily occurrence.) The teacher knew these facts: Mary lived with her grandparents; her parents were divorced, and the father worked in another state. The child created fantasies of her father coming to see her; he never came. Several months earlier the mother had taken employment as a waitress in a large city several hundred miles away and had not been home to visit her daughter during this period. The grandparents fulfilled the child's physical needs, and she was fairly well-dressed and clean. They completely failed to help the child in her emotional problem, which stemmed from feelings of rejection and attendant guilt feelings about her own contribution to parental rejection.

While all of this history was known to everyone in the small community, including Mary's two previous teachers, none had sensed the child's loneliness or great need for someone to tie to, until Miss Blank. The important point is that Miss Blank did not feel that she was doing something "nice" for Mary. She did not think of what she was doing as therapy. Her problem, as she saw it, was to protect Mary by concealing from the other children the fact that Mary was monopolizing the teacher. No change had yet occurred in Mary's reading behavior, but gradually she was able to bring some energy to bear on learning. Meeting the needs of children is therapy, and the more flexible and creative the reading teacher is in discerning the child's real needs, the more likely it is that she will alleviate present reading problems and forestall the appearance of others.

Being aware of children's psychological needs and observing their social behavior can help a teacher detect many signs of maladjustment which are, or may become, related to reading behavior. Figure 10 is a personal inventory containing items which focus the teacher's attention on social-emotional behavior and which may reveal the presence of unresolved problems.

NAME: _____
ADDRESS: _____
AGE: _____
GRADE: _____
Father: Living ( ) Deceased ( ) Occupation: _____
Mother: Living ( ) Deceased ( ) Occupation: _____

	Above Average	*Average*	*Below Average*
Feeling of security	( ) ( ) ( )	( ) ( ) ( )	( ) ( ) ( )
Acceptance by peer group	( ) ( ) ( )	( ) ( ) ( )	( ) ( ) ( )
Attitude toward school	( ) ( ) ( )	( ) ( ) ( )	( ) ( ) ( )
Degree of self-confidence	( ) ( ) ( )	( ) ( ) ( )	( ) ( ) ( )
Reaction to frustration	( ) ( ) ( )	( ) ( ) ( )	( ) ( ) ( )
Language facility	( ) ( ) ( )	( ) ( ) ( )	( ) ( ) ( )
Ability to follow directions	( ) ( ) ( )	( ) ( ) ( )	( ) ( ) ( )
Independent work habits	( ) ( ) ( )	( ) ( ) ( )	( ) ( ) ( )
Concentration span	( ) ( ) ( )	( ) ( ) ( )	( ) ( ) ( )
Background and experiences which relate to reading	( ) ( ) ( )	( ) ( ) ( )	( ) ( ) ( )
Parents' attitude toward child's reading	( ) ( ) ( )	( ) ( ) ( )	( ) ( ) ( )
Parents' acceptance of child	( ) ( ) ( )	( ) ( ) ( )	( ) ( ) ( )
Estimate of home:			
(Socio-economic status)	( ) ( ) ( )	( ) ( ) ( )	( ) ( ) ( )
(Emotional climate)	( ) ( ) ( )	( ) ( ) ( )	( ) ( ) ( )

Observed behavior which is related to judgments on above items:

_____
_____
_____
_____

Figure 10

Personal Adjustment Inventory.

SUMMARY

There are large and significant differences among children as they begin learning to read. Teachers are generally aware of this fact, but classroom practices and habits of thought prevailing in the school and community sometimes tend to slight the significance of these pupil differences. Our society places a high value on reading ability, and as a result, all children in the group are expected to progress at a somewhat uniform rate. Failure to do so is a very noticeable failure. When some children in the group do not meet fixed arbitrary standards of achievement, pressures from both school and home increase. Reading is particularly sensitive to pressure because it involves learning a complicated symbol system.

Knowing how to teach reading is very important for a reading teacher. Most pupils in a class will learn when they have such a teacher. However, in some instances, knowing how to teach reading is not quite enough. One must also know how to *teach children to read.* In these situations the teacher must be able to read the signs of human growth and behavior. Noting, understanding, and reacting to children's feelings, attitudes, rate of growth, independence (or lack of it), will prove to be as important as methodology.

Children as beginning readers are quite pliable, yet there are many who cannot adjust to, or profit from, a lock-step educational philosophy which treats pupils as interchangeable parts in the classroom. Teachers must be able to use what children bring to the classroom as well as what they themselves bring.

YOUR POINT OF VIEW?

Would you defend or attack the following statements?

1. The teacher, the school environment, and the curriculum inescapably function as barriers to, or means of, fulfilling the psychological needs of children.
2. Inadequate reading ability, or failure to learn to read well enough to meet the demands of the school curriculum, is a factor in producing antisocial behavior and delinquency.
3. A thoroughly differentiated instructional program in grade one which is based on sound ongoing diagnosis would materially reduce the difference between the reading achievement scores of boys when compared with girls.
4. Emotional factors are no more important in the learning of reading than in any learning situation.
5. The teacher is not a causal factor in the disproportionate number of reading failures among boys as compared with girls.

Respond to the following problems:

A. Assume you have worked closely with a group of six-year-olds who learned to read before entering school. Describe these children, touching on the behavioral characteristics you think they would display.

B. Assume a forced choice item on a test required you to select one of the following broad categories as being the most influential causal factor in the production of sex differences in beginning reading. Which would you choose? Why?
    1. Physiological—maturational factors.
    2. Social—cultural—environmental factors.

BIBLIOGRAPHY

1. Alden, Clara; Sullivan, Helen B.; and Durrell, Donald, "The Frequency of Special Reading Disabilities," *Education* LXII (1942): 32–36.

2. Allen, C. N., "Recent Research on Sex Differences," *Psychological Bulletin* XXXII (1935): 343–54.

3. Anderson, Irving H.; Hughes, Byron O.; and Dixon, Robert W., "Age of Learning to Read and Its Relation to Sex, Intelligence, and Reading Achievement in Sixth Grade," *Journal of Educational Research* (February 1956): 447–53.

4. Axline, Virginia, "Nondirective Therapy for Poor Readers," *Journal of Consulting Psychology* XI (1947): 61–69.

5. Ayres, Leonard, *Laggards in Our Schools.* New York, Russell Sage Foundation, 1909.

6. Bell, John E., "Emotional Factors in the Treatment of Reading Difficulties," *Journal of Consulting Psychology* IX (1945): 125–31.

7. Blanchard, Phyllis, "Reading Difficulties in Relation to Difficulties of Personality and Emotional Development," *Mental Hygiene* XX (1936): 384–413.

8. Bond, Guy L. and Dykstra, Robert, "The Cooperative Research Program in First-Grade Reading Instruction," *Reading Research Quarterly* (Summer 1967): 5–142.

9. Burns, Paul C. and Schell, Leo M., eds., *Elementary School Language Arts,* second ed. Chicago: Rand McNally College Publishing Co., 1973. Part 3.

10. Carroll, Marjorie W., "Sex Differences in Reading Readiness at the First Grade Level," *Elementary English* (October 1948): 370–75.

11. Cramer, Ronald L., "Reading to Children: Why and How," *Reading Teacher* 28 (February 1975): 460–63.
12. Durkin, Dolores, "The Achievement of Pre-school Readers: Two Longitudinal Studies," *Reading Research Quarterly* (Summer 1966): 5–36.
13. Dykstra, Robert, "Summary of Second-Grade Phase of the Cooperative Research Program in Primary Reading Instruction," *Reading Research Quarterly* (Fall 1968): 49–70.
14. Ekwall, Eldon E., ed., *Psychological Factors in the Teaching of Reading.* Columbus, O.: Charles E. Merrill Publishing Co., 1973.
15. Fabian, A. A., "Reading Disability: An Index of Pathology," *American Journal of Orthopsychiatry* (April 1955): 319–29.
16. Gates, Arthur I., "Sex Differences in Reading Ability," *Elementary School Journal* (May 1961): 431–34.
17. Glass, Gerald G., "Students Misconceptions Concerning Their Reading," ✗ *The Reading Teacher* (May 1968): 765–68.
18. Heilman, Arthur W., *Effects of an Intensive In-Service Program on Teacher's Classroom Behavior and Pupil's Reading Achievement.* Cooperative Research Project No. 2709, USOE, 1965, p. 53.
19. Hillerich, Robert L., "Kindergartners Are Ready! Are We?" *Elementary English* (May 1965); 569–73.
20. Hughes, Mildred C., "Sex Differences in Reading Achievement in the Elementary Grades," *Clinical Studies in Reading II,* Supplementary Educational Monographs no. 77. Chicago: University of Chicago Press, pp. 102–6.
21. Johnson, Dale D., "Sex Differences in Reading across Cultures," *Reading Research Quarterly* 9, no. 1, 1973–74, pp. 67–86.
22. McCollum, Mary E. and Shapiro, Mary J., "An Approach to the Remediation of Severe Reading Disabilities," *Educaton* (March 1947): 488–93.
23. McNeil, John D. and Keislar, Evan R., *Oral and Non-Oral Methods of Teaching Reading by an Auto-Instructional Device.* Cooperative Research Project No. 1413, USOE, 1963.
24. Means, Chalmers, "Sex Differences in Reading Achievement," *Improving Reading through Classroom Practices.* Joint Proceedings of the Twenty-seventh Reading Conference and the Third Intensive Summer Workshop, Pennsylvania State University, 1966.
25. Micucci, Pat, "Let's *Not* Teach Reading in Kindergarten!" *Elementary English* (March 1964): 246–51.
26. Miller, Wilma H., "Home Prereading Experiences and First-Grade Reading Achievement," *Reading Teacher* (April 1969): 641–45.

27. Missildine, W. H., "The Emotional Background of Thirty Children with Reading Disabilities with Emphasis on Its Coercive Elements," *Nervous Child* (July 1946): 263–72.

28. Monroe, Marion, *Children Who Cannot Read*. Chicago: University of Chicago Press, 1932.

29. Newman, Robert E., "The Kindergarten Reading Controversy," *Elementary English* (March 1966): 235–39.

30. Nila, Sister Mary, "Foundations of a Successful Reading Program," *Education* (May 1953): 543–55.

31. Page, William, ed., *Help for the Reading Teacher: New Directions in Research*. Urbana, Ill.: National Conference on Research in English, 1975.

32. Prescott, George A., "Sex Differences in Metropolitan Readiness Test Results," *Journal of Educational Research* (April 1955): 605–10.

33. Preston, Mary J., "Reading Failure and the Child's Security," *American Journal of Orthopsychiatry* X (1940): 239–52.

34. Preston, Ralph, "Reading Achievement of German and American Children," *School and Society* XC (1962): 350–54.

35. Quick, Donald M., "Toward Positive Self-Concept," *Reading Teacher* 26 (February 1973): 468–71.

36. Rich, Anita and Bernstein, Joanne E., "The Picture Book Image of Entering School," *Language Arts* 52 (December 1975): 978–82.

37. Robinson, Helen M., "Factors Which Affect Success in Reading," *Elementary School Journal* (January 1955): 266.

38. St. John, Charles W., "The Maladjustment of Boys in Certain Elementary Grades," *Educational Administration and Supervision* XVIII (1932): 659–72.

39. Shepherd, Terry and Iles, Lynn B., "What Is Bibliotherapy?" *Language Arts* 53 (May 1976): 569–71.

40. Smith, C. A. and Jenson, M. R., "Educational, Psychological and Physiological Factors in Reading Readiness," *Elementary School Journal* (April 1936): 689.

41. Smith, Richard J. and Johnson, Dale D., *Teaching Children to Read*. Reading, Mass.: Addison-Wesley Publishing Co., 1976. Chapter 10.

42. Staiger, Ralph C., "Self Responsibility and Reading," *Education* (May 1957): 561–65.

43. Stroud, J. B. and Lindquist, E. F., "Sex Differences in Achievement in the Elementary and Secondary School," *Journal of Educational Psychology* (1942): 657–67.

44. Terman, Lewis M. and Tyler, Leona E., "Psychological Sex Differences," *Manual of Child Psychology*, second ed., L. Carmichael, ed. New York: John Wiley & Sons, Inc., 1954. Chapter 17.

45. Tibbetts, Sylvia-Lee, "Sex Differences in Children's Reading Preferences," *Reading Teacher 28* (December 1974): 279–81.

46. Vorhaus, Pauline G., "Rorschach Configurations Associated with Reading Disability," *Projective Techniques XVI* (1952): 3–19.

47. Wilson, Frank T.; Burke, Agnes; and Flemming, C. W., "Sex Differences in Beginning Reading in a Progressive School," *Journal of Educational Research* (April 1939): 570–82.

48. Wright, Benjamin, "Postscript on Permissiveness," *Elementary School Journal* (April 1965): 393–94.

49. ———, and Tuska, Shirley, "The Price of Permissiveness," *Elementary School Journal* (January 1965): 179–83.

50. Young, Robert A., "Case Studies in Reading Disability," *American Journal of Orthopsychiatry VIII* (1938): 230–54.

Chapter 4

Beginning Reading I: Methods and Materials

Instructional materials, which are viewed as a blueprint for every classroom contingency, may pose a threat to teachers' creativity. Teachers can become overdependent on or dominated by materials. If one starts from the premise that poor instruction is the trademark of our schools, then "teacher-proof materials" might seem desirable. On the other hand, if one believes that "teachers are the most important variable in classroom learning situations," then one might expect teachers to be a major source of *input* into teaching strategies.

It is quite obvious that teachers cannot and should not develop all of the materials they will need in teaching reading. It is also obvious that materials which are alleged to be equally useful for all children simply cannot be. Differences among learners call for differentiation of instruction.

This chapter deals with materials prepared outside the schools but designed specifically for teaching reading in the schools. Each set of materials represents a philosophy of instruction. Different materials will have some instructional goals in common and some philosophical premises and instructional goals that differentiate them from other approaches. Perhaps one of the main differences between available materials will be found in the degree of emphasis placed on teaching certain skills. The materials discussed are

Basal Reader Series
Initial Teaching Alphabet (*ita*)
Programmed Reading Materials
Words in Color
Linguistic Regular Spelling Approach
Computer Assisted Instruction (CAI)

The Basal
Reader Approach

For decades, basal reader series have served as one of the chief instructional materials used in the elementary grades for teaching reading. Throughout the 1950s and early 1960s, basal series tended to be very much alike. Significant innovations were held to a minimum, and a number of criticisms were leveled against these materials. Critics alleged that

1. The materials were dull, insipid, and too repetitive.
2. The language used was somewhat removed from the child's own language usage.
3. Story material often lacked literary merit.
4. Too little emphasis was placed on teaching letter-sound relationships in grade one.
5. Content dealt almost exclusively with characters and incidents drawn from middle class strata; and conversely minority groups were practically ignored (26).

Some of these criticisms were justified, and authors and publishers made a number of changes in basals that most observers feel enhanced the value of these materials. There was another type of criticism, which in reality should not have been aimed at the basal materials, but rather at their misuse. These particular practices were neither suggested or condoned by any basal program. However, certain critics of basals contended that these practices were inevitable outcomes of using basals. For instance, when using basals, teachers would

teacher problems —

1. Have a group of children read "round-robin" every story they read. Each child would be asked to focus her attention on the same line at a given time.
2. Resort without exception to "three groups" within a classroom, and these groups would remain static throughout the year.
3. Make no provision for individual differences beyond this "three-group" pattern.
4. Hold the more facile reader to the basal material only, forcing her to move through this material at a pace far below her capacity.
5. Prohibit children from selecting and reading other books in which they may be interested.

Unfortunately, the above practices could be found in certain classrooms. Removing basals from these classrooms, however, would not get at the basic problem which, essentially, is poor teaching. The following is a description of the materials usually found in any basal reading series. These materials are arranged to parallel the grade-level system. They range in difficulty from a work-type readiness book (containing pictures, geometrical forms, and letter-matching exercises) to rather massive anthologies at seventh- and eighth-grade levels.

Readiness Books

At the readiness level one might find picture books in which a picture, or series of pictures, suggests a child-centered story. From the pictures, the teacher and the pupils develop a story. The more skillful the teacher is in providing background and involving the pupils in participation and interpretation, the more successful the use of these materials will be. Other readiness books may call for children to identify and mark similar objects, letters, or words, and to facilitate the development of visual perception. To strengthen auditory discriminations, the child will identify two pictures in a group whose naming words rhyme. Identifying other pairs of pictures which start with the same sound gives practice in the discrimination of initial sounds.

The readiness books are followed by a series of three or four pre-primers in which the characters are the same ones the children met and talked about in the readiness books. The preprimers introduce pupils to printed words *along with pictures.* The first few pages may have single words which are "naming words" to go with the picture. Gradually more words and sentences per page are used.

Many basal materials are characterized by a rather rigid vocabulary control in the preprimer and primer stages. This control does not involve *which* words are introduced, but rather the *rate* at which they are introduced. Thus the introduction of twenty to twenty-five different words would be representative of most first preprimers (pp[1]). Usually there are three or four preprimers in a given series, and each of these will introduce approximately this same number of new words while systematically repeating those words previously introduced.

Since stories in the first preprimer are limited to two dozen different words, the story, of necessity, lacks literary merit. Adult critics have described this material as "dull, insipid, contrived, and offensive to the eye and ear." It is much easier to level such criticisms against materials than it is to solve the problem of how to present vibrant prose to six-year-olds who cannot as yet read anything in print. In defense of criticism, the truth is that for several decades, basal materials did remain quite static. During this period, the frequent "revisions" of these materials were quite meaningless.

Until the mid-1960s, the primary difference between competing basals was to be found in the names of the characters who pulled the little red wagons and called to the housebroken doggies. However, at the present time, there are basal materials available which represent a wider philosophical continuum. Some basals stress meaning and an early emphasis on sight vocabulary, others emphasize code cracking, and some attempt to achieve a balance between these two polar positions. Story characters and life situations involving minority groups are now the rule rather than the exception. The literary quality of materials for use beyond the beginning stage has been upgraded. While basals have changed more in the past decade than during the previous thirty years, some critics hold that the changes are more apparent than real.

Primers

The primer is the first hardback book in the series. It carefully builds on what has gone before, using the same characters the children are familiar with and reviewing the words already met, while it introduces 100 to 150 new words.

First Readers

Some series contain a single first reader; others have two (1^1 level and 1^2 level). Different series vary as to vocabulary load introduced, but a range between 315 and 400 words for first grade is representative.

Graded Readers

Each subsequent grade level introduces one or more basal reading books. Many series provide two books at each of the grade levels, second through fourth, and one book at grades five and beyond. These are usually designated by grade number plus a subscript which indicates first or second half of the year (2^1–2^2, 3^1–3^2, 4–5–6–7–8).

Workbooks

Separate workbooks which parallel each level (preprimers, primers, first readers 2^1–2^2, etc.) are available. The workbooks present material arranged as teaching exercises. These are usually designed so that one concept or skill is dealt with on each page. The exercises reinforce the teaching of skills which are being dealt with in the readers. In some cases, workbook pages are tied to specific stories in the reader. In others, skill-building exercises are independent of story content and could be used whether or not a particular basal reader were available.

Supplementary Materials

It is becoming more common at all grade levels for basic reader series to include some supplementary books to be used in conjunction with the regular graded series. There has always been an abundant supply of these supplementary materials available at the intermediate level. Recently, good supplementary books have appeared at the early primary level where they are sorely needed. Some of these are easy to read, introducing very few words other than those already met in the regular basal texts. Others are designed for the more advanced readers and are more difficult and more challenging than the regular graded series.

There are two keys to learning: *supplement* and *adapt;* and there are hundreds of adaptations that facilitate language learning.

Other supplementary materials include large poster-size wall charts or spiral-book charts which exactly duplicate a preprimer. The large picture and large print have obvious advantages for classroom use. There has been considerable emphasis on filmstrips designed for use with basic readers series. The reading gains reported as resulting from the systematic use of filmstrips and other visual aids are encouraging (21, 22).

Teacher Manuals

Teacher manuals or guide books, containing suggestions for effective use of materials, accompany each reading level. That is, a separate manual is available for the preprimer, primer, and first reader stages as well as for each subsequent level. These manuals are discussed in more detail in the following section.

Using a Basal Reader Series

(Advantages)

The purpose here is to deal with the framework of basal programs as designed for the first year of instruction. Major advantages of using a good series include

1. Modern reader series are characterized by excellent use of pictures and art work.
2. A number of the first books used deal with the same characters, giving children a feeling of familiarity with the material and adding to their confidence in reading.
3. The books are graded to provide systematic instruction from the prereadiness level through the upper elementary grades.
4. These graded materials permit teachers a great deal of flexibility in dealing with individual differences and in working with children grouped according to attained reading skill.
5. Excellent teacher guides are provided for each book or level. These provide suggestions for a step-by-step teaching program.
6. If used properly, the basic reader series deals with all phases of the reading program, guarding against overemphasis on some aspects and neglect of others.
7. Practice of new skills is introduced in a logical sequence.
8. A great deal of review is provided in deliberate, well-thought-out procedures.
9. The vocabulary is rigidly controlled to prevent frustration in beginning reading.
10. Use of prepared materials saves teachers considerable time.

A Well-balanced Program

Providing a well-balanced program is a virtue of basal series, particularly in the beginning reading stage. They provide for silent and oral reading, and by means of grouping and through individual work, the teacher can vary the emphasis for different pupils. The preparation of pupils for tasks is thoroughly outlined in the teacher's manual. During the readiness period, the children have used a prereading book which included a number of pictures. Through these pictures, the children were introduced to the characters that they will meet again in the preprimer, primer, and first reader. The teacher acquaints the children with the names of these characters and prints their names on the chalkboard, thus preparing them for the first words they will encounter in the preprimer. The pictures are specific in that they represent *particular* persons, but they are general in that the characters in them are doing things that most children understand. Out of these picture situations, discussion can grow and provide an introduction to formal reading in basal materials.

The first few pages of the preprimer may be only pictures, but very soon words are introduced. These will probably be the names of the boy and girl who have been met previously in pictures—Jane, Sally, Ted, or Jack. The teacher will probably use the chalkboard and flash cards for both teaching and reviewing words. During seatwork, the children will draw a line from the word (*Sally, father, Ted.* etc.) to a picture the word represents. They might be asked to underline one of three sentences which describe a picture:

Sally rides in the wagon.
Sally plays with Spot.
Sally plays with Father.

Such exercises help children learn words in the first preprimer. Soon, more than one familiar word will appear on each page but rarely more than one *new* word.

The repetition of words in beginning reading can dull the child's appetite for reading. The teacher must guide the pupils into both imaginative and reminiscent "building of ideas and stories." The book may contain the words "Look, Mother" under the picture. These words, with the help of the picture, can serve as the basis for a great number of interesting and logical questions and conjectures. Perhaps from the following, one might easily visualize the picture that accompanies "Look, Mother."

"Who is in the picture?"
"Yes, what is Tom doing?"
"Does Spot like to wear Tom's hat?"
"What is Tom's mother doing?"

Good teaching uses Basal Readers as a tool, which need not be a form of tyranny over the minds of children.

"Is she watching Tom?"
"Would he like for her to see Spot?"
"Does Spot look funny?"
"What does Tom say to his mother—who will read what he says?"

Many other points could have been discussed—such as pets in general and kindness to pets (Tom was not hurting Spot, but playing). Why wasn't mother watching? (Sometimes mothers are busy.) Why was she picking flowers? (Innumerable good responses.) What season of the year was this? As the child learns more words, she has less need for pictures which suggest the context or hold attention. As the pupils move through the basal series and master sight words, they need less story analysis by the teacher.

Comprehension and meaning are emphasized as children select the best titles for paragraphs or short stories or as they recall sequences of events. Concepts of time, number, size, and direction are developed through seatwork which calls for children to follow directions, to perceive relationships, to grasp main ideas, and to anticipate events. Auditory discrimination exercises are provided in the form of rhyming exercises and an emphasis on the initial sounds of words. Motor coordination of small muscles is developed in exercises such as tracing, coloring outlined forms, drawing connecting lines between matching words, and copying words from a model.

One of the greatest advantages in using a good series is the availability of excellent teacher guides. These guides are carefully worked out by the authors with the total reading program in mind. Sound laws of learning are followed, specific techniques are suggested, lesson plans are given in great detail, and the reasons for using certain approaches are explained. The beginning teacher would be remiss in not following the teacher guides and in not becoming very familiar with the rationale and concrete suggestions they contain. Experienced teachers might find the detail of these manuals a bit tedious, but they know that they can take what is offered and adapt it in light of their own experience.

The thorough and extensive treatment typical of teacher guides is exemplified in the manual for the readiness book, *Getting Ready to Read.** This teacher guide contains over one hundred pages of suggestions and directions for use with a prereading program. In the Robinson et al. series, a teacher's guide consisting of over 250 pages is available for use with two preprimers.† Considering that these preprimers contain seventy-five different words, it is obvious that the guide is thorough and goes beyond the mechanical aspects of instruction at this level. Separate manuals for the primer and first reader each contain approximately 250 pages of material addressed to the teacher.

With this type of meticulous concern for every facet of the reading program, the various guides can be excused for sometimes stressing the inevitable as if it were a deliberately planned virtue of the basic readers. It is common practice to find teacher's guides making much of the fact that preprimers, primers, and first readers "do not require children to deal with concepts beyond their experience level." Considering the small number of words found in these materials, it would be a challenge, using only this vocabulary, to confront the child with concepts beyond her experience level. She uses twenty to thirty times the number of words and understands many more.

The foregoing discussion has touched on the alleged major weakness of the basic reader series. The concern for controlling the introduction of new words puts a limit on the variety of reading material

---

* Paul McKee and M. Lucile Harrison (4th ed.; Boston: Houghton Mifflin Co., 1966).

† Helen M. Robinson et al., *The New Basic Readers Guidebook, Second and Third Pre-Primers* (Chicago: Scott, Foresman and Co., 1965).

which can be accommodated within the desired framework. The teacher must motivate children to identify themselves with the characters and the situations depicted, even though these may be somewhat alien to children of certain socio-economic groups. Without identification, the vicarious experiences gained from reading about a set of middle-class siblings, their parents, and their dog, may not seem half as fascinating as television. If one reads the guides carefully, it will be obvious that a major portion of their content is devoted to suggesting ways and means of bringing in background and of extending the concepts and the meanings actually found in the reading materials. This is important because the child's interest must not be permitted to lag.

Use of
Workbooks

As pointed out previously, workbooks constitute one of the important supplementary features of basal reader series. The educational value of using workbooks has been debated for years. It is true that seatwork in the form of workbook exercises can deteriorate into nothing more than "busy work" if teachers permit this to occur. However, this is only a potential danger not an inevitable outcome. A child may "learn" to daydream or doodle in workbook sessions. But with the right type of guidance, she can develop self-reliance and independence in work habits.

Workbooks properly used can have considerable educational value. Since a wide variety of skills are dealt with, it is likely that some exercises can be found that provide needed and meaningful practice in mastering essential skills. Workbooks can serve as diagnostic instruments since they will identify those children who do not understand a particular step in the reading process. A study of errors made by children will suggest to the alert teacher where further instruction is needed.

For some children, workbook exercises have value in that they are brief—usually one page. This factor is especially appealing to the child with a short attention span. A given workbook or developmental series deals with a wide variety of tasks. This provides work on new skills as well as review of skills partially mastered. Workbooks, like all other instructional media, are neither inherently good or bad. The way they are used can result in either of these outcomes.

Responses made in workbooks serve as diagnostic clues for diligent teachers.

Economy of Time

Economy of teachers' time is a major factor in the widespread use of basal series. This is closely related to the previous point of a balanced reading program. No teacher would ever have the time to match the meticulous planning that is reflected in the total program of a good basal series. When a teacher has materials available for teaching and drill on every facet of reading, he will have more time to prepare supplementary exercises as needed. It will still be necessary to prepare these for certain pupils, since the basal program cannot possibly meet all individual needs. However, it is easier to prepare supplementary lessons for a few than it is to build the entire program for all pupils.

Providing for
Individual Differences

Since a basal series includes many levels of difficulty, the teacher who understands his pupils and who is not compulsive in his teaching will be able to use these materials to advantage. Proficient readers may complete grade level materials much more rapidly than do the other children. These readers should then be encouraged to read supplementary trade books. The poorest reader should not be expected to read the same book month after month or year after year. Other basal materials (at the child's reading level) should be available. Impaired readers will have more success with "graded" materials than they will with books which reflect a minimum of vocabulary control.

From the standpoint of the busy teacher, one of the major contributions of any good basal series is the seatwork which is provided in workbooks. A separate workbook is available at every level—readiness, preprimer, primer, and first reader. Many exercises are tied to particular stories in the reading text; others are independent of actual stories but closely parallel or supplement the new tasks. This varied nature of the workbooks in the basal series allows for flexibility in assignments, which is an aid to the teacher searching for ways to accommodate individual differences. Figure 11 attempts to illustrate the different levels one is likely to find among children in a given first grade and the correlative materials available in a basal reader series.

Review

Adequate review is systematically provided in basal series. Children do not learn sight words, the sound of letters, initial blends, inflectional endings, and the like, as a result of one or two experiences. The introduction of new words is carefully controlled, and once a word or concept is introduced, it will be repeated many times. Tests, designed to show pupils' mastery of all skills previously introduced, are provided in workbooks. These workbooks, when used properly, can serve as diagnostic tools to indicate where more teaching or review is needed.

The previous discussion is not meant to imply that basal reader series *are* the reading program. A teacher may rely quite heavily on these materials and still teach reading through the use of bulletin boards, labeling objects, drawings and pictures, experience charts, and reading stories and poetry. These reading experiences are not incidental but are deliberately planned.

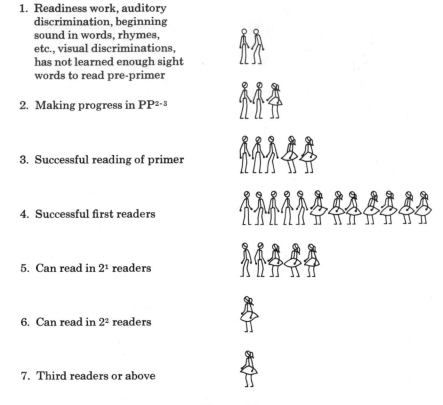

1. Readiness work, auditory discrimination, beginning sound in words, rhymes, etc., visual discriminations, has not learned enough sight words to read pre-primer

2. Making progress in PP$^{2-3}$

3. Successful reading of primer

4. Successful first readers

5. Can read in 2^1 readers

6. Can read in 2^2 readers

7. Third readers or above

Figure 11

A graphic representation of the reading levels which could be expected for a given class near the end of grade one.

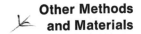

**Other Methods
and Materials**

As outlined earlier, basal reader series attempt to provide an instructional program for the entire "learning to read" period. In recent years, many other materials have become available, most of which have a narrower range of goals. In general, these materials emphasize one particular facet of instruction and focus on one stage of development called *beginning reading*.

Instructional Materials and
Philosophy of Instruction

The materials available for beginning reading instruction reflect different philosophies which in large measure determine initial instructional strategies. The major differences in materials can be traced to the way the following pedagogical issues are treated.

1. The way initial reading-vocabulary is controlled.
2. The amount of phonics (letter-sound relationships) taught.
3. The emphasis on *meaning* in beginning instruction.
4. The degree to which various facets of the total language-arts program are integrated, specifically the emphasis on children's writing.
5. The temporary use of respellings or alphabet modifications.
6. "Content" of materials. (This of course is determined by prior decisions made in regard to items 1, 2, 3 above.)

In this section we will discuss a number of materials which have the following common characteristics.

1. Each in its own way emphasizes "cracking the code" and achieving a *fast start* in beginning reading.
2. Each has its own specific set of instructional materials which are an integral part of the methodology.
3. Each focuses on beginning reading instruction offering little in instructional strategy beyond this stage.

English writing is based upon twenty-six letter symbols and follows the alphabetic principle of graphic signs representing speech sounds. While approximately half of the letters are quite consistent with the sound they represent, other letters and letter combinations represent several sounds. There is little room to doubt that the degree of inconsistency of letter-sound relationships adds to the difficulty of learning to read English. There have been numerous attempts to devise modifications of the English printing so as to mitigate this inconsistency.*

---

* See: Edward Fry, "New Alphabet Approaches," *First Grade Reading Programs,* Newark: International Reading Association Perspectives in Reading, no. 5 (1965): 72–85.

All attempts thus far to resolve inconsistent letter-sound relationships have centered on two approaches (or a combination of the two): (1) The use of additional printed signs to represent particular sounds; (2) respelling of English words so that the orthography parallels speech sounds heard. The first of these might be illustrated by Fry's (12) *Diacritical Marking System:* a bar over vowels representing long vowel sounds; a slant line through silent letters; underlining of digraphs; a dot over vowels indicating the *schwa* sound; and a bar under letters representing irregular sounds for that letter. A sample sentence follows:

"Onçe upon a time Little Red Hen livéd in a barn with her five chiçks." This system preserves the traditional spelling of words but adds clues to pronunciation.

Learn English the New Way by Frank C. Laubach utilizes a slant line following any vowel which has its long sound, and in addition respells many words: *smile*—smi/l; *quite*—qui/t; *snake*—sna/k; *told*—to/ld; *woman*—wuumun; *Asia*—A/zhaa; *cease*—seass; *deceive*—de/seev; *pronounced*—pro/nounsst.*

i/t/a
(Initial Teaching Alphabet)

Sir James Pitman of England devised a new orthography which consists of a forty-two character alphabet. This alphabet dropped the letters Q and X and added eighteen new characters to the traditional English alphabet. Materials printed in this initial teaching alphabet (i/t/a) were used experimentally in certain English schools beginning in 1960. Since that time a number of American schools have used beginning reading materials printed in this augmented alphabet.

The purpose behind the development of this orthographic system was to permit a specific character to represent only one English sound or phoneme. Allowing for some irregularities in phoneme-grapheme relationships, the augmented alphabet does approximate a one-to-one relationship between letters seen and speech sounds heard. Use of the augmented alphabet was proposed only for teaching beginning reading. In general, this was envisioned to be the first year of formal instruction for the average child, and possibly less for the accelerated learner.

---

* Frank C. Laubach, *Learn English the New Way,* Syracuse, N.Y.: New Readers Press, 1962.

Issues

1. Transfer to traditional English writing. The questions most fre- *problems*
quently raised regarding this approach to beginning reading focus on
the issue of "what will the reader do when she transfers from the one-
to-one relationship of letter-sound found in i/t/a materials and meets
the frequently inconsistent graphic representations (i.e., spellings) of
traditional English writing?" In some quarters this problem was somewhat summarily dismissed with the response that "there appears to be
no problem of transfer." This opinion was often tied to "early reports
from experimentation carried out in England" which conceivably lost
something in translation.

Discussion by John A. Downing of the early English experiments
reveals caution on this point. He writes

> If teachers *opinions* are supported by the results of the objec-
> tive tests conducted last month [March 1963], we may feel en-
> couraged in our *hopes* that all children will pass through the trans-
> fer stage with success, but *we must urge the greatest caution in
> drawing final conclusion or taking action on the basis of this pre-
> liminary trial* . . . the full effects of the transfer cannot be judged
> until the majority of these children have been put on to books in
> conventional print for their everyday reading. *Even then the final
> assessment cannot be made until some years have elapsed* and we
> can determine the extent to which (i/t/a) pupils, at various ability
> levels, are able to maintain the advantage made possible through
> their early (i/t/a) experience. [Emphasis added.] (7)

Some evidence as to the ease with which pupils transfer from i/t/a
to regular print is supplied by several studies of American pupils.
Mazurkiewicz (24), reporting on a population of 451 i/t/a taught pupils
(1963–64 school year), indicates that only 26 percent made the transition. In a second study covering the academic year 1964–65 and involving 417 i/t/a taught pupils, "almost half the i/t/a population had not
made transition to the T.O. [traditional orthography] standard in instruction." Hayes and Nemeth (18) report a lower figure, 26 percent
having not made the transfer.

2. Amount of phonics instruction involved in i/t/a. There are numerous studies which indicate that emphasis on phonics instruction in
grade one has a salutary effect on reading achievement, as measured
by first grade achievement tests, when such programs are compared
with others which include significantly less phonics. The i/t/a program

does include intensive systematic teaching of letter-sound analysis. The child's first learnings center on the sound associated with each graphic symbol. This stress is logical because the underlying principle of the system is uniformity of letter-sound relationships.

This discussion is not concerned with judging the value of such early phonics emphasis. The issue is that the intensive phonics emphasis found in i/t/a is an important factor which is ignored if reading achievement is attributed exclusively to the variable of the i/t/a orthography.

3. Emphasis on children's writing in i/t/a programs. In i/t/a instructional programs there is considerable stress on children's writing, using the i/t/a symbols. This is also a feature of the language-experience approach and other integrated language arts programs. Although available data are inconclusive, it is generally hypothesized that such integration of reading and writing enhances the learning of the reading process. If this hypothesis proves tenable, the heavy emphasis on children's writing is a second variable which clouds the efficacy of the initial teaching alphabet.

A second and more immediate question is, if the child is to transfer from the initial teaching medium to traditional orthography within the first year of instruction, why should she learn and reinforce the augmented alphabet in her own writing? The question does not relate to the value of children's writing in grade one, but upon the medium in which that writing will be done. It is true that many letters are exactly the same in both systems, and in these particular cases, transfer should be 100 percent. On the other hand, there is no question that using i/t/a symbols in writing is more difficult than writing using traditional orthography, because one meets such letter characters as æ, ᴇᴇ, œ, ᴅh, ᴛh, ŋ, ω, ꞷ, and the like.

4. Respelling of irregularly spelled English words. In the promotional materials for i/t/a, it is claimed that there is a high degree of compatibility between spellings in i/t/a and traditional orthography. The question is asked, "Are the traditional alphabet and spelling of English important causes of failure in beginning reading?" The answer is that problems in learning to read English do not stem from the traditional alphabet, but from the spellings of words. A fact that is often overlooked is that in addition to the changed alphabet in i/t/a, a great number of words are changed to phonetic spellings. The following examples come from one small first grade book of less than primer difficulty.*

---

* "A Seesied Holidae for Jaen and Toeby," Ann Thwaite (Cunstabl and Company, Limited, Lundon). [*sic*]

was—woz	watched—wotcht	walked—waukt
excited—eksieted	enough—enuf	thought—thaut
called—cauld	once—wunz	next—nekst
large—larj	find—fiend	boxes—boksez
busy—bizy	some—sum	George—Jorj
come—cum	one—wun	six—siks

i/t/a actually attempts to follow the traditional "rules" found in most phonic approaches, particularly with regard to the "two vowel" and "final e" rules. When words do not follow the rules, they are spelled phonetically:

one—wun	said—sed
some—sum	board—bord
once—wunz	couple—cupl
more—mor	head—hed
have—hav	laugh—laf

In such instances, i/t/a ceases to be a method for "cracking the code" (which is English writing) and becomes a substitute code. The respellings are logical; but the issue is that children will soon be exposed to the irrational spellings, and they will have to learn these word symbols as sight words whether or not they begin reading with i/t/a or regular orthography. Since all words met in i/t/a writing can be sounded out by heeding the individual letters, the learner will inevitably develop a set to utilize this approach. This habit will not serve her well when she meets hundreds of irregularly spelled words following the transition.

5. *Results of i/t/a instruction.* Data from various studies have failed to indicate any significant superiority in reading achievement at the end of grade one which accrues from the use of i/t/a. Hahn compared the reading achievement of three groups of children taught respectively by i/t/a, basal programs, and a language arts approach (16). His conclusion was that no one approach was consistently superior to the others although significant differences favoring each approach were found on some particular reading subtests. Fry found no significant differences in silent or oral reading achievement of first-grade children taught by i/t/a, the Fry Diacritical Marking System, or the Sheldon Basal Readers (Allyn-Bacon) (13).

Tanyzer and Alpert (32) compared the efficacy of i/t/a, the Lippincott basal program, and the Scott Foresman basal program. Reading achievement of pupils taught by both the Lippincott materials and i/t/a were significantly superior to that of pupils taught by the Scott Foresman basals on each of the subtests of the *Stanford Achievement Test*. The group taught by the Lippincott materials was significantly superior to the group taught with i/t/a on vocabulary and spelling. No significant differences were found between these groups on Word Reading, Paragraph Meaning, and Word Study Skills.

Mazurkiewicz (25) found no significant differences in reading achievement between children taught by i/t/a and traditional orthography as measured by the subtests Word Reading, Paragraph Meaning, Vocabulary, and Word Study Skills, on the *Stanford Achievement Test*. Pupils taught in traditional orthography were significantly superior in spelling.

Hayes and Nemeth (18) compared four instructional approaches: i/t/a, Lippincott basal series, Scott Foresman basals, plus the use of *Phonics and Word Power** and Scott Foresman basals alone. It should be noted that the first three include a considerable amount of phonics, while the Scott Foresman basals introduce a relatively small amount of letter-analysis in grade one materials. On the word reading subtest, no significant differences were found between i/t/a and Lippincott approaches but both were superior to the Scott Foresman basal program alone. There was no significant difference between i/t/a and Scott Foresman materials supplemented by the Phonics and Word Power Program. On paragraph meaning, no significant differences were found between i/t/a and any of the other approaches. On word study skills, no significant differences were found between i/t/a, Lippincott, and Scott Foresman supplemented by *Phonics and Word Power*, while each of these was significantly superior to Scott Foresman basals alone.

One important finding which emerges from a number of these studies is that when programs which utilize extensive phonics instruction are compared, no significant differences in reading achievement appear at the end of grade one. However, phonics-emphasis programs appear to result in higher reading achievement (as measured by existing standardized tests) than do programs which include significantly less letter-sound analysis.

This tends to support the contention that studies which have purported to be dealing with the efficacy of i/t/a orthography as compared with traditional orthography have failed to control an important variable—the amount of phonics instruction in the programs being compared. The contribution of the augmented alphabet in learning to read can be evaluated only if the stress on phonics instruction is equated in comparative studies.

---

* American Education Publications, Columbus, Ohio, 1964.

Programmed Reading Materials

Programmed reading materials fall into two categories: (1) those the purpose of which is to teach facts and understanding in any one of the numerous subject areas; (2) those whose chief aim is to teach the child *how* to read, i.e., dealing with various skills which make up the reading process. This discussion will deal only with the latter in the form of workbook-type programmed materials.

There are a number of such materials available. One example which may be considered fairly representative is *Programmed Reading* (Webster Division, McGraw-Hill Book Company). The materials in this program, which are designed for grade one, consist of seven conventional-sized workbooks. The pupil writes a letter or word or circles a response in each frame. There is considerable emphasis on "phonics," or associating printed letters with speech sounds. Initial teaching involves short vowel sounds and consonant sounds in words which enjoy "regular spellings." This term implies that the sound represented by individual letters is the most common or characteristic sound of those particular letters (cat, rat, fat, mat, etc.)

Before beginning to work with the programmed materials, the child must have mastered a sizable number of phonic skills including the following:

1. The names of the letters of the alphabet (capital and small).
2. How to print all the capital and small letters.
3. That letters stand for sounds.
4. What sounds to associate with the letters *a, f, m, n, p, t, th*, and *i*, which are used as the points of departure for the programmed readers.
5. That letters are read from left to right.
6. That groups of letters form words.
7. The words *yes* and *no* by sight, how to discriminate the words *ant, man*, and *mat* from each other, and how to read the sentences, *I am an ant, I am a man, I am a mat, I am a pin, I am a pan, I am tan, I am thin, I am fat.*

These skills are taught in a stage called *programmed prereading* which, by the nature of what is taught, represents a rather heavy saturation of phonic analysis early in beginning reading.

One strength of programmed reading is that it makes possible individualized instruction. While every child would be using the same material, each may progress through it at her own rate. A second virtue is that even though programmed materials deal primarily with mechanical aspects of the reading process, many of these skills have to be practiced until they become automatic responses on the part of the learner. Thus, a well-planned program can relieve a teacher from a certain amount of repetitive drill and leave him more time for other important aspects of instruction. This assumes, of course, that programmed materials represent only one part of the instructional program.

Words in Color

This is a system for teaching beginning reading, developed by Caleb Gattegno (14). Initial instruction involves the use of visual stimuli which provide two visual clues: (1) the traditional letter configurations, and (2) color. In this approach, thirty-nine colors are used, each of which represents a speech sound in English. Any letter or combination of letters which represent a given speech sound will be presented as a visual stimulus in the particular color assigned to that speech sound. For instance, the long vowel sound of $\overline{A}$ is represented by the following combinations:

a—able	*eigh*—weight
ey—they	*aigh*—straight
ay—play	*ei*—their
ai—mail	*ea*—great

Each group of italicized letters above would be one color (green). The sound of ă, regardless of letters which represent it, is shown in white; the sound of $\overline{e}$ is represented by vermillion, etc.

The actual teaching of this color code is done through the use of a number of large wall charts. Twenty-one charts contain words, and eight phonic-code charts contain letters and letter combinations which represent given sounds. The only other learning experiences which utilize color are those in which the teacher may write on the chalk board using different colored chalk. *ALL other printed material which the child uses is printed in black on white.* Thus, the wall charts are nothing more than "keys" to which the child may turn to see the color of particular letters. The following are some pertinent facts about *Words in Color.*

1. This approach places considerable emphasis on phonics instruction. Children learn "sounds" of letters rather than letter names. Instruction starts with short vowel sounds and then moves into consonant sounds. These are taught systematically and with a good deal of repetition.

2. At the time of this writing, there has been no research which suggests that the addition of color to *letter forms* has any positive effects on learning either letter configuration or sounds associated with letters.

3. The use of thirty-nine colors can make the learning process quite confusing. In the absence of letter configuration clues, many adults have difficulty in determining whether certain color samples are actually the "same" or "different." It is likely that some six-year-olds also have trouble in discriminating between colors which are very much alike. One series of color shades includes: dark green, olive green, cadmium green, yellow green no. 15, yellow green no. 47, light green, deep green, emerald green no. 45, emerald green no. 26, leaf green, yellow ochre, and brown ochre.

4. It is difficult to justify the emphasis on colored letters considering the fact that the child never reads any material printed in colors. Her contact with words in color is limited to classroom charts composed of individual words, but no sustained reading matter.

5. Children who learn to *rely* on *color cues* could not read outside of class since the charts they depend on are large, bulky and expensive. It is highly improbable that these "aids" would ever become household fixtures.

The "Linguistic" Regular Spelling Approach

In the April and May 1942 issues of *The Elementary English Review*, Leonard Bloomfield outlined an approach for beginning reading instruction. In essence, Bloomfield suggested a very rigid vocabulary control in which children's first attempts at reading would be limited to "words with regular spellings." Regular spellings are those words in which each grapheme (written letter) represents the one sound most frequently associated with that letter. Thus the words *cat* and *hum* enjoy regular spellings while *cent* and *come* are irregular (*c* in *cent* represents *s*; *o* in *come* represents the short sound of *u*).

Opposition to Phonics Instruction

The regular spelling approach is similar to i/t/a, *Words in Color,* and *Programmed Reading* in that it deals with beginning reading instruction and calls for use of special materials. However, it differs from these methodologies in one important way. They emphasize phonics instruction (or the systematic teaching of letter-sound relationships) and Bloomfield was unequivocally opposed to this method. Present day proponents of Bloomfield's method have remained loyal to this dictum.

In order to understand certain important methodological considerations in Bloomfield's proposal, one must be aware of his position as outlined in *Let's Read: A Linguistic Approach* (5). His opposition to phonics instruction is based on two erroneous premises. The first of these is the misconception voiced by Bloomfield that the purpose of phonics instruction is to teach the child how to *pronounce* words by teaching him speech sounds. Bloomfield writes

> The inventors of these (phonic) methods confuse writing with speech. They plan the work as though the child were being taught to speak. . . . If a child has not learned to utter the speech sounds of our language, the only sensible course is to postpone reading until he has learned to speak. As a matter of fact, nearly all six-year-old children have long ago learned to speak their native language; they have no need whatever of the drill which is given by phonic methods. (5: p. 27).

The second misconception about phonics which one finds in the writing of Bloomfield and others is found in their belief as to how phonics is taught. Bloomfield states

> The second error of the phonic methods is that of isolating the speech sounds. The authors of these methods tell us to show the child a letter, for instance *t*, and to make him react by uttering the

t-sound; that is the English speech sound which occurs at the beginning of a word like *two* or *ten*. This sound to be uttered either all by itself or else with an obscure vowel sound after it (5: p. 28).

This description of phonics instruction was valid for an earlier era, but this practice had largely disappeared by the time Bloomfield inveighed against it. It is true that one cannot separately pronounce letter sounds, which taken together constitute the pronunciation of English words, and children are not asked to do so. They are taught that a particular letter represents the same speech sound in many different words, and they are invited to think or subvocalize this sound when the letter occurs in a word they are attempting to solve.

The Program

The materials and methodology described here are outlined by Bloomfield and Barnhart in *Let's Read: A Linguistic Approach* (5). The program consists of 245 separate lessons which present five thousand words. The first 97 lessons deal with words with regular spellings. The remaining 148 lessons present words with irregular spellings. Prior to instruction in reading, the child must have developed certain prereading skills which include the ability to identify (name) the letters of the English alphabet. Capital letters are learned first, then lower case forms. Letters are taught in alphabetical order stressing left-to-right progression.

Teaching "Regular Spelling" Words

Each of the lessons 1–36 introduces a different series of words which contain identical final phonograms (*at, an, op, ag, ip, ed, un, ot,* etc.). Thus, the words in a given lesson differ from each other only in the initial letter (sound) *cat, bat, mat, hat*. The teaching of CVC (consonant, vowel, consonant) words is followed by lessons dealing with other patterns such as CVCC (*lamp*); CCVC (*snap*); CCVCC (*stamp*); CVVC (*deep*), etc.

Lesson one presents the words *can, Dan, fan, man, Nan, pan, ran, tan, an, ban, van.* Bloomfield describes the method of teaching as follows:

> The word *can* is printed on the blackboard or a card. The child knows the names of the letters, and is now asked to read off those names in their order:
>
> see   aye   en
>
> The parent or teacher says, "Now we have spelled the word. Now we are going to *read* it. The word is *can.* Read it: *can*" (5:41).

Other words are taught in the same manner. It is suggested that no more than two or three words be presented per lesson since this learning calls for "a severe intellectual effort."

Bloomfield is quite precise as to *what* the child is to learn from the presentation of two words such as *can* and *fan.* "The aim is now to make the child distinguish between the two words—that is, to get him to read each of the words correctly when it is shown by itself, and, when the two words are shown together, to say the right one when the parent or the teacher points to it, and to point to the right one when the parent or the teacher pronounces it" (5:41).

In this teaching method children are asked to learn every word as a sight word, or to arrive at its pronunciation by saying the letter names. "All he (the child) needs to do is read off the names of successive letters, from left to right" (5:36). Bloomfield's example "*see aye en*—read it *can*" is all the evidence one needs in order to understand why the alphabet method (the spelling of words to arrive at their pronunciation) was discarded years ago. Letter *names* do not coincide with the sounds that letters represent in words.

**Teaching
Irregular Words**

It should be pointed out that words with regular spellings consti-tute less than 40 percent of the five thousand words listed in the *Let's Read* program.* Bloomfield's suggestion for teaching words with ir-

---

* This statement is based on Bloomfield's designation of words. It should be pointed out that he used much stricter criteria for regular spellings than is necessary if one's goal is teaching reading.

regular spellings is somewhat astounding: "When it comes to teaching irregular and special words each word will demand a separate effort and separate practice" (5:206). Elsewhere in criticizing the sight word method, Bloomfield correctly points out the difficulty (or impossibility) of teaching many thousands of words in this manner. The child who has been taught phonics will find that she can apply something of what she has learned to a majority of irregular words. Since letter-sound relationships are not taught with the regular spelling words, the proponents of this approach cannot talk in terms of *transfer*. Thus they must fall back on the vague and impractical suggestion that each new word demands a separate effort and separate practice.

This is not to say that there is no virtue in presenting "family words," "word patterns," or words with minimal grapheme-phoneme differences in teaching reading. Gray*   wrote favorably on this practice under the trade name "mental substitution of initial consonant sounds." Research by Wylie and Durrell† supports the fact that first grade children find it easier to identify words when they work with rhyming phonograms (i.e., identical final letter-combinations). However, these individuals also advocate the systematic teaching of letter-sound relationships which turns out to be the missing ingredient in Bloomfield's approach.

Meaning and Reading

The methodological decision to teach regular spelling words (and include all words that fit a given "pattern") definitely limits story content or material that will be meaningful to children. Both Bloomfield and others, who have developed materials based on regular spellings, reject the thesis that beginning reading instruction should be concerned with meaning. The rejection of meaning is not so much a well-founded pedagogical principle as it is an expediency when one is limited to using only those words which qualify as regular spellings. Normal English sentences are difficult to build when one decides to use only words which follow regular spelling patterns. For example, in Bloomfield's material, after sixty-six words have been taught (roughly equivalent to

---

* William S. Gray, *On Their Own in Reading* (Chicago: Scott, Foresman and Co., 1960).

† Richard E. Wylie and Donald D. Durrell, "Teaching Vowels through Phonograms," *Elementary English* (October 1970): 787–91.

three preprimers in a representative basal series), one finds only the most contrived sentences and absolutely no story line:

lack of meaning

Pat had ham.   Sam ran.
Nat had jam.   Can Sam tag Pam?
Sam had a cap.   Can Pam tag Sam?
Dan had a hat.   Dan had a ram. (5:65)

After 200 words have been learned, the child reads these sentences:

Let Dan bat.   Let us in, Sis!
Did Al get wet?   Sis, let us in!
Van had a pet cat.   Let Sid pet a pup.
Get up Tad!   Jim let Pam tag him. (5:87)

Computer
Assisted
Instruction (CAI)

While computer programmed instruction is quite different from the materials and methodology just discussed, it does meet the criterion of being a newer approach. Thus far (in reading) it has been used for initial instruction, and has focused mainly on teaching the code-cracking skills.

A decade ago both proponents and critics of computerized instruction agreed that "within a few years" computers were destined to play a major role in classroom instruction. There were an unprecedented number of mergers of big business (technology) and educational publishers. Apparently it was believed that simply bringing these two elements under one management would lead to very rapid development of computer-instructional programs.

While no miracles have been wrought, it has been demonstrated that given time and enough resources, instructional programs for teaching mathematics, beginning reading, science, spelling, and even methods courses for teachers could be developed. At the moment most program development has been experimental in nature, involving only a few hundred or at most a few thousand students. Most programs, after being used in this limited fashion, were stored, shelved, and forgotten. The major stumbling block in the path of widespread use of computer assisted instruction has not been program development, but the problem of delivery to where the students are.

There is little reason to believe that computerized instruction will not increase in our schools. As far as reading instruction is concerned, it appears that computer technology is ideally suited for teaching a number of the essential skills associated with beginning instruction. Included would be letter recognition, association of letter forms with the sounds they represent, recognition of words which undergo structural changes (plurals, affixes, compounds), and teaching irregularly spelled sight words. The computer also has potential for bridging the instructional gap between dialect speakers and the standard English of the school.

Computer Capabilities
for Teaching Reading

Teachers of reading should understand the capabilities of computer assisted instruction as these relate to reading. The purpose here is not to explain the hardware, program writing, circuitry, and the like. When the program has been written, the system is in operation, and a child is sitting at the terminal, this instructional system has the following capabilities. The terminal at which the child works can consist of any or all of the following:

1. The child views a television set (cathode ray tube) on which can be shown:
   a. Anything that may appear in a workbook, or any material ordinarily presented via chalkboard or overhead projector.
   b. The child can "register" responses directly on the tube by use of a light pen which leaves no marks but electronically registers the response made.
   c. A typewriter keyboard may also be part of the circuit in which case the learner types responses.
2. The auditory (voice) component can provide explanations, give directions, or present supplementary data.
3. The computer has the capacity to function much like an animated cartoon. A stick man can appear and take away a letter that is not sounded—(k)nee, (w)rap—or these letters can drop down the screen and disappear while the audio explains that the letter is not sounded but that it will always appear when these words are met in print.
4. If all goes well electronically, the learner can within a second's time receive a response to her response. This instant feedback can be visual, auditory, or both.
5. Every response a learner makes can be recorded and stored.
6. A child can be absent for a period of time. Upon her return, the "system" can pick her up at exactly the spot she was prior to her absence.

If she has forgotten a crucial principle, the program can ascertain this by her error pattern and she can be "branched" back through a review or to easy material that fits her present need.

The possibilities above represent those capabilities already achieved in programming. Rapid changes and improvements can be expected.

Limitations

Computer instruction involves a highly complex electronic system. It does break down, and when it does the party is over until an expert gets the lint out of the carburetor. If the system is crowded (maximum use), the instant feedback can be delayed a few seconds. During such intervals the student may wander mentally or physically; if the learner is "gone," the teaching can't go on.

Research reports have avoided mention of learners being "turned off" by computer instruction. It is highly unlikely that everyone has the same threshold of tolerance for this type of instruction. There is a hint of a problem in reports of how learners deliberately make "errors" in order to see how the computer will handle them. While the system is adept at recognizing and recording errors, it is vulnerable in analysis of what *caused* the error. In some cases this is of minor importance, in others it can be a crucial issue in the learning process.

One of the virtues of CAI is that it *can* maximize individual instruction. Through meticulous programming, it can provide child x and child y with exactly what they need in instruction. When designing a program to be used by many thousands of students, the cost of developing, storing, and delivering an ideal program for each child becomes prohibitive (just as it is without computers). In essence, while the potential is there, it is highly unlikely that it can be used to its maximum.

YOUR POINT OF VIEW?

Would you defend or attack the following premises? Why?

1. One's definition of reading would have considerable impact on practices followed in teaching the reading process.

2. Programmed reading materials permit different pupils to be working on different skills and to work at different rates. This statement applies with equal validity to any workbook or series of workbooks.

3. Using basal reader series as the basic instructional approach has less efficacy with accelerated readers than with those pupils who, on the basis of reading achievement, rank in the lower half of their grade.

4. Early experiences in learning to read have a considerable influence on pupils' later work habits and attitudes toward the school.

5. All reading-instruction materials which follow the structure and patterns of English usage can be said to be "linguistically sound" or "linguistic methods."

6. A justifiable criterion for judging good teaching in beginning reading is the extent to which a teacher uses different methods in his classroom. (Basic readers, experience method, individualized reading, etc.)

7. Since children use thousands of words in oral language, stories which they dictate will depart from the practice of controlled vocabulary and repetition.

8. "Context clues" are of little importance in first grade when instruction centers around a basic reader series because of "controlled vocabulary." (Be sure to use a representative basic reader series to illustrate your point of view.)

9. There is little evidence that the reading material found in basal readers is inappropriate for children who come from depressed socioeconomic backgrounds.

BIBLIOGRAPHY

1. Atkinson, Richard C. and Hansen, Duncan N., "Computer-Assisted Instruction in Initial Reading: The Stanford Project," *Reading Research Quarterly* (Fall 1966): 5–25.

2. Aukerman, Robert C., *Approaches to Beginning Reading.* New York: John Wiley and Sons, Inc., 1971.

3. Bammon, Henry A.; Dawson, Mildred A.; and McGovern, James J., *Fundamentals of Basic Reading Instruction.* New York: David McKay Co., Inc., 1973.

4. Bliesmer, Emery P., "Problems of Research Design in Classroom Studies," *Journal of Reading Behavior* (Winter 1970): 3–17.

5. Bloomfield, Leonard, and Barnhart, Clarence L., *Let's Read, A Linguistic Approach.* Detroit: Wayne State University Press, 1961.

6. Bond, Guy L., "First-Grade Reading Studies: An Overview," *Elementary English* (May 1966): 464–70.

7. Downing, John A., *Experiments with Pitman's Initial Teaching Alphabet in British Schools*. New York: Initial Teaching Alphabet Publications, Inc., 1963, p. 25.

8. ———, *Evaluating the Initial Teaching Alphabet*. London: Cassell and Co., L.T.D., 1967.

9. ——— and Lathram, W., "A Follow-Up of Children in the First i.t.a. Experiment," *British Journal of Educational Psychology* (November 1969): 303–05.

10. ———, "The Bullock Commission's Judgement of i.t.a.," *Reading Teacher* 29 (February 1976): 379–82.

11. Feldhusen, Hazel J.; Lamb, Pose; and Feldhusen, John, "Prediction of Reading Achievement under Programmed and Traditional Instruction," *Reading Teacher* (February 1970): 446–54.

12. Fry, Edward, "A Diacritical Marking System to Aid Beginning Reading Instruction," *Elementary English* (May 1964): 526–29.

13. Fry, Edward Bernard, *First Grade Reading Instruction Using a Diacritical Marking System, The Initial Teaching Alphabet and a Basal Reading System*. USOE Cooperative Research Project No. 2745, 1965.

14. Gattegno, Caleb, *Words in Color*. Chicago: Learning Materials, Inc., 1962.

15. Green, Donald Ross; Henderson, Richard L.; and Richards, Herbert C., "Learning to Recognize Words and Letters on a CAI Terminal," *Reading and Realism*. Proceedings, International Reading Association 13, Part I, pp. 658–64.

16. Hahn, Harry T., *A Study of the Relative Effectiveness of Three Methods of Teaching Reading in Grade One*. USOE Cooperative Research Project No. 2687, 1965.

17. Harris, Albert J. and Serwer, Blanche L., "The Craft Project: Instructional Time in Reading Research," *Reading Research Quarterly* (Fall 1966): 27–56.

18. Hayes, Robert B. and Nemeth, Joseph S., *An Attempt to Secure Additional Evidence Concerning Factors Affecting Learning to Read*. USOE Cooperative Research Project No. 2697, 1965, p. 34.

19. Kerber, James E., "The Tasks of Teaching Reading," *Language Arts* 53 (April 1976): 414–15.

20. Kerfoot, James F., ed., *First Grade Reading Programs*. Perspectives in Reading no. 5. Newark, Del.: International Reading Association, Inc., 1965.

21. McCracken, Glenn, "The Newcastle Reading Experiment: A Terminal Report," *Elementary English* (January 1953): 13–21.

22. ———, "The Value of the Correlated Visual Image," *Reading Teacher* (October 1959): 29–33.

23. Marsh, R. W., "Some Cautionary Notes on the Results of the London i.t.a. Experiment," *Reading Research Quarterly* (Fall 1966): 119–26.

24. Mazurkiewicz, Albert J., "Lehigh-Bethlehem—I/T/A Study Interim Report Six," *Journal of the Reading Specialist* (September 1964), p. 3.

25. ————, First Grade Reading Using Modified Co-Basal Versus the Initial Teaching Alphabet. USOE Cooperative Research Project No. 2676, 1965.

26. Niemeyer, John H., "The Bank Street Readers: Support for Movement toward an Integrated Society," *Reading Teacher* (April 1965): 542–45.

27. Ohanian, Vera, "Control Populations in I/T/A Experiments," *Elementary English* (April 1966): 373–80.

28. Singer, Harry; Samuels, S. Jay; and Spiroff, Jean, "The Effect of Pictures and Contextual Conditions on Learning Responses to Printed Words," *Reading Research Quarterly* 9, no. 4, 1973–74, pp. 355–67.

29. Serwer, Blanche and Stolurow, Lawrence M., "Computer-Assisted Learning in Language Arts," *Elementary English* (May 1970): 641–50.

30. Smith, Frank, *Understanding Reading.* New York: Holt, Rinehart and Winston, Inc., 1971.

31. Southgate, Vera, "Approaching i.t.a. Results with Caution," *Reading Research Quarterly* (Spring 1966): 35–56.

32. Tanyzer, Harold J. and Alpert, Harvey, *Effectiveness of Three Different Basal Reading Systems on First Grade Reading Achievement.* USOE Cooperative Research Project No. 2720, 1965.

33. Tovey, Duane R., "Children's Perceptions of Reading," *Reading Teacher* 29 (March 1976): 536–40.

Chapter 5

Beginning Reading II: Instructional Activities

Beginning Reading Instruction: Objectives

Regardless of the materials one elects to use in beginning reading, the goals of this level of instruction would be much the same. Instruction will focus on a number of specific skills which are related to the larger long-term goal of producing facile and critical readers. It is understandable that the teaching of a process as complicated as beginning reading will include many objectives, some of which have been dealt with in previous discussions: to structure experiences so that the child feels accepted and develops desirable attitudes toward reading and toward self; to provide for group participation, development of verbal facility, listening ability, and auditory and visual discrimination; to teach left-to-right sequence; and to encourage contact with books, stories, and pictures.

Despite the fact that these activities are very appropriate in the reading readiness program, it is apparent that the teacher must not neglect any of these goals when instruction in reading becomes more formal.

The main objective in beginning instruction is to arouse and sustain the child's interest in reading. When this is achieved she becomes ego-involved in reading. Achieving the following objectives is crucial if the child's ego is to be kept harnessed to the reading task. Experiences must be provided so that beginning readers

Objectives

1. Expand their sight-recognition vocabulary.
2. Master letter-sound relationships.
3. Understand that printed words are made up of letters. These letters represent speech sounds that must be blended to arrive at the pronunciation of printed words that are not recognized.
4. Develop the necessary visual and auditory discrimination skills that are needed for these code-cracking activities.
5. Grasp the fact that reading is a meaning making process; that meaning is conveyed in sentence units; and one arrives at meaning by supplying the intonation patterns that recreate the melody of spoken language.
6. Practice oral language usage and understand that reading is working with language.
7. Develop and expand concepts, noting that ideas are expressed through language.
8. Learn that some words have many different meanings and that the various meanings are "signaled" by context clues.
9. Develop critical thinking through experiences which sharpen both critical listening ability and analysis of printed messages.
10. Gradually acquire independent work habits.
11. Progress smoothly in the mastery of the mechanics of reading such as heeding punctuation, reducing the number of regressions, and combining words into phrases.

These and other goals can be achieved when the results of individual on-going diagnosis are used as a blueprint for instruction. Obviously, some provision will have to be made for individual and small group instruction to assure that teaching becomes flexible and meaningful.

In order that we may partially recapture the challenge of learning a symbolic process like reading, let us look at a number of familiar symbols and a number which are new. On the left of the list below are pairs of short word-symbols which are very much alike. For an adult it is extremely simple to distinguish between them. On the right are the same word symbols built from a different alphabet which at this point is unknown to the reader. The new word symbols are no more alike than the words on the left, but it is much more difficult to distinguish between them.

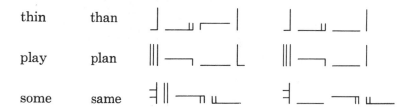

thin	than
play	plan
some	same

The unknown symbols on the right are actually easier to learn than the ones on the left for these reasons:

1. All letters are composed of three or fewer straight lines.
2. The lines are always horizontal or vertical (no slanting lines like *A, X, K, M;* no curved lines like *S, C, U;* no combinations of straight and curved lines like *D, B, P,* etc.).
3. The first thirteen letters of this alphabet are composed of long horizontal lines and short vertical lines and the last thirteen letters are composed of long vertical and shorter horizontal lines.

This new alphabet, with its equivalent in English, is found in Figure 12.

Two short reading passages using this new symbol system are presented below Figure 12. The purpose is not to present a situation analogous to beginning reading, since the reader will have to study the new alphabet in Figure 12 prior to reading. Attempting to read

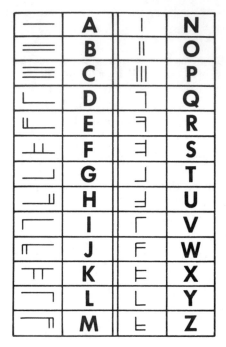

Figure 12

Passage A   *Passage B*

the passages will illustrate the difficulty of mastering a symbolic task in which the symbols are unknown. In this respect, the task is similar to beginning reading.

There are eleven different letter symbols and twelve word symbols in Passage A. Among the twelve words there are only six different words. Thus the vocabulary was carefully controlled. All of these words are found in the first few pages of preprimers and have been used thousands of times by the reader. These factors might suggest that this reading exercise will be quite easy. Passage B should be extremely easy to read since, in this sixteen-word passage, only four new letters and four new words are introduced. Seventy-five percent of the words are repeated from the first lesson.

If you had a little trouble reading these simple passages (translations below*), the experiment was worth the effort. The objective was to demonstrate that any symbolic process is potentially difficult and that when the symbols appear very much alike, it becomes doubly so. Before the child is confronted with a task as exacting as reading passages A or B (above), she will have had many hours of practice aimed at helping her make finer and finer visual discriminations. She will also have had many experiences with the printed form of words in readiness books, in experience charts, and on bulletin boards.

Three Major Instructional Tasks

Insofar as mastering the reading process is concerned, there are three instructional tasks which represent the major thrust of beginning reading instruction. Their importance diminishes little, if any, throughout the entire process of learning to read. These instructional tasks are helping the child

1. develop and expand a sight vocabulary.
2. learn to associate visual symbols with speech sounds.
3. see that reading is always a meaning making process, and that printed word symbols represent speech.

Some instructional materials tend to treat the first two of these facets of instruction as independent skills which should be taught in sequence, either 1. first or 2. first, over an extended period of time. Children can learn much of what is taught in such an instructional approach, but in doing so they run the risk of developing attitudes and habits which "color" their concept of the reading process. When beginning reading instruction overemphasizes letter analysis, learning sight words, or reliance on context, children tend to become overdependent on the particular skill emphasized.

---

* Passage A:	look oh look	Passage B:	baby likes to play
	see baby play		look at baby play
	look at baby		oh oh see baby
	play baby play		play with me baby

It is easy to inculcate pupils with a "set" which may neglect one or more of these important clues. This is uneconomical and may result in habits which handicap the reader in her later development. For instance, a child may develop a set to sound out every word she meets. This means she will be sounding out the same word the tenth, twentieth, or even the fiftieth time it is met in reading situations. She has learned that reading is "sounding out words," and this becomes her goal in all reading situations.

On the other hand, overemphasis on learning sight words in the absence of letter-sounding techniques overburdens the child with the task of making minute visual discriminations, where minimal sounding techniques would have made her task much easier. Sight words, plus context, plus the use of the minimal sounding clues necessary to solve unknown printed words, is more efficient than overreliance on one technique alone.

The premise underlying this discussion is that the major instructional tasks identified above are inseparable parts of one total instructional process. Each of these skills—expanding sight vocabulary, learning letter-sound relationships, and using context—are essential at each point on the learning continuum. They interact and complement each other in every reading situation. Thus, the major task of reading instruction is to arrive at the proper blending of those three instructional components.

What makes reading instruction complicated is that there is no blueprint which spells out precisely where and how much instructional time and effort should be devoted to each of these skills. And second, there is no blueprint which tells us what particular instructional techniques will have the most efficacy with particular learners. Understanding individual differences among learners become the key to these questions.

Developing and Expanding Sight Vocabulary

The normal child's experience with reading will result in her acquiring a constantly enlarging stock of sight words. She will have established automatic stimulus-response patterns for dozens of frequently used words such as: *that, with, will, be, come, are, and, some, was, it, an, the, in, which, to, than, no, what, stop, you, they, now, us, said, when, him, go, little, can,* and the like. A number of these structure words and other frequently used words must be "overlearned" to the point where recognizing them is automatic.

There is a difference between overlearning certain frequently used words and learning to overrely on one approach to beginning reading, whether that approach be whole words, letter analysis, or context. The normal pattern of learning dictates that the child develop a sight vocabularly or learn some words "as wholes." The purpose of the following discussion is to illustrate a limited number of approaches which may help to facilitate learning.

Learning to Read Children's Names

1. Probably the first printed word a child learns is her name. Many first grade teachers tape each child's first name on the front of her desk.

Mary	Mike	Sarah	Sandy

Children learn the names of other children, and many learn very quickly to recognize a number of names in printed form. The practice of learning names in printed form provides the basis for teaching letter-sound analysis, discussed later.

2. Use of blackboard announcements involving pupils' names.

Hand out books	*Water the plants*
John	Jean
Helen	Billy

Labeling Objects in the Room

The teacher prints a naming word on separate oak tag cards.

door	book	plant	blackboard	table

Each card is held up and a volunteer is selected to say the word and place the card on the object it names.

Association of Printed Word with a Picture It Names

1. Secure a number of pictures which depict objects or animals within the children's range of experience. Paste the picture on cardboard and print the naming word beneath it.

cat   cow   horse   house

2. To add the kinesthetic sensory mode to the words, duplicate a page of outline drawings and leave space for the children to write (copy) the names from models displayed on the chalk tray. In the first experience the printed words may be outlined with dots. The child then marks over the dots writing the words.

  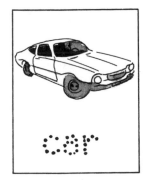

3. A later exercise may be one which omits the dotted outlines and the child copies from the printed models on the chalk tray, chalk-board, or bulletin board.

Building a Picture Naming Dictionary

Secure a number of small pictures from workbooks, magazines, and the like. Have one page devoted to each letter of the alphabet. Pupils paste pictures and teacher prints *picture naming word* beneath each picture. A partial M-m page is illustrated in Figure 13.

Drill Cards for Irregular Words

Prepare a number of cards containing *words we learn*. Each card presents five to ten sight words. Any word card can be studied or "practiced" by a child or by two or more partners. When a student is ready to volunteer to read card A or C etc., she reads the words to the

A picture dictionary is one type of
bridge between what is known and
what must be learned.

teacher or a *word helper* (a child who has received credit for knowing
all the words on that particular card).

Examples of cards are illustrated below:

A	B	C	D
the	have	two	could
once	for	any	I
to	they	been	says
you	one	does	too
of	very	said	come
is	your	love	eye
was	but	would	shoe
are	some	many	want

Figure 13

How, What, When, Where, and Why *Words*

Write the above words on the chalkboard, say the words, then have volunteers point to and identify different words. Use the chalkboard, overhead projector, or duplicated materials to present materials similar to the following (see top of page 141).

Circle A:

a. *How* many dots?	four
b. *How* did you learn this?	We counted them.
c. *When* did you count them?	Just now!
d. *What* color are they?	black
e. *Where* is the circle?	Around the dots!
f. *Why* is the circle around the dots?	So we could ask *how, what, when, where,* and *why* questions!

Circle B:

Where are the letters? *How* many letters? *What* are they? *Which* letters are also words? (A and I), *what* is around the letters? *Why* is it around the letters?

There are dozens of other formats that can be used involving squares, triangles, boxes, numbers, and small and capital letters. After a few trials, children will want to build games which can be edited

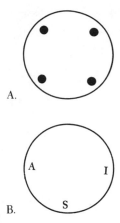

A.

B.

and used with the class or groups. Each experience with these important words helps children learn them as sight words.

Position Words: in, on, above, below, over, under, *etc.*

Use a format similar to the circle-square-table shown below. Provide each participating child with three or four word cards. Each card has the same "position word" printed on both sides. (As children hold up the card requested, the teacher can check for accuracy).

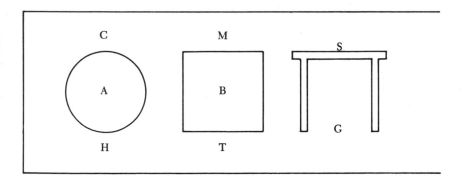

Reading the following directions:

a. "Hold up the word *IN* (pause) what letter is *IN* the circle?"
b. "Hold up the word *OVER* . . . . . what letter is *OVER* the square?"
c. "Hold up the word *ON* . . . . . what letter is *ON* the table?"

Continue using all of the word cards issued to the children. Each can be used more than once if desired, *i.e.*, *in* the circle, *in* the square, *under* the circle, square, table, etc.

Feed the Word-Eater (*Game for Pairs or Teams*)

Prepare two "word-eaters" by pasting or drawing faces on cardboard boxes. The mouths are cut out so that word-cards can be inserted. Print a number of word cards each of which contains one "sight word." These are placed face down on the table. Players take turns drawing a card. If the child can read the word, she feeds the card to the word-eater. If the word is not pronounced, the card is handed to the opponent or the next player of the opposing team who now has an extra chance to feed her word-eater. If this player fails, the card is placed in a study-pile and the game continues. At the end of the game, the person's (or team's) word-eater that has eaten the most cards wins.

High Frequency Words often Confused

Use the chalkboard, overhead projector, or duplicated materials consisting of sentences each containing two words frequently confused in early reading. Teacher and class (or group) read these sentences in unison, paying heed to the underlined words.

1. Their house is over there.
2. Every one said it was very cold.
3. When were they taken there?
4. These sell four for a dollar.
5. Which boy will go with you?

Follow-up Approach

Prepare sentences which contain two blank spaces. In front of each sentence write the two words that will complete the sense of the sentence. Students are to write the correct word in each blank space.

to
two
1. The ____ boys were going ____ the store.

for
four
2. These boxes sell ____ ____ a dollar.

think
thank
3. I ____ you should ____ him for it.

very
every
4. ____ teacher was ____ busy.

you
your
5. Have ____ had ____ dinner?

Reading Teacher-printed Sentences

1. Today is Tuesday.
   Today we have our music lesson.
   Miss Rogers comes to our room at 10:00 o'clock.

   The teacher reads each sentence, then asks the class to read with him. Following this, he may ask different pupils to go to the board and underline particular words such as *have, our, today, room.*

2. Assembling scrambled sentences.

   Individual words, from sentences used previously on the chalkboard, are printed on separate cards. These are presented in scrambled order, and volunteers are chosen to arrange the words in proper order to be followed by a card bearing the proper punctuation mark.

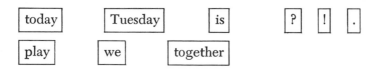

This is one of the many ways to provide repetition with particular frequently used words.

Joint Teacher-pupil Planning and Reading of Experience Charts

Teacher prints on large easel or blackboard:

1. Daily happenings in classroom or school
2. Trips or visits
3. Special events charts (Valentine's Day, Halloween, Thanksgiving Day, National Elections, Lincoln's or Washington's birthday, etc.)

Sentence Completion Exercises

The child selects the correct word from a pair of *look alike* words, which completes the meaning of a sentence.

1. Child circles the correct word.
   a. Let's play _____ . ball, tall
   b. In winter it is _____ . hold, cold
2. At the next level of difficulty, the child may *write* the correct word in the blank space

Use of "Classifying Games" to Teach Common Words

animals	clothing	food
dog	hat	milk
cat	shoes	cookies
cow	dress	pie

Place the underlined classification words on the board. The teacher points to and reads each word. Pupils repeat each word after the teacher pronounces it. Each of the other words to be used in the exercise is printed on oak tag or cardboard. The teacher holds up one word at a time and selects a volunteer to *pronounce* the word and to tell under which heading it belongs.

Variations include duplicated seatwork pages with headings such as *Toys, Plants, Months, Days.* A number of appropriate words are placed in a box at the bottom of the page and pupils copy the words under the correct heading.

Sight words are learned in myriad ways: from television, road signs, bulletin boards, labels on cartons, and the like. Obviously the most important source of learning is from meaningful reading situations as provided by charts, individual teacher-written stories, pre-primers, and easy to read trade books.

Thus far, the rationale for reading sight words has stressed only that to be a facile reader, one must acquire an ever-increasing stock of "instant recognition words." The degree to which printed words are mastered as sight words is one of the most meaningful ways of differentiating between poor and accomplished readers at all grade levels. A skill of such significance to the total reading process should be taught effectively. A number of justifications for learning words as wholes are briefly summarized.

1. If a child knows a number of words as sight words (instant recognition), she can be taught to see and to hear similarities between these known words and the new words she meets. Having a sight vocabulary is an invaluable tool in helping her "unlock" other words.

2. When words are recognized instantly, analysis is not necessary. The reader can put known words together in phrases, thus achieving intonation patterns that facilitate reading for meaning.

3. There are numerous high-frequency words which should be learned as units simply because they are met over and over in any reading situation. In addition, many of these words have irregular spellings which militates against "sounding them out."

Teaching Phonic Skills

Simultaneously with developing a sight vocabulary, children must also acquire skills which will permit them to unlock or identify words which they do not instantly recognize as sight words. Since various English words are very much alike in their visual patterns, the child must learn that letters and letter combinations represent speech sounds. The application of phonic analysis is undoubtedly the chief means used by readers to identify unknown words.

In the early stages of reading it is possible for a child to learn some "sight words" without noting letter-sound relationships. When she recognizes a word configuration as a whole (cat), she is not forced to translate letter-to-sound and to blend the sounds to arrive at the pronunciation *cat*. However, as more and more word symbols are met, the ability to sound and blend becomes an absolute necessity. For example the following words differ from *cat* in only one letter: *cut, cab, bat, fat, hat, can, cap, car, mat, pat, sat*. These minimal visual differences become harder to detect with the absence of phonics clues.

Formal instruction in associating printed letters with speech sounds heard in words has been preceded by years of experience with related learnings. The child can discriminate rather minute differences in spoken words (*Ted, bed, fed, led, red*) (*sat, sad, Sam, sack*). She hears and learns these words globally, rather than perceiving that each consists of three sounds (phonemes). Nevertheless, the six-year-old does distinguish thousands of words on the basis of minimal phoneme differences.

Cracking the letter-sound code
provides a tool for cracking the
meaning code.

She understands that *cat, rat, sat* and *call, tall, ball* rhyme. She notes that the words *cat, bet, cot* do not have this quality even though they have a common concluding sound. Children cannot "explain" what is being pointed out here, but they have mastered the auditory discriminations involved.

The reading readiness program has extended the child's knowledge of language sounds by providing much practice in this area. A fairly large percent of children entering grade one have learned to make visual discriminations between some letter forms and all other letter forms. That is, they can name the letters *B, O, M, S, L, T,* etc., whenever they see these symbols. Most readiness programs now include formal instruction in letter recognition. The next step after learning to discriminate letter forms is to associate speech sounds with known letter forms. To achieve independence in reading, a child must master these letter-sound associations and be able to apply them in reading situations when she meets unknown printed words.

Phonics instruction in the schools today starts in the readiness period and extends through all stages of reading instruction. The teacher works with the children to make sure that they hear the similar beginnings or similar endings of these words. The next step is instruction on seeing that letter combinations correspond to the similar sounds in the beginnings or endings of words.

If the child recognizes *m*ine and *m*any, she is then led to perceive that *m*ilk and *m*ud begin with the same symbol and thus, the same

sound. While she is learning sight words, she is also learning the sounds
that initial letters contribute to words. If she knows the words *tell* and
sell, she may be able to work out the word *bell,* since she also knows
the words *be, by, boat,* and *boy.* Gray* calls this process "initial consonant substitution" and points out that this process can work only in
relation to other *known* words. In addition to the clues just mentioned,
if the child knows all of the words in the sentence except the one new
word *bell,* the context in which the new word is found will also aid   *context*
her in arriving at the correct choice.

The question is sometimes heard, "When should phonics instruction be introduced?" The question seems to imply that this instruction
is not seen as an on-going integral part of the total reading program,
but rather as a block of skills which might be plugged in at one or another point on the learning continuum. A further implication suggested
by certain instructional materials is that when one decides to plug in
phonics, this is done with a degree of emphasis which neglects related
teachings. Evidence that balance can be achieved is provided by one
teacher who describes her first phonics lesson as follows:

> I usually have a phonics lesson the first day of school. Prior
> to the opening of school, I print on oak tag the first name of every
> child assigned to my room. As the children enter, each is given
> his name tag. I introduce the children on a first name basis,
> "Class, this is Mary. Does anyone else have a name that begins the
> same way as Mary?" If I get a correct response, I build on it. If
> not, I say, "Now I want to introduce Mike, I think Mike's name
> begins like Mary's. Listen, children, as I say these two names;
> *Mike, Mary.* I hear the same sound at the beginning of both
> names." I then have these two children stand at the front of the
> room and hold their name cards so everyone can see them. I point
> out that if the children look closely they will *see* that each name
> begins with the same letter and that this letter is called M. I then
> print both names on the board; we pronounce the names and look
> carefully at the initial letter. We then move to other names such as
> *Bobby, Billy;* or *Henry, Harry, Helen.*

Observing in this teacher's classroom, one is impressed with the
variety of approaches she uses to teach reading. All of these include
some emphasis on word analysis. Every day she writes the day of the
week, the month, and date, both in numbers and spelled out in words.
These writings often contain words which begin with the same sounds:

---

* William S. Gray, *On Their Own in Reading,* rev. ed. (Chicago: Scott, Foresman
& Co., 1960).

Today is Tuesday, September sixth, November ninth. In response to her questions, the children note that *Today* and *Tuesday* begin with a *T* that represents the same sound in both. They add other words which begin with the sound heard in *Today* and *Tuesday,* and the teacher writes these in a column on the chalkboard. They see the letter and say the words *tomorrow, time, take, tooth.*

The teacher introduces the children to a game which involves participation, language usage, listening, observation of the environment, and word analysis. "I'm thinking of something in the room—its name begins like *dog*—what is it?" The children look around and respond *door, desk, David, dominos;* as well as *duck* and *dolphins,* which are seen in pictures on the bulletin board.

Every day the teacher lets three or four children come to the front of the room and dictate a "sentence story." If the child's story is a "run-on account" and becomes lengthy, the teacher and child abstract it to a sentence. This is placed on the board and read by the teacher. Then the child who dictated the story reads it to the class and chooses a pupil to underline a particular word in the sentence. This work on sight vocabulary is usually followed by some work on letter sounds. "Which two words begin with the same sound?" "There are two words that rhyme; what are they?" "Who can give a word that rhymes with *hand?*"

Interdependence of Visual and Auditory Discrimination

Although visual and auditory discrimination may be discussed separately and lessons may be devised which emphasize one or the other, the two skills invariably work together in the reading situation. The child who learns to rely exclusively on visual clues will experience extreme difficulty as she meets hundreds of new printed words which have only minimal differences in letter configuration (*thumb, thump*). On the other hand, one cannot profit from learning letter-sound relationships if she cannot visually distinguish letters.

Attempting to teach the characteristic sound of *b* and *d* in such words as *big-dig, day-bay, dump-bump, bread-dread* cannot help the child "sound out" words unless she can instantly recognize the *b* and *d* configurations. First graders have learned to make hundreds of minute auditory discriminations required for understanding oral language. They can build upon this previous learning only if they learn to

1. Focus on sounds (phonemes) which are blended into whole words.
2. Associate these speech sounds with the proper graphic representations (letters).

Eye and Ear Training

Combination eye and ear training usually come after children have learned to recognize letters and some words. A series of work sheets can be prepared using single letters, letter blends, or words. This type of exercise may be viewed as moving beyond readiness activities, since the child must be able to recognize printed words.

Phonics instruction is "associating"
a visual stimulus with the sound it
represents.

1. The teacher says one of the letter symbols in each box and the child circles what he hears (*N—P—B—D*).

| (N)　　M　　R | B　　(P)　　D | S　　C　　(B) | T　　B　　(D) |

2. The teacher pronounces one word in each series (*flap, cap, tap, went*) and the child underlines that word.

clap		cap		map		*went*
flap		clap		top		want
slap		cat		*tap*		won't

3. The child marks the word in each box which rhymes with the stimulus word the teacher pronounces (*am, land, jump, day*).

hand		lamp		Jane		said
any		*sand*		came		sail
ham		fan		*dump*		*say*

4. Duplicate a number of three-word series of rhyming words:

a. look	book	took
b. pick	sick	kick
c. name	game	fame

The teacher identifies the line and pronounces one of the words: "line a: *book*; line b: *pick*; line c: *name*." The children circle that word. In addition to providing practice in auditory and visual discrimination, such sheets have diagnostic value for the teacher. At a glance, he can see which children are experiencing difficulty on particular letter-sound combinations.

5. The same type of exercise can be devised to teach and test consonant blends and digraphs as well as short and long vowel sounds.

*tr*ip	*dr*ip	grip
cheat	*w*heat	*sh*eet
b*a*t	bet	b*i*t
beet	b*oa*t	b*i*te

Pick a pair of pictures (with Rhyming Names). Secure a number of pictures making sure that there are several pairs of pictures whose naming words rhyme. Children take turns picking a pair of pictures whose names rhyme. If pages are duplicated, lines can be drawn connecting pairs of pictures whose names rhyme. See Figure 14.

Techniques for teaching phonic skills are practically unlimited. A few examples follow:

1. Match two or more pictures of objects whose names begin with the same sound. The teacher secures pictures and pastes each one on cardboard. One picture from each letter series is placed on the chalk tray. As the children select a picture from the remaining pile, it is placed beside the picture whose name begins with the same sound:

fish	lamp	cake	tent	bus	horn
fence	lake	comb	turtle	book	horse

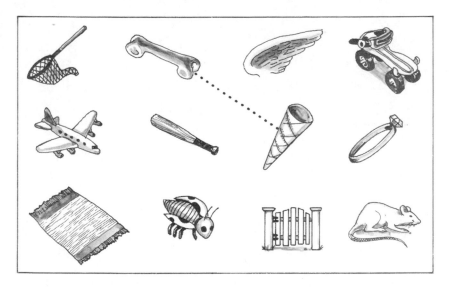

Figure 14

2. The final sounds in words may be stressed by using a different set of pictures:

hat	lamp	frog	book	bell	bus
boat	cup	flag	desk	towel	grapes

Working with Initial Consonant Sounds

A. *Substitute initial letters to make new words.* There are many frequently used words which end with the same two or three letters. These common elements are referred to as phonograms and words containing them were once referred to as "word families." Substituting initial letters in such words often helps children see and hear the letter-sound relationships.

Make a new word by placing a letter in the blank space in front of each word.

__at	__all	__and
__at	__all	__and
__at	__all	__and

The exercise can be made easier by providing letters which can be used (*b, f, h, s*).

Variations

1. "Add a '*b*' in front of each word and listen carefully as you pronounce the new word."

    __and   __ it   __old   __ eat   __end

2. "Add an '*s*' in front of the same words and listen carefully as you pronounce the new word."

    __ and   __it   __old   __eat   __end

3. *Add:*

add F →	__an	__ail	__ill	__at	__ear
add P →	__an	__ail	__ill	__at	__up
add M →	__an	__ail	__ill	__at	__end
add H →	__and	__ail	__ill	__at	__eat

B. *Change the first letter and make a new word that names an animal.*

Sample bolt   olt (c)olt

boat	__oat	meal	__eal
wear	__ear	big	__ig
sat	__at	pull	__ull
half	__alf	fog	__og
box	__ox	house	__ouse

C. *Put the letter* c *in any blank space where it will make a word.*

| __ap | *__eg | __up | __ub |
| *__im | __ot | __ap | __an |

If the letter *b* makes a word, put it on the blank space.

| __at | *__ap | __et | *__eb |
| __ed | __ag | *__ot | __ox |

---

* Space left blank.

More consonant-vowel-consonant (C.V.C.) words can be developed for most initial consonants than are shown above. This is true for all but a very few consonant letters.

D. *In each box write a* different *letter on the blank space to make a word.*

__ at	__ ed	__ ug	__ ip
__ at	__ ed	__ ug	__ ip
__ at	__ ed	__ ug	__ ip
__ at	__ ed	__ ug	__ ip

E. *Initial consonant blends.* The teacher can guide the reading of the following materials when used with children who may have difficulty reading the clues. The materials may be duplicated and used as seat work by students who can read the clues.

1. These pairs of letters are called blends (or clusters).

$$SK \quad SM \quad SC \quad SN \quad SP \quad ST \quad SW$$

This group of blends begin with the letter *s*. You always hear the sound of both of the letters:

say *mile—smile*; say *wing—swing*

Read the clue, then write one of the blends to make a word that fits the clue. Example: To say something _ _eak (write *SPeak*)

Clue		Clue	
"fish do it"	_ _im	"use your nose"	_ _ell
"not moving"	_ _ill	"cute but smelly"	_ _unk
"for eating soup"	_ _oon	"leader, goes ahead"	_ _out
"slow as a"	_ _ail	"where there's fire"	_ _oke

2. More blends. These all end with *r*. You hear both the letter-sounds.

say *ring—bring*; say *rag—drag*.

Clue		Clue	
"trains run on it"	_ _ack	"played with sticks"	_ _um
"a pretty color"	_ _een	"many people"	_ _owd
"what it costs"	_ _ice	"not the back"	_ _ont
"use on teeth"	_ _ush	"on king's head"	_ _own

3. Here are some blends that end with *l*:

$$bl \quad cl \quad fl \quad gl \quad pl \quad sl$$

You always hear the sound of both letters:

say *led—sled*; *lock—clock*

	Clue			Clue	
"could make rain"	_ _oud		"a big fire"	_ _aze
"too much rain"	_ _ood		"wear on hand"	_ _ove
"it can fly"	_ _ane		"icy rain"	_ _eet

Vowel Letter-sounds

A. *See and Say* (minimal contrast in vowel sounds). Many children who have no difficulty in speaking and understanding words which have only minimal phoneme differences do have difficulty when attempting to read such words. Vowel letter-sounds are usually the most troublesome. Brief periods of drill which focus on these minimal letter-sound contrasts can be helpful to some children. Too much drill can lead them to believe that what they are doing is reading. They should understand that they are playing a visual-auditory game that can help them later in their reading.

The material on the drill cards focuses on medial vowels in C.V.C. words (to be read across the boxes).

ĭ	ĕ		ŭ	ă		ĭ	ŭ		ă	ŏ
pin	pen		mud	mad		rib	rub		cat	cot
bit	bet		fun	fan		fin	fun		map	mop
lid	led		cup	cap		bit	but		rag	rug
sit	set		but	bat		hit	hut		hat	hot
tin	ten		rug	rag		big	bug		tap	top

hat	hit	hut	hot
big	beg	bag	bug
pat	pot	pet	pit
him	hum	ham	hem

sit	sat	set	sit
pin	pan	pun	pen
ten	tan	tin	ton
but	bit	bet	bat

B. *Teaching short-long vowel "patterns."* Many children will profit from a simultaneous visual presentation of letter patterns and the speech sounds that these patterns represent in words. This provides an immediate contrast. Material such as found in Figure 15 can be developed and used for class, group, and individual study. Then the materials can be placed on the bulletin board to serve as "models" for those children who may need such reinforcement. The use of pictures assures that the child will properly identify the printed words. Although only one vowel series (e - ēₐ̸ - ēȼ) is illustrated in Figure 15, picture words that can be used for the other vowel letter-sounds are listed.

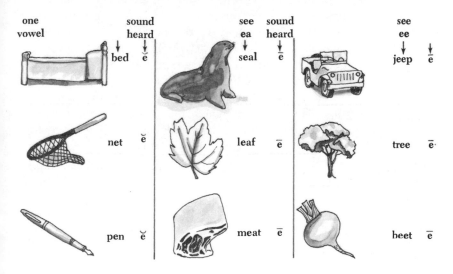

one vowel		sound heard	see ea		sound heard		see ee	
	bed	ĕ	seal	ē			jeep	ē
	net	ĕ	leaf	ē			tree	ē
	pen	ĕ	meat	ē			beet	ē

Figure 15

Picture words that illustrate other vowel patterns:

a	āi̸	ā-ȼ	o	ō-ₐ̸	ō + ȼ	i	i̸ȼ	ī + ȼ
cap	pail	cake	mop	goat	nose	pig	pie	pipe
pan	sail	rake	box	soap	rope	lid	tie	tire
bag	tail	vase	pot	boat	bone	"6"		kite
map	nail	gate	top	coat	cone	pin		"9"

C. *Effect of final* e. "Make a new word by adding the vowel 'e' to each word in column B. Pronounce the old word under A and the new word under B. What happens to the vowel sounds you hear?"

A	B	A	B
at	at__	pin	pin__
past	past__	dim	dim__
cut	cut__	plan	plan__
rid	rid__	tub	tub__

Reading
for Meaning

Much emphasis and instructional energy goes into cracking the "letter-sound code" in beginning instruction. It is also essential that children have experiences that focus on the meaning code. Many of the materials which the school adopts or which the teacher uses will make provisions for doing this, (basal readers, Chapter 4; language experiences, Chapter 6; individualized, Chapter 9).

The sentence is the meaning bearing unit of language in both speech and reading. The materials which follow emphasize this fact, while illustrating ways in which language skills and reading for meaning can be stressed. Beginning instruction is not too early to teach that a written statement may be true or false. Or, that in some situations, one must decide whether what is being read is a fact or the writer's opinion.

Children need experience in both combining sentences for precision and economy, and expanding sentences to include needed details. Riddles should be part of the reading program because they hold children's interest and motivate them to read. Riddles also represent a sophisticated use of language and involve the manipulation of language. Sentences can provide enough data from which to draw inferences. Written directions can be simple enough for beginning readers, while others can be difficult enough for high school or college level readers. The same is true of analogies.

These language-reading skills and dozens of others are developmental in nature. This means that if the difficulty level is controlled, working with analogies can begin in kindergarten or first grade. Relationships can be expressed orally or via pictures. Each succeeding instructional level can increase the difficulty level of the task, adding new types of relationships and new modes of presentation. This developmental nature of reading will be shown throughout various chapters devoted to instruction.

Combining Sentences

Beginning readers need experience with various sentence patterns. Many beginning reading materials consist primarily of short sentences, presumably because of the child's limited reading activity. Children also tend to string short sentences together in their oral language usage. One way to help children master and use more difficult syntactical patterns is to have them combine two or more short sentences into one statement. The introduction to this activity may involve the entire class with the teacher writing the stimulus material on the chalkboard. Later, smaller groups or individuals can work with cards, each of which contain one sentence reduction task, or with duplicated pages which contain several items.

Combine the numbered sentences into one sentence.

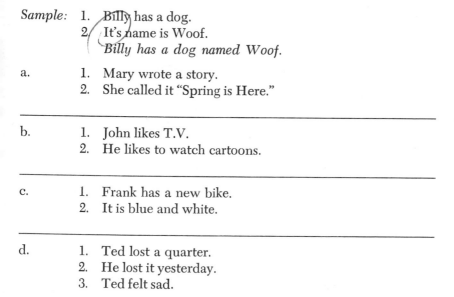

Sample: 1. Billy has a dog.
2. It's name is Woof.
    Billy has a dog named Woof.

a. 1. Mary wrote a story.
    2. She called it "Spring is Here."

b. 1. John likes T.V.
    2. He likes to watch cartoons.

c. 1. Frank has a new bike.
    2. It is blue and white.

d. 1. Ted lost a quarter.
    2. He lost it yesterday.
    3. Ted felt sad.

Building Sentences from Scrambled Word Order

One way for children to become familiar with English syntax is to provide them with opportunities to build sentences. Children enjoy manipulating series of words into meaningful units. This practice helps them develop an awareness of the role of structure words (*the, this, that, and, when, those,* etc.) and of permissible sequences in stringing words together.

Building sentences from a series of scrambled words can be introduced to the entire class through use of the chalkboard. A series of words which can be arranged into a sentence are written in jumbled order:

horse hay the ate the

The children suggest how to make this into a sentence.

The horse ate the hay.

Capital letters and punctuation are discussed and are included in the second writing. A second example might illustrate that the same words may be arranged in more than one way:

horse hay the eating was

The horse was eating hay.

Was the horse eating hay?

A second format could be the writing of each word separately on oak tag cards and placing the cards in an envelope.

A   Jack   my   is   name
B   eyes   Mary   brown   has
C   happen it   ?   how   did

Pupils select an envelope and arrange the words into a sentence. The sentence can then be checked by the teacher, a classroom helper, or a self-checking key can be made available.

A third format is to duplicate a page containing several scrambled sentences, leaving space for the students to write correct sentences.

1. won who game ball the

_____

2. girls boys the beat the

_____

_____

Expanding
Kernel Sentences

Expanding sentences is a language-reading activity that pays high returns on any time invested in its use. One can start with any kernel sentence (*Birds fly; John said "no;" Frank watched T.V.*) written on the chalkboard. Then invite children to answer questions by supplying a word which will then be added to the sentence. They can also tell where the word is to be added and, in their own words, why it fits there. There need be no use of terms like *adjectives, modifiers, adverbs,* etc. In addition, as words are added, the pupils can make observations as to where and what type of punctuation would be helpful in reading the expanding sentence.

Example: Mary had a lamb.

Question: "What size?" *little* "Where do we put little?"
Mary had a little lamb.

"Describe the lamb:" *woolly* "Where do we put woolly?"
Mary had a woolly little lamb.
Mary had a little woolly lamb.

"The lamb's name?" *woolly?* "Can we do this?" "How?"
Mary had a woolly little lamb named Woolly.

"What color is the lamb?'" *white*

"How white?"   *as snow*

"What is white as snow?" *Its fleece; its coat.*
"Mary had a woolly little lamb named Woolly, whose fleece (coat) was white as snow."

There are, of course, many other ways the sentence might have been developed, and expanded farther. If desired, the class can play "shorten the sentence." Ask for a volunteer to erase the word that is not needed if we do not care what the lamb's name is, or its color, or its size etc. This technique integrates many language-reading skills. Children experience how their language operates, how words can be strung together to convey a message, how sequence controls the stringing, how adding a word or words affects intonation.

**How Many
Ways?**

This language game demonstrates that words can be arranged in many patterns each of which results in meaning. Select three or four words that can be arranged in different ways to produce different sentences. Write these words in jumbled order on the chalkboard. Ask the class (or individual) to arrange the words so they make a sentence.

Example: friend is my Mary
Response A: "Mary is my friend."

Leave this sentence on the board and ask if the words can be arranged in another way and still make a sentence (no words can be added).

Response B: "My friend is Mary."
(Suggest there may be another way)

Response C: "Is Mary my friend?"
(and another . . . ?)

Response D: "Is my friend Mary?"

Example 2:   say I say you what

a. You say what I say.
b. I say what you say.
c. What I say, you say.
d. What you say, I say.

Variations: Once the game has been played by the class it can be used for independent seat work by individuals, pairs of students, or teams. Write the words separately on oak tag:

| answer | the | no | is |

These are placed in an envelope. The pupil(s) then arrange the words into a sentence and write it on a card. The words are arranged into another sentence which is copied on the card. This continues until no other sentences can be formed. Then the children compare their work with the answer card key which reads:

The answer is no.
No is the answer.
Is the answer no?
Is no the answer?

The next level of participation is to encourage individual pupils, pairs, or teams to develop sentences whose words can be rearranged into several different sentences. Those that merit selection can be added to the stack of envelopes.

Using
Riddles

     Riddles should be used in beginning reading because they are fun, highly motivating, and can lead to valuable insights about language. Teachers have observed pupils' behavior in their reading of children's newspapers (*My Weekly Reader*, etc.). When children are permitted to "self-select" what they wish to read first, they tend to choose the language games such as riddles, puzzles, and jokes. We should profit from such observations, since children are indicating they enjoy humor and the challenge of sophisticated language usage.

     There are all types of riddles ranging from the factual, (which are only good for openers), to those involving a ridiculous play on words. There are numerous ways that this language game can be used in the classroom, ranging from "riddle time" to riddle banks and bulletin boards. A few varieties of riddles are illustrated here.

What am I? These are factual and their chief value is introducing riddles and teaching that "listening to the clues" is essential.

1. What eats hay and gives milk?
2. What has 4 legs and a trunk?
3. What has black and white stripes and looks like a pony?
4. What turns red and green and yellow?
5. What is soft and furry and rhymes with *mitten?*

Factual "with a twist."

1. What is bigger than a cow, has one horn and gives milk? (a milk truck)
2. What goes up and down without moving? (a staircase)
3. What is full of holes and still holds water? (a sponge)
4. What gets wetter the more it drinks? (a towel)
5. What is it that the more you take away from it, the larger it gets? (a hole)

Play on letter names and sounds.

What letter:

1. do we see with?   (I)
2. makes honey?   (B)
3. usually starts a question?   (Y)
4. is a blue bird?   (J)
5. is a girl's name   (K) $\mathcal{D}$ β

Parts of the body riddles (overused, but fun at first).

What has:

1. legs but can't walk?   (chair, table, etc.)
2. a neck but no body?   (a bottle)
3. teeth but no gums?   (a comb)
4. a tongue but can't talk?   (a shoe)
5. eyes but can't see?   (a potatoe)
   (adapt to needle, Mississippi river, etc.)

Play on words.

1. What is the longest word in the world?
   (Smiles, there's a mile between its first and last letter)
2. When are bus drivers not people?
   (When they turn into a parking lot)
3. What should you do if your left toe falls off?
   (Call a "toe" truck)
4. What is the only word you can make shorter by adding letters?
   (The word *short*—then add *er*)
5. What did the dog say when it sat on the sandpaper?
   ("Ruff-Ruff")

Crazies.

1. What is pointed, yellow and writes?
   (a ball point carrot)
2. Ad infinitum

Use a "cluebox" (or double the reading). Duplicate a page containing five or six riddles. At the bottom of the page include a cluebox which provides the answers in random or mixed order. Children use cluebox as needed. (NOTE: They *always read* all of it.)

Moral riddle: What's worse than a day without riddles?
Answer: (two days in a row without riddles).

Working with Fact or Opinion Statements

In the process of becoming readers, children should develop questioning attitudes toward what they read. The school, being factually oriented, is frequently interested in "what the book says." This emphasis can lead learners to believe that if information is in a book (or in print), it must be correct. The goal in analyzing statements is not to establish that X statement is a fact (or opinion), but to sharpen the process for achieving such a goal in the future.

When Paula responds that "Sunday is the best day of the week" is a fact, she may learn that it is for her, but not for Stanley. Could she and Stanley, with help from the class, rewrite the statement so that a majority of the class would agree their statement is a fact? Doug says the statement "Learning to read is fun" is not a fact, but the next day notes that "Learning to read should be fun" is a fact. Perhaps his reasoning and analysis may lay the groundwork for saving the schools. More likely, the chief logician at the nearby university would say, "that kid would flunk in my class." However, if children have experiences which lead to the understanding of and manipulation of language, they are growing—and that's the point of the game.

The following fact-opinion statements are only illustrative. Add a few each day.

1. Americans are friendly people.
2. Watching cartoons on T.V. helps develop your mind.
3. First-grade girls can run faster than first-grade boys.
4. Big cities are not good places to live.
5. School work should be done in school—no homework!
6. The best team always wins.
7. If you do the same thing every day, it gets boring.
8. There should not be taxes on food.
9. Someday, people will live on the moon.
10. The Earth is the only planet on which there is life.

Reading is often defined as a "thinking process," or at least as a task involving thinking. There is no more powerful reading task than solving analogies, which are simply expressions of a relationship between two things or word meanings. Analogies can be introduced as a listening-thinking game by using relationships within the child's experience.

"What do we wear on our feet?" (socks, *shoes*)
"When its cold, what do we wear on our hands?" (gloves)
"Listen carefully and tell me what word we need to finish this sentence:"
shoe is to foot as glove is to _____
glove is to hand as shoe is to _____
shoe is to foot as *hat* is to _____

Other easy relationships can be used such as synonyms or antonyms: (big-large/tiny-small); (hard-soft/hot-cold). After oral presentations, analogies similar to those above may be placed on the chalkboard. Children need not be able to read these perfectly as long as the teacher reads them several times. Volunteers then supply the missing word. A series of pictures may also be used. Children name the pictures, discover the relationship, and indicate which picture completes the analogy. A page of picture analogies can be duplicated for independent work as illustrated in Figure 16. A variation is to place four pictures in an envelope. The child then arranges these in sequence to express a given relationship.

In describing relationships, adult terminology should not be forced upon the pupils (i.e. "function," "classification," "origin," etc.). However, children should be encouraged to verbalize in their own words why a particular choice was made.

Plurals

Analogies can be a highly motivating method of working with or teaching plurals, homonyms, classification, irregularly spelled words. One of the virtues is that the difficulty level can be controlled. For example, the first lesson of analogies involving plurals can deal only with adding *s*, the next group with adding *es*, and a third set with *change y to i and add es;* a fourth format can include all of these in mixed order:

```
boy   boys   (as)   girl   _____
box   boxes  (as)   fox    _____
city  cities (as)   penny  _____
```

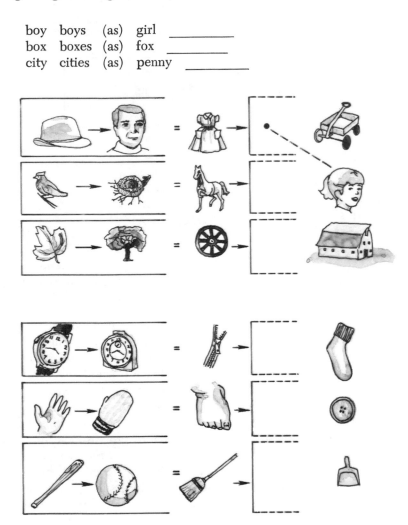

Figure 16

Homonyms

Difficulty level can also be controlled by providing clueboxes which include all of the words that the child will need to complete a series of analogies. One or more foils may be included to increase difficulty. The following material could be used after a lesson or two on homonyms.

Directions: Use a word from the box to complete each line

clue box	by	too	rode	rap	meat

1. see   sea   (as)   to   _____
2. tail   tale   (as)   road   _____
3. week   weak   (as)   buy   _____
4. sail   sale   (as)   meet   _____
5. wring   ring   (as)   wrap   _____

Developing Intonation Skills

Reading with acceptable intonation patterns is an essential skill that should be developed from the very beginning of instruction. By the age of six, most children have already made tremendous progress in applying intonation patterns in oral language usage. However, they need guidance in understanding that reading demands much the same application of stress, pitch, juncture, and phrasing.

The major difference between speaking and reading is that when the child speaks, she is in charge of the entire process. The message originates with the speaker, and intonation *is part of the message.* One does not make up the words and then decide how they will be delivered. Reading is somewhat different. The reader is interpreting someone else's message. The proper intonation is still an essential part of the message, but only limited clues can be provided via print. This is why beginning readers frequently "decipher the words" and then sense that something is lacking. They then reread, this time utilizing the proper *expression.*

When inexperienced readers focus on each of the words, they obviously are less effective in decoding the entire string of words. If each word is treated as if it were a message, the message is lost. The following are a few ways in which beginning readers can be helped to read with intonation.

Provide Good Models

In beginning reading instruction, it is essential that children hear and experience good models of oral reading. Most teachers involved with beginning instruction are quite skilled at conveying feelings, building suspense, and arousing interest. Teachers who *enjoy* reading usually find that children give rapt attention to stories that are told or read well. Recordings of stories or poems read by skillful readers provide other useful listening models. Parallel with providing models, there should be encouragement for children to develop good intonation patterns in their reading.

Demonstrating Stress or Emphasis

After explaining the meaning of stressing or emphasizing a word, write a sentence on the chalkboard. Tell the children you will read the sentence and stress one word more than the others. They are to listen carefully and tell which word was emphasized.

Sample: "Which <u>word</u> did I stress the most?" Repeat, using the same sentence but stressing a different word each time.

"Which word did I stress the <u>most</u>?"
"Which word did <u>I</u> stress the most?"
"Which word did <u>I</u> <u>stress</u> the most?"

Variation. Write another sentence on the board and read it with the class in a normal voice. Next, underline one word and invite the group to again read the sentence this time stressing the underlined word. Continue by erasing the line and underlining a different word each time.

Stress and Rhyme. Explain that you will read a rhyming sentence and will stress <u>two words</u>. However, the pupils must supply the last word which will complete the rhyme. In order to do this, they must listen carefully and provide a word that means the opposite of the last word stressed. This word must also complete the rhyme.

1. "Think of a word that rhymes with <u>go</u>.
   It isn't <u>fast</u>, it must be ____ ." (slow)
2. "Give me a word that rhymes with <u>best</u>.
   It isn't <u>East</u>, it must be ____ ."
3. "Give me a word that rhymes with <u>gold</u>.
   It isn't <u>hot</u>, it must be ____ ."
4. "Think of a word that rhymes with <u>track</u>.
   It isn't <u>front</u>, it must be ____ ."
5. "Give me a word that rhymes with <u>dress</u>.
   It isn't <u>more</u>, it must be ____ ."

Change the Meaning (*Punctuation and Dialogue*)

This exercise demonstrates how punctuation provides clues to meaning and to intonation patterns. One of the peculiar characteristics of many beginning reading materials is the high frequency with which dialogue is used. This is one of the most difficult types of reading material. Yet, first graders are exposed to more of it than they will meet in later learning situations. Examine a preprimer or primer and you may be surprised at the number of times you meet ...he said, ...said Jack, ...she said, ...asked Mary, ...said Mom, ...called Jimmy, ...said the man.

In order to cope with this difficult aspect of reading, children need explanations and practice in seeing punctuation and solving its role. Place a sentence (similar to number 1 below) on the chalkboard. Read it to the class using a minimum of intonation—hopefully some degree of ambiguity will result. Ambiguity is a big word, and children can experience it without using the term. The fact that something is missing can be established by questions such as what does it mean? Who said what?

1. "The teacher said the principal is your friend" Next, punctuate the sentence as shown in 2. Read this to the class, and then read it in unison with the class. Discuss what the punctuation does for the reader.
2. "The teacher," said the principal, "is your friend" The punctuation can be erased from sentence 2 and new punctuation added, as found in 3. Have the children read the sentence and discuss how the meaning was changed.
3. The teacher said, "the principal is your friend"

Obviously many follow-up experiences will be needed by most children. In addition to the teacher-class work, materials can be designed for individual work or work by pairs or teams. In these exercises, the student simply adds the punctuation called for in the directions.

One item assignments.

Directions: fix the sentence so that John is absent
John said Mary is absent today

Larger units of work. A series of cards or duplicated pages can be prepared, each containing several items. In some instances, punctuation can simply be added to the material. In other situations, it may be desirable to have the pupils "rewrite the sentences" and include the needed punctuation.

		Use punctuation to show that:
1.	Mike said Mary is always hungry.	(Mary is talking)
2.	Mike said Mary is always hungry.	(Mike is talking)
3.	That little boy said the teacher is smart.	(The boy is smart)
4.	The doctor said his friend is ill.	(The doctor is sick)
5.	The doctor said his friend is ill.	(The doctor is speaking)

"*Add a word.*" The following exercise is designed to help children understand how intonation signals the end of a sentence. Write a kernel sentence on the chalkboard. Have children note what the voice does at the end of the sentence.

The doctor is in.

Erase the period at the end of the sentence and add a word or two. Have children note that the signal no longer follows *in.*

The doctor is in a hurry.

(*Continue one more step:*)

The doctor is in a hurry to leave.

A series of cards can be typed or printed, each containing two or three sentences that illustrate the above.

The rain fell. The rain fell faster.	Sally came in. Sally came in first. Sally came in first again.	John is late. John is late again.

No child in first grade will master all of the intonation skills needed in reading for meaning, but all children should have experiences that will help them gain insights as to how intonation functions in reading.

SUMMARY

During the past few years beginning reading instruction has received more attention than any other facet of the school curriculum.

A *breakthrough* in reading is when
a child learns *how* to read.

Practically all of the "newer approaches to reading" were, in essence,
materials and methodology focusing primarily on the beginning reading period. Materials were designed to emphasize certain premises
which promised to be the best approach to reading instruction. Representative examples are augmented English alphabet, diacritical markings, basals following various philosophies, trade books, concomitant
stress on reading and writing, programmed reading workbooks, boxed
materials, and reading kits stressing particular facets of reading ranging
from phonics to appreciation of literature.

The proliferation of teaching materials undoubtedly held some
promise for the teaching of reading since teachers and schools would
have many different materials available. However, there developed a
tendency to place unwarranted faith in "new" materials and approaches. This false hope was undoubtedly nourished by the producers
of some of the new materials. Advertisements and brochures attributed
qualities to these materials which had not yet been established in the
classroom. "Breakthroughs in reading instruction" were announced
with startling frequency, and the popular press joined in building shaky
hypotheses into specious proofs for many of the newer materials.

After a decade or more of disillusioned search for a reading instruction panacea, the consensus is that none will be found. There is
less of a tendency today to become a partisan for or against particular
materials. Many observers feel that the more rigid the teaching, the

more likely one is to find reliance on one set of materials; conversely, creative teachers are less bound by loyalties to specific materials and methodology.

The fact that so many of the new materials emphasized the early and systematic teaching of letter-sound relationships has made this the foremost issue in reading instruction. Data from recent studies have reaffirmed the position that instructional programs which include considerable emphasis on phonics result in higher achievement at the end of grade one than do programs which include significantly less phonics instruction. Nevertheless, there are still a number of unanswered questions relative to beginning reading instruction, if one views learning to read as a long-term developmental process.

YOUR POINT OF VIEW?

Would you defend or attack the following premises? Why?

1. Deliberately teaching children to note and use context clues for solving unknown words is self-defeating since the possibility for "wrong guesses" is always present.
2. Many "trade books" for children deliberately limit the use of different words (i.e., follow the practice of "controlled vocabulary"). This is inevitably bad, as it curtails story content.
3. If every child in the class were ego-involved in the learning tasks, there would be practically no discipline problems in the classroom.
4. Parents' ego-involvement in their child's learning to read is a causal factor in many reading failures and is a major problem for the schools and first-grade teachers.
5. Recently, reading instruction has tended to focus more on materials and methodology than on "the child as a learner."

Defend or attack the following statements.

A. In most reading situations methodology is less important in changing reading behavior than is the type of relationship established between teacher and child.
B. *Premise:* "If a given instructional technique is effective with a given child and does not inhibit her later growth in reading, the use of this technique is justifiable." State whether or not you accept this premise and support your decision.

BIBLIOGRAPHY

1. Barr, Rebecca, "The Effect of Instruction on Pupil Reading Strategies," *Reading Research Quarterly* 10, no. 4, 1974–75, pp. 555–82.
2. Burns, Paul C. and Roe, Betty D., *Teaching Reading in Today's Elementary Schools*. Chicago: Rand McNally College Publishing Co., 1976. Chapter 7.
3. Eller, William, "Contributions of the First and Second Grade Studies," *Reading and Realism*, J. Allen Figural, ed. Proceedings, International Reading Association 13, Part 1, 1969, pp. 585–88.
4. Emans, Robert, "Linguists and Phonics," *Reading Teacher* 26 (February 1973): 477–82.
5. Fleming, James T., "Oral Language and Beginning Reading: Another Look," *The Reading Teacher* (October 1968): 24–29.
6. Harris, Albert J. and Jacobson, Milton D., "Some Comparisons between Basic Elementary Reading Vocabularies and Other Word Tests," *Reading Research Quarterly* 9, no. 1, 1973–74, pp. 87–109.
7. Hillerich, Robert L., "Word Lists—Getting It All Together," *Reading Teacher* 27 (January 1974): 353–60.
8. Jones, Daisy Marvel, *Teaching Children to Read*. New York: Harper and Row, 1971.
9. King, Ethel M. and Muehl, Siegmar, "Different Sensory Cues as Aids in Beginning Reading," *Reading Teacher* (December 1965): 163–68.
10. King, Ethel M., "Beginning Reading: When and How," *Reading Teacher* (March 1969): 550–53.
11. Lefevre, Carl A., "The Sounds and Tunes We Read By," *New Dimensions in Reading*. University of Pittsburgh Conference Proceedings, 19, 1963, pp. 61–68.
12. ———, *Linguistics and the Teaching of Reading*. New York: McGraw-Hill Book Co., 1964.
13. MacGinitie, Walter H., "When Should We Begin to Teach Reading?" *Language Arts* 53 (November 1976): 878–82.
14. Mattleman, Marciene S., "Building Reading Vocabulary: A Treat, Not a Treatment," *Reading Teacher* 27 (October 1973): 51–53.
15. Melaragro, Ralph J., "Beyond Decoding: Systematic Schoolwide Tutoring in Reading," *Reading Teacher* 28 (November 1974): 157–60.
16. Meltzer, Nancy S. and Herse, Robert, "The Boundaries of Written Words as Seen by First Graders," *Journal of Reading Behavior* (Summer 1969): 3–14.
17. Pikulski, John, "Effects of Reinforcement on Word Recognition," *Reading Teacher* (March 1970): 516–22.

18. Porter, Para, "Pictures in Reading," *The Reading Teacher* (December 1968): 238–41.

19. Rosner, Jerome, "Perceptual Skills—A Concern of the Classroom Teacher," *The Reading Teacher* (March 1971): 543–49.

20. Ross, Ramon Royal, "Fannie and Frank and the Flannelboard," *Reading Teacher* 27 (October 1973): 43–47.

21. Schell, Leo M., *Fundamentals of Decoding for Teachers.* Chicago: Rand McNally College Publishing Co., 1975.

22. Shuy, Roger W., "Some Considerations for Developing Beginning Reading Materials for Ghetto Children," *Journal of Reading Behavior* (Spring 1969): 33–43.

23. Singer, Harry and Ruddell, Robert B., eds., *Theoretical Models and Processes of Reading*, second ed. Newark, Del.: International Reading Association, 1976.

24. Sister Marilyn, O.S.F., "Reading for Meaning," *Catholic School Journal* (September 1965): 56.

25. Smith, Dora V., "Children's Literature Today," *Elementary English* (October 1970): 777–80.

26. Smith, Nila Banton, *American Reading Instruction.* Newark, Del.: International Reading Association, 1965.

27. Speer, Olga B. and Lamb, George S., "First Grade Reading Ability and Fluency in Naming Verbal Symbols," *Reading Teacher* 29 (March 1976): 572–76.

28. Stauffer, Russell G., *The Language-Experience Approach to the Teaching of Reading.* New York: Harper and Row, 1970.

29. Weiger, Myra, "Puppetry," *Elementary English* 51 (January 1974): 55–65.

Chapter **6**

Language: The Key to Child Growth and School Instruction

Language and Growth

By the age of six years, the normal child's linguistic achievement is so great that it is difficult to evaluate or comprehend. It is one of those miracles described by John Donne when he wrote, "The ordinary things in nature, would be greater miracles, than the extraordinary which we admire most, if they were done but once."* Since practically all children master the language process, this "miracle" is often treated as commonplace. Even though the school curriculum is almost totally language dependent, educators may be underestimating the potential for learning which most preschool children have developed.

---

* *The Complete Poetry and Selected Prose of John Donne* (New York: The Modern Library, Random House, 1946), p. 380.

Children upon entering school

1. have a very well developed control of the language system involved in their native language. In regard to the mastery of the syntactical structure of language they are closer to being "miniature adults" than in any other aspect of development.

2. have an amazing understanding of the language heard in their environment.

3. have a partial mastery of the *supra-segmental phonemes,* which account for intonation patterns found in their language.

4. have the ability to make very fine auditory discrimination among words which sound very much alike (*bath-path; drink-drank; feed-feet*).

5. have mastered the meanings of and ability to pronounce thousands of words. They can also string words into sentences and larger language units.

All of these skills and abilities are developmental in nature. Each must be expanded and refined if normal growth is to be maintained.

Social, emotional, and intellectual growth reflect and interact with language growth. Individuals learn and use language in social-emotional settings, and the language used is a key to ego needs, frustration, and self-concepts. It is important that teachers *read* these clues if they hope to teach all children to read. Learning, and particularly learning to read, is a process related to and controlled by other facets of growth.

The concept of "teaching the whole child" has been muted or deleted from current educational philosophy. Yet, any experienced teacher knows that children cannot be taught to read if their energies are being consumed by unresolved social-emotional problems.

Language and Socialization

The school is very much involved in guiding the social growth of its pupils. In the case of normal children, socialization is almost exclusively built around communication. Up to the time children reach school age, spoken language is the chief means of communication. There is no better tool than language facility for gauging the social needs or social maturity of children. Among the first experiences provided in the modern school's curriculum are those which have to do with social growth. The logic of this is apparent. Many children have

Individuals who interact with language are developing the tool for later interaction in groups.

had little or no experience in a group as large as that in which they will find themselves upon beginning school. There will be many learning situations which will call for group coherence. Each member of the group will have to follow certain social patterns in order not to disrupt the learning situation for the others in the group.

Gradually, step by step, the teacher moves in the direction of establishing social control within the class so that learning can take place. Whether the teacher structures this control on an authoritarian basis or has the group control evolve out of the group itself, the medium for establishing control will be language. Many group activities in the classroom, if they are to end successfully, will call for cooperation and sharing among pupils. Language is the most important basis for cooperation. Cooperation and sharing help the child grow and develop from a very self-centered organism into a social being. If the process breaks down and the individual, for any reason, does not learn the social rules, or does not within certain limits follow them, his behavior

sets him apart from the group. When his peer group reacts to this behavior, he and the group are out of adjustment.

These maladjustments among children beginning school are almost
inevitable because some children have further to go in order to live up
to the group standards, some learn slowly, and some have learned to use
anti-social responses when attempting to satisfy their needs. A teacher
who does not perceive the symptoms of maladjustment fairly early may
soon have cases of nonaffiliation in her class. These can develop rapidly
into isolates, or children rejected by the group. The teacher may be the
best teacher of reading in the district, but if she lets the security of
some children become seriously threatened in the school situation, the
odds are that she will not teach them reading. In their unskilled efforts
to strike back at threats they do not understand, these pupils may disrupt the learning for others in the group.

Language and Emotional Adjustment

Clinicians state that language is the most sensitive indicator of maladjustment and psychological needs. The classroom, the playground,
in fact the total environment, is one never-ending projective technique
if one but heeds the language of children. Both as adults and as
teachers, we sometimes learn very little about children from children.
This happens when we consciously or unconsciously feel that what
children say is not important. The truth of the matter is that their language mirrors their needs, feelings, aspirations, and fears; and if one's
job is to help children grow, sensitivity to these is essential.

A child's need for ego satisfaction seems to increase by a geometric
ratio in the face of frustration. That is, a little denial of love, attention,
and acceptance, or a little threat to self-worth and integrity, is reacted
to by an increased drive for these goals. If rebuffed, the child seems to
redouble his efforts to maintain his prestige and self-worth. It is apparent that when children are trying to fulfill ego needs, they invariably
use behavior which by adult logic seems ill-conceived and not likely to
achieve the child's goal. The child who wants and needs friendship and
is rebuffed may resort to the use of aggressive, hostile, or abusive language, perhaps feeling that he can force acceptance or that his language will reduce the stature of those persons to whom it is addressed.
Another child, after each failure, may withdraw more and more and
make very few language overtures to others in his peer group. This non-

When emotional needs are met,
energy is focused on learning.

use of language is itself a clue which should have diagnostic value for the teacher. Here is a child who has elected to withdraw from the arena, but the fight to salvage his ego will go on within himself. This child, at the moment, poses no problem to the teacher or society, but his response is potentially more dangerous than overt aggression.

Language and Mental Growth

Psychologists agree that the most valuable insights into the child's mental growth are gained from a study of the development of language facility. A brief though acceptable definition of intelligence is that it is "the ability to do abstract thinking." Stated another way, it is the ability to manipulate in a meaningful manner symbolic materials of which language is our best example. Intelligence itself cannot be measured but is inferred from behavior that can be measured. We measure certain behavior which by agreement is said to be representative of intelligence. The one kind of behavior most universally measured on intelligence tests is language behavior. Our society puts a high value on the ability to use and understand language. The degree of the child's mastery of communication skills determines to a large extent his readiness to do school tasks and to profit from instruction. Although he cannot read, spell, or write when he starts school, he has had years of experience with language. His language proficiency is used as an index of his mental growth, just as it provides data for appraisal of social and emotional growth and adjustment.

Furthermore, when we wish to assess what the student has learned at any grade level, we rely on language usage. Language reveals the number and breadth of concepts acquired. All concepts exist within the framework of some symbolic process, and all are arrived at and refined through thought processes, which in turn depend on the manipulation of language symbols. In other words, a change in language behavior is often the sole criterion of learning.

A society such as we have today could not have evolved without language. It is equally obvious that education would not have developed along the lines it has without language. Language provides a bridge which permits ideas, information, and data to pass between parent and child, teacher and pupil, and child and peer. As an individual masters new forms of language usage, he is developing "mind tools" which he can use from that time forward in the pursuit of knowledge. Reading is our best example of such a tool.

Language and Reading

While language usage provides the teacher with information about all aspects of a child's development, previous language experience is probably most important as it relates to the specific task called *reading*. Reading is a language process. When we read we translate graphic symbols into the language they represent.

The teaching of reading has a unique relationship to and with language. The school's success depends in large measure on how well students develop language facility. This is because practically all learning in the school is language dependent. From the time the nation's first schools were founded, reading has been the chief means of achieving the school's goals. However, there are practically no concepts that the schools teach that could not be learned even if the student could not read what the school assigns.

The schools elect to depend on reading ability of students, and the society which supports the schools places a high value on "learning to read." Perhaps unconsiously, the society agrees with Thomas Paine's observation that "Every man of learning eventually becomes his own teacher." It is quite obvious that the *learning* referred to cannot be achieved in the absence of reading ability. The school and all segments of mass media hold the learner as a hostage to some degree, since the learning they provide is selective. In a free society, the ability to read is just as much a prerequisite as is freedom to read.

Learning to Read: Cracking Two Codes

— letter-sound code
— meaning code

　　Learning to read involves the learner in cracking (solving) two codes. One is the relationship between letters seen in print and the speech sounds these letters represent. Knowing this letter-sound code permits the reader to "say," "pronounce," "decode," "solve," or "approximate" the pronunciation of words not recognized as sight words. The second code focuses on meaning or decoding the "message." For instance, by the end of third grade many students can get the speech sounds correct, that is, pronounce all the words, in the following passage.

The louder he talked of his honor, the faster we counted our spoons.

Many high school students and some college students are at a loss to crack the meaning code.*

　　Reading "for meaning" is actually closer to children's previous experiences than is associating visual symbols with phonemes. Prior to reading instruction, they have for years, been listening to and speaking meaningful language. The relationship between oral language and reading is apparent to most adults. Unfortunately, the way that adults sometimes teach children to read masks this relationship. The process of learning to read can take place under circumstances that minimize the language component. The child who is learning to read may fail to see that he is really involved in a language process, mainly because we have developed ways to teach reading that pretty thoroughly divorce the act of reading from language involvement. This outcome is trace-

---

* A few interpretations of college students: "It simply doesn't make any sense;" "The after-dinner speaker was giving a boring speech, so *we* counted the spoons at our place setting;" "The more this guy boasted of his great feats at the banquet the more we ignored him by eating our soup."

able to the fact that instruction can (and sometimes does) overempha-size the letter-sound code while failing to stress the language-meaning code. The lack of balanced instruction may or may not be deliberate—the issue is "how the learner perceives what is going on."

Cracking the letter-sound code can provide its own motivation for only a limited time—it is not a self-sustaining activity. Teaching the myriad of reading skills must be accompanied by a sense of involve-ment with language*

The Curriculum
as an Enemy

The school has two major functions, which are to help children

1. develop and expand concepts.
2. develop the language tools that will permit them to continue this process in or out of school.

These goals appear to be totally compatible yet, in actual practice, the school has not been successful in providing the ideal mix or maintaining the proper balance between teaching concepts and developing lan-guage facility. One often reads in the professional literature that reading is a tool. It might be better to go back one step and establish the fact that language is the *tool* and that reading is the manipulation of or a specific use of that tool.

Over the years the curriculum materials that are widely used in the schools have focused primarily on teaching concepts that can be characterized facts. This has been prevalent in the various content areas, such as social studies, science, health. Teachers and other ob-servers of the educational scene are aware that "fact-oriented" reading materials do not always grab students' minds or hold their interest. One of the most frequently heard questions among reading teachers is, "How do you motivate children to read?"

The answer lies in achieving the proper balance between teaching facts (which are both mundane and transitory), and helping students develop and sharpen language usage and facility. Children must ex-perience the power and beauty of language since this is the only magic

---

* This concept was presented by Jerome Bruner in his International Reading Association address, Detroit,1972.

available to the school. Everything else in the curriculum is "The Way It's Spozed to Be."[*] A book can be a frigate to bear us lands away only when the reader transforms the book into a frigate. The captain of such a ship knows that both sail and rudder are synonyms for language. This is not a plea for the child's hasty entrance into great literature, but rather that he will have a chance to work with jokes, rhymes, riddles, proverbs, and both brief and lengthy language samples. Man is the only talking animal, and his language has a tremendous potential fascination for him. We must find ways to smuggle language into reading.

Linguistics and Reading

Various facets of linguistics are discussed throughout this book. For example, both the phonology and syntax of nonstandard dialect speakers are treated in Chapter 11, The Culturally Different Child as a Learner. The linguistic (regular spelling) approach to beginning reading is described in Chapter 4, and exercises for teaching intonation in reading are found in the primary instruction section. This discussion will explore some of the areas in which linguistics appear to be contiguous with reading instruction. In order to understand what linguists have proposed, why they disagree about reading instruction, and why they, as a group, will never develop "The Linguistic Method of Teaching Reading," we must have some understanding of the terms *linguist* and *linguistics.*

In attempting definitions of these terms one might keep in mind a linguist's advice, "We must define a linguist rather strictly because the term has become dangerously popular, emulating the more extensive term scientist."[†]

Linguists are trained individuals who make a scientific study of human language. Such study implies accurate observation and recording of data.

The linguist studies and identifies the building blocks of language, speech sounds or phonemes. He discerns how these are combined into words and word parts which have assigned meanings (morphemes). This is the groundwork for further study of language, namely the *pat-*

---

[*] J. Herndon, *The Way It's Spozed to Be* (New York: Simon & Schuster, 1968).
[†] Raven I. McDavid, Jr., "The Role of the Linguist in the Teaching of Reading," *Changing Concepts of Reading Instruction,* International Reading Association Proceedings 6 (1961): 253–56.

terns in which words may occur and those patterns which cannot occur in a particular language. When these discoveries are made, one has the key to the structure or the grammar of a language.

The linguist discovers facts which are unique to each language and others that are common to various languages. The layman can verbalize some of these findings without grasping their full significance. For instance, the linguist states, *language is arbitrary*. This applies to all facets of language. The normal child growing up in an English-speaking environment learns to make many speech sounds which he will have to discard if he restricts his language usage to English. The sounds he will use are not a matter of individual choice. This matter has been arbitrarily established, along with the patterns or sequence in which sounds may be combined.

The order in which words may be combined into utterances has also been established. Language has a definite structure. The linguist notes that this structure permits a sentence like, "I runned all the way home," but that common usage dictates, "I ran all the way home," and English structure cannot accommodate, "I all the ran home way." While six-year-old children have mastered a tremendously large portion of English grammar, they project certain characteristics into word meanings which do not exist. When asked Piaget's question, "Can the sun be called the moon?" they answer: "No, because the moon comes up at night," or "No, because the sun is brighter." This reaction that the meaning resides in the word is not confined to children.

Adults can also have hazy concepts about language. An example is the manner in which adults think the grammar of a language might best be taught to students who have already mastered it in practice. Fries (6) states that traditional grammar starts with the assigning of meaning to any given sentence and then moves to the labeling of words or groups of words and whole utterances. Thus, sentences become *declarative, interrogative,* or *imperative*. Within each sentence there is a subject and verb; to this may be added a direct object and an array of modifiers attached to each of those parts.

This approach, according to Fries, starts with an assumption that *grammatical meanings* are intuitive. A number of structural linguists reject this assumption. They posit that grammatical meanings are of considerable importance and that meanings are conveyed by signal or structure words which permit certain meanings and exclude others. A few examples of these structure words are *a* man, *the* man, *these* men, *that* man, *this* man, *some* men, *no* man. A further discussion of structure words will be found later in this chapter.

Linguistics is a broad term which can cover many orientations to language study. One linguist may be primarily interested in comparing different languages, another with the sound patterns of a language, another with the structural (grammatical word order) features of one or more languages, and another in the changes (phonological and structural) which occur in any living language. While linguists rarely deal with only one isolated facet of language, they do tend to become somewhat specialized.

Linguistic science has moved rapidly in the past fifty years because linguists were able to agree on the precise meaning of many crucial terms. Linguists were the first and possibly the only group who thus far agree on the definition of language. Their definition is that "language is oral." To reading specialists, psychologists, and general semanticists, this definition may seem to be somewhat narrow, but the mark of a science is that its basic terms are unequivocal.

On the other hand, the field of reading provides many examples of terms which are used frequently but for which there is no universal agreement as to meaning. Examples include *reading, phonics method, individualized reading, critical reading, sightword method, reading disability, traditional method, remedial reading* and *phonics instruction.* All of these represent concepts, but none have a fixed meaning for all of the people who use them. Obviously, confusion results. The problem is accentuated when persons in different disciplines attempt to cooperate in the absence of an agreement on the meaning of the terms both groups use. An illustration is provided in the use of the term *language* at a national reading conference.

A linguist, speaking to teachers of reading, remarked that he had little patience for the educators who made such absurd statements as, "English is not a phonetic language," or "English is not phonetically lawful." He stated that "English is perfectly phonetic—100 percent phonetic." He was followed on the same platform by a teacher of reading who, probably not having heard his predecessor, stated: "One of the major problems of teaching children to read is the fact that English is not phonetic. The language contains a large number of phonetically irregular words."

Each of the speakers started from different premises based on different connotations for the words he used. Each was correct if one granted his original premise. The linguist worked from the linguistic definition of language that "language is oral—language is speech." Thus, all English language (speech) is 100 percent phonetically regular. Such words as *freight, light, come,* and all other words can be transcribed within the framework of English phonemes.

The teacher of reading used language to mean written English. The linguist, of course, would refer to this as "a graphic representation of language." The teacher of reading meant that many English spellings were irregular; that there was not a one-to-one relationship between printed letters seen and speech sounds heard when one is reading English. With this the linguist would agree, but he would convey this information by using the terms *phoneme-grapheme relationship*.

Communication between reading teachers and linguists depends on each making an effort to understand the other. In recent years terminology from the science of linguistics has been used frequently in material addressed to the reading teacher. These terms have fixed meanings, and there is little point in not adopting them for use in discussion of reading instruction.

Phoneme. This is the smallest unit of sound within a language. When the word *man* is pronounced, three phonemes are utilized: /m/ /ae/ /n/. The basic consonant and vowel sounds are called *segmental phonemes*. In addition to these thirty-one to thirty-three basic sounds, the English language utilizes twelve intonational phonemes.

Morpheme. This is the smallest meaningful unit of language. Thus, *son* is a morpheme composed of three phonemes. If one adds an *s* to form a plural, *sons*, the final *s* in this situation is a morpheme. Here, the same grapheme (s) functions in the initial part of the word as a phoneme, and when it is used at the end of the word to change the meaning to "more than one son," it functions as a morpheme. When used to show possession, *his son's house*, it illustrates another morpheme.

There are two classes of morphemes determined by function. A *free morpheme* is one that functions independently in larger language units (cat, man, son). *Bound morphemes* must combine with another morpheme. This class includes affixes and inflectional endings. The prefix *un* in *un*lock is a bound morpheme while the same graphemes in *union* do not represent a morpheme.

Alphabetic Principle. English is one of the many languages for which an alphabet has been devised for writing. We use twenty-six letters to represent graphically the sounds of English. Thus, English is an alphabetic language. English writing follows an alphabetical principle, i.e., certain graphic signs represent speech sounds. However, English spellings used in writing of words do not follow a one-to-one relationship of grapheme seen, phoneme heard. Exceptions are discussed in relation to phonics instruction (Chapter 7).

The irregular spellings of English words creates a problem for the person attempting to learn to write or read English. The fact that a large majority of English words follow regular grapheme-phoneme patterns leads some individuals to minimize the effect of irregular spellings on learning these two derived language processes. Establishing what percent of the 10,000 most frequently used words happen to be regular in grapheme-phoneme relationships and then generalizing from this data to the reading process ignores the *frequency of the use* of irregularly spelled words. This point becomes clearer as we examine structure words.

Structure Words. This term is used to cover some three hundred or more frequently used words which have no concrete referent. Various other descriptive terms have been used to describe these words. These include *signal words, glue words, service words*, and for reasons discussed below, they have also been referred to as *basic sight words*. Each of the above has some validity. Structure words do signal the listener, or more important, the reader, that a particular syntactical pattern is coming.

Lefevre (19) refers to structure words as "empty" words used primarily to signal the coming use of noun or verb phrases, dependent clauses, and questions. In one analysis he indicates that approximately half of the words on the *Dolch Basic Sight Word Test** are structure or empty words. A few examples of markers are

Noun markers: *my* house, *any* house, *this* house, *a* house, *some* houses, *the* house.
Verb markers: *am* coming, *are* coming, *is* coming, *was* coming.
Clause markers: *now, like, until, if, although, since, before, however.*
Question indicators: *when, where, who, which, why.*

It is easy to see why structure words have been called "the glue words of the English language," or *service words*. Both of these concepts are consistent with the way these words function in sentences. They both introduce and bind together utterances while not conveying meaning in and of themselves. Many structure words have irregular spellings, which accounts for their being designated *sight words*. Both their irregular spellings and their high frequency of usage make it mandatory that they be instantly recognized in print.

The frequency with which particular words are used will of course vary with the material under consideration. The previous sentence uses

---

* *The Dolch Basic Sight Word Test* consists of 220 words and is available from Garrard Press, Champaign, Illinois.

eight different structure words for a total of ten running words (the, with, which, used, will, of, course, with, the, under). Whether one is talking about reading material specifically designed for the primary grades or the professional writing of historians and linguists, these words will comprise from 25 to 50 percent of all running words, regardless of how many different words are encountered.

Structure words pose no problem for facile readers. But with seriously impaired readers, these are the words they have been unable to learn or recognize even after hundreds of experiences of seeing them in print and various types of drills designed to facilitate their becoming sight words.

Syntax. This term is used to describe the meaning patterns found within any language, in essence, the *grammar* of that language. Syntax includes the various order patterns in which words can be strung together. The following word orders represent a correct sentence in English, an extreme regional expression, and a non-English pattern: "I go up the steps;" "I go the steps up;" "Up the go I steps."

Syntax includes the ways in which words may function in different patterns. The same word may function as a verb, noun, or adverb: *Light* the fire; She saw the *light;* He danced *lightly* across the ring and threw a *lightning* punch. English syntax rules out "He danced *lightning* across the ring and threw a *lighted* punch." A careful study of the syntax of a language will permit one to describe the basic sentence patterns which occur in that language, as well as the ways in which these patterns may be varied by means of expansion, substitution, and inversion.

Intonation

Speech consists of a flow of words arranged in particular patterns which result in distinctive rhythms or melodies that are unique to English. The melody is created in part by several levels of pitch, several degrees of stress or emphasis on word components, and by pauses or stops in the flow of speech. Linguists have labeled these variations in pitch, stress, and juncture as *supra-segmental phonemes.* These are illustrated in the following discussion.

Junctures and terminals. Speech includes a number of pauses which serve as signals to the listener. In general, four classes of junctures and terminals are identified in English speech. These are:

Open Juncture / – / which represents the most minute interruptions which occur between some syllables within words and between words. These breaks in speech enable one to follow such patterns as:

"I *am a Tory* but not an *amatory* Tory."
"He used a jar to keep the door ajar."
(*amiss—a miss; a bet—abet; add dresses—addresses*).

Level juncture is a pause between parts of a total utterance in which the pause does not demand a rise or falling off of pitch. In the following illustrative sentence, examples A and B represent level terminal where everything preceding the phrase *was blind* is spoken without noticeable variation in pitch. Example C indicates a different reading.

A. The man ➤ speaking to me ➤ was blind.⟩
B. The man speaking to me ➤ was blind.⟩
C. The man speaking to me ⟩ was blind.⟩

Rise and fall terminals are examples of speech signals which terminate all sentences and which are frequently found separating major groupings of words within sentences. (Sentence C above.) The symbol / ⟩ / represents a falling off or fading pitch accompanied by a pause which characteristically terminates declarative sentences. Many interrogative sentences end with a fading, higher pitch, indicated by the symbol / ⟋ /. Both of these terminals contain a signal which goes beyond the mere pause in the flow of words.

"The train arrives at six o'clock."⟩
"What time does the train leave?"⟋

Pitch, as this term is used in describing a particular characteristic of human speech, should be thought of as a continuum. However, this continuum does not consist of innumerable points, but rather a discrete number of segments or ranges. These ranges have been labeled low, normal, high, and extra high, and are frequently designated by the numbers 1–2–3–4. The absence of pitch variations in speech is called *monotone*, or in essence, one-level pitch.

Pitch interacts with stress and juncture, and every statement in English has a "pitch contour" which can be plotted using one or another marking system such as /1–2 3 4 /;/ low normal high etc/.

Stress indicates the degree of emphasis placed on syllables or words in utterances. As in the case of pitch, there are four levels or degrees of stress: heavy, medium, light, weak.* As noted earlier, the graphic representation of speech provides a rather incomplete record of intonation. Stress, pitch, and juncture are represented only partially by means of punctuation marks, such as beginning a sentence with a capital letter and the use of the comma, semi-colon, period, exclamation mark, and question mark. In addition, one may indicate emphasis through underlining or italicizing a particular word.

He was really a tall man.
He was *really* a tall man.
He was really a *tall* man.

Intonation and Reading

Individuals learn the intonation patterns of their native tongue without being aware of the significance of these signals and certainly without any conscious labeling of the variations in pitch, stress, and pace. The preschool child with normal hearing inevitably "picks up" the intonation patterns of the particular language he hears around him. Later, as an adult, he may experience considerable difficulty in mastering the intonation patterns of a foreign language. He may have little difficulty in learning the pronunciation and meaning of *words* (vocabulary). The problem lies in stringing the words together, in acquiring the flow or the melody of the new language.

In learning to read, the child must understand that part of the translation of print to speech involves recreating the melody of spoken language. One of the problems in learning to read is that writing cannot accurately depict intonation, or the melody of speech. The readers' task now becomes that of putting the intonation back into the graphic signs. He has some very useful hints in the form of punctuation which suggests some pauses and stops. He is aided by other orthographic devices, such as underlined or italicized words. But in the final analysis, the reader is left to project or "think in" much of the meaning-making melody which is not depicted in print.

---

* Levels of stress are also designated as primary ($\diagup$), secondary ($\diagup\!\!\diagdown$), tertiary ($\diagdown$) and weak ($\smile$). See Henry Lee Smith, Jr., "The Teacher and The World of Language," *College English* 20 (January, 1959): 172–78.

Lefevre (19) in *Linguistics and the Teaching of Reading*, states, "The basic fault in poor reading (viewed as a crippled language process) is poor sentence sense, demonstrated orally in word-calling, or in reading various nonstructural fragments of language patterns as units." If a child reads word by word, he treats each separate word as an utterance and will utilize a fade-fall terminal /⤸/ after each word.

The/boy/went/to/the/store/.

This habit will inevitably destroy the melody of spoken English and thus preclude reading for meaning.

Tyler (36) makes a number of references to the melody one must seek out when reading. "A writer wants his reader to hear the unspoken melody of his words;" primary-grade pupils have "an extensive lexicon of sentence melodies." Stress patterns are referred to as an "upward-downward melody." Lloyd (21) states, *"The ability to relate the melody of speech to the written page is the key to good reading.* Good readers do it; poor readers don't do it." Stevens (31) suggests that once pupils are able to recognize words in print, "they must be taught to see the sentence that they already hear. Only with help in perceiving this melody in its varied patterns will they ultimately become literate."

Although there is general agreement that children must learn to recreate the melody of language in their reading, there is little research data that bears on this issue. The results of two studies do suggest that intonation is closely related to reading comprehension and that intonation can be taught in beginning reading.

Means (23) studied the relationship between third-grade children's use of intonation in oral reading and reading comprehension. He reported statistically significant relationships (.01) between appropriate use of each of three intonation variables (pitch, stress, and juncture) and comprehension scores on reading tests. Those children making the lowest number of "errors" on a measure of intonation made significantly higher scores on measures of both oral and silent reading.

Ahlvers (1) demonstrated that first-grade children can profit from instruction which focuses on teaching intonation patterns. She designed a program consisting of thirty lessons, each of approximately ten minutes duration. Children who received this instruction scored significantly higher on a test of intonation than did children in a control group who had no special training in intonation. However, no significant difference in reading achievement was found between the two groups on a reading test administered near the end of grade one. A hypothesis related to this finding was that possibly the content of first-grade reading achievement tests may not reflect the contribution of intonation skills to the same degree as do tests designed for later grade levels.

The concept of melody of language does not concern itself with the selection of words, but rather with the structural arrangements found in English. The child comes to school with an ear for this melody already developed. His use of oral language fits the pattern, and his understanding of oral English rests on this tremendous accomplishment. The seven-year-old speaks a melodic English comparable to that of his teacher. Both have learned the same structure.

In another sense, the child has much to learn from his teachers and from experience which will enhance his use and understanding of the melody of language; this is in the choice of words which he can fit into the sentence structures permitted in the English language. This is illustrated by the title of a book of poems by Emily Dickinson, *Bolts of Melody*. This title is a most apt choice of words to describe the poet's art, the manipulation of language.

Structuralists emphasize that the sentence is the meaning-bearing unit and that reading instruction should not focus on words but on the sentence. Some theorists hold that the child should start with oral reading of sentences and that instruction should emphasize his noting and practicing intonation patterns he uses in his speech.

This position is somewhat reminiscent of a methodology used some years ago which was labeled the *sentence* or *memory approach*. Using material on the chalkboard or from a book, the teacher would read a sentence orally. Immediately following, the children would recite the sentence while hopefully noting the printed equivalent. This practice was not effective in teaching children how to read and it was soon replaced by various types of "skills" emphasis, which moved from sounding out individual letters to drill on recognition of sight words.

The problem, of course, is that reading involves the simultaneous application of many skills. When one essential skill is neglected, we produce unwanted reading behaviors. Thus, while proponents of a melody of language emphasis may be justified in criticizing reading instruction that overemphasizes skills, the fact remains that children without the necessary skills cannot project intonation into their reading.

In order to read a sentence with proper intonation, the child must recognize or instantly solve all or most of the words that make up the sentence. His ability to deal with all of the parts of a sentence enables him to combine the parts and arrive at the proper intonation. An unknown word interrupts the melody as does miscalling or substituting words. Thus it is a mistake to attempt to dichotomize mechanical skills and intonation.

Translating
Linguistic Insights
into Reading Instruction

Linguists as scientists are in no way responsible for finding applications for their discoveries. Few have actively engaged in relating their discoveries to the school curriculum. As a result, linguistics has had little impact on the content of the curriculum, particularly at the elementary level. University faculties have devised courses of study for students whose educational goal is to become linguists or specialists in a particular language. Certain related fields, such as speech therapy, draw heavily on linguistics since therapists must distinguish speech sounds and understand the anatomical involvement in their production.

How children learn to read and how the reading process should be taught is not a part of linguistic science. Thus, there can be no official linguistic approach to reading instruction. However, any linguist is free to theorize and experiment in the area of reading instruction. Some theories relative to instructional materials and methodology have evolved, but these have not been tested longitudinally in the classroom.

A body of literature is rapidly accumulating on the general topic of psycholinguistics, and more specifically on *psycholinguistics and reading*. In defining the term Smith writes, "Psycholinguistics, as its name suggests, is a field of study that lies at the intersection of two broader disciplines, psychology and linguistics" (27).

The perception that reading instruction is a panacea-prone enterprise and that terms are frequently invested with magical properties has led to many warnings not to expect salvation through faith in this new educational *buzz* word. Fortunately, these cautions are frequently found in books and articles whose titles are (or include) *Psycholinguistics and Reading*. Smith, after expressing the opinion that the field has something to offer teachers of reading, warns, "But I must admit that I feel a growing anxiety about the word 'psycholinguistics' itself. Already there are signs that 'psycholinguistic' is becoming one of those faddish labels that suffer a brief career of indiscriminate application in education in order to deceive, dissemble, or convey an image of totally false authority" (27).

Since linguistic science has not been concerned with *how children learn to read*, there is little research data upon which to base conclusions. For this reason, it has been difficult for linguists to apply the same scientific rigor to reading instruction that they apply to the study of language. Nevertheless, linguistics provide a number of important concepts which focus on and hold promise for improving reading instruction. The following are illustrative.

1. Despite irregularities in English spelling, important phoneme-grapheme *patterns* do exist, and possibly these should be exploited to a larger degree in reading instruction.

2. Reading instruction can overemphasize dealing with words as units. Graphic symbols must be read to parallel normal sentence tunes. The reader must "put together meaning bearing patterns."

3. The printed page represents language which is oral. The child beginning to read knows the melody (i.e., grammar or syntax) of oral language. However, the printed pages do not contain all the language clues found in speech. The "graphic representation" of language does not indicate various levels of pitch and stress. Punctuation (which indicates junctures) is the only graphic intonational help that is provided; and it too is somewhat imperfect. Intonation (juncture, stress, and pitch) are part of the language, not optional additives.

4. The purpose and function of structure words need to be better understood for the mastery of the reading process. These approximately three hundred words, sometimes referred to as *glue words* or *service words*, have little or no meaning in and of themselves; but they provide significant clues as to the type of patterns they introduce (questions, noun markers, verb markers, parallel constructions).

5. Language has a definite structure, and this structure plays an important role in conveying meaning. Structure is revealed in sentence patterns, not by word units.

6. Linguists describe language as *it is used*, not as they or others think it should be used. Thus, a given dialect is not incorrect, nor is standard English superior to other dialects.

7. While linguists have and will continue to provide accurate descriptions of the phonology and syntax of various nonstandard dialects, the problem of how to teach reading to dialect speakers is still unresolved.

8. The science of linguistics should not be moved downward into the elementary school curriculum. However, linguistic findings can and should be *translated* into meaningful curricular changes in the school. Teachers of reading should place more emphasis on teaching

children *about* language and how it functions since reading is a language function.

The Language Experience Approach to Reading

The process of learning to read is not dependent upon moving through a particular body of content. It consists of mastering a derived language process which is a long-term developmental endeavor. The child can learn needed reading skills through the use of any of a number of printed passages. These materials may be children's books, stories dictated by the child himself, basal texts, experience charts, myths, biographies, riddles, children's newspapers, programmed workbooks, or subject matter content in any area. The one criterion that any material would have to meet is that of appropriateness to the reader's present level of development.

The major question in reading instruction is not what printed material to teach from, but rather to determine what skills to teach and when and how to teach them. However, when an individual addresses himself to these questions, he usually develops a set of materials which reflect previous decisions about what to teach and where on the educational continuum to teach particular skills. Materials also reflect *how* to teach particular facets of reading.

Regardless of what other materials may have been adopted by schools or used by teachers, most teachers of beginning reading include teacher-written charts and stories in their reading programs. Pupil experiences used as the content for writing charts and stories is a practice of long standing. Throughout the years, modifications and extensions have resulted in renewed emphasis on this procedure. For a comprehensive history of the language experience approach, the reader might consult Smith (29) and Hildreth (13). In addition to these sources, two early publications devoted to descriptions of experience-based materials are Gans' *Guiding Children's Reading through Experiences* (8) and Lamoreaux and Lee's *Learning to Read through Experience* (17).

The latter work (1943) describes the rationale as well as concrete procedures for using teacher-written experience charts. These materials, written by teachers, were envisioned as the basic instructional program.

A revision (1963) by Lee and Allen (18) deals not only with experience charts for use with the class as a whole, but stresses the advantages of teachers' writing individual stories for individual students.

**The Experience
Chart**

The experience chart is a means of capturing the interest of children by tying their personal experiences to reading activities. The chart, which tells about a shared activity, is a story produced cooperatively by the teacher and the class. This is a natural extension of earlier and less difficult experiences wherein the teacher wrote single words, short sentences, days of the week, names of months, the seasons, children's birthdays, and holidays on the chalkboard. The experience chart provides practice in a number of developmental skills which are closely related to reading. For example:

1. Oral language usage in group-planning prior to a trip and in recounting the experience, for chart building, after a trip.
2. The give-and-take of ideas as the experience is discussed.
3. Sharpening sensory acuity, particularly visual and auditory, while on excursions.
4. Expanding concepts and vocabulary.
5. Reinforcing the habit of reading from left to right.
6. Experience in learning words as wholes, thus building sight vocabulary.
7. Reading the sentence as a unit.
8. Reading about one's own experiences, emphasizing that reading is getting meaning from printed words.

All of the points cited above are appropriate both to readiness and to beginning reading, and the experience chart should not be thought of as belonging exclusively to one stage of development. The experience chart has merit in proportion to the degree to which certain logical practices are followed. For instance, vocabulary must be simple and sentences short; a minimum of sentences must be used, and each sentence must contribute to the story. There should be deliberate repetition of common sight words.

A teacher and children plan for a visit to the zoo, a nearby farm, or the library. Let us assume that the teacher has been able to make all of the necessary arrangements for a trip to the community library. She has arranged for the use of the school bus and has spoken to the librarian, who has volunteered to read the class a story and set up a display of children's books. When she has the attention of the entire class, the teacher might say, "I talked to Mrs. Winters, the librarian, the other day and she invited all of you to come to the library and look at the new books—maybe some of you would want to take a book home with you. I wonder if it would be fun if we took a trip to the library?"

CHILDREN:	"Let's go!" "I'd like that."
TEACHER:	"If we go, we'll have to make plans first. What are some things we should decide?"
BILLY:	"Can we go today?"
TEACHER:	"Billy asks when can we go? We can't go today; we have to make our plans first."
CHILD:	"Let's go tomorrow."
TEACHER:	"How many would like to go tomorrow?" *(General agreement)*
TEACHER:	"How shall we get to the library?"
MIKE:	"Let's walk."
MARY:	"Can we go in a car?"
TEACHER:	"Mike suggests we walk, but it's quite a long way from here; Mary suggested we go in a car, but it would take a lot of cars for all of us. Maybe we could go in the school bus." *(Excitement heightens in the class.)*

The class and the teacher talk about what they should do and what they should not do at the library. Following each discussion, the teacher writes the decision on the board; from this activity an experience chart emerges. The chart itself may not be the most important outcome of this educational endeavor. The children have experienced how the group process works; cooperative planning and individual contributions have resulted in identifying and structuring a goal. The children are now ego-involved in a trip to the library. Their experience chart follows:

Plans for Our Trip

We will go to the library.
We will go tomorrow.
We will go in the school bus.
This will be fun.
We can look at books.
We will sit in our chairs.
We will hear a story.

The children enjoyed the trip to the library. Mrs. Winters, the librarian, had three tables of children's books available; she showed where the children's books were kept on the shelves and on a book rack. She talked about how to treat books—not to fold pages or tear the paper cover. The children were permitted to look at the books and the pictures. Finally, Mrs. Winters read them the story *Stone Soup*.*
The children clapped their hands when Mrs. Winters finished the story. They thanked her and then returned to their classroom on the school bus.

That same day they discussed their trip and the things they saw and did and heard. The natural outcome was to "write a story" about their experience. The teacher asked questions and occasionally substituted words to keep the vocabulary reasonable. The following discussion developed the title for the story.

TEACHER: "What shall we call our story?"
BOB: "What we did at the library."
TEACHER: "That's a good suggestion; does anyone else have a name for our story?"
MARY: "I think it should be called 'We have a nice time at the library.' "
TEACHER: "Fine—anyone else?"
RUTH: "Things we did on our trip to the library."
TEACHER: "Those are all fine—we did have a very nice visit, we did learn many things, and we did enjoy the story Mrs. Winters read us. Would it be all right to call our story 'Our Trip to the Library'?"

Since the children agreed to the title, she printed it on the chalkboard, saying each word as she wrote it and then reading the entire line, being careful to move her hand slowly from left to right as she

---

* Marcia Brown (New York: Charles Scribner's Sons, 1947).

read. Next, she inquired what incidents should be related in the story and accepted the various suggestions while attempting to keep the vocabulary as simple as possible. Each line of the story was developed in much the same way as the title was. The teacher was careful to see that all of the students participated. The following chart is the result.

Our Trip to the Library

We rode in the school bus.
The bus took us to the library.
We looked at many books.
We sat at tables.
We looked at books and pictures.
Mrs. Winters read us a story.
The story was *Stone Soup.*
We thanked Mrs. Winters.
Our trip was fun.

After the teacher and children read the complete story, a child was asked to point out the line that told how they had traveled to the library, the line that told the name of the story they had heard, the line that told where the children sat in the library, and so forth. In each case, the child pointed out the desired line and attempted to read it.

The same chart may be used in other ways. Each line in the chart may be duplicated on a strip of heavy paper: *We thanked Mrs. Winters.* A child is handed a sentence and is asked to find this line on the chart. Individual words may also be printed on oaktag or cardboard and held up by the teacher while a child points out that particular word on the chart: *books, us, bus.* Word cards may be prepared for each word in a particular line. These are handed to a child in mixed order, and he is to arrange them in proper order to correspond with the line on the chart. These tasks can be either seatwork or boardwork. The experience chart can be used with the class as a whole and also with various reading groups. After its main use with a unit, it may be referred to incidentally when certain words used on the chart come up in other contexts and in other activities.

Individual Experience Stories

Children enjoy talking about their experiences, particularly about incidents which involve them, their families, their pets, and the like.

One of the best ways to take advantage of such motivation is to write individual experience stories. These language productions are usually brief, ranging from one to several sentences which deal with one incident. In the early stages of reading, the stories are usually dictated by the pupils and written by the teacher.

Some of the major principles which provide the rationale for language experience stories have been outlined by Lee and Allen (18) and include

1. What a child thinks about, he can talk about.
2. What one talks about can be expressed in writing.
3. Anything the child or teacher writes can be read.
4. One can read what he writes and what other people write.
5. What a child has to say is as important to him as what other people have written for him to read.

Since these brief stories relate the child's own experiences, they involve his ego with the reading situation. The stories are always meaningful and are written in complete sentences which closely parallel the child's own language usage. In some cases, the teacher can write brief stories based on her observation of children and events which occur in class. An excellent description of how one teacher introduced the writing of experience stories is provided by Lindberg:

> "I have something to share with you, too," the teacher says to the first graders. "I like to write books for boys and girls. Here are the ones I wrote last night. Let me read them to you."
> She holds up a gay booklet, "This one is called *Susan's Red Shoes*." Susan looks up. Can it be! She does have new red shoes. The other children look at Susan. They are very aware of her bright new sandals because she talked of nothing else yesterday.
> The teacher opens the cover and reads the first page, "Susan has new red shoes." She turns to the next page. "Her father bought them for her at Smith's Shoe Store. They cost $7.98." Now the children know for certain that it is their Susan, and Susan is beaming.
> The teacher continues to read. "See me stand on one foot," says Susan. "Now see me stand on the other. Now watch me jump."
> "I have written the story," says the teacher to Susan, "but there are no pictures in the book. Perhaps you can make some."
> The other children lean forward. What is in the other books?
> "Read some more. Read one about me," are the cries from the

first graders. So they are read. *Terry's Tooth, Jane's Trip to the Farm, Harry and His Big Brother, Roy's Birthday Cake, Cowboy Joe, Here Comes Josephine* are the titles.

"But there wasn't one about me!" is the refrain when all of the books have been read.

"See that pile of books on my desk? There isn't anything written in them. Why don't you tell me what to write—then you will have a book, too."

During their work period, several children dictate stories. These will be read to the others the next morning (20).

Experience stories need not be limited to accounts of personal experiences. Observations of the world outside the classroom can also serve as story topics: a seed growing into a plant, astronauts exploring the moon, squirrels gathering nuts in the fall, a hurricane in the news for several days striking a community, an oilspill threatening wildlife. As children talk, describe, and interpret such events, their own language is written down. As they practice reading, they also expand their concepts and enlarge their world; the magic of language is thus transferred to reading.

The amount of magic that gets into the method depends on the teacher. The experience approach can be open-ended, flexible, and highly motivating. It can also become highly structured or overly dominated by the teacher. Obviously the most difficult task is to somehow make the transition between the child's highly developed language usage and his developing ability to cope with the graphic representation of that language. Sessions devoted to skills development must somehow be included in the instructional program. Good teachers are learning that *language* can be smuggled into the teaching of skills.

The Experience Approach as a Method

Experience charts and stories can be used in any method of teaching reading. When a program limits instructional materials to this one type, the resulting instruction might be referred to as the *experience method*. Any procedure may have both merits and limitations, and this seems particularly true of the experience approach to teaching reading. The major strengths of experience stories and charts have been discussed previously; some potential weaknesses which may result from overreliance on teacher-written materials are *potential weaknesses*

1. It is difficult to control vocabulary. Too many words may be introduced at one time.
2. Basic sight words may not be repeated often enough to insure mastery.
3. When used exclusively as a method, it puts too much of a burden on the teacher, demands much time, and a high level of training.
4. It is difficult to adapt this type of instruction to the needs and abilities of all children.
5. It encourages memorization rather than mastery of sight words.

The strengths and weaknesses of the experience method are relative and not inherent in the method itself. Under certain conditions, all of the advantages of the method might be lost through overemphasis, misuse, or lack of understanding. In other situations the effects of certain of the cited disadvantages could be held to a minimum through a teacher's skill, experience, and clear understanding of objectives. In our opinion, the experience approach is most vulnerable when advocated as a complete method in itself. Most teachers prefer to use the experience chart as a supplement to basals and other materials. This permits certain of the weaknesses to be minimized. The basic readers provide drill on sight vocabulary and control over the introduction of new words. The use of experience charts adds flexibility and interest to the program.

A Broader View

The concept of language experience has been extended far beyond the group chart and the writing of individual stories. Today, the term *language experience* applies to practically every type of self-expression through language and every experience that involves the manipulation of language of others. Allen (2) in *Language Experience in Communication* provides an excellent blueprint for expanding language experiences throughout the school curriculum.

The role of teachers has undergone considerable change also. They have assumed responsibilities far beyond that of being scribes to write down stories children tell. Harnessing the child's ego by means of the personal story is still a widely used procedure. However, teachers have become more active partners in helping children expand concepts and language proficiency through the use of many other language stimuli. (See Table 3.)

Children write poetry, read poetry, and solve riddles (and make up some of their own). Language learning centers are widely used, and they focus both on learning about language and on using language as a tool for further learning. Working with homonyms and homographs, children learn that different words may be spelled the same and have

Classrooms should provide space and time for many forms of "language manipulation," such as reading-writing poetry, riddles, and analogies.

different meanings and pronunciations—or spelled differently and have the same pronunciation. They learn about relationships through experience with *analogies,* through combining sentences, and arranging sentences into larger units. In working with language, students learn that *a* word may have dozens of different meanings, that plurals are written in many ways, that new words are constantly being added to our language, and that over periods of time, the meanings of words change.

Language experience is, thus, experiencing language. The teacher's role is to help children understand that

> writing a word is an achievement
>
> writing a story is a larger achievement
>
> combining stories into a book is quite a production.

Table 3

Language Experience

Part I: Charts and Stories

What It Is   How It Functions

| Any Experience |

| Children provide the language |

| This involves thinking, recall, sequence, choice of words, etc. |

| Material is familiar | | Reading is ego-involved |

| Translate thoughts into language |

| Leads to success in reading | | High motivation for reading |

| Language can be written |

| Transfer to other reading situations
a. confidence
b. interest
c. ego-satisfaction |

| Writing can be read |

Part II

| Broader range of language experiences
Move from personal stories to any and all language stimuli |

| It can be said (written) many different ways
A word may have many meanings
A statement may be true or false—fact or opinion
How you say (read) it can change meaning
Learning—mastery of and ability to manipulate language |

Saying something one way is an achievement
Saying it another way and
noting what you did the second time
permits you to control language!

When you can control language
you can, mold words like clay
mix words like paints
use words to draw pictures.

The next step is to let children try it. Let them tell or write the answer to

How many ways can a leaf fall?
"Down" you say.
Surely there's another way.

A leaf can
just fall—
  fall gracefully
glide—
  glide like a glider
  glide and swerve
sail—
  sail like a rudderless ship
  sail like it had a mind of its own
dip—
  dip and glide
  dip and rise and bank gracefully to a landing
dance—
  complete its solo dance
  dance with the wind
fall with no map to guide it—
  map its own course
  try many detours
  twist slowly in the wind.

How many ways can a leaf fall that we didn't write today?
"No other way", you say?
Don't you think leaves like to play?

  playfully! (*of course*)
    If in a hurry?

plummet
   with memories of summer?
reluctantly

Since language is developmental in nature, any stimulus can provide language experiences at any level of language usage. The poet Cyrano de Bergerac is nearing death. A dear friend notices the falling leaves and says:

"The leaves—
what color,
Perfect Venetion red! Look at them fall."
Cyrano replies:
"Yes—they know how to die.
A little way from the branch to the earth,
A little fear of mingling with the common dust—
and yet they go down gracefully
A fall that seems like flying" (14)

Any teacher can suggest:

"We could,
if you like,
write a book called
"One hundred ways that leaves can fall"
(or) "Two hundred ways that leaves can fall"
(or) "Three hundred ways that leaves can fall"

Someday, maybe tomorrow, we must think about how many ways dogs can

   bark,
      clouds can drift,
         fish can swim,
            children can write!

**Writing
Poetry**

Any language experiences, the above included, can serve as a basis for leading children into writing poetry. As they write, they develop an understanding of and appreciation for poetry. Many teachers have discovered that children have tremendous talent for the use of language. One poetic form that is a favorite of many children is Haiku, or stanzas composed of exactly seventeen syllables divided into three lines of five, seven and five syllables respectively. The following are examples of fourth graders' writing. The third poem titled *Now* illustrates an interesting pattern of repetition of the title.

See the small bird fly
He is just a beginner
Oops! He fell again.

Trees now with no leaves
Plants gone to their winter beds
All waiting for spring.

Now

Winter has come now
The snowflakes are falling now
Winter has gone now

Winter has gone now
And spring is in the air now
The birds are back now

Spring too has gone now
And summer has filled the air
Soon it will be gone

Summer is gone now
Now all the leaves are falling
The trees are bare now

Children and teachers working together can devise their own poem forms. One class* wrote poems patterned on the Cinquain form of five lines, but did not follow the syllable requirements of this form. Their poems were based on the following stanza form.

1st line:	one word (usually a naming word)
2nd line:	two words which constitute a synonym for line one
3rd line:	three words describing action
4th line:	four words which build on line three
5th line:	a one-word summary

---

*The author regrets not having the data which would permit giving proper credit to the individual students and teacher(s) whose work is cited here.

The following are illustrative examples written by fourth- and fifth-grade pupils.

Maps	Earth
Giant papers	Small planet
On the wall	Spinning fast around
Colors red and blue	Rotating on its axis
Useful	Neat
Deer	Leaves
Little fawns	Shapes, colors
Jumping far, playing	Falling slowly down
Jumping over big stones	Through brown tree branches
Happy	Lonely

Expanding Concepts

There are innumerable ways in which teachers can involve students in exciting, growth provoking language-reading experiences. Individual differences among students make it mandatory that approaches be adapted to fit student's abilities. A creative teacher can structure activities so that they hold the student's interest and lead to the expansion of reading skills and language facility.

Having children complete language exercises is only one step in the learning process. Group discussion may produce more significant gains and insights. Encouraging children to build their own language games and exercises is the highest level of working with language. One third-grade teacher found that students very quickly developed the ability to solve analogies written at their level. However, they learned much more about language relationships when they themselves attempted to dictate or write analogies.

The following materials are illustrative of a few teaching procedures which focus on developing reading skills and language facility. Several different approaches or "teaching formats" are provided in order to suggest that any teaching can be adapted both as to difficulty level and method of presentation. Other language-reading stimuli are found in the chapters dealing with beginning, primary, and intermediate level instruction.

Different Meanings
for the Same Word

Native speakers of English are frequently unaware that so many words we use have five, ten, twenty, or more different meanings. This does not imply that we do not use or understand many connotations for a given word. The point is we rarely think about the extent to which this feature of our language operates (5). Thus, working with "different meanings" is an excellent way for children to learn about language while developing and expanding concepts.

The fact that many words have a large number of connotations adds to the problem of developing a precise order of difficulty of words, or the order in which words should be introduced and taught. Thus, the word *rhinoceros,* while very concrete in meaning, might be considered more difficult than the word *heavy*—but only if one is discussing a particular and limited connotation for *heavy.*

A child may acquire *a* meaning for *heavy* (opposed to light in weight) before he acquires a concept for, or the ability to, pronounce the term *rhinoceros.* But once he has had the experience of seeing a rhinoceros, or even a picture of one, he will have established a workable concept. He can learn many more details about this animal, such as its average weight, height, habitat, feeding habits, aggressiveness, and economic value. However, he will not have to develop a series of different meanings for the word rhinoceros.

The word heavy has dozens of connotations which range from fairly concrete to highly abstract.

They had a *heavy* load on the wagon.
The voters registered a *heavy* vote.
The guide led them through a *heavy* fog.
Meet the new light *heavy*weight champion.
Time hung *heavy* on his hands.
Their eyes became *heavy* with sleep.
He carried a *heavy* load through life.
The sad news made him *heavy*-hearted.
The actor complained, "I am always cast as the *heavy.*"

After selecting a word (such as *head* used next), explain that volunteers are to use this word in a sentence. They must *listen carefully* as the game proceeds, trying not to use a meaning that has already been given previously.

1. John scratched his *head*.
2. Mother bought a *head* of lettuce.
3. The candidate called his opponent a cabbage *head*.
4. That ranch supports 100 *head* of cattle.
5. You must be "out of your *head*" to talk like that.
6. The captain will *head* the ship into the storm.
7. Two *heads* are better than one.
8. The sheriff said "We'll *head* them off at the pass."
9. The coach said, "Don't lose your *head*—play it cool."
10. They couldn't make *heads* or tails of the code.
11. John was selected to *head* up the committee.
12. He gave an opinion off the top of his *head*.
13. May I speak to the *head* waiter please.
14. This course is over my *head*.

One fifth grade class decided to start each of their sentences the same way using *Joe* as the subject and using different meanings for the word *broke*.

Joe broke the dish.
Joe said, "I'm *broke*."
Joe watched as dawn *broke*.
Joe broke a rule.
Joe broke the bank (at Monte Carlo).
Joe broke the record.
Joe finally *broke* the silence.
Joe broke his $20 bill.
Joe broke in his catchers mitt.
Joe broke the news.

Joe broke into the big leagues.
Joe threw a curve that *broke* outside.
Joe watched as the crowd *broke* up.
Joe, playing fullback, *broke* into the open.
Joe broke up when he heard the story.
Joe said to the team, "Let's go for *broke!*"

The number of connotations for a given word may be enlarged if the various inflected forms and different tenses of a word are used. The class added the following: Joe finally got a *break;* . . . sounds like a *broken* record; . . . jammed on the *brake;* . . . played for the *breaks;* . . . struck out on a *breaking* pitch; . . . was *broken* up by the news; . . . saw the waves *breaking* over the hull; . . . said, "the new cars have more *braking* power," etc.

The *Different Meanings* game provides an excellent medium for the development of written exercises. Children may work on these individually, as pupil pairs, or in teams of various sizes. Two teams may select the same word from a list and see which team can develop the most meanings for that word. Children's work can then be used for developing teaching exercises which consist of a duplicated page showing an extensive number of sentences, each of which illustrates a different connotation for the chosen word. Children can then select a lesson sheet and study the meanings of any word in which they may be interested. Examples which might be used are unlimited: fence, light, handle, read, match, pack, state, pike, dead, free, grace, set, etc.

Each of the sentences below contains the same underlined word.
This word has a different meaning in each sentence.
Select a definition from the box which conveys the meaning of the word in each sentence.
Write the correct definition (or its number) in the space following the sentence.
Note: one definition in the box will not be used.

Level 1

Definitions

1 rub, create friction	4 discover
2 begin, carry-on	5 to agree
3 to hit, punish	6 to stop work

1. The Union members voted to <u>strike</u>. _____
2. Never <u>strike</u> a child in anger. _____
3. "I hope we <u>strike</u> oil soon," he said. _____
4. He tried to <u>strike</u> up a conversation. _____
5. The guide said "<u>strike</u> a match". _____

Level 2

Definitions

1 take a course, to go	4 seem to be
2 to hit, punish	5 a defined area
3 lower the flag	6 take out, delete

1. The rookie pitcher couldn't find the <u>strike</u> zone. _____
2. The admiral shouted "do not <u>strike</u> the colors." _____
3. "Let's <u>strike</u> out across the river," he suggested. _____
4. "<u>Strike</u> out the paragraph," the editor mumbled. _____
5. "Does that <u>strike</u> you as being odd?" _____

In each series of sentences the same word is underlined. *In the space provided, write the meaning of the word as used in each sentence.*

1. a. The guide said, "no, I can't <u>figure</u> this out."
        (   )
    b. Don't be upset, it's only a <u>figure</u> of speech.
        (   )
    c. Did you get a <u>figure</u> on the cost of this project?
        (   )
    d. Who will explain <u>Figure</u> 2 on page 37?
        (   )

2. a. The waitress whispered, "Don't <u>order</u> the fish plate."
        (   )
    b. The Benevolent <u>Order</u> of Beavers were in the midst of a membership drive.
        (   )
    c. The corporal said, "get this room in <u>order</u> immediately."
        (   )
    d. The military code states that an <u>order</u> from a superior must be carried out.
        (   )

Light or heavy?

Complete each sentence below by filling in the blank space.
Write *light* or *heavy*—or both of these words if each makes "sense".

1. Soon we'll see the (   ) at the end of the tunnel.
2. The weatherman said "we can expect a (   ) rain."
3. It was so (   ) he couldn't lift it.
4. The team's (   ) hitters come to bat this inning.
5. The voters registered a very (   ) vote.

6. Who owns that (   ) blue pick-up truck?
7. The guide said, "be sure and wear (   ) clothing."
8. The news made him feel (   ) hearted.

The sentences below are completed by writing the words set *and* move *in the correct blank space. Notice the variations of meaning for these words.*

1. The machine was ____ to ____ at a fixed speed.
2. "I will buy you a new chess ____ after we ____," said father.
3. After each ____ of tennis the teams would ____ to another court.
4. The coach said, "when you hear ready, get ____, go, I want you to ____!"
5. Mother said, "you can ____ your hair after we ____ the furniture."

Figurative Language

Working with figurative expressions is a natural follow up to teaching multiple meanings of words. The preceding material illustrates that many of the different meanings are figures of speech ("Two *heads* are better than one;" "off the top of his *head;*" "couldn't make *heads* or tails of it;" light hearted, light headed, light fingered, etc.). The English language is rich with expressions, and even though children may be able to "read the words," they frequently need experience in arriving at the author's intended meaning.

A study by Holmes (15) indicated that children in the intermediate grades have difficulty with the meanings of many figurative expressions found in reading and social studies textbooks. The problem involved more than not knowing meanings. When a child did not arrive at the intended meaning, he tended to fall back on a concrete meaning for the words, which resulted in misconceptions.

Groesbeck (11) reported that significant transfer of learning occurred when children were given spaced systematic instruction in understanding figurative expressions and were later tested on materials which were not part of the instructional program. Considering the large number of idiomatic expressions found in textbooks, it appears that working with this facet of language is of considerable value to readers. The following are techniques which might be adapted to various instructional levels.

1. Match expressions with concrete meanings.
   Identify each definition on the right with the letter of the expressions that it explains.

Expressions	*Definitions*
a. Business will soon *pick up.*	____ pay attention
b. March came in *like a lamb.*	____ does not understand
c. *Jack stood up* for his friend	____ will improve, become better
d. "*Mark my words,*" said father.	____ very pleasant weather
e. I don't *dig the jive.*	____ defended

2. *After each expression, write in your own words what it means.*
   a. *bury the hatchet.* _____
   b. *out of step with the times.* _____
   c. *lost in thought.* _____
   d. *chip off the old block.* _____
   e. *flew off the handle.* _____

3. *In each sentence below, a figurative expression is underlined. Rewrite each sentence so that it carries the same meaning but do not use the underlined phrase.*

   Sample: Old Mr. Brown was a man who often *flew off the handle.*
   Old Mr. Brown frequently got mad and lost his temper.

   a. The broadcast warned against dealing with *fly-by-night* business concerns.
   _____

   b. The bandit had a *price on his head.*
   _____

   c. "That fellow *rubs my fur the wrong way,*" said big Bill.
   _____

   d. Wearing a suit and tie to the picnic, Wylie *stuck out like a sore thumb.*
   _____

   e. Old Mr. Jones was a *jack-of-all-trades.*
   _____

4. Prepare a study sheet that will help children in understanding and interpreting figurative expressions. The following is one example:

Just an Expression

Some groups of words have special meanings. If someone writes "It was raining cats and dogs," he means it was raining very hard. He does not want the reader to take his words *literally*. (Is the meaning of the last word clear?) Basketball players are not "tall as mountains" or "as fast as greased lightning." However, this is a much more colorful and vivid way of saying one is very tall or that he moves quite rapidly.

Expressions such as "strong as an ox," "patient as Job," "flew off the handle" are called figures of speech. They help us to draw vivid word images. With them we can make picturesque (*pik sure esk*) comparisons. With figures of speech, we can exaggerate or convey meaning by stating the opposite of what is meant. A few of the more common types of figurative language are:

a. Hyperbole (hy. per′ bow. lēē): To exaggerate—an obvious overstatement.
   "so hungry I could eat a bear"

b. Simile (sĭm′ ĭ. lē): Is an actual comparison between things that are basically different. Usually these comparisons include the words *like* or *as*.
   "Hearing this, he turned as *white as a sheet*."
   "He drifted about town *like a ship without a rudder*."
   "He was so tired he *slept like a kitten*."

c. Irony (ī′ rō. nĭ): Humorous light sarcasm.
   If you hand in a rough copy of a theme which contains misspellings, marked out passages, improper punctuation, and no evidence of organization, your teacher may say,
   "This is a *fine* piece of work," but your grade on the theme should provide a clue as to what she meant.

d. Metaphor (met ă for): An implied comparison between two different things.
   "The *ship plowed the ocean*."
   "Tom remained *rooted to the spot*."
   "The king had a *heart of stone*."

5. Illustrate over use of expressions: Prepare a passage or story in which the child is to underline each example of a figurative expression (underlining is provided in the following sample).

Directions: The following story contains too many figurative expressions! Many of the examples are used so often that we
say they are *threadbare, shopworn, worked-to-death*
expressions or *cliches (klee shays)*. Figurative language
is to the writer as seasoning is to the cook. Overuse may
spoil the flavor. Underline each example of a figure of
speech in the passage. (To illustrate, expressions have
been underlined.)

Our hero Horatius Algerman left home at a tender age to seek
his fortune in the cold and heartless city. He was a person of sterling
qualities and had a burning desire to prove his worth. (Also his
mettle.) One day he found himself lost in the heart of the (heartless)
city. So with a lump in his throat he decided to follow his nose,
meanwhile keeping one eye out for Indians. Remaining true to his
upbringing he kept his other eye on the ball, his nose to the grind-
stone, shoulder to the wheel, and feet on the ground. However, he
never let the grass grow under his feet. This was particularly difficult in the heart of the city as the grass sprang up fast as lightning
and spread like wildfire.

Soon our hero was as hungry as a bear—so hungry in fact that
he could eat a horse. Having no horse of his own, he declined to eat
another's horse as this was a horse of a different color to Horatius.

The next day good fortune smiled on our hero. He was elected
mayor of the cold heartless city. He vowed he would be a good
servant of the people. He decided to learn the mayor business from
the ground up. Since he always kept a straight face, he soon earned
the nickname "old oval jaw." That year March came in like a lion,
but Horatius kept a clear head, frequently put his foot down,
weathered many storms, stormed every obstacle in his path, pushed
his way to the top, rarely lost his head, and when he did he would
find his tongue at the right moment. He also learned to hold his
tongue at the right moment (some people thought he was odd).

Nevertheless, our Hero never wasted a minute and always made
up for lost time, was up with the sun and never slept on the job,
burned the candle at both ends, and became a Jack of all trades. We
hear little more of our hero except for two conflicting stories. One
has it that he threw his heart into his work and ended up a clinker.
The other version—equally heart rending—is that one dark night,
black as pitch, he was swallowed up by the city.

Children may "translate" or rewrite selected sentences, paragraphs,
or the entire passage, substituting other words for the underlined
expressions.

6. Reserve space on the bulletin board where members of the class may put up examples of figurative language that they meet in their reading. A committee may then select the best of these and duplicate them for distribution to all members of the class.

Eyeball to Elbow

Children working in pairs, teams, or as a class enjoy making an exhaustive list of figurative expressions that focus on one theme, such as *eyes, parts of the body* or *terms involving animals*. This can be an ongoing language game in which the product is displayed on the bulletin board and new items added as children discover them. Dozens of items can be found for each of the above topics. A few examples follow:

Eyes. Keep your *eye* on the ball, he caught the waiter's *eye*, the prophet cast his *eyes* to the heavens, that's an *eye*-opener; her *eyes:* burned like coals, twinkled like stars, were full of wonder, were swimming in tears, lighted up.

Parts of the body. Nose of a boat, *head* of a hammer, *eye* of a hurricane, *foot* of the mountain, he's all *thumbs,* get to the *heart* of the matter.

Animals. Sly as a *fox,* hungry as a *bear, wolfed* his food, gentle as a *lamb,* clumsy as an *ox,* a memory like an *elephant.*

Imagination

This is a variation of the above activity. Here children develop their own expressions. These are often related to immediate experiences with school, reading, television, news. A few examples from children:

"As determined as army ants"
"As busy as a ball of yarn in a basket of kittens"
"As noisy as a school bus"
"About as funny as a broken toe"
"Funnier than an elephant joke"
"As gentle as a 300 lb. tackle"
"Tender as a hawk's beak"

Word Analogies

Working with analogies is an excellent way to develop skill in seeing relationship, associating or contrasting word meanings, and applying analytical processes. Exercises involving analogies can be developed for working with practically any concepts with which the school deals and can be adapted to any difficulty level. The materials which follow illustrate working with a limited number of areas, such as synonyms, irregular plurals, homonyms, sports, irregular verbs, mathematics, science, and social studies. Two different formats are shown. Each illustration can easily be expanded into larger units or full page exercises.

Explain that word analogies involve a relationship or similarity between words. The following might be used to illustrate some of these relationships.

Part to whole:	(finger–hand; toe–foot)
Sequence:	(six–seven; f–g)
Origin:	(paper–tree; wheat–bread)
Class:	(orange–fruit; carrot–vegetable)
Function:	(shoe–foot; glove–hand)
Opposites:	(weak–strong; cold–hot)
Synonyms:	(hate–despise; expand–enlarge)

1. *Complete the following analogies by underlining the one word on the right that completes the sense of the statement.*

Synonyms

a. Expand is to enlarge as
   contract is to: shrink   sign   annual
b. Awkward is to clumsy as
   funny is to: joke   luminous   childlike
c. Miniature is to small as
   average is to: ordinary   rare   peculiar
d. Huge is to massive as
   often is to: hasten   forever   frequently
e. Perfect is to flawless as
   exact is to: legal   peruse   accurate

Sports

a. Glove is to baseball as
   stick is to: tennis   wrestling   hockey
b. Football is to gridiron as
   baseball is to: diamond   summer   stadium
c. Five is to basketball as
   eleven is to: baseball   football   volleyball
d. Baseball is to sport as
   tennis is to: ball   net   sport

   e. Swimming is to pool as
      hockey is to: ice   teams   soccer

Math

   a. Foot is to yard as
      one is to: twelve   three   six
   b. One is to four as five is to: ten   fifteen   twenty
   c. Ten is to 100 as one is to: ten   twenty   1/10
   d. Radius is to diameter as
      three is to: 6   1½   9
   e. Minute is to hour as
      second is to: first   hour   minute

Science

   a. Magnet is to nail as
      light is to: dark   moth   electrons
   b. Soft is to hard as
      bituminuous is to: deposit   anthracite   coal
   c. Stem is to flower as
      trunk is to: elephant   traveler   tree
   d. Canal is to water as
      vein is to: leaves   blood   mining
   e. Bark is to tree as
      scales are to: markets   music   fish
   f. Caterpillar is to butterfly
      as tadpole is to: frog   fishing   pond

Process

   a. Cream is to butter as
      apple is to: tree   bushel   jelly
   b. Leather is to shoe as
      flour is to: doughnut   wheat   mill
   c. Wood is to paper as
      sand is to: break   glass   clear
   d. Milk is to cow as
      wool is to: clothing   farmer   sheep
   e. Grass is to cow as
      mouse is to: trap   cat   rat

2. *Complete the following analogies by writing the one word in the English language that will complete the sense of the statement.*

Homonyms

   a. Piece is to peace as pain is to _____.
   b. Steel is to steal as sun is to _____.

    c. Deer is to dear as eight is to _____ .
    d. Tale is to tail as reign is to _____ .
    e. Blue is to blew as weight is to _____ .

Irregular Verbs

    a. Sing is to sang as bring is to _____ .
    b. Write is to written as speak is to _____ .
    c. Give is to gave as dive is to _____ .
    d. Fly is to flew as cry is to _____ .
    e. See is to saw as flee is to _____ .

Irregular Plurals

    a. Nickel is to nickels as penny is to _____ .
    b. Dog is to dogs as fox is to _____ .
    c. Cow is to cows as deer is to _____ .
    d. Pan is to pans as tooth is to _____ .
    e. Book is to books as child is to _____ .

SUMMARY

The preceding exercises dealing with *different meanings, figurative expressions,* and *analogies* illustrate several different approaches for using these particular language-expanding activities. There are, of course, unlimited highly motivating techniques for developing and expanding concepts. A number of these are found in the chapters which deal with teaching reading at various instructional levels.

YOUR POINT OF VIEW?

Would you defend or attack the following premises? Supply a rationale for each of your choices.

1. Reading instruction in American schools tends to neglect helping the child to see reading as a language process.
2. Normal developmental growth in reading reduces the efficacy of writing individual stories for pupils who are beyond the stage of beginning reading.
3. Many children master the mechanics of reading, but fail to understand the role of intonation as it functions in reading for meaning.

4. Materials used for instruction in reading should include a sizable portion of content that "teaches the child about his language and how language operates."

5. Any given experience-chart story will not be equally motivating for all pupils in a class.

6. At each successive grade level, a smaller percentage of children are avid readers, i.e., fewer children love to read as a free-choice activity.

7. The study of *language* is unquestionably neglected in our schools.

BIBLIOGRAPHY

1. Ahlvers, Elizabeth R., *A Study of the Effect of Teaching Intonation Skills on Reading Comprehension in Grade One.* Unpublished Doctoral Dissertation, The Pennsylvania State University, 1970.

2. Allen, Roach Van, *Language Experience in Communication.* Boston: Houghton Mifflin Company, 1976.

3. Attea, Mary, "Teacher Education in Reading and Language Arts," *Reading Teacher 27* (November 1973): 139–41.

4. Elkins, Deborah, *Teaching Literature Designs for Cognitive Development.* Columbus, O.: Charles E. Merrill Publishing Co., 1976. Chapter 6.

5. Emans, Robert, "Use of Context Clues," in *Reading and Realism*, J. Allen Figurel, ed. Proceedings, International Reading Association 13, Part 1, 1969, pp. 76–82.

6. Fries, Charles C., *Linguistics and Reading.* New York: Holt, Rinehart and Winston, Inc., 1963.

7. Galloway, Charles G. and Mickelson, Norma I., "Improving Teachers' Questions," *Elementary School Journal 73* (December 1973): 145–48.

8. Gans, Roma, *Guiding Children's Reading through Experiences.* New York: Bureau of Publications, Teachers College, Columbia University, 1941.

9. Furner, Beatrice A., "Creative Dramatics in a Language Arts Program: Personal Growth and Self-Expression," *Elementary English 51* (January 1974): 41–44.

10. Golub, Lester S., "A Critical Age Model of Language Learning," *Language Arts 52* (December 1975): 1097–1103.

11. Groesbeck, Hulda, The Comprehension of Figurative Language by Elementary Pupils: A Study of Transfer. Unpublished Doctoral Thesis, Oklahoma University, 1961.

12. Hall, Mary Anne, *Teaching Reading as a Language Experience*, second ed. Columbus, O.: Charles E. Merrill Publishing Co., 1976.

13. Hildreth, Gertrude H., "Experience-Related Reading for School Beginners," *Elementary English* (March 1965): 280–97.
14. Hooker, Brian, *Cyrano De Bergerac*. New York: Holt, Rinehart and Winston, 1937, pp. 242–43.
15. Holmes, Elizabeth Ann, Children's Knowledge of Figurative Language. Unpublished Masters Thesis, Oklahoma University, 1959.
16. Kendrick, William M. and Bennett, Clayton L., "A Comparative Study of Two First-Grade Language Arts Programs," *Reading Research Quarterly* (Fall 1966): 83–118.
17. Lamoreaux, L. A. and Lee, Dorris M., *Learning to Read through Experience*. New York: Appleton-Century-Crofts, 1943.
18. Lee, Dorris M. and Allen, R. V., *Learning to Read through Experience,* second ed. New York: Appleton-Century-Crofts, 1963.
19. Lefevre, Carl A., *Linguistics and the Teaching of Reading*. New York: McGraw-Hill Book Co., 1964.
20. Lindberg, Lucile, "This Is Reading," *Improving Reading Instruction.* Joint Proceedings of the Twenty-fifth Reading Conference and First Intensive Summer Workshop, Volume I, University Park, Pa., 1963, p. 15.
21. Lloyd, Donald J., "Reading American English Sound Patterns." New York: Harper and Row, Publishers, 1962, Monograph No. 104.
22. Manzo, Anthony, V. and Martin, Deanna Coleman, "Writing Communal Poetry," *Journal of Reading 17* (May 1974): 638–43.
23. Means, Chalmers Edward, *A Study of the Relationship between the Use of Intonation Patterns in Oral Reading and Comprehension in Reading.* Unpublished Doctoral Dissertation, The Pennsylvania State University, 1969.
24. Pflaum, Susanna Whitney, *The Development of Language and Reading in the Young Child*. Columbus, O.: Charles E. Merrill Publishing Co., 1974.
25. Pikulski, John J., "Linguistics Applied to Reading Instruction," *Language Arts 53* (April 1976): 373–77.
26. Robertson, Jean E., "Pupil Understanding of Connectives in Reading," in *Forging Ahead in Reading*, J. Allen Figural, ed. Proceedings, International Reading Association 12, Part 1, pp. 581–88.
27. Smith, Frank, *Psycholinguistics and Reading*. New York: Holt, Rinehart and Winston, Inc., 1973.
28. Smith, James A., *Adventures in Communication*. Boston: Allyn and Bacon, Inc., 1972.
29. Smith, Nila Banton, *American Reading Instruction*. Newark, Del.: International Reading Association, 1965.
30. Stauffer, Russell G., *The Language-Experience Approach to the Teaching of Reading*. New York: Harper and Row, Publishers, 1970.

31. Stevens, Martin, "Intonation in the Teachings of Reading," *Elementary English* (March 1965): 231–37.

32. Thomas, Owen, "Teaching Children about Language," *Elementary English 51* (January 1974): 11–19.

33. Thompson, Ruby L. "Word Power: How to Use What They Like to Give Them What They Need," *Journal of Reading* (October 1971): 13–15.

34. Turner, Thomas N., "Figurative Language: Deceitful Mirage or Sparkling Oasis for Reading?" *Language Arts 53* (October 1976): 758–61.

35. Tway, Eileen, "Language Experience: All Together," *Reading Teacher 27* (December 1973): 249–52.

36. Tyler, Priscilla, "Sound, Pattern and Sense," *Changing Concepts of Reading Instruction.* Proceedings, International Reading Association 6, 1961, pp. 259–63.

37. Vaughn, Joseph L.; Estes, Thomas H.; and Curtis, Sherry L., "Developing Conceptual Awareness," *Language Arts 52* (December 1975): 1141–44.

38. Weber, Rose Marie, "The Study of Oral Reading Errors: A Survey of the Literature," *Reading Research Quarterly* (Fall 1968): 96–119.

39. Wilson, Robert M. and Hall, Mary Anne, *Reading and the Elementary School Child.* New York: Van Nostrand Reinhold Co., 1972.

Chapter 7

The Role of
Phonics in Reading
Instruction

This chapter introduces phonics instruction by attempting to develop some basic premises, or to identify a philosophy of instruction. To do this, agreement must be reached in regard to certain questions, such as what phonics instruction consists of, the purpose for teaching it, what it can and cannot do for individuals who are learning to read.

Further, do we believe that phonics is an "additive" that goes into the reading curriculum at a particular stage of learning? Or, is it an integral part of beginning reading instruction which supplements and interacts with other skills which are being taught concomitantly with phonics instruction?

Do we always think of phonics instruction as it relates to "learning to read;" or do we sometimes confuse or equate phonics instruction with that vast body of knowledge on phonology that has been amassed by linguists? The point of this question is to determine if we sometimes teach certain letter-sound data because they exist, rather than because we believe they contribute to learning to read.

When we do not have a clear understanding of what we expect phonics instruction to accomplish, we may be equally vague on how to implement instruction to achieve nebulous goals. It is easy to get emotional in the face of that which is not understood. If one knows that phonics is essential in learning to read, the term takes on the connotation: *good.* To consider the proposition that a child could get too much of a good thing might be interpreted as lack of fervor.

On the other hand, there are a great many things that can, and often do, go wrong as a result of fervid systematic teaching of phonics. If the final result is bad, something must be attacked with fervor! In the past, criticism was not limited to excesses in phonics instruction, but phonics instruction per se was damned.

Criticism
and Controversy

Learning to read is very highly valued in our society, and not learning how to read has a tendency to become highly visible. Since "instruction" does not always result in the looked for gains in reading achievement, reading instruction in American schools has always generated criticism and controversy. It is still difficult to explain how phonics—one small ingredient in the instructional program—has managed to generate so much controversy.

No other aspect of the entire curriculum receives so much critical attention. No controversy from evolution to sex education has demonstrated the "staying power" of phonics instruction. Each generation of reading teachers is faced with both old and new controversies which focus on phonics instruction. Occasionally a "new debate" is nothing more than substituting new labels for old issues. An example is found in the *sight word* versus *phonics* controversy which centered on the relative merits and shortcomings of these two alleged "methods" of teaching reading. After years of heated but fruitless argument, a truce was reached in the mid-1960s. It was based on the acknowledgment by partisans from both sides that these labels were meaningless. No such methods, or materials for carrying them out, really existed.

The void was filled immediately by a publication, *The Great Debate* (6), which continued the debate by substituting the terms *code emphasis* and *meaning emphasis*. The ground rules were changed slightly since one did not have to embrace one and decry the other, but simply decide *which must come first* in reading instruction.

This debate was costly because the energy burned up on a dead-end controversy should have been expended on real problems. Teachers of reading need to develop a philosophy of reading instruction that comes to grips with the realities found in the classroom. One way to do this is to pose and answer questions which focus on important educational issues related to phonics instruction. A few such questions are listed below and are followed by discussion or rationale.

1. What is the purpose of phonics instruction as it relates to learning to read?
2. Is the learning of letter-sound relationships an absolute essential for learning to read?
3. Should beginning reading instruction stress:
   a. reading for meaning?
   b. systematic teaching of letter-sound relationships?
   c. learning sight words, or words as wholes?
4. Will phonics instruction produce readers who overrely on letter-sound relationships?
5. What is the optimum amount of phonics instruction for every child?
6. Is it good strategy to teach phonic rules or generalizations?

While most of these questions could be answered with a *yes* or *no*, such brevity should be avoided. When dealing with phonics instruction, *why* we believe and practice certain things must be clearly understood. The following discussion attempts to provide a rationale as to why a particular position is advocated.

The Purpose Of Phonics Instruction Is

1. to teach beginning readers that printed letters and letter combinations represent speech sounds heard in words.*
2. to teach the learner to blend the sounds represented by the printed letters when she meets a word she does not recognize.

This skill is important because the beginning reader inevitably meets many words that she does not instantly recognize as sight words.

---

* Speech sounds heard in words are quite different from teaching sounds in isolation. To read the word *cat,* three phonemes are blended just as they are in saying the word *cat.* Beginning readers are not taught to produce three syllables kuh·ah·tuh = cat.

She cannot solve these unknown print jumbles by staring at them, and sometimes she cannot solve them by using the available context clues. The only other alternative is to use the letter-sound relationship to "unlock," "solve," or arrive at the word's pronunciation.

Most likely, the written word that puzzles the child is a word she has pronounced many times. So the purpose of phonics instruction is not to teach learners "how to pronounce words." Applying the letter-sound code simply reveals the pronunciation, or yields an approximate pronunciation of the unknown word symbol.

The purpose of phonics instruction as outlined above is compatible with the frequently met statement that "phonics is taught so that children can become independent readers."

Phonic Skills—
Essential for
Learning to Read?

During recent years it would have been difficult, if not impossible, to find disagreement on this question among reading teachers, critics of reading instruction, or members of the "reading establishment." All would answer with an unqualified yes that phonics skills are essential in learning to read. Debate and differences of opinion could have been found on such instructional issues as *how, when* and *how much* phonics should be taught.

An individual who does not master the letter-sound code can progress only so far in learning to read. It would be futile to attempt to say exactly how far each child can go in terms of words she can learn in the absence of phonics skills. However, it is fairly safe to say that no child will function as a facile reader, or even an average third-grade reader, if she does not learn to apply letter-sound relationships in her reading.

It is also safe to say that the farther a learner progresses in beginning reading without applying the letter-sound code, the smaller will be her rate of growth per unit of instruction, or time spent in reading. The reason for this is obvious to the person who has worked with individuals who are learning to read. The terms *learning to read* and *beginning readers* imply a limited experience with the written symbol system. The beginning reader is faced with the burden of making many visual discriminations among printed words that contain only minimal differences in visual cues.

A word not recognized which is essential to the meaning of a sentence will likely contribute to the beginning reader's uncertainty as to the intended message. Many plausible alternatives as to the identity of the word may come to mind even when some context clues are available. But if the initial letter-sound clue can be utilized, this will drastically reduce these options. This is a very important reduction of reader uncertainty. If more letter-sound clues are needed and if the reader is capable of applying them, she can in most cases establish the identity of the printed word.

To make progress while learning to read one must constantly be developing a more effective set of skills which reduces the uncertainty resulting from attending to visual clues alone. Unless letter-sound clues are added, the visual discrimination circuit overloads and the reading process breaks down.

Phonics and the Expert Reader

An expert reader is someone who no longer functions like a beginning reader. The term *expert* implies that one is a facile, experienced reader. Psycholinguists and other theorists have observed that such readers rely very little, if at all, on letter-sound relationships. They obviously pay no heed to individual letters and cannot be observed applying phonics skills. This is one of the major reasons why they merit the designation skilled, accomplished, or expert readers.

Sight words learned reduces one's need to rely on phonic analysis.

The beginning reader is crippled if she cannot use letter-sound relationships, and an adult reader cannot be called an expert reader if she continues to heavily rely on this technique. To some observers, myself included, this suggests that the activity of learning to read involves a quite different set of behaviors than those used by an expert reader. If this is true, one should not analyze skilled readers and then generalize to beginning readers.

A potentially dangerous generalization is that since skilled readers do not appear to use phonics, perhaps children learning how to read need not be taught letter-sound relationships. If such an hypothesis is advanced, it should be accompanied by a description of how the learner will *learn* to read. One suggestion is that possibly "memory" for word forms, that is, visual memory, may be all that is really needed. Smith writes, "we can both recognize and recall many thousands of words in our spoken language vocabulary, and recognize many thousands of different faces and animals and plants and objects in our visual world. *Why should this fantastic memorizing capacity suddenly run out in the case of reading?*" (18:75 emphasis added)

It should be pointed out that Smith does not come out flatly against phonics instruction. However, the question raised seems to invite the conclusion that visual memory of word configurations should be sufficient for learning to read. If this point of view gains adherents we shall have made full circle back to the sight word versus phonics debate. This debate should not be reopened unless evidence is provided that children can learn to read without applying letter-sound relationships in the beginning reading stage.

Beginning Instruction— Meaning? Phonics? Whole Words?

Previous discussion has attempted to establish that phonics, or letter-sound relationships, must be learned and applied by beginning readers. Over the years, some individuals apparently felt that accepting this premise precluded emphasizing reading for meaning. Conversely, believing that beginning reading should always be a meaning making process was often interpreted as implying some restriction about teaching letter-sound relationships.

The problems may have been accentuated by some of the labels that have become attached to instructional practices. For instance, phonic analysis is frequently called a *mechanical skill*. Such a label bestows a much lower status on an instructional activity than if we choose to call it a "reading for meaning" activity. The labels may interfere with noting that the mastery of certain mechanical skills is a prerequisite for the application of *comprehension* skills.

Thus, many people believe that sounding out a word is the natural enemy of reading for meaning. This has some surface validity since the act of sounding interrupts the melody of the sentence. But the real purpose of this interruption is to guarantee that the melody and the meaning of the sentence can be achieved.

In most cases an unknown word in a sentence destroys the melody of the language unit and, in many cases, prevents one from getting the meaning. The first objective in sounding out the word is to establish its identity, but this is not the end of the process. The word is identified so that its contribution to the meaning of the sentence can be utilized. If a child sounds out a word without pursuing the meaning of the sentence, she is a casualty of poor instruction, or not quite enough instruction. Unlike climbing a mountain, you do not identify a word because it is there, but because your objective is to read the passage for meaning.

Adhering to an either-or position in relation to phonics meaning is not necessary. Once it is accepted that beginning instruction should include both, there is still one more either-or stance to avoid. This is the question, "which one should be emphasized first?" The best answer is neither because they are both essential to growth in reading. Also, stressing one skill and slighting the other will mislead the learner as to the nature of reading.

Developing a Learner's Set

It is inevitable that what transpires during the initial stage of reading instruction will develop a *set* within the learner that "this is reading." The only way a child can miss the fact that reading is a meaning making process is if she receives initial instruction that masks this fact. An extensive time block devoted to phonics instruction leads the child to view reading as sounding out words. On the other hand, a lengthy instructional period without insight into letter-sound relationships leads a child to see reading as a process in which, "when you don't know the words, you stare a while and then guess." Serious damage to the learner can result from either "set."

The ultimate goal of phonics instruction is to "internalize the cues"
to such a degree that no one will
know if and when you use phonics.

Mastery of
Sight Words

It is difficult to understand how so much misunderstanding, confusion, and controversy could become associated with a spurious issue
labeled *sight word* versus *phonics*. Children learning to read have no
choice except to learn and constantly expand their stock of sight words.
This is true for several reasons.

First, there are a number of words which have highly irregular
spellings. These words cannot be sounded out by applying letter-sound
analysis. Examples include *once, a, the, eye, one, know, isle, Mr., you,
could, eight, aisle, cough, Mrs., enough, ocean, do, through, weight,
sew*. There are hundreds of other words whose spellings are irregular
to some degree and learning some of them as sight words would represent a real economy.

A second reason why sight words are learned is found in the nature of the English language. Certain words are used over and over in
speech and writing. These are called *high frequency* words and have
also been referred to as "service words," "structure words," "glue

words," and "sight words." The laws of learning are not suspended simply because the task is learning to read. The repetition involved in seeing the same word dozens of times will eventually cause it to be recognized as a unit. In the limited time period represented by first grade, some high frequency words will have been met hundreds of times in reading situations.

The repetition of high frequency words does not diminish in later grades. Any child attempting to learn how to read who does not systematically expand her stock of sight words is in trouble as a reader. In fact, if this phenomenon persists for any length of time, the child must be thought of as an impaired reader. She is not developing a skill she must have.

There is a third reason why normal growth in reading results in learning more and more sight words. The key is what happens in the reading situation when the learner applies letter-sound analysis. When phonics is used in identifying a word, the visual pattern of the word remains intact. The reader must attend to the visual pattern of the word in order to use letter-sound clues. Thus, visual recognition of words is reinforced even while the reader is applying phonic analysis. The contribution of the sounding clues to the recognition of a given word diminishes with each successive encounter with that word. After X encounters, the word becomes a sight word and will never be sounded out again.

Phonics Instruction— Limitations

English spelling (writing) does not approximate a one-to-one relationship between letters seen and speech sounds heard in the pronunciation of many words. This was alluded to in the discussion as to why some words must be learned as sight words. The problem is more severe than was suggested by the few words cited as examples. Irregular spelling of words undoubtedly limits what phonics instruction can contribute to learning to read.

A few years ago some linguists were stressing that English spelling was not as irregular as reading teachers suggested. Figures were cited such as, "85 per cent of English words have regular spellings." Fries wrote, "modern English spelling is not hopelessly chaotic" (11). This statement was based in part on the premise that if the etymological evaluation of certain words was taken into consideration, their spellings might not be considered irregular.

More recently other linguists and psycholinguists have taken the position that the irregularities of English spelling are so serious as to almost preclude the practice of teaching letter-sound relationships in reading instruction. Such a conclusion is too pessimistic and was probably drawn in part from data on spelling, or sound-to-grapheme relationships. Computers were programmed with all possible letter combinations which could represent a given speech sound. In some cases this might total fifteen to eighteen letter or letter-combinations for a single sound.

In addition, the computer stored data as to how other letters in a word might affect the spelling. Children sometimes store similar data, as illustrated in the old spelling-clue ditty, "*i* before *e* except after *c*, or when sounded like $\overline{A}$ as in neighbor or weigh." Using the data mentioned above, the computer was then instructed to spell many thousands of words. Needless to say, this undertaking severely taxed both programmers and the computer since an enormous number of variables in the form of rules or generalizations was involved.

If one generalized from data on spelling rules to applying letter-sound relationships in reading, the latter task appears monumental. The two tasks are not analogous for several reasons. The computer was restricted exclusively to clues within the word and choices had to be exactly right to be correct. The reader could use context clues provided by an entire meaning-bearing chunk of language; and in many cases an approximation of the sounds would unlock the identity of the unrecognized word. In other words, the computer was not "reading" and the reader is not "spelling" when applying letter-to-sound associations.

Rejecting extreme positions, one would likely conclude that irregular spelling patterns do limit what phonics instruction can achieve for beginning readers. These irregularities also emphasize the necessity of augmenting or supplementing letter-sound analysis with every other clue available in the reading situation. These vagaries of English spelling will not be discussed in detail, but a few will be noted for the purpose of illustration.

1. The English language contains thousands of words "borrowed" from other languages. The spelling of these words is often confusing (yacht, beret, chassis, adieu, alias, naive, chaos, fjord, reign, chamois, bizarre, etc.).

2. Words with the same pronunciation will have different spelling patterns both of which meet the criteria of regular spellings:

   pain–pane; waist–waste; beat–beet; steel–steal; wail–whale; plain–plane; weak–week.

3. Some pairs of words have the same pronunciation, one following a regular spelling pattern, the other being irregular: ate–eight; sun–son; brake–break; wood–would; herd–heard; way–weigh.
4. The most troublesome grapheme-phoneme relationships involve vowel letters. The material below illustrates a few spelling patterns that represent long vowel sounds in English writing.

ā	(ay)	(a + e)	(ai)	(ea)	(ey)	(ei)
	pl*ay*	c*a*ke	m*ai*l	br*ea*k	gr*ey*	w*ei*gh
ē	(ee)	(ea)	(e)	(ie)	(ey)	(eo + e)
	b*ee*t	s*ea*t	m*e*	n*ie*ce	k*ey*	p*eo*ple
ī	(i + e)	(i + gh)	(e + e)	(ai)	(ui + e)	(y)
	b*i*te	h*igh*	*eye*	*ai*sle	g*ui*de	m*y*
ō	(oa)	(o + ld)	(o + e)	(ow)	(oe)	(ou + e)
	s*oa*p	g*old*	b*o*ne	sl*ow*	h*oe*	c*ou*rse
ū(ü)	(u + e)	(ue)	(ui)	(u)	(ui + e)	(ew)
	r*u*le	gl*ue*	s*ui*t	R*u*th	j*ui*ce	fl*ew*

Letter-sound irregularities involving consonants pose less of a problem in learning to read than do vowel letter-sounds. A few of the major consonant irregularities follow.

c	represents two sounds: c = k candy · cook · cube
	c preceding i-e-y = s *c*ity · *c*elery · *c*ycle
g	represents two sounds: goat · gum · gate
	g preceding i-e-y often = j giant · gentle · gym
s	represents several sounds: (s) = some · sat · sister
	s = z: i*s* · wa*s* · ha*s;* (s = ch) sure · sugar
ch	represents several sounds
	ch: *ch*urch · *ch*air · *ch*imney
	ch = sh: *ch*ef · *ch*amois
	ch = k: *ch*rome · *ch*emistry
ph = f:	*ph*one · ne*ph*ew · Philadel*ph*ia
gf = f:	rou*gh* · lau*gh* · cou*gh*
dge = j:	ju*dge* · bri*dge* · le*dge*
qu and que:	the letter *q* represents no sound of its own and is always followed by the vowel u.
Initial *qu* = *kw*:	quick (kwick); quite (kwite)
Final que = k:	plaque (plak); brusque (brusk)

In many instances a consonant letter (or letters) does not represent a sound.

Initial *kn:* ̷knew ̷knot ̷kneel
Initial *wr:* ̷wring ̷write ̷wreck

Double consonants: dollar   ladder   summer
gh: night   sigh   light
Final *mb:* comb   thumb   crumb
Syllable *ten:* fasten   often   listen

There are other irregularities, many of which occur in only a very
limited number of words in beginning reading.

Phonics and
Rules

The irregular spelling of words makes it difficult to devise rules
that will cover all of the letter-sound relationships encountered in beginning reading. More specifically, there will be exceptions to any rule
advanced. For this reason, the term *phonic generalization* is frequently used instead of rule. An example of a rule is that a vowel letter
usually represents its short sound if it is the only vowel in a syllable
or word and does not come at the end of the word or syllable. (Also
stated "one vowel in medial position usually has its short sound.")

The above generalization is considered one of the better ones since
it applies in most three-letter words and in a number of four- and five-
letter words. Even so, there are many words which meet "the one vowel
within the word" criterion but which violate the rule. When we meet
gold, sold, told, bold, cold, fold, hold, etc., we amend the rule to "o
followed by *ld* usually represents its long sound." Also, the vowel *i*
followed by *nd* or *ld* usually has its long sound (*mind, find, blind, kind;
mild, child, wild*).

There are a number of studies which have explored the degree to
which phonics rules can be depended upon. That is, what percent of
words that meet the criterion specified in the rule actually follow the
rule. Oaks (17) analyzed the vowel situations occurring in a number
of basal series, primer through third grade. From among all the phonic
generalizations that were advanced to cover these letter-sound relationships, she concluded that only eight principles applied often
enough to merit their being taught. In this study, the eight generalizations were applicable in only about 50 percent of the cases that the
rules were designed to cover.

In another study, Clymer (7) tested the percent of cases in which
various rules or phonic generalizations actually applied in words met
in four basal series (grades 1–3), plus the words on the *Gates Primary
Reading Vocabulary* (not found in the basals). Some twenty-six hundred

words constituted the sample. Forty-five phonic generalizations were applied to these words to determine what percent of the words followed the rule and what percent were exceptions.

Clymer suggested that two criteria be met in order for a rule to be classified as useful. First, the situation covered by a rule must occur in a minimum of twenty words found in the twenty-six-hundred-word sample; second, the rule should apply in at least 75 percent of the cases it was designed to cover. Of the forty-five phonic generalizations studied, twenty-three covered vowel situations. Only five of this number met the criteria stated above. Ten vowel rules applied in less than 50 percent of the cases; seven rules applied more than 50 percent (but in fewer than three out of four instances); and one rule-situations occurred in only ten words in the entire sample.

Burrows and Lourie (5) report an intensive study of the frequency with which one widely taught vowel rule applied to the five thousand highest frequency words on the Rinsland List. The rule under discussion states, "when there are two adjacent vowels in a word, the first usually has its long sound and the second is silent." Children are often taught this rule as, "when two vowels go walking, the first does the talking." In the five-thousand-word sample, a total of 1,728 words met the two-vowel criterion. However, only 628 (approximately 40 percent) followed the rule.

Emans (9) tested the frequency with which phonic generalizations applied to words found in materials written for pupils above the primary grades. In regard to the utility of phonic rules, intermediate-level materials did not enjoy a significant advantage over beginning materials. Studies by Bailey (1) and Burmeister (3, 4) reported data that were in general agreement with the findings cited above. However, different researchers have suggested different criteria for assessing the "utility" of phonic generalizations.

The majority of phonic generalizations focuses on vowel letter-sound relationships. It should be noted that many consonant sound relationships are taught without reference to rules. For instance, in teaching the sound of *M* as it occurs initially in words, the child is simply told, "when you see *M*, think or make the sound you hear in *man, mine* or *most*." These or other words beginning with *M*, which the children have met and now recognize, can be placed on the chalkboard to serve as visual models while teaching the visual-auditory relationship.

This teaching-learning will suffice for all words beginning with *M* except *mnemonic*, which will not be met in beginning reading. This same rule-less procedure is used to teach the letter-sound association for b-d-f-h-j-l-n-p-r-t, etc. Most generalizations covering consonant letter-sounds are designed to cover exceptions. In the manner described above, the child is taught that K or W or C at the beginning of words is sounded like the first sound heard in *k*ite, *w*ait, and *c*at. Eventually the following generalizations, all relating to exceptions, are introduced.

"If a word begins with KN—don't sound the K."
"If a word begins with WR—don't sound the W."
"C is sounded like S when it precedes *i, e,* or *y.*"

A phonics program need not be based on children memorizing rules. In fact, knowing the rule does not assure that the child will be able to apply it while reading. The main value of generalizations is that they focus attention on visual letter patterns, such as *oa-ea-ee-ai*-ae, etc. while simultaneously associating such patterns with the sounds they represent in words. Many teachers prefer that children experience the rule or deduce the generalization while working with a series of words the rule covers.

Apparently, there are misconceptions as to how phonics is taught and the degree to which instruction relies on rules. Smith writes, "The aim of phonics instruction is to provide rules that will predict how a word will sound from the way it is spelled. The value of phonics would appear to depend on how many rules are required to establish correspondences between the letters and sounds of English, or to what extent our phonemes can be predicted by the rules of phonics" (18:84).

The aim of phonics is to have the learner react to visual stimuli (letters) with speech sounds heard in words. This is to be done only when a word form is not recognized. Since the reader is reading for meanings, she will also be aided by meaning or context clues. All regular consonant letter-sound relationships are simply taught as visual-auditory associations—no rules are involved.

Phonics Instruction:
How Much?

What is the optimum amount of phonics instruction for each child learning to read? It is apparent the answer cannot be in terms of the number of hours to be devoted to instruction or review. Obviously, different learners will need differing amounts of phonics instruction. Meeting individual pupil needs has always been the number one priority in our schools, but the hundreds of plans, procedures, grouping techniques, etc. have never been able to provide the teacher with anything more than a set of ground rules for instruction.

Phonics is a crutch you use until
you can walk through the page
without it.

This is particularly true in regard to phonics instruction. Teachers must first know what skills are needed for learning to read. Then through observation and diagnosis they must discover what each child has mastered and which skills are still needed. As in the case of all instruction, the teacher holds the key to good practice. When answering the question posed above, one should keep in mind the purpose and the limitations of phonics instruction and that letter-sound analysis is most effective when used in combination with other skills. The *optimum* amount of phonics instruction for any learner is the *minimum* needed to become an independent reader.

SUMMARY

Learning letter-sound relationships is essential for learning to read. However, reliance on these clues should diminish quite rapidly as a result of reading experiences.

Beginning reading instruction must provide for growth in three broad areas:

1. Learning letter-sound relationships.
2. Developing and expanding sight vocabulary.
3. Using context clues for reading for meaning.

These are not to be developed in *any* sequence, but rather to be taught concomitantly. They aid and abet each other. Overreliance on any one will cause the child to develop an erroneous set as to the nature of the reading process.

YOUR POINT OF VIEW?

What is the basis for your agreement or disagreement with each of the following statements:

1. An examination of how adult expert readers function in reading situations will not lead to an understanding of "how children *learn to read.*"
2. Children can learn to read without gaining insights into letter-sound relationships.
3. Highly competent readers rely very little on applying letter-sound relationships in their reading.
4. Early reading instruction inevitably causes children to develop a *set* relative to "what is reading?"
5. The spelling patterns found in English writing constitute a major obstacle in learning to read English.
6. "Phonics instruction" implies the learning of rules which apply to letter-sound relationships.
7. Teaching both sight words and letter-sound analysis as parallel or concommitant learnings will inevitably lead to confusion.

BIBLIOGRAPHY

1. Bailey, Mildred Hart, "The Utility of Phonic Generalizations in Grades One through Six," *Reading Teacher* (February 1967): 413–18.
2. Brzeinski, Joseph E., "When Should Phonics Instruction Begin?" *Reading as an Intellectual Activity.* International Reading Association Proceedings 8, 1963, pp. 228–32.
3. Burmeister, Lou E., "Vowel Pairs," *Reading Teacher* (February 1968): 445–52.
4. ———, "Final Vowel-Consonant-e," *The Reading Teacher* (February 1971): 439–42.

5. Burrows, Alvina Trent and Lourie, Zyra, "Two Vowels Go Walking," *Reading Teacher* (November 1963): 79–82.
6. Chall, Jeanne, *Learning to Read — The Great Debate*. New York: McGraw-Hill Book Co., 1967.
7. Clymer, Theodore, "The Utility of Phonic Generalizations in the Primary Grades," *Reading Teacher* (January 1963): 252–58.
8. Dzama, Mary Ann, "Comparing Use of Generalizations of Phonics in LEA, Based Vocabulary," *Reading Teacher* 28 (February 1975): 466–72.
9. Emans, Robert, "The Usefulness of Phonic Generalizations above the Primary Grades," *Reading Teacher* (February 1967): 419–25.
10. ———,"Phonics: A Look Ahead," *Elementary English* (May 1969): 575–582.
11. Fries, Charles C., *Linguistics and Reading*. New York: Holt, Rinehart & Winston, Inc., 1963.
12. Fry, Edward, "A Frequency Approach to Phonics," *Elementary English* (November 1964): 759–65.
13. Goodman, Kenneth S., "A Linguistic Study of Cues and Miscues in Reading," *Elementary English* (October 1965): 639–43.
14. Kavanagh, James F. and Mattingly, Ignatius G., ed. *Language by Ear and by Eye*. Cambridge, Mass.: The MIT Press, 1972.
15. Potts, Marion and Savino, Carl, "The Relative Achievement of First Graders under Three Different Reading Programs," *The Journal of Educational Research* (July-August 1968): 447–450.
16. Marlin, R. G., "Decoding and the Quest of Meaning," *Journal of Reading Behavior* (Fall 1969): 22–29.
17. Oaks, Ruth E., "A Study of the Vowel Situations in a Primary Vocabulary," *Education* (May 1952): 604–17.
18. Smith, Frank, *Psycholinguistics and Reading*. New York: Holt, Rinehart & Winston, Inc., 1973.
19. Smith, Carl Bernard, "The Double Vowel and Linguistic Research," *Reading Teacher* (April 1966): 512–14.
20. Soffietti, James P., "Why Children Fail to Read: A Linguistic Analysis," *Harvard Educational Review* (Spring 1955): 63–84.

Chapter 8

Phonics Instruction

Learning to read is an activity that involves the mastery of a wide array of cues. Applying letter-sound relationships is very important in the learning process, but equally important is an understanding of how all *available cues* must be used simultaneously. The child has already learned several cue systems simply from learning to speak his native tongue. The first of these relate to the syntax and structure of the language. This includes the system which governs how words can and cannot be strung together in meaningful units.

The second cue is that speech (and writing) must meet the criterion of being meaningful. These are important ground rules applying to spoken and written English. These are what the learner can transfer from the mastery of spoken language to mastery of the reading process.

This chapter deals with some of the "new learnings" involved in reading; specifically, translating *visual stimuli* into what they represent. What one reads is not written speech, but rather an imperfect but fairly adequate graphic representation of language. Intonation is discussed elsewhere and involves certain components of language that cannot transfer to reading until the meaning of a passage is grasped. The difficulty in learning to read is that one must decipher the squiggles—printed words—in order to decipher the meaning.

Learning to read involves cracking two codes: (1) "What are the printed words?" and (2) "What do they mean in this setting?" It is totally unrealistic to equate reading with the former. On the other hand, it is impossible to derive the meaning if one cannot translate the graphic representation of language into language.

Options

Phonics instruction consists of teaching letter-sound relationships. These techniques are taught so that the learner will be able to *identify* (figure out, solve, attack, analyze) words that he does not recognize. Fortunately for the learner, there are several other options which can be exercised in identifying unknown words. Several umbrella terms have been used extensively to refer to this group of skills, including *word recognition skills, word analysis skills,* and *word identification skills.*

To avoid distorting how children actually learn to read, all of the methods that can be used in identifying unknown words will be listed and briefly discussed. The justification for this is that many of these skills work together for the learner, and each makes its maximum contribution when it is used in combination with others.

**Word
Identification
Skills**

The major methods children may use in identifying unknown words include

1. Unique letter-configuration clues
2. Structural analysis
3. Phonic analysis

4. Context clues
5. Any methods in combination

The Unique Appearance of Words

With the exception of a limited number of homographs (*re cord–rec ord; tear–tear; wind–wind*), all words in English writing have unique visual patterns. While many children use this "uniqueness" cue in the earliest stages of learning to read, its utility diminishes with each new experience with reading.

The word *look* may be recognized because of the *oo* pattern. Then the child meets the word *book*. These words are different but they cannot be differentiated on the basis of the original unique cue *oo*. As the child meets *took, hook, door, floor, flood,* this *visual* clue ceases to be unique.

Using only partial clues (*oo* in look, *tt* in little, *y*—"a tail on the end of monkey," *mm* in summer, etc.) has such limited utility that it is safe to say that such clues should not be taught. If a child notes such clues on his own and learns to rely on them, confusion will result very early. The *tt* will not help the child to differentiate between be*tt*er, le*tt*er, ki*tt*en, ma*tt*er, ba*tt*le, pa*tt*ed, ra*tt*le, and many other words that contain this pattern.

However, paying heed to a whole word is a different matter since the child will see the entire word configuration each time the word is met. Many words should be learned as sight words because:(1) they occur with very high frequency, or(2) they have highly irregular spelling and must be learned as sight words.

Structural Analysis

Using structural analysis, the child gains mastery of a great number of words whose visual patterns are changed as a result of adding
a. Inflectional endings (*s, ed, ing, ly*)
b. Prefixes and suffixes (*ex, pre, un; tent, ment, ous,* etc.)
c. Root to root to form compounds (*sidewalk, farmyard, playground, sailboat*)

Obviously, the use of some of these techniques is predicated on previous learnings. For instance, for a child to use structural analysis in unlocking words with inflectional endings, he must recognize the root word (*help*) as a familiar unit or be able to sound out the root word. Then he solves the ending (*ing*) and blends the two (*helping*). A bit later this type of analysis should be uncalled for since he perceives the word *helping* as one familiar unit.

In applying structural analysis skills to solve unknown words, the child is aided if he recognizes parts of words that he may already have studied. These familiar parts may be roots, inflectional endings, affixes, and the combining elements in compounds. He must also understand that a number of identical letter-units are added either to the front or end of many different words to form new words (*pre, un, re, dis; s, ed, ing, ment, tive, able, ness,* etc.). Exercises which illustrate these frequently-met structural changes are often helpful to the learner. A few teaching examples follow:

1. Adding *s, ed, ing* to words.
   "In the space provided, add *s, ed,* or *ing* to the stimulus word. Then pronounce each word."

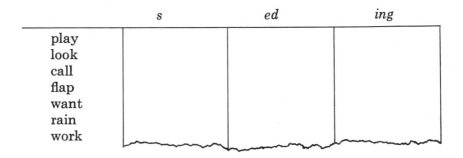

	s	*ed*	*ing*
play			
look			
call			
flap			
want			
rain			
work			

2. Adding *er, est, ly* to words.
   In the space provided add *er, est, ly* to the stimulus word. Then pronounce each word.

	er	*est*	*ly*
warm			
great			
high			
soft			
kind			

3. "In each blank space add a prefix or suffix to make a word." Use: *in, dis, re;* and *ment, able, ness.*

____agree	disagree____	____agree____
____direct	indirect____	____direct____
____fill	refill____	____fill____

4. Working with compounds (different levels of difficulty).

  a. Each line below contains one compound word. Underline the compound word and write it on the blank space at the end of the line.

    1. children   dancing   hotdog   _____
    2. someone   beaches   crawling   _____
    3. alike   mousetrap   puzzle   _____
    4. downpour   happily   permitted   _____
    5. autumn   mistake   handbag   _____

  b. Illustrating how the same word may be used in a number of compound words. Write three compound words for each group of words.

    Example:

air	plane	craft	port
	___	___	___
1. book	case	keeper	worm
	___	___	___
2. door	way	man	mat
	___	___	___
3. candle	light	maker	stick
	___	___	___
4. moon	glow	shot	light
	___	___	___

  c. Complete each sentence by writing a compound word in the blank space.

    1. A player can hit a home run in the game of _____ .
    2. The teacher wrote on the _____ with a piece of chalk.
    3. November 25 is _____ Day.
    4. The front window in a car is called the _____ .
    5. The mail carrier puts mail in our _____ .

5. Working with suffixes.
Read the clue—and add a suffix.
Add a suffix to the italicized word.
The new word must fit the clue.

Examples: clue

a. "full of *fear*" = fearful
b. "has no *fear*" = fearless

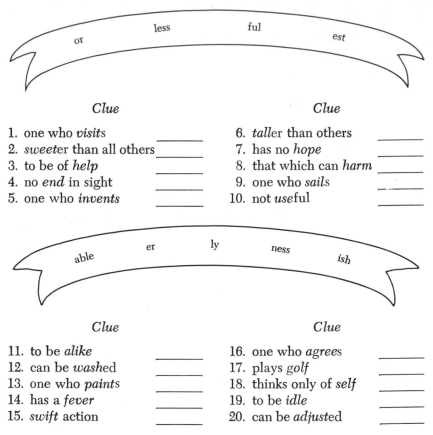

Clue

1. one who *visits* _____
2. *sweeter* than all others _____
3. to be of *help* _____
4. no *end* in sight _____
5. one who *invents* _____

Clue

6. *taller* than others _____
7. has no *hope* _____
8. that which can *harm* _____
9. one who *sails* _____
10. not *use*ful _____

Clue

11. to be *alike* _____
12. can be *wash*ed _____
13. one who *paints* _____
14. has a *fever* _____
15. *swift* action _____

Clue

16. one who *agrees* _____
17. plays *golf* _____
18. thinks only of *self* _____
19. to be *idle* _____
20. can be *adjus*ted _____

Other exercises for developing structural analysis skills are found in chapters dealing with instruction.

Context Clues—Phonic Analysis

A child can use context clues only when he has the ability to recognize or sound out most of the words in a sentence that contains perhaps one unknown word. It should be emphasized that phonics is only one of many skills needed for facile reading. For instance, when a child does not know the meaning of a word, arriving at its *exact* pronunciation through phonic analysis will not help him. In the following sentence there is an unknown symbol:

"The man was attacked by a marbohem."

Everyone reading this page can sound out *mar-bo-hem,* but no one knows what attacked the man since saying *marbohem* does not convey meaning to the reader. Words can be substituted for *marbohem,* and some readers would still have trouble with the meaning even though they successfully analyze the speech sounds in the words. For example:

1. The man was attacked by a peccary.
2. The man was attacked by a freebooter.
3. The man was attacked by an iconoclast.
4. The man was attacked by a fusilier.
5. The man was attacked by a hypochondriac.

Analysis is only a tool for use in the reading process and should not be confused with the process. It is a valuable technique in reading, but is not in itself a method of teaching reading.

Context clues can be useful aids in solving unknown words if the reader demands meaning from what he reads. Context plus a minimal amount of letter analysis focused on the beginning of the words is much superior to context alone. This combination of clues is also much superior to intensive analysis on a word-by-word basis which ignores the contextual setting of the unknown word.

In the following illustrations a blank line is used to represent an unknown word.

"The boy waved goodbye as the train left the _____." Even when the sentence has a blank line substituted for the word, most readers have no problem in supplying the correct word. One would have to strain in order to miscall the unknown word if he heeded the first letter supplied below:

"The boy waved goodbye as the train left the s_____."

Other reading situations will present more difficult problems. For example:

"The girl waved goodbye to her _____."

Here quite a number of possible word choices would make meaning: friend, mother, sister, teacher, brother, parents, family, playmate, aunt, cousin, uncle, etc. Select *any* word that makes meaning and insert only its first letter in the blank space. Note how many of the words that were possibilities are now eliminated when the reader heeds the sound associated with that initial letter.

The efficacy of combining skills is often more dramatically illustrated in larger contexts. In the first version of a story provided below, it is possible to get the sense of the story even if one is not sure of the

identity of a number of the missing words. The second version provides only the initial letter of each missing word.

> John and his Cousin _____ started on their fishing trip. John
> said, "I have my trusty _____ pole, a _____ full of lunch,
> and a can of _____." After walking a long time, John said,
> "Not far from here there is a _____ across the stream. We
> can sit on the _____ and fish." When they started fishing,
> John said, "I'm not going to _____ from this _____ until
> I catch a _____." Finally _____ said, "I am tired of sitting
> on the _____. I am going to take a walk along the _____."
> _____ had walked only a short way when he lost his _____
> and fell into the stream. The water was not very deep and he
> waded out. "Hey," said John, "you're lucky. You won't have to
> take a _____ when we get home."

The version below inserts the initial letter in each unknown word,
which in all cases happens to be the letter *b*.

> John and his Cousin B_ _ started out on their fishing trip. John
> said, "I have my trusty b_ _ _ _ _ pole, a b_ _ full of lunch,
> and a can of b_ _ _." After walking a long time, John said,
> "Not far from here there is a b_ _ _ _ _ across the stream. We
> can sit on the b_ _ _ _ _ and fish." When they started fishing,
> John said, "I'm not going to b_ _ _ _ from this b_ _ _ _ _
> until I catch a b_ _ b_ _ _." Finally B_ _ said, "I am tired of
> sitting on the b_ _ _ _ _. I am going to take a walk along the
> b_ _ _." B_ _ had walked only a short way when he lost his
> b_ _ _ _ _ _ and fell into the stream. The water was not very
> deep and he waded out. "Hey," said John, "you're lucky. You
> won't have to take a b_ _ _ when we get home."*

The preceding discussion emphasized the importance of using
word identification skills in combination. Learning to read is a very
complicated task. From the very beginning, the learner attempting to
identify unfamiliar words should look for and accept help from all
available clues. This simultaneous usage of all options helps simplify
beginning reading. While it is occasionally true that phonics will be the
only key that works, this is not true all of the time. Applying letter-
sound analysis should be held to a minimum.

---

* Words in order of their omission are: Bob, bamboo, bag, bait, bridge, bridge,
budge, bridge, big bass, Bob, bridge, bank, Bob, balance, bath.

Tasks Involved in Phonics Instruction

There is a series of instructional tasks which, taken together, constitute the phonics program. Different phonic teaching materials will include a number of techniques which are common to all approaches. They may differ as to the sequence in which skills are introduced, the emphasis on children learning rules, the number of different steps taught and how much phonics instruction is included in beginning reading. An outline of the major phonics tasks which must be taught would include

1. Auditory discrimination of speech sounds in words.
2. Written letters are used to represent these speech sounds.
3. The sound represented by a letter or letters in a known word can be used to unlock the pronunciation of unknown words in which these particular letters occur.
4. Sounds of consonants.
   a. Initial position in words
   b. Final position in words
5. Consonants which are blended.
6. Special consonant digraphs (*th, ch, sh, wh*).
7. Vowel sounds.
   a. Short vowel sounds
   b. Long vowel sounds
   c. Double vowels
      (1) Digraphs
      (2) Diphthongs
   d. Vowels followed by *r*
   e. Effect of final *e*
   f. Final *y* sounded as long *i*
8. Silent consonants.
9. Syllabication.
10. Accent.

It should not be inferred that each of the above steps is of equal importance in learning to read, or that each should receive the same amount of instructional time. The steps listed are simply the framework, since some steps include many specific tasks. For instance, under syllabication one would deal with such teachings as "prefixes and suffixes are usually syllables; there are as many syllables as sounded vowels; two consonants coming between vowels usually divide (*gar·den*); double consonants usually divide (*let·ter, sum·mer*); the letter combinations *cle, ble, gle, dle, kle,* and *tle* at the ends of words are single syllables." There is no agreement as to the number of such rules or principles that should be taught in the reading process. Even a summary of all the suggestions found in the literature of teaching reading would be beyond the scope of this book.

The actual learning of phonics as it relates to reading usually begins quite early in the preschool years. The child learns a sound like *mommy,* and can easily differentiate it from similar sounds. He may have a pet *kitty* and a playmate *Kathy* and will differentiate if asked "where is *Kathy?*" even though the kitty is also present. Phonics instruction begins when an adult talks with an infant, thus providing the child with a model.

When a child associates sounds with objects and does not confuse sounds that are very similar such as *mommy, money, monkey,* and *maybe,* he is mastering auditory discrimination, which is a prerequisite for phonic analysis in the reading process. None of the later "steps" in learning phonics can take place in the absence of mastery of this basic language function. Beginning reading instruction in the school builds on the child's previous language experiences. In reading, the child will have to make visual discriminations among written word symbols and learn that the written symbols represent the speech sounds of words he speaks and understands.

Brief Review of
Past Practices

Some knowledge of the history of phonics teaching in American education is undoubtedly helpful in understanding the problems, attitudes, and misconceptions observable in education today. The following discussion is a very brief summary of phonic practices advocated in the past.*

Beginning around 1890 and continuing for a period of years, the cornerstone of reading instruction in American schools was a synthetic

---

* The reader who wishes a more detailed account of past practices will find the following sources helpful:

Nila B. Smith, "Phonics Then and Now," *Education* LXXV (1955): 560–65.

W. S. Gray, *On Their Own in Reading* (Chicago: Scott, Foresman & Co., 1948), Chap. 1.

E. A. Betts, "Phonics: Practical Consideration Based on Research," *Elementary English* XXXIII (1956): 357–71.

Nila B. Smith, *American Reading Instruction* (Newark, Del.: International Reading Association, 1965.)

phonics method. Prior to this era, much time was spent on the rote learning of the ABC's. Apparently, it was believed that unknown words could be identified by saying the names of the letters which comprised these words.

Rebecca Pollard's "synthetic method," introduced about 1890 (22), advocated reducing reading to a number of mechanical procedures, each of which focused on a unit smaller than a word. Reading became very mechanistic and, when mastered, often produced individuals who were adept at working their way through a given word. The result among both teachers and pupils was that reading became equated with "facility in calling words." A few of the teaching procedures recommended during this period included

Isolation of sounds. Drills in articulation were to precede any attempt at reading. The child was to drill on the "sounds of letters." Then he would be able, it was reasoned, to attack whole words. This was a form of phonics drill unrelated to meaning and in some instances unrelated to words in English. Children drilled on isolated sounds as illustrated below:

da	*ha*	*la*	*ma*	*pa*	*ra*
be	*se*	*te*	*ne*	*le*	*re*
pi	*mi*	*ti*	*si*	*li*	*ri*

This drill was not in context with reading, since the drills preceded the child's learning of words. It is easy to see that this type of introduction placed little, if any, emphasis on reading as a process of discovering meaning.

Single consonants were "sounded." Each consonant was given a sound equivalent to a syllable. Thus *b, c, d, p, h,* and *t* were sounded *buh, cuh, duh, puh, huh,* and *tuh.*

Use of diacritical marks. Diacritical markings were widely used in beginning instructional materials. Children also practiced "marking sentences" by inserting diacritical marks which parallel the usage found in their instructional materials, for example:

The gh̆ost wăs ā cŏmmŏn sigh̆t near the wreck. He knew the ῑsl̆and was ĕmpty.

Different diacritical marking systems varied as to the number of signs employed. Undoubtedly a few such "helpers" would be more effective than adding a great number of these signals, since they do drastically change the orthography. In the sentence marked above, the slant lines indicate letters that are not sounded; the Macron (–) signals a long vowel sound; the breve (◡) a short vowel sound. Other markings might be underlining digraphs which represent one sound (*church*) and underlining single consonants which represent an "irregular sound" such as hi*s* (s = z); *c*ity (c = s) or *g*ym (g = j).

Word family drills. Drill on word families was stressed. This was unrelated to meaning. Sometimes children memorized lists of words ending in such common family phonograms as *ill, am, ick, ate, old, ack.*

A number of widely used reading texts adopted the suggestions of Pollard and, in many cases, extended them. For instance, if the objective of a unit was to teach the phonogram or "family" *ick*, a story might be built primarily from words in that family, without regard to meaning or lack of it in the passage. The following example is illustrative and, it is hoped, exaggerated.

Nick, flick the tick from the chick with a stick. Prick the tick from the chick with a thick stick. Nick, do not kick the brick, kick the stick.

The discerning reader will see the close relationship between this practice and one of the linguistic approaches to beginning reading which has recently enjoyed widespread publicity.

It is not implied that teaching word families is an indefensible practice, but rather that some practices seem to have more merit than others. Drill on a column of words entirely unrelated to meaningful reading might be a poor learning technique. On the other hand, when children have learned the words *make* and *take* as sight words, and they meet the new word *lake* in a reading exercise, it would not be poor instruction to point out that this word, and certain others whose meanings are known, contain the common letters *ake* which in every case represent the same speech sound (*cake, bake, wake, snake, rake, shake*).

There is little point in opposing the teaching of "family groups" on the basis that a relatively small number of English words contain these families. This is not a sound argument because so many small, often used words *are* formed from some thirty such families, and these words are among those most frequently occurring in beginning reading materials (specifically such families as *an, at, it, am, in, as, ate, ake, et, ick, eat, arm, en, ing, ot, est, un, all, ell,* and *ame*). There are enough common or service words which are *not* phonetic to be learned as sight words that any clue, such as word families, that a child can pick up early in learning to read can be useful.

Wylie and Durrell (31) report that "whole phonograms are more easily identified by first-grade children than the separate vowels contained in the phonograms, suggesting that the recognition unit is the phonogram rather than the separate vowel." They report that approximately fifteen hundred primary grade words include ending phonograms which contain a stable vowel sound.

Finding little words in big words. Since some of the regular spelling families are also words (*am, is, and, ate, an, all, old, it, at, eat*), the practice of "looking for small words in large words" was advocated. The justification for this practice was that the little words were familiar to the child, and he could pronounce them. If he found little words he knew in larger unknown words, he had a start toward mastering the unknown larger word.

The procedure of looking for small words in larger words fails for two reasons. First, there is little logic in having the child see the word *ill* in the monosyllabic words *will, Bill, fill, mill, kill,* and *pill,* unless it is the association of *ill* with *pill,* which leaves much to be desired. In teaching reading today, the clue will not be the word *ill* but the sound of *ill* in conjunction with the sounds of various initial letters: *w, b, f, m, g, k, p,* and *h.*

The second charge against finding little words appears to be so serious as to remove the practice from the list of justifiable procedures. Many of the little words which retain some degree of pronounceable autonomy in single-syllable words lose this characteristic in words of more than one syllable. In *pan, can, man, fan, tan, ran* or in *ham, jam, Sam,* noting the little words *an* and *am* would not destroy the pronunciation of the words. However, seeing or pronouncing the *am* in *among, amend, amen, amuse, amass* would prevent a correct phonic analysis. Likewise, seeing or saying the word *as* in *ashore, Asia, aside, asleep; it* in *item; at* in *atomic* and *athlete;* or *all* in *allow* or *allege* would hinder attempts at word analysis.

The total emphasis on phonics brought the method into disrepute during the 1920s. Reform was not advocated, but rather the discarding of the teaching of phonics. It was commonly alleged that the abuses of phonics teaching were responsible for the reading problems found at that time. Thus, what was *pre*scribed at one moment was *pro*scribed the next.

Teaching Consonant Sounds

Why Begin with Consonant Sounds? A large majority of instructional materials used in beginning reading advocate that the teaching

Learning to read is not effortless,
but it must not become a grind.
Balance the drill with the magic of
language.

of letter sounds begin with consonants. This position is supported by
the following factors:

1. A number of consonants (*b, f, d, h, j, k, p, m, l, r, t,* etc.) have only
   one sound. Once the child masters these letter-sound associations,
   this skill can be transferred in attacking other words in which these
   letters occur. On the other hand, vowels in written words are notori-
   ously inconsistent as to the sound they represent.
2. Children must learn to read from left-to-right. Since most English
   words begin with consonants, the first letter or letters a child must
   sound out in an unknown word will be consonants.
3. If a reader uses context along with sounding, the initial sound in the
   word helps eliminate most alternative possibilities. To illustrate,
   each of the following blank lines represents an unknown word.
   a. _____
   b. n_____
   The blank space in (a) can represent any word in English, while in
   (b) *all* words which do not begin with the *n* sound are eliminated.
   Below, each sentence contains a different unknown word. It is likely
   that the one-sentence context and the initial consonant will permit
   you to solve the unknown word. Larger contexts would make the
   task easier.
   c. "Pull that n_____ out of the board," said Grandfather.

d. "What's the n_____ of that song?" asked Mary. "It's on the n_____ record I bought yesterday."

e. "The big right hander struck out in the last of the n_____."

The rationale for introducing vowel sounds first rests on the following assumptions. These have been gleaned from writings favorable to this practice and represent all of the justification this writer has found to date.

1. All words contain one or more vowels.
2. Vowels provide more important clues to pronunciation of words.
3. Consonants are blended with vowels and thus should not be sounded in isolation.

At first glance the above statements appear to have validity, but upon analysis they are seen to be relatively weak arguments. One might reverse the first statement and say, "all words contain consonants," but this is not a reason for teaching either consonants or vowels first. In the following sentence all consonant clues are removed:

$$\_e\_ \_ \_ \_y \_o \_ou\_ \_ \_ \_e\_e \_o\_ \_ \_$$

It would be a most difficult task to decipher the preceding sentence. The following sentence shows consonants and omits vowels.

$$L\_t's \ tr\_ \ t\_ \ s\_ \_nd \ th\_s\_ \ w\_rds.$$

Reading this sentence is a much simpler task. Many other samples could be cited and the result would be to cast doubt on the premise that vowels provide the most important clues to pronunciation.

In regard to the third point above, *neither* consonants nor vowels should be sounded in isolation (*cat* = kah-ah-tuh). Since no instructional materials advocate sounding letters in isolation, the statement has little relevancy as an argument for teaching vowels first. It should be kept in mind that one of the most important clues to the sounds of vowels is provided by consonants which follow vowels. A consonant-vowel-consonant pattern usually results in a short vowel sound—*cat, den, can*. The same is true if the vowel is followed by two consonants (*cattle, dentist, canvas*).

Teaching Initial Consonant Sounds

Starting from the premise that the child has learned to recognize a few words, which for illustrative purposes we will assume includes any of the words *be, back,* or *ball,* he is now ready to associate the sound of *b* in these words with the written symbol *b.*

The teacher prints a capital *B* on the chalkboard and says, "Today we will learn all about the letter *B.* Next to the big *B* I will print a little *b.* This big *B* is called a capital *B.* Now I am going to write some words which begin with little *b.*" (She writes *be, back,* and *ball.*) "Who can give us another word that begins with the *b* sound? Yes, *bear, boat, big—Bobby* we write with a large (or capital) *B* because it is somebody's name."

B b
be
back
ball
boat
Bobby

When a number of examples have been given, the teacher asks, "What do we notice about the sound of each of these words?" "That's right, they all begin with the sound of *b—bear, ball, boat, bat, big, bomb.*" As the words are called out by the children, they are added to the list on the board and the teacher asks, "What do we *see* that is the same in all of these words? That's right, they all begin with *b.*" It should be noted that in no instance were the children asked to sound the letter *b* in isolation, although it may have been emphasized without distortion.

In addition to the group work just described, there will be workbook exercises giving each child an opportunity to do seatwork which parallels the concept taught. These exercises use both visual stimuli and sounds associated with pictures, letters, and words. A few typical examples are:

1. In the row of pictures below, the child is to mark those objects whose names begin with the same sound as the name of the object in the picture on the extreme left.

Figure 17

2. A picture of a familiar object is shown along with the word represented by the object in the picture. The example is a bell (Figure 18). Here the child can see and hear the *b* sound. He is then to mark all the other words in a supplied list which begin with the same sound.

bell

be	play
lake	boat
book	

Figure 18

3. Figure 19 shows a series of words in columns, some of which begin with the same sound and the same letter. The child is to draw a line from the word in column *A* to the word in column *B* which begins with the same sound.

A   B   A   B

me   be   big   did
ball   said   dog   but
sail   make   car   call

Figure 19

A word of caution should be injected here to point out that many exercises found in workbooks which aim to provide auditory practice can result in nothing but visual discrimination exercises, unless the teacher is careful to see that each child actually *sounds* the word symbols which are given as stimuli. To illustrate, the following exercise is patterned after Figure 19 and can be correctly marked using only visual clues. Incorporating auditory practice would require associating sounds with each initial symbol.

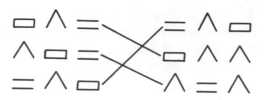

Figure 20

4. A pictured object is shown, followed by four words, none of which stand for the picture, but one or more of which begin with the same sound as the name of the pictured object.

| house | baby | cup | bath |

Figure 21

5. A series of boxes is shown, each containing three words. The teacher pronounces one of the words and the pupil underlines the word pronounced. (See Figure 22.) He need not know all of the words as sight words, provided he is familiar with the initial sound of each. In the following example, the teacher could pronounce *bank, tell, bill, may, bat.* There are many other types of exercises and many variations of those illustrated.

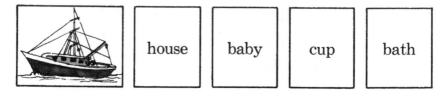

1	2	3	4	5
call	*tell*	hill	*may*	hat
bank	sell	fill	pay	show
play	fell	*bill*	say	*bat*

Figure 22

**Substitution of
Initial Sounds**

The next important skill to be learned is to substitute known letter sounds in attacking unknown words. Assume the child knows the words *take* and *make* and meets the unknown word *rake*. He should be able to combine the *r* sound (which he knows in words like *run, rain,* or *ride*), with the sound of *ake* in *take*. By this process of "thinking the sounds," he should unlock the new word (16). If the reader has mastered the steps in phonics previously introduced, this step also starts from that which is known, i.e., sight words and the sounds initial consonants contribute to words.

In beginning reading it is a common practice to teach a number of monosyllabic words which contain frequently used phonograms. Practically all workbooks use these "word families" as a means of teaching new words. Work on the substitution of initial consonants parallels the primers and first readers. Moving through the primer, the child meets such words as *back, came, day, fun, gate, hand, just, king, lake, met, not, pin, rest, sun, tall,* and *wet*. Each of these words contains a familiar and often occurring phonogram. Children should not receive drill on these word endings in isolation (*ack, ame, ay, ate, est, ust, ing, ake, ot, in, un, all, et*). Nevertheless, a number of important words can be solved independently when the child knows some sight words containing often used letter combinations and can substitute initial letter sounds.

Figure 23 illustrates how pictures may be used in teaching letter-sound substitutions.

Name the picture.
Listen to the first sound in the picture name.
Write the letter that represents this sound.

Figure 23

Substitution of
Single Consonant Sounds
at the Ends of Words

Some teachers prefer to teach consonant sounds at the ends of words at the same time that they deal with a particular initial consonant sound. Other teachers work through the initial sounds and then work on single consonant sounds at the ends of words. Regardless of which procedure is followed, the child is taught to notice visually and auditorily the final consonants in short words. He knows words such as *men, log, pen, bold, leg* and the sounds of letters, including *t.* He is now asked to substitute the *t* sound at the end of the words to get *met, lot, pet, bolt,* and *let.*

Initial
Blends

In dealing with many words that the child will meet early in the process of learning to read, sounding only the initial consonant will result in confusion. These words fall into two classes: simple consonant blends, and a smaller group of two-consonant combinations representing special speech sounds in English (*th, sh, ch, wh*).

The twenty-five two- and three-letter blends may be divided into three major groups on the basis of a common letter:

1. Those which begin with *s: sc, sk, sm, sn, sp, st, sw, str*
2. Those which conclude with *l: bl, cl, fl, gl, pl, sl, spl*
3. Those which conclude with *r: br, cr, dr, fr, gr, pr, tr, scr, spr, str*

The above arrangement is not intended to suggest a particular order in which blends should be taught. A logical sequence would probably be determined by the vocabulary found in the instructional materials actually used in beginning reading.

There is a great deal of variance among teachers as well as among basal readers as to (a) when blends are dealt with, (b) which are taught first, and (c) how rapidly the blends are covered. Most materials suggest teaching initial blends first and later stressing blends and special consonant sounds at the ends of words (chur*ch*, tra*sh*, che*st*, che*ck*, fla*sh*, fre*sh*, fro*st*, smoo*th*, whi*ch*, thi*ck*). While there are numerous approaches for teaching consonant blends, the objectives of all methods are to lead the child

1. To see the printed letters involved.
2. To understand that in every instance the letter sounds combine into a blended sound.
3. To discriminate auditorily among the sound of individual letters and blends—*d*ug, *r*ug, *dr*ug; *s*old, *c*old, *sc*old.

Any procedure for teaching initial consonant sounds can be utilized for teaching each of the different consonant blends. A few techniques are illustrated next.

1. Secure a number of pictures of concrete objects whose names begin with a blend. Show the pictures one at a time and have the children write, or say orally, the blended letters. (They are not to simply name the picture.) Examples: *sk*ate, *tr*ain, *br*idge, *pl*ate, *gr*apes, *sl*ed, *fr*og, *cl*ock, *st*ar, *bl*anket, *sn*ake, *st*ore, *pl*ow, *cl*own, *sw*ing, *sch*ool.
2. Prepare and duplicate a series of sentences which contain a number of blends. Have pupils underline each blend.
   a. The *bl*ack *cr*ow *fl*ew away *fr*om the *tr*ee.
   b. *Pr*etty *br*ight *fl*owers *gr*ew near the *br*idge.
   c. What is the *pr*ice of the *gr*een *dr*ess in the *st*ore window?
   d. We will re*st* when we reach the coa*st* about du*sk*.
3. Add one of the letters *c, g, p, t* in front of each word to produce a consonant blend. Underline the letters which blend .

__reat	__roud	__rain	__rop
__reek	__rail	__rice	__ruly
__rint	__reen	__row	__rize
__rip	__rack	__ree	__rand

4. *Step 1.* Place on the chalkboard a list of words which begin with *p* and to which *s* can be added as a first letter to form the *sp* blend. Pronounce these words with the children.

   Step 2. Write the *sp* blend word to the right of each word. Have the children note the visual pattern *sp* at the beginning of each word. Guide the children in pronouncing the two words in each pair in rapid succession and in noting the

Step 1	*Step 2*
pot	spot
pin	spin
pill	spill
peak	speak
pool	spool
poke	spoke
park	spark

blended sound in the second word in each pair (*p*in = *sp*in; *p*ot = *sp*ot, etc.).

Most of the other initial blends can be handled in much the same manner. Illustrative word pairs with *tr:* race–*tr*ace; *r*ain–*tr*ain; *r*ip–*tr*ip; *r*ust–*tr*ust; *r*ap–*tr*ap; *r*ail–*tr*ail; *r*ay–*tr*ay, etc. In teaching *sl:* *l*id–*sl*id; *l*ap–*sl*ap; *l*ip–*sl*ip; *l*ed–*sl*ed; *l*ow–*sl*ow; *l*ack–*sl*ack; *l*ick–*sl*ick.

5. Use "reading clues" in teaching initial blends. Write the blend that spells the word that fits the clue. Examples:

             clue

  a. "think with it:" _ _ain (br)

  b. "mountain side:" _ _eep (st)

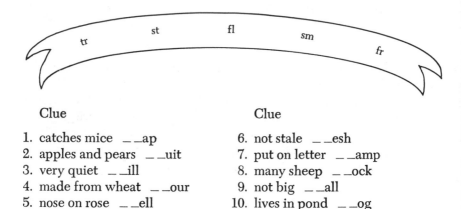

Clue

1. catches mice _ _ap
2. apples and pears _ _uit
3. very quiet _ _ill
4. made from wheat _ _our
5. nose on rose _ _ell

Clue

6. not stale _ _esh
7. put on letter _ _amp
8. many sheep _ _ock
9. not big _ _all
10. lives in pond _ _og

Teaching Consonant Digraphs

A digraph is a combination of two letters which when pronounced results in one speech sound. This sound is not a blend of the two letters. Some digraphs have more than one sound (*ch* = *k* in character; *sh* in chiffon; *ch* in church). Techniques used in teaching consonants and blends and the illustration of teaching *ch* which follows will apply to teaching other digraphs.

Teaching the Sound of ch and sh

1. a. Place words beginning with *ch* on the board.
   b. Direct children's attention to these initial letters.
   c. Pronounce each word, inviting pupils to *listen* to the sound of *ch* in each word.
   d. In pronouncing, emphasize but do not distort the *ch* sound.
   e. Have pupils pronounce words.

Ch

chair
child
chance

f. Ask class to provide other words which begin with the *ch* sound heard in *chair, child,* etc.

2. Contrast single initial consonant sounds and initial digraph sounds in words.

    Place words shown in Column A on the chalkboard and pronounce these words with the children.

    Next, write the words in Column B, inviting children to note the visual pattern *sh* at the beginning of each word. Have the children pronounce each pair of words (*hip–ship*) to contrast the initial sounds in each pair of words.

A	B
hip	ship
hop	shop
hot	shot
hark	shark
hare	share
harp	sharp

3. The procedure outlined above may be used with words that begin with *s* or *sh*.

    As the children contrast the initial sound in the words in each pair they note the visual pattern (*s–sh*) and hear the initial sound represented by these letters.

sell	shell
sort	short
sip	ship
save	shave
self	shelf
sock	shock

4. Use "reading clues" in teaching initial digraphs. Read the clue—spell the word by adding a digraph. Example:

    a. Part of leg—rhymes with *chin:* _ _in (sh)

    b. Doesn't cost much: _ _eap (ch)

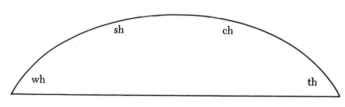

Clue

1. used in bread _ _eat
2. find on seashore _ _ell
3. can sit on it _ _air
4. never do it! _ _eat
5. use your head _ _ink

Clue

6. not open _ _ut
7. largest in ocean _ _ ale.
8. not fat _ _in
9. sun can do it _ _ine
10. must be round _ _eel

At a later time children will be taught that

ch = *k*: *ch*orus, *ch*emistry, *ch*rome, *ch*aracter.
ch = *sh*: *ch*auffeur, *ch*amois, *ch*ef, *Ch*icago.
Other frequently met digraphs include *sh, wh, th, gh, ng, ph*. The sounds of these letter combinations are:

sh = Sound heard in *sh*oe, *sh*op, *sh*ell, *sh*ort, wi*sh*, fi*sh*.
wh = *hw:* when—*hw*en; wheel—*hw*eel; which—*hw*ich.
wh followed by *o*, the *w* is silent: whole—*h*ole; whose—*h*ooz; whom—
*h*oom.
th = two sounds, voiced: *th*em, *th*ere, *th*ey, wi*th*.
    voiceless: *th*in, *th*ree, *th*row, wid*th*.
gh = sound of *f* in: lau*gh*, tou*gh*, cou*gh*, etc.
    silent in: ni*gh*t, bou*gh*, ei*gh*t, thou*gh*t, etc.
ng = sounded as in: sa*ng*, wi*ng*, so*ng*, ru*ng*.
ph = usually sounded as *f: ph*one, ne*ph*ew, gra*ph*.

Teaching Vowel-letter Sounds

Vowels are the worst offenders in any audit of grapheme-phoneme irregularities. Regardless of these irregularities, mastering letter-sound relationships is absolutely essential. The function of the teacher and school is to provide guidance, and most children gain proficiency in phonic analysis more quickly and more surely with guidance that leads to insights. To require rote memorization of a great number of rules will hinder some children in understanding the relationship between the rule and their reading. They may become so involved with learning the rules that they miss the application. On the other hand, having a generalization verbalized is often a help to learning.

Short Vowel Sounds

Techniques for teaching letter-sound relationships are unlimited. Each illustration presented will deal with only one vowel-letter sound since all of the other vowel sounds can be taught in the same manner simply by changing stimulus words. Practically any lesson can be presented via the chalkboard, overhead projector, or on duplicated pages for seatwork.

1. Visual-auditory association (illustration using short ĕ). (a) Select a few easy words which have been used previously and which contain the vowel pattern being taught. (b) Write these words in a column and pronounce each word with the children. (c) Have children note the vowel letter in the middle of the word and emphasize the sound it represents in *met, set, pet,* etc.

The efficient reader varies his rate
of reading to fit the reading terrain.

The material below might constitute three different presentations
on different days. Column A contains one pattern CVC words, Column
B mixed patterns, and Column C longer words.

A	B	C
met	leg	desk
set	men	bell
pet	bed	dress
bet	pep	sled
let	wet	best
jet	hen	help

2. *Discriminating rhyming elements* (illustration using short ă). Pronounce pairs of words selected so that the first word in each pair contains the short sound of ă. The second word either rhymes with the
first or differs only in the vowel sound. As a pair of words is pronounced,
children tell whether the words rhyme (both contain ă) or whether the
vowel sounds differ.

268   Foundations for Teaching Reading

Stimulus word-pairs	Children's responses
map–cap	Both have the short sound of ă.
rag–rug	Different vowel sounds.
dad–mad	etc.
pat–sat	etc.
hat–hit (tag–bag, fan–fun,	
dad–did, man–can, had–hid,	
pan–ran, bat–bet, bag–tag, etc.)	

3. *Reviewing all short vowel sounds.* Pronounce stimulus words, each of which contains a short vowel sound. Call on a volunteer to repeat the word, name a rhyming word, and identify the vowel sound heard in the two words.

Stimulus-word	Illustrative children's responses
mop	mop–hop have the short o sound.
bug	bug–rug have the short u sound.
wig	wig–pig have the short i sound.
set	set–met have the short e sound.
had	had–bad have the short a sound.

4. *Contrasting short vowel sounds in words.*
   a. Write a column of identical initial and final consonants leaving a blank space for adding a vowel letter (Step 1).
   b. Insert a vowel letter to complete the first word; call on a volunteer to name the word.
   c. Continue using a different vowel letter for each blank space.
   d. When the column is complete, have the children read the words in rapid succession to contrast the vowel sounds.

   Example:

Step 1	Step 2 (Insert vowel)	Step 3 (Children name word)	Step 4
b_g	(i)	big	(Pronounce the
b_g	(e)	beg	series of words
b_g	(u)	bug	in rapid succession)
b_g	(a)	bag	

Other stimulus patterns: (bud bid bad bed; pan pun pin pen; pat pet pit pot; hut hit hot hat).

5. *Working with final phonograms.* Have children name the picture, then blend the initial letter (shown beneath the picture) with each of

the phonograms at the right of the picture. Student then writes the correct letter pattern on the blank spaces to complete the naming word.

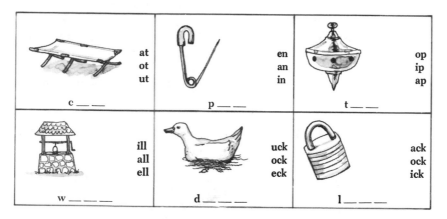

at ot ut	en an in	op ip ap	
c _ _	p _ _	t _ _	
ill all ell	uck ock eck	ack ock ick	
w _ _ _	d _ _ _	l _ _ _	

6. *Using sentence context.* Prepare simple sentences each of which contains a blank space. Each sentence is followed by two words which differ only as to vowel letter. One of these words fits in the sentence. If done orally via the chalkboard, a child *names* and *spells* the correct word which is then written in the blank space to complete the sentence. (If the exercise is seatwork, the child reads both words and then writes the correct word in the blank space.)

Example sentences:

1. The cat drank milk from the _____ .   (cap/cup)
2. Tom hit the ball with the _____ .   (bat/bit)
3. The _____ was in the pen.   (peg/pig)
4. We have _____ fingers.   (tin/ten)
5. John had a _____ of candy.   (bag/bug)

Long Vowel Sounds

Generalizations covering vowel letter-sound relationships are quite numerous. Illustrative teaching procedures will be cited for two adjacent vowels (*ea, ai, ee, oa* patterns), effect of final *e*, long vowel sounds at the end of short words, and vowels followed by consonant controllers, and diphthongs.

Adjacent Vowels (*same syllable*)

When two adjacent vowels represent a single sound they are referred to as vowel digraphs (*feet, boat, sail, mean*). One of the more widely quoted generalizations relates to vowel digraphs. "When two vowels come together they usually represent the long vowel sound of the first vowel," or "the first vowel has its long sound and the second is not sounded." When this rule is applied to all two-vowel situations, there are about as many exceptions as instances where it applies. Clymer found this rule to apply less than half the time in the sample he tested (10). However, he also reported that for specific vowel situations it holds much more frequently. For instance, words containing *ee* (98 percent), *oa* (97 percent), *ea* (66 percent), *ai* (64 percent).

Contrast single-double vowel patterns. Prepare lists of words selected so that the first has a single vowel (m*e*t), the second is identical except for an added vowel (m*ea*t).

Children read the first word under A and listen for the short-vowel sound. Then they read the first word under B, note the two-vowel pattern and listen for the long vowel sound.

As a final step, read each pair in rapid succession to note the contrasting vowel sound (met–meat; led–lead, etc.).

A	B	A	B	A	B
e	*ea*	*a*	*ai*	*e*	*ee*
met	meat	man	main	fed	feed
led	lead	lad	laid	met	meet
men	mean	pal	pail	pep	peep
bed	bead	ran	rain	bet	beet
stem	steam	bat	bait	wed	weed
set	seat	plan	plain	step	steep

Words containing *o–oa*: cot–coat; got–goat; rod–road; cost–coast.

Different visual patterns represent the same sound. Prepare lists of homonyms in which one word in each pair contains either the *ai* or *a–e* pattern. Other pairs contain either the *ea* or *ee* pattern.

The following exercise may be used for group work at the chalkboard or duplicated for independent seat work.

Two words may sound alike
but not be spelled alike

Are these words		Spelled alike? (Yes/No)	Pronounced alike? (Yes/No)	Vowel Sound you hear
1	2			
sail	sale	_____	_____	_____
weak	week	_____	_____	_____
heel	heal	_____	_____	_____
made	maid	_____	_____	_____

pail	pale	_____	_____	_____
beet	beat	_____	_____	_____
plain	plane	_____	_____	_____
steel	steal	_____	_____	_____

Association of long vowel sounds with letter patterns. Line A shows picture and three words which differ only as to vowel pattern. Child pronounces words and circles the naming word. Line B shows series of pictures and vowel patterns. Children name each picture; then blend each set of vowels (shown at right of picture) with letters shown below it. The correct vowel pattern is then written on the blank spaces to complete the naming word.

Recognizing different vowel patterns as rhyming elements. Prepare a number of four-word series each of which includes two rhyming words with different spelling patterns.

Underline the two words that rhyme

boat	not	note	both
can't	cane	ran	rain
met	feet	seat	felt
sail	tall	walk	whale
sold	soap	rose	rope
paid	made	path	hand
while	well	wheel	meal
pain	plan	plane	land

The Effect of Final e

1. Write a column of CVC words on the chalk-board, each of which contains the medial vowel *a*.

Step 1	Step 2
can	cane

(Step 1) As these words are pronounced have the children tell which vowel sound they hear in the words (ă).

hat	hate
mad	made
pal	pale
rat	rate
plan	plane

Explain that you will change each word by adding the letter *e* at the end of each word (print the words shown in Step 2).

As these words are pronounced, have the children note the *a–e* pattern and tell the vowel sound heard in each of the words (ā).

Have the children explain what vowel sound they hear in words with two vowels when one is a final *e*. Their explanations may then be restated, "In many short words showing two vowels, a final *e* is not sounded while the first vowel has its long sound."

Word pairs for other final *e* series: bit–bite, pin–pine, hid–hide, kit–kite, rid–ride, slid–slide; not–note, hop–hope, rod–rode, rob–robe.

2. Prepare an exercise for either chalkboard presentation or independent seatwork. Supply a list of CVC words some of which can be changed to another word by adding a final *e*.

Children read the stimulus word and "think the long vowel sound" to determine if this will make a known word. The word is named (if an oral exercise) or they write the word on the space provided.

Directions. If the word can be changed into another word by adding a final *e*, write the new word on the line provided. If adding an *e* does not make a word, leave the line blank.

can ____		hid ____	
rat ____		sob ____	*
top ____	*	mad ____	
plan ____		bit ____	
kit ____		not ____	
hop ____		tap ____	
cat ____	*	rob ____	
cut ____		big ____	*

(*spaces left blank)

Exceptions to final e rule. A number of high frequency *final e* words do not follow the rule and these irregularities should be pointed out to children. The material which follows focuses on these exceptions.

According to the rule, words under A and B should have a long vowel sound. Each pair of words should rhyme since they end with the same letters. One of the words is an outlaw and will not follow the rule. Write the outlaw word in the box.

A	B	Do they rhyme?	Outlaws
some	home	____	some
brave	have	____	
move	stove	____	
bone	done	____	
wove	love	____	
give	hive	____	
come	dome	____	
cone	gone	____	
none	tone	____	

Long Vowel Sounds at the End of Short Words

There are two generalizations which cover single vowels at the end of words: "If a word has only one vowel which ends the word, the vowel sound usually is long;" and, "If a word has no other vowel and ends with *y*, the letter *y* serves as a vowel and is pronounced as long *i*." These generalizations apply in a limited number of high frequency words and can be taught at the chalkboard using columns of words.

be	by	try	go
me	my	sky	no
he	cry	fly	so
we	why	fry	ho
she	dry	shy	yo-yo

Vowel Affected by Particular Consonants

The long and short vowel sounds are by far the most important vowel clues in helping children unlock the pronunciation of words. In addition, there are other vowel situations which should be explained, even though they may be of lesser importance in phonic analysis. When a vowel is followed by *r*, the sound of that vowel is affected by the *r*.

Usually a blend results, which is neither the long nor the short sound of the vowel (*car, curl, fir, for, park*). When the vowel *a* is followed by *l* or *w*, the resultant sound is a blend (*awl, tall, awful, talcum, awning, ball*).

While a number of words contain a vowel followed by *r*, it is debatable whether this particular letter-sound combination causes beginning readers much trouble. That is, if children master the long and short vowel relationships they are not likely to experience serious trouble with vowels followed by *r*. Undoubtedly there are many successful readers who are unaware of the difference between the vowel sounds in the words *can* and *car*.

Diphthongs

Diphthongs are two adjacent vowels, each of which is sounded, as the *ou* in *house*, *oi* in *oil*, *oy* in *boy*, *ow* in *how* (but not the *ow* in *blow, grow, throw,* or *sow,* where the sound is long *o*). It is doubtful that teaching diphthongs is of major importance in the total phonics program. These sounds are met in a number of words that are learned as sight words, and certain of these words can serve as key words to help the pupil hear the sound (*house, oil, boy, how*).

1. To teach that the visual pattern *ow* has two sounds, place two columns of words on the board. In column B the *ow* represents long *o;* in Column A the *ow* is a diphthong.

	A	B
Have children note that words in a column rhyme, but that words under A do not rhyme with those under B.	now	low
	how	snow
	cow	grow
	plow	blow

2. Write some three-word series and have the children identify the two words that rhyme.

1. plow	cow	slow	4. grown	clown	brown
2. snow	now	grow	5. crow	cow	low
3. how	now	low	6. clown	own	down

3. Write several columns of words selected so that each word contains the same diphthong and represents the same sound. Have the children read the words in unison, noting the visual pattern and sound represented.

oil	out	saw	boy
boil	mouth	jaw	joy
soil	south	law	Roy

to*i*l	sh*ou*t	p*aw*	t*oy*
sp*oi*l	f*ou*nd	r*aw*	

The Schwa
Sound

In a large number of words of more than one syllable, there is a diminished stress on one of the syllables. The sound of the vowel in these unstressed syllables undergoes a slight change which is referred to as "a softening of the vowel sound." This softened vowel sound is called the *schwa* sound, and is represented by the symbol ə.

All of the vowels are represented by the schwa sound as illustrated by each of the italicized vowels in the following words.

bedl*a*m = bed′ ləm
beat*e*n = bēt′ ən
beaut*i*f*u*l = bū′ tə fəl
beck*o*n = bek′ ən

In other words, if vowels were interchanged in unstressed syllables, the spellings would change but the sound heard would remain the same for the different vowels. For instance, read both of the following sentences without stressing the second syllable in any word.

a. "Button, button, who has the button?"
b. "Buttun, buttan, who has the butten?"

If, in reading sentence b you give each second syllable the same stress as it was given in the word directly above it, the sounds remain constant. Thus, teaching the schwa sound in the initial stages of reading would have little impact on one's ability to sound out words. However, once the child begins to use a dictionary which utilizes the schwa symbol, ə, the points discussed above would have to be explained.*

Summary of Rules
Related to Vowel Sounds

1. A single vowel followed by a consonant in a word or syllable usually has the short sound: *can* or *cancel.*

---

*From Arthur W. Heilman, *Phonics in Proper Perspective*, 3rd ed. (Columbus, Ohio: Charles E. Merrill Publishing Co., 1976), p. 76.

2. A single vowel which concludes a word or syllable usually has the long sound (*me, ti ger, lo co mo tive*).
3. In the vowel digraphs *oa, ea, ee, ai, ay,* the first vowel is usually long and the second is silent (*coat, reap, bead, wait, play*). The digraphs *oo, au,* and *ew* form a single sound which is not the long sound of the first vowel (*food, good, haul, few*).
4. In words containing two vowels, one of which is final *e,* the final *e* is usually silent and the preceding vowel is long.
5. Single vowels followed by *r* usually result in a blend sound (*fir, car, burn, fur*). The vowel *a* followed by *l* or *w* usually results in a blend sound (*awl, tall, claw, awful*).
6. The letter *y* at the end of words containing no other vowel has the long sound of *i* (*my, try, sky, shy*).
7. Diphthongs are two-vowel combinations in which both vowels contribute to the speech sound (h*ou*se, b*oy*, c*ow*).

Syllabication

A syllable is a vowel, or group of letters containing a vowel, which is pronounced as a unit. A child must be able to break unknown polysyllabic words into syllables if he is to approximate the pronunciation of these words. This ability grows out of knowing both the structural and the phonetic features of words. Children usually learn a number of one-syllable root words prior to meeting polysyllabic words. As they meet longer words, they learn that most prefixes and suffixes and some inflectional endings constitute syllables. During the child's early experience with high frequency affixes, he breaks the word into parts and then combines the parts into the whole: *re* read *ing, pre* heat *ed, bi* week *ly, dis* appear *ance.* After many experiences, he reduces his reliance on this type of analysis, and the blending of the parts into the whole becomes much smoother.

Providing Practice in Hearing Syllables

A series of pictures may be used to help children develop the ability to distinguish syllables in words. In Figure 24, the picture name is pronounced and the child circles the number that matches the number of syllables heard.

A knowledge of vowel behavior within words is the second major aid in breaking words into syllables. The sounds of vowels and letter combinations are not as consistent as prefixes and suffixes. Nevertheless,

Figure 24

many phonetic generalizations are useful. Although the following examples are not words, the letter combinations can be broken into syllables:
comration, ragmotex, obsebong, fasnotel. The likely syllabication is:
com·ra·tion, rag·mo·tex, ob·se·bong, fas·no·tel. Most facile readers
would pronounce these nonsense words in substantially the same way.
These readers probably would not recite rules to themselves before
attempting to pronounce the above words, but they would probably
be subconsciously influenced by rules they had learned.

When generalizations applicable to syllabication are taught, children should be provided with a number of examples and then led to
see for themselves what happens. Out of this experience, rules can develop. Starting with the question, "What usually happens when two
consonants come between vowels?" the teacher can place on the board
a number of words such as:

af ter	win dow	rab bit	let ter
gar den	can dy	din ner	sum mer
fas ter	pen cil	lit tle	cot ton

The generalization will then emerge that "when two consonants come
between vowels, the syllable division comes between the consonants"
or "one consonant goes with each vowel." It should be pointed out that
this rule will not always hold, but that it is the best guess to make when
trying to pronounce an unknown word. In the case of double consonants (le*tt*er, su*mm*er), there are few exceptions to the rule.

To teach what happens when one consonant comes between two
vowels, a list of known sight words may be placed on the board:

be gin	fe ver	to tal	de cide
o ver	di rect	ti ger	me ter
fa tal	mo ment	pu pil	ho tel

From these examples children will both see and hear that "the single consonant goes with the following syllable." They will also note that when "the syllable is a vowel or ends with a vowel, it usually has the long sound." These two generalizations should be taught together because they work together. In cases where the first of two vowels separated by a single consonant has its short sound, the single intervening consonant closes the first syllable (*cam el, mag a zine*).

A few generalizations about common word endings as they relate to syllabication might be taught. Children have had experience with prefixes and suffixes and may follow these rules even though they are not able to verbalize them.

1. Common endings which begin with a vowel such as *ing, est,* or *er* are usually sounded as syllables (look *ing,* long *er,* long *est*). This is not true of *ed* except when preceded by *t* or *d* (want*ed,* need*ed*).
2. Most one-syllable words remain intact as syllables when endings are added. In many instances this violates the "divide between consonants" rule stated earlier. This is not a problem to children if they have learned to see prefixes and suffixes as units. Examples might include spell *ing,* want *ed,* tell *ing* (not spel *ling,* wan *ted,* tel *ling*).
3. Certain letter combinations, when found at the ends of words, are rarely divided and thus stand as the final syllable.

un *cle*	fa *ble*	bu *gle*	sad *dle*
cir *cle*	tum *ble*	sin *gle*	can *dle*
bicy *cle*	mar *ble*	ea *gle*	nee *dle*
mus *cle*	dou *ble*	strug *gle*	bun *dle*
sam *ple*	gen *tle*	puz *zle*	an *kle*
tem *ple*	rat *tle*	daz *zle*	spar *kle*
sim *ple*	whis *tle*	muz *zle*	ran *kle*
pur *ple*	ti *tle*	fraz *zle*	twin *kle*

The generalizations are

1. The letter combinations *cle, ble, gle, dle, zle, kle, ple, tle* at the end of words usually stand as the final syllable.
2. The final *e* is silent, and the sound contains the *l* blended.
3. This final syllable is not accented.

Accent

Certain words in sentences receive more stress than others, and this is also true of syllables in polysyllabic words. As he learns his native language, the child masters the stress and intonation patterns of sentences and longer words. To say that a child knows the pronunciation of a word implies that he knows its pattern of stress in normal speech. However, when one is attempting to sound out a word not known as a sight word, determining the syllable stress is important.

Teaching accent is usually one of the later steps in phonic analysis, primarily because the learner must be at a stage of development where he can use a dictionary and note primary and secondary accent marks. Memorization of a set of rules to apply in determining accent is probably not desirable since there are numerous exceptions to most such rules. However, structuring learning situations in which the child is invited to make observations and note certain "pronunciation clues" is undoubtedly defensible. To facilitate such learnings, one might provide brief lists of words and have the child or class mark the accent and then state an observation which applies to the group of words. Several illustrations follow.

1. Two-syllable words

dentist	den' tist	anvil	an' vil
barley	bar' ley	wisdom	wis' dom
wizard	wiz' ard	column	col' umn
journal	jour' nal	local	lo' cal
symbol	sym' bol	tailor	tai' lor

Observation: In two-syllable words, the first syllable is accented. Present following new data:

appoint	ap point'	parade	pa rade'
subdue	sub due'	complain	com plain'
receive	re ceive'	reveal	re veal'
proceed	pro ceed'	astound	a stound'

Modify observation: In two-syllable words, the first syllable is usually accented *unless* the second syllable contains two vowels, in which case it is usually accented.

2. Compound words

evergreen (ever' green) underdog (un' der dog)
newscast (news' cast) makeshift (make' shift)
shoehorn (shoe' horn) passport (pass' port)
censorship (cen' sor ship) drawbridge (draw' bridge)
waterfall (wa' ter fall)

Observation: Compound words are usually accented on or within the first word.

3. *Three syllable words*

an' ces tor	sta' di um	syl' la ble
cap' i tal	fan tas' tik	ho ri' zon
sat' el lite	pa' tri ot	in' ci dent
in dig' nant	col' o ny	chem' is try
fi na' le	bat tal' ion	al' ma nac

Observation: Three-syllable words are usually accented on the first or second syllable.

4. *Words containing primary and secondary accent*

con' den sa' tion	su' per sti' tions
op' po si' tion	ad' van ta' geous
sep' a ra' tion	in' ter mis' sion
sen' ti men' tal	mi' cro scop' ic

Observations: a. Words of four or more syllables have a primary and secondary accent.
b. The primary accent usually falls on the syllable preceding suffixes such as *tion, ous, al, ic, sion*.

5. *Shift in accent*

sep' a rate → sep a ra' tion
re spon' si ble → re spon si bil' i ty
sen' ti ment → sen ti men' tal → sen ti men tal' i ty

Observation: Primary accent often shifts in derived forms of root words (adding suffixes).

SUMMARY

In order to become an independent reader, a child must learn to associate printed symbols with the sounds these symbols represent. When a child successfully applies phonics skills, he blends a series of sounds so as to arrive at the pronunciation of a word he does not recognize on sight. Phonics is undoubtedly the most important of the word identification skills which also include word configuration, structural analysis, and context clues. The facile reader does not overrely on one skill, but tends to use various clues in combination. In teaching phonic skills, the following principles should be kept in mind.

The independent reader is not a
hostage to what he has learned previously. He does not overrely on
any particular skill.

Principles to Follow in Teaching Phonics

One of the principles cited in chapter one recognizes the importance of phonics: "Early in the learning process the child must acquire
ways of gaining independence in identifying words whose meanings
are known to him but which are unknown to him as sight words."

As one begins teaching children letter-sound relationships, more
concrete guidelines can be formulated and added to this general
statement:

1. Before a child is taught that a given letter represents a particular
   sound in words, he must be able to discriminate visually that letter
   form from other letter forms.
2. Also, he must be able to discriminate auditorially the sound under
   consideration from other speech sounds in words. These considerations are valid even in methodological approaches which temporarily
   bypass the teaching of letter names but which invite learners to associate sounds with letter symbols directly.

3. There is an unlimited number of ways that letter-sound relationship can be taught. Any technique that proves successful for a child is a justifiable procedure for him providing:
   (a) What he is taught today does not inhibit his later growth, and (b) that the instructional approach is reasonably economical in time and effort expended.

4. Children should not be taught to overrely on phonic analysis techniques. Examples of overreliance include sounding out the same words hundreds of times (sight recognition must replace analysis); and attempting to sound out words which do not lend themselves to letter-sound analysis: *once, knight, freight, some, one, eight, love, know, head, move, none, have, laugh,* etc.

5. Children differ as to how much instruction is needed while they are learning letter-sound relationships. Diagnosis that reveals what a child knows and does not know is essential for good instruction. In the final analysis, the *optimum* amount of phonics instruction for every child is the *minimum* that he needs to become an independent reader.

YOUR POINT OF VIEW?

Space limitations prohibit a thorough discussion of all of the educational issues involved in phonics instruction. Therefore, as a conclusion to this chapter a number of questions will be posed, followed by brief answers which do not cite research findings. In some instances these questions and answers may serve as a stimulus for further discussion and library research.

1. In learning to read, how important are phonic (letter-sound analysis) skills? The child learning to read English writing *must* learn to associate printed letters with speech sounds. One cannot become an independent reader without this skill. It follows that if a cluster of skills are this important, they should be well taught.

2. What is the purpose of phonics instruction as it relates to learning to read? Applying phonic skills permits the reader to "work out" the pronunciation or the approximate pronunciation of printed words NOT known as sight words. The child is not learning "how to pronounce" the word in question, she is learning that a particular series of letters represents a particular word which is part of her speaking vocabulary.

3. Should children be taught to learn words-as-wholes (sight words)? All facile readers at *every* grade level recognize words as wholes and their stock of sight words is constantly enlarged month by month and year by year.

4. Is it possible to teach children to overrely on phonic analysis? It is possible to teach children to overrely on any word recognition technique (sight words, context, letter analysis). Learning to read involves the *simultaneous* application of all of these approaches; each is part of a unitary process called *reading*. When children overrely on phonics analysis, they have a "set" to sound out each word (a habit which precludes getting meaning from larger language units). They sound out the same words many times, continuing to do so long after they should have learned the word as a unit. The child who sounds out every word in a story *is a seriously impaired reader.*

5. What is the optimum amount of phonics instruction? The optimum is the minimum amount of phonics which permits the child to become an independent reader. Ongoing diagnosis provides the teacher with information as to what skills are needed.

6. What is the relationship between memorizing "phonic rules" and applying them in reading situations? It is likely that some children profit from familiarity with certain phonic generalizations. On the other hand, it is known that some children can memorize "rules" and yet be unable to apply them in reading situations. It is debatable whether children should be asked to memorize rules which have very limited application to words they will meet in reading.

What is the basis for your agreement or disagreement with each of the following statements:

1. There is little justification for the deliberate teaching of letter names to first grade children.

2. The sequence in which phonic skills are taught is of little significance.

3. Since a child must learn letter-sound relationships before she can become an independent reader, this skill should be taught before "reading for meaning" is stressed.

4. Reform of English spelling would have little impact on children's learning to read English writing.

BIBLIOGRAPHY

1. Agnew, Donald C., *Effect of Varied Amounts of Phonic Training on Primary Reading.* Durham, N. C.: Duke University Press, 1939.

2. Bagford, Jack, *Phonics: Its Role in Teaching Reading.* Iowa City: Sernoll, Inc., 1967.

3. Bear, David E., "Two Methods of Teaching Phonics: A Longitudinal Study," *Elementary School Journal* (February 1964): 273–79.

4. Betts, Emmett Albert, "Phonics: Three Word Patterns and How to Use Them," *Reading Teacher* 27 (May 1974): 825–27.

5. Bliesmer, Emery P. and Yarborough, Betty H., "A Comparison of Ten Different Beginning Reading Programs in First Grade," *Phi Delta Kappan* (June 1965): 500–04.

6. Botel, Morton, "Strategies for Teaching Sound-Letter Relationships," *Vistas in Reading*. International Reading Association Proceedings 2, Part I, 1966, pp. 156–59.

7. Burmeister, Lou E., *Words—From Print to Meaning* . Reading, Mass: Addison Wesley Publishing Co., 1975.

8. Burns, Paul C. and Schell, Leo M., "Instructional Strategies for Teaching Usage of Context Clues," *Reading World* 15 (December 1975): 89–96.

9. Chall, Jeanne; Roswell, Florence G.; and Blumenthall, Susan Halm, "Auditory Blending Ability: A Factor in Success in Beginning Reading," *Reading Teacher* (November 1963): 113–18.

10. Clymer, Theodore, "The Utility of Phonic Generalizations in the Primary Grades," *Reading Teacher* (January 1963): 252–58.

11. Cohen, Alice Sheff, "Oral Reading Errors of First Grade Children Taught by a Code Emphasis Approach," *Reading Research Quarterly 10*, no. 4, 1974–75, pp. 555–82.

12. Cordts, Anna D., "When Phonics is Functional," *Elementary English* (November 1963): 748–50.

13. ———, *Phonics for the Reading Teacher*. New York: Holt, Rinehart & Winston, Inc., 1965.

14. Dechant, Emerald V., *Improving the Teaching of Reading*, second ed. Englewood Cliffs, N. J.: Prentice-Hall, Inc., 1970. Chapters 10 and 11.

15. Durrell, Donald D., "Phonics Problems in Beginning Reading," in *Forging Ahead in Reading*, J. Allen Figurel, ed. Proceedings, International Reading Association 12, Part I, 1968, pp. 19–25.

16. Gray, William, *On Their Own in Reading*, rev. ed. Chicago: Scott, Foresman & Company, 1960.

17. Gurren, Louise and Hughes, Ann, "Intensive Phonics vs. Gradual Phonics in Beginning Reading: A Review," *Journal of Educational Research* (April 1965): 339–46.

18. Heilman, Arthur W., *Phonics in Proper Perspective*, third ed. Columbus, O.: Charles E. Merrill Publishing Co., 1976.

19. Hull, Marion A., *Phonics for the Teacher of Reading*, Columbus, O.: Charles E. Merrill Publishing Co., 1976.

20. King, Ethel M. and Muehl, Siegmar, "Different Sensory Cues as Aids in Beginning Reading," *Reading Teacher* (December 1965): 163–68.

21. Marchbanks, Gabrielle and Levin, Harry, "Cues by Which Children Recognize Words," *Journal of Educational Psychology* (April 1965): 57–61.

22. Pollard, Rebecca S., *Pollard's Synthetic Method*. Chicago: Western Publishing House, 1889.

23. Rystrom, Richard C., Perceptions of Vowel Letter-Sound Relationships by First Grade Children," *Reading Research Quarterly 9*, no. 2, 1973–74, p. 170.

24. Samuels, S. Jay; Bergy, Gerald; and Chen, Chaur Ching "Comparison of Word Recognition, Speed, and Strategies of Less Skilled and More Highly Skilled Readers," *Reading Research Quarterly 11*, no. 1, 1975–76, pp. 72–86.

25. Schell, Leo M., *Fundamentals of Decoding for Teachers*. Chicago: Rand McNally College Publishing Co., 1975.

26. Sparks, Paul E. and Fay, Leo C., "An Evaluation of Two Methods of Teaching Reading," *Elementary School Journal* (April 1957): 386–90.

27. Weintraub, Samuel, "A Critique of a Review of Phonics Studies," *Elementary School Journal* (October 1966): 34–41.

28. Wilson, Robert M. and Hall, Mary Anne, "Programmed Word Attack for Teachers," second ed. Columbus, O.: Charles E. Merrill Publishing Co., 1974.

29. Winkley, Carol K., "The Applicability of Accent Generalizations," *Academic Therapy Quarterly* (Fall 1966): 2–9.

30. ———, "Why Not an Intensive-Gradual Phonic Approach," *The Reading Teacher* (April 1970): 611–17.

31. Wylie, Richard E. and Durrell, Donald D., "Teaching Vowels through Phonograms," *Elementary English* XLVII (October 1970): 787–91.

Chapter 9

Organizing
the Classroom
for Instruction

Administrative Practices Affecting Instruction

There are really two types of administrative practice which relate to instruction. The first has to do with administrative input into the "climate for learning," which becomes an identifying characteristic of every school or school district. This climate is determined by administrative leadership and the assignment of resources. Learning climate is also influenced by whether the administration is perceived as being receptive to or resistant to teacher input—oriented toward rule enforcement or the expediting of instruction.

The second type of administrative practice that affects instruction are those which have become traditional or fixed within the system. It is doubtful whether many administrator's could make sweeping changes in practices such as the following:

School entrance based on chronological age.

The grade-level system.

Use of graded instructional material (which cannot be equally effective for all students).

Promotion criteria.

Too early termination of systematic reading instruction.

School entrance based on chronological age can be a factor in producing problems in the teaching of reading. Educators generally agree that instruction should be based on readiness for attempting the tasks to be performed. Once the school and community accept the chronological-age criterion for entering school, it is a simple step for parents and communities to reason, "Johnny is six years old. Therefore, he is ready for school. If he is in school, he is ready for reading."

Evolvement of the grade-level system followed urbanization and growth in school enrollment. The first publicly supported schools in America were one-room rural schools which housed pupils of all ages and achievement levels. However, with larger numbers of students attending a given school, the number of classrooms also increased. This gave rise to the question, "When there are a number of classrooms in a building, why should each room contain pupils ranging from six to thirteen or fourteen years of age? Why not group pupils in such a way as to reduce the wide age and achievement differences?"

Thus, the graded system replaced the totally heterogeneous classroom. The theory on which the graded system rested was that pupils would move upward through the grades on the same basis as they entered school—chronological age—and further, that pupils exposed to the same instruction for a school year would be similar in achievement at the end of that period. Therefore, all children would be equally ready to move to the next higher level of instruction.

The development of graded instructional materials was a natural outgrowth of this new organizational pattern. There was logic in the assumption that the learning tasks found in the school could be arranged on an ascending scale of difficulty. The formal curriculum evolved into a "sequence of tasks" which were placed at particular levels or grades. Once there was a general agreement as to sequence and grade placement of tasks, graded instructional materials were developed so that over the years instruction became more and more dependent on such materials.

Gradually, it became apparent that the game plan was not working as smoothly as expected. The differences among pupils of a given chronological age were so great that the fixed curriculum was not equally effective for all children. Some were not mastering the skills they needed in order to function at the next grade level.

Nonpromotion of these students was tried as a solution to the problem. Students who had not mastered necessary skills to do satisfactory work in the next grade were held back a year. It has been estimated that during one period of our history between 20 and 25 percent of all students reaching the sixth grade had been retained in a grade at least once. Nonpromoted pupils simply went through the same educational experience with the same teacher. This had little salutary effect upon the nonpromoted child. Soon nonpromotion came under attack and was rejected because it emphasized failure by making it highly visible. In this sense it was a form of punishment which could, and often did, affect the child's chance of returning to a normal growth pattern.

Social promotion (or universal promotion) then became popular. It was reasoned that practically all children should continue through the graded system with their age-group peers. This practice caused further confusion by moving a child to a higher grade in which mastery of prescribed learning tasks was dependent upon skills which she had not previously acquired. Inevitably this also doomed the child to failure.

As school systems adopted the practice of social promotion, one might expect that the grade-level concept would be abandoned or drastically revised. In the majority of our schools neither of these things happened. The result is that today we find children moving from grade to grade mainly because they have been physically present in a particular grade for an academic year. True, many children master the skills required for the next year's curriculum, but many do not. And when many do not, the grade-level concept is unsound because it was not designed to function under these conditions. The higher the grade level under consideration, the more apparent becomes the inadequacy of our efforts to impose automatic promotion on a graded system. When we attempt to justify automatic promotion on the grounds that it is psychologically sound because promotion prevents failure, we are being unrealistic in our concept of failure. Children who progress through the grades without adequate skills to deal with the tasks expected of them experience failure everyday they attend school.

The foregoing is not intended to imply that nonpromotion is desirable. Such data as we have on retaining students in the same grade for another year indicate that this is also an ineffective practice. An alternative to the practices just cited is found in the proposal of "ungraded school" (2). Here the concept of promotion or nonpromotion is replaced by the mastery of skills concept. A series of skills are identified and pupils move through the sequence at their own pace without reference to a grade level. Further discussion of this concept is found later in the chapter.

The lack of systematic reading instruction beyond the elementary grades is a source of many serious educational problems. This practice is largely the responsibility of the school administration. As we go upward in the grades, more reading is required, but instruction in reading is not as systematic as in the lower grades. In practice, reading seems to be regarded as a skill to be acquired in the elementary and intermediate grades and used in all areas of the curriculum from that point on. Although most school administrators and teachers realize that many children need thorough, planned, deliberate instruction above the sixth grade, they are also aware that systematic instruction at these levels is lacking.

At the junior high and high school levels we tend to rely more on slogans than planned instruction. "Every teacher is a teacher of reading" is such a slogan. The slogan does not fit the facts because some teachers are not qualified to teach reading. The job calls for specific training, knowledge, and skills, just as it does at lower grade levels. It is wrong to assume that poor readers will outgrow poor reading habits when they reach these grades, and it is wrong to assume that poor readers will read widely and better because they have more reading assigned in these grades. If children entering seventh and eighth grades had mastered the fundamental reading skills required for the reading tasks in these grades, present practices in our schools would be justified. Research data for these upper grades tell a different story. It has been found that in these grades, about one in four students functions at a level one grade below actual placement; more than 10 percent function at a level two grades below, and 5 percent at three grades below placement (35).

We hear more and more criticism that students are not proficient readers and that they cannot meet the demands of the curriculum. There is a growing consensus that one of the major ills of our educational system is that the systematic teaching of reading is terminated too early.

There are other policy decisions and practices which affect instruction, over which teachers have little control. Examples include decisions relative to class size; the hiring of teacher-aides; and providing logistical support for development of teaching materials. On the other hand, in some schools teachers may share in making these decisions. If aides are available, a given teacher may choose not to request one. If there are provisions for producing and duplicating teacher-made materials, some teachers may not build an original exercise all year. It is probably true that in some important matters school "administration" and "classroom teaching" may not be harnessed to the same goals. Partial blame for the less than optimal conditions for learning may be traceable to either or both parties. We turn now to those facets of classroom management which traditionally are considered the responsibility of the classroom teacher.

Differentiation of Instruction

A history of American education dealing primarily with classroom practices would be, in essence, a history of the attempts to deal with pupil differences. Some of the more important differences are previous learnings, present instructional needs, the rate at which learning can take place, and pupil attitudes toward themselves as learners. These factors provide the basis for the fact that whatever instructional approach a teacher may use, it will not be equally appropriate for all pupils in her class. During the past fifty years, numerous plans or procedures for differentiating instruction have been advanced. A few examples are listed below, some of which will be discussed throughout this chapter.

The Dalton Plan
Winnetka Plan
Various other "contract" plans
The Unit Approach
Individualized Reading
The Ungraded School
The Joplin Plan
All types of homogeneous grouping

The several "tracks" approach
Programmed materials
Individually Prescribed Instruction (I.P.I.)
Programmed Learning According to Need (P.L.A.N.)
Team teaching

Reports of the success of new approaches always hold out hope for reform. Once the initial enthusiasm for a new practice begins to wane, teaching tends to fall back on the old established order. Perhaps this occurs because any plan of individualizing instruction takes more skill and energy than simply treating a classroom of pupils as interchangeable parts. As Smith notes, "It seems, however, that the seeds of these passing innovations lie dormant for a time and then spring up again in revised and better forms." There is no question that teaching individual learners is a most difficult task. It is easier to pledge support for the proposition that every child has the "right to read" than it is to deliver on that promise (30).

Grouping for Instruction

Grouping of pupils is one means of classroom organization, the purpose of which is to provide differentiated instruction. It is important to note that one should not group pupils *because* of individual differences they exhibit. We resort to groupings in order to utilize teaching strategies that were designed to cope with those differences, at least that is the theory behind the practice. It is well known that this distinction is not always reflected in our schools.

For decades, the concept of grouping was very narrow and ritualistic. If a free association test had been given to educators and the phrase "grouping for instruction" appeared as a stimulus, the majority of responses might have been, "divide the class into three groups." This old traditional format for in-class grouping is only one of an unlimited number of ways that children can be brought together for learning activities.

Types of Grouping

1. Two (or more) children:
   a. playing a phonics game.
   b. writing different meanings for the word *light*.
   c. listening to a recorded story or a taped spelling lesson.
   d. tutoring other children individually.
   e. working on any number of jobs related to preparing a class newspaper.
   f. writing a mock radio program.

2. All children:
   g. reading a "self-selected" story or book.
   h. working on a "self-selected" skill-building exercise.

   i. illustrating a story the teacher has read to them.
   j. writing an ending for an uncompleted story.
   k. working on a "language-expander" exercise selected from the learning center (examples: analogies, fact-opinion statements, cloze sentences or paragraphs, expanding kernel sentences, etc.).

While any or all of the above activities are being carried out, the teacher will function as an observer, helper, and resource person. As an alternative, he could call up a previously identified group of children for work on a given reading skill. In this role the teacher will be more than an observer-helper, but rather will serve as the catalyst that causes the desired change in behavior to occur. The groups above were selected on the basis of need for a particular skill or ability.

Ability Grouping

Grouping pupils on the basis of previous learnings and present instructional needs is a practice of long standing in our schools. It is probably unfortunate that the term *ability grouping* was applied to this practice. Ability grouping is an accurate description when it refers to *present achievement* without reference to potential ability. However, it was sometimes used to imply innate or intellectual capacity. When this occurred the mere act of grouping suggested a final judgment, rather than an initial step in on-going diagnosis.

There were certain other widespread but indefensible practices which resulted in criticism of ability grouping. It was observed that once groups were established, there was very little change in their composition. Pupil mobility between groups did not seem to be synchronized with any performance criteria. Another practice, difficult to explain, was that some teachers followed the same practice and procedures with the high, medium, and low groups. All read, or attempted to read, the same book(s) and attempted to *cover* the same number of pages. Since there was no differentiation of instruction, it had to be assumed that grouping was a ritual unrelated to instructional strategy.

It is realistic to assume that grouping per se is neither inherently good nor bad. Practices carried out under any plan of grouping may enhance pupil growth or become a meaningless and even harmful educational ritual. Grouping pupils on the basis of instructional needs can provide the framework within which an alert teacher can develop meaningful differentiated instruction. Grouping can narrow the range of differences and reading problems with which a teacher has to cope during a given instructional period. As a result, one can focus on particular short-term goals for specific pupils.

There are always practical considerations which influence grouping practices. Attempting to work with five or six groups might result in instructional time blocks that are too small to be effective. Two groups could result in too heterogeneous a collection of pupils in both groups. Such problems emphasize why grouping practices should be quite flexible. When teachers are primarily concerned with the *goals* of grouping, the mechanics tend to fall into place. Figure 25 illustrates a few possible groupings that might occur in self-contained classrooms. Logical grouping patterns emerge as a result of what the teacher plans to do with each group.

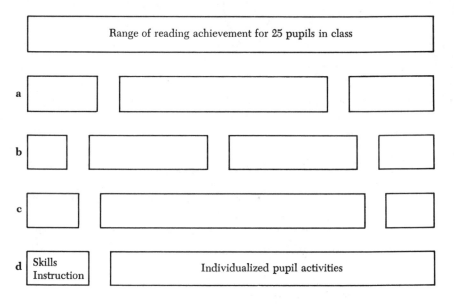

Figure 25

Illustrative options for grouping
self-contained classrooms.

School-wide Homogeneous Grouping

Some provision for grouping students may be handled on a schoolwide basis. For instance, if a school has several classrooms for each grade level, pupils may be assigned to classes on the basis of "present reading achievement." Assume there are three second grade classrooms. One would house the lowest third of all second grade students. The middle achievers would be assigned to another class and the top third, in reading achievement, would comprise the remaining second grade class. All grade levels would be treated in a similar manner. This is only the first step, since the teachers of the various classes will undoubtedly have to resort to some additional grouping practices. However, it does reduce the "range of abilities" found in each classroom.

A second type of school-wide grouping cuts across grade levels (one example is called The Joplin Plan). In this arrangement, all pupils are tested to determine their present reading levels. All students, regardless of their *grade-level placement,* who read at second grade level meet together for reading instruction. Other instructional groups will be those pupils reading at third, fourth or fifth grade level. Almost any grouping procedure will have some potential merits. But many also have potential disadvantages such as uneconomical use of time or posing an ego threat to some pupils.

The Psychological Impact of Grouping

Grouping is sometimes discussed as being potentially threatening to pupils. There are various points of view as to how the grouping within a classroom is to take place so as not to introduce comparisons between children. Suggestions include calling the groups group one, group two, and group three; giving the groups some irrelevant titles such as bluebirds, redbirds, robins; referring to the groups by the names of children in the group. The latter has the merit of being a straightforward approach. No one is being humiliated on the basis of reading ability, and it does not appear that the teacher thinks every pupil should have a certain ability in reading. Psychologically, it is inadvisable for a teacher to attempt to hide differences among beginning readers. It is impossible to fool the children about their reading, and when the poorer readers see through the bluebirds versus the blackbirds, they too start attaching a stigma to poor reading ability. This, of course, is what the teacher has done, but he did not do it openly.

A wise teacher has had different groups of children doing different things at the same time throughout the year, and no significance was attached to this by either the teacher or the pupils. This teacher probably did not start all children reading from the preprimer on the same day. He observed children closely and identified those who were ready. When he started this group on a preprimer, other groups worked on reading also. Some children worked in a readiness workbook, some

When what is done in the group
justifies the grouping arrangement,
there will be no side effects from
grouping.

worked on teacher-prepared readiness materials, and some did preparation for making an experience chart. The teacher, in a natural way,
had planted the idea that groups of pupils would be reading from different books and would be working on different pages of workbooks.
The teacher who is successful in doing this helps his pupils in many
ways.

1. He helps children build a foundation for independent work habits.
2. Competition and feelings of failure are reduced, since children are
   not arrayed against each other on the same reading tasks.
3. Tension and bad attitudes toward reading are held to a minimum.
4. Each child is permitted to progress at her own rate, and intergroup
   rivalry is minimized.
5. The teacher is prevented from embracing, consciously or unconsciously, a grouping system that is too rigid.
6. The teacher is granted flexibility in reducing the size of a group he
   works with by having some children work independently while he
   works intensively with others.

Alternative Approaches to Classroom Management

Organizing the classroom for instruction involves making provisions for individual differences among learners. As noted earlier, finding ways to differentiate instruction has been, and remains, a top priority in American education. This is a justifiable preoccupation since success in this endeavor is the key to successful school programs. The following discussion outlines several types of classroom management which deal with individualizing instruction, promotion practices, and other factors related to instruction.

The Ungraded School

The term *ungraded* is applied to an administrative-instructional organization that (1) deemphasizes or suspends the grade level structure, and (2) emphasizes continuous pupil progress. This concept and practice represents another approach for dealing with pupil differences. Attempts at *ungrading* have been most successful at beginning instructional levels. Thus, much of the literature focuses on the *ungraded primary school* which embraces the first three years of formal schooling.

The ungraded primary has a highly structured curriculum which accommodates a wide range of student achievement. All tasks are placed within a series of "levels" arranged in order of ascending difficulty. Pupils move through the sequence at their own pace. As they master one level, they move on to the next, thus, maintaining continuous pupil progress. At the end of a year's instruction, each pupil is located somewhere on an identified continuum of skills. The next year's instruction begins at this point, meeting the student where she is in relation to skills mastered. Both philosophy and practice defuse the emphasis and concern usually associated with "end of the year promotion."

While instruction in the conventional grade-level system is geared to the mean, experience tells us that pupils do not cluster closely around an achievement mean. Differences in achievement are marked, and they increase with instruction. The ungraded primary starts from the premise that each child should progress at her own rate, and the instructional program centers on each child's need at the moment. This is accomplished by breaking the primary years into a number of units of accomplishment or levels of competency. As each child develops competency at one level, she is moved on into work at the next level. The number of levels and the skills to be mastered at each level are worked out cooperatively by teachers in the program.

Austin (2) describes an ungraded primary school that was eminently successful from the standpoint of both teachers and parents. No official reference is made to grade level; all primary grades, which cover the first three years of school, are simply designated primary rooms. Parents are always kept informed of their children's progress. Teachers are encouraged to work with the same group of children for more than one year, and new teachers are initiated into the program with a workshop held before the opening of school.

No single learning curve fits first graders' achievement, and pupil variability in achievement increases in succeeding grades. There is evidence that if the children are allowed three years of instruction to achieve the third-grade level, there will be fewer failures than there would be if all of the children had had to meet arbitrary standards at the end of grades one and two. Maturity and growth cannot be forced, and growth is characterized by both spurts and plateaus. The ungraded primary encourages continuous pupil progress without specifying precise amounts of growth which are to take place in a given year. Such a plan has particular merit for the child who starts slowly but later shows rapid progress (12, 13).

Some of the educational advantages believed to be inherent in the ungraded primary plan are

1. It is easier to provide for the child's reading growth *early* in her reading career if one is not thinking of "grade level norms" the first year.
2. There is likely to be less failure and frustration in the reading situation if there is less emphasis on comparison and promotion.
3. A teacher often stays with the same group of students two years or longer. This gives him an opportunity to know pupils better. He is less likely to push a student beyond her ability during the first year, since he expects to work with her the next year.
4. Students always work at the level on which they need instruction; i.e., they are not likely to miss some facet of instruction because they were absent several weeks.
5. The slower learner will not repeat the first or second grade, but she may take four years to move up from the primary level.

6. The ungraded plan is flexible in allowing pupils to cover some phases of learning quite rapidly when they are capable of doing so and in giving them more time when it is needed.
7. Bright pupils would not "skip a grade" and possibly be deficient in some skill taught there. They would simply go through the entire primary curriculum at a faster rate.

No method of grouping will automatically solve all instructional problems, and the ungraded primary plan is certainly not a panacea. If a shift to the ungraded plan is not accompanied by an understanding of the goals to be achieved, none of the potential benefits are likely to be realized. If teachers or parents continue to think in terms of a grade-level system, the plan is doomed from the start. On the other hand, if the philosophy of the plan is believed sound and the chief reason for adopting it is to help children grow in reading, problems which do arise will not be insurmountable.

The Unit Approach

The unit approach has a long history of successful classroom use. Although it can be considered a method of instruction, it is discussed in this chapter because of its classroom management potential. The unit provides many ways for coping with individual differences, differentiating instruction, and grouping pupils for specific short- and long-term activities.

This approach provides the teacher with so many options that it has been discussed under a wide array of titles including *resource units, teaching units, activity centered instruction, core approach,* and *survey units.* Use of a unit approach permits the integration of reading instruction and related language skills in numerous learning activities, all of which focus on a specific curricular theme.

A unit may be devised for any subject area and can cover a time span of a few days during which pupils attempt to find the answer to a particular question or, as is usually the case, may extend over a period of weeks and culminate in some class project. The culmination might be a play, a school program, or a science fair consisting of many individual and committee projects, all related to the central theme. While the unit approach is not new, it is consistent with the aims of modern curriculum planning. Unit study can help avoid the tendency toward fragmentation of the curriculum into isolated, seemingly unrelated parts.

1) Units lend themselves to two types of major emphasis. The first
type emphasizes pupil experiences built around a specific topic, such
as *How We Get Our Food.* Experiences related to this topic might include visits to various types of farms, to a cannery, a cold storage plant,
a meat packing plant, a dairy, or a bakery. Pupils may plant and care
for a garden or a window box. The second major emphasis is on wide
2) reading. It is likely that emphasis on the experience approach will come
at the early elementary level, shifting to reading in the subject areas in
the intermediate grades. These two methods are extremely compatible,
and the proper combination of the two approaches undoubtedly makes
for a better total learning situation.

Advantages of the Unit Approach

The potential advantages of the unit approach are quite numerous.
The actual benefits resulting from its use will vary with such factors
as the teacher's skill, the reading ability and work habits of the pupils,
and the amount of supplementary reading material available. Some of
the more frequently mentioned advantages of the unit approach are
summarized below.

1. The unit serves as the framework within which learning experiences
   are shaped into larger, more meaningful wholes. The unit permits

Units can "open up the system" for
both teachers and learners. Then,
good teaching makes good things
happen.

more than the superficial study of a topic and encourages wide and varied reading.

2. Units can be used in any area of the curriculum.

3. The pupils learn that reading is the key to getting information on all subjects and not just an operation performed in the basal reader and accompanying workbooks.

4. The unit approach can and should include a great variety of experiences related to reading, such as excursions, field trips, and small group participation in working on various facets of the problem.

5. Units structure the learning situation to make reading more varied, more meaningful, and more interesting.

6. Units permit pupils of widely different reading abilities to work on different facets of the same project. Reading materials at many levels of difficulty can be used, and children need not be directly compared as readers.

7. The unit approach gives the teacher flexibility and freedom to work with a child or a group of children engaged in some reading activity at their own level. The retarded and the accelerated reader can be working independently and successfully on something that is challenging.

8. Units aid independent reading and help to foster independence in research reading.

Examples of Units

A unit on weather designed for a fourth-grade class may be used as an illustration. The teacher had aroused the interest of the class through an assignment of watching weather reports on television, finding interesting pictures of weather stations, and a class discussion of stories dealing with weather. Out of this grew the class decision to have a study unit on weather. Pupils worked cooperatively in identifying objectives, finding questions to be answered, and working on individual projects which fell within the limits of the unit. These are listed below.

1. Objectives of unit on weather:
   a. To learn ways in which weather helps or harms man.
   b. To learn what causes various types of weather and changes of seasons.
   c. To learn the causes and effects of rainfall, temperature, fog.
   d. To become familiar with the instruments used in measuring or predicting weather changes.

2. Questions to be answered:
   a. How is a thermometer constructed and how does it work?
   b. What is fog?
   c. What causes hail?
   d. What is lightning? Why is it followed by thunder?
   e. Why do we have seasons such as winter and summer?
   f. Why are some parts of the earth always hot and others always cold?
   g. Why is there very little rainfall in one part of a country and a great deal in another part?
   h. Why is it important for people to be able to predict weather?
   i. What is a barometer? How does it work?
   j. What is humidity?

3. Representative activities or projects, both individual and group:
   a. Keeping a daily record of temperatures. Securing temperatures registered in cities in different parts of the country.
   b. Preparing charts and graphs which illustrate some aspect of weather.
      (1) Average rainfall for different states and countries.
      (2) The relationship between rainfall and the type of crops raised in a particular area.
      (3) The effect of rainfall on density of population.
      (4) Maps showing occurrence of tornadoes, hurricanes, or floods during past decade.
   c. Explaining and demonstrating a thermometer and barometer.
   d. Doing research on the work of the U.S. Weather Bureau in predicting weather—how it is done and why.
   e. Studying the effects of weather on human dress, shelter, or diet.
   f. Measuring rainfall during a rain.
   g. Securing pictures which illustrate any facet of weather or the effect of weather, such as floods, erosion, storms on land and sea, barren deserts, and permanent snows.

4. Culminating activity:
   It was decided that at the end of the unit the class would have a Weather Fair. All individual and group projects would be displayed, including posters, graphs and charts, picture series, pupil-made instruments for measuring weather, and all written projects. Parents were invited to visit the class on a particular afternoon, and other classes in the school saw the display at certain times that day. Children explained their projects and received a great deal of ego-satisfaction from this culminating activity.

Units Integrate Work in All Areas

This well-planned unit provided a variety of purposeful learning experiences; the teacher had structured activities so that all facets of the curriculum received attention.

Spelling. Many words were learned incidentally as children printed them on their posters or charts. New words were assigned and studied as part of the unit (*weather, thermometer, mercury, rainfall, temperature, erosion, bureau*).

Health. One popular topic, *How Weather Affects Our Health,* almost became a unit within a unit. The entire class participated, and each pupil was asked to write a brief account of anything she had found in her reading that answered the question. The teacher had a few references for those children who needed help in finding material. What was ostensibly a health lesson also became a lesson in communication skills as the children worked on their written assignments. Practice in oral language usage also received attention as children discussed or reported their findings to the class.

Arithmetic. A lack of understanding of the problems to be solved is more of a stumbling block in arithmetic in the intermediate grades than is lack of computational skills. Failure to read problems critically will result in hazy concepts. In unit work the arithmetic problems which are met emerge from the immediate experience of the learner. Problems such as finding the average rainfall, average temperature, or total foodstuffs raised are related to larger goals and become meaningful in the goal-directed activity. The need for accurate measurement becomes apparent in building a barometer or measuring a rainfall.

Science. Basically the unit was a science unit. One topic that received emphasis at this particular grade level was how science predicts and tracks weather and the scientific instruments used in the process. In studying the thermometer and barometer, many scientific principles and questions evolved, such as the principle of expansion, the principles of gravity and pressure, and the questions of whether mercury is a metal, why it is used in these instruments, what the function of heat is in causing a thermometer to work.

Social Science. The discussion above on health led into social science topics. A discussion of diet in relation to health led to questions and discussion on how weather affects diet or the production of foodstuffs. A discussion of the economic value of climate would logically follow. The relationship of climate to certain natural resources was discussed, i.e., to forestry, deposits of coal, and petroleum. The relationships between rainfall, temperature, winds, forests, and the types of crops were discussed. Methods of cultivation and crop rotation were studied in relation to erosion of the land.

Reading. Reading was the process which provided the raw material for all of the curricular activities mentioned above. The unit stressed, in the pupils' minds, that they were getting information for science, health, and geography. This reading was purposeful. Neither the reading nor the teaching of it were the compulsive "let's get this workbook page finished" approach. The teacher kept in mind all the principles of teaching reading. He had to be particularly careful not to expect all children to read the same materials and to provide a variety of supplementary materials at many grade levels.

Use of the unit method in no way restricts the teacher in developing the reading skills of his pupils. In fact, once the preliminary planning of a unit is done, the creative teacher will find that he has as much time and opportunity to help individual pupils or small groups as he had when working with a conventional grouping arrangement. Most unit work introduces a fairly heavy vocabulary load. It follows that some time must be spent on sight word recognition problems. As the teacher has different children read for him and as pupils ask for help with unknown words, he can prepare several word lists of new words to be studied during the course of the unit. One such list might be taken from the more difficult sources and be used exclusively with the advanced reading group. Lists of easier words can be used in sight word exercises with average and poor readers. Many new and unknown words can be used for teaching phonic analysis and for stressing the importance of context clues in solving meaning difficulties.

In developing a unit, the teacher may find that his first important task is to secure materials at various levels. The references available will vary from school to school. Basal readers at all levels could serve for such a unit as well as selected reading from subject-matter texts. *My Weekly Reader* files would provide materials on many topics, and a child is often pleased to bring to school her own books on some special topic. The following is a partial list of materials the teacher was able to assemble and make available.

Primary level (from basal readers)

The Thermometer	The Storm
Winter Is Coming	Adventures in Science
Rain-Sleet-Snow	The Wonderworld of Science
Changing Weather	The Thunderstorm
How Spring Came	What Time of Year

Intermediate level (basal materials)

Dogs and Weather (Poem)
Inside a Thunderhead
Weather Control
The Snowstorm (Poem)
Ways of the Weather

Trade Books

"Our Friend the Sun," Polgreen (Holt, Rinehart & Winston, Inc., 1963)

"The Sun and Its Planets," Hawkins (Holt, Rinehart & Winston, Inc., 1964)

"Air Is All Around You," Branley (Crowell, Collier & Macmillan, Inc., 1962)

"Weather and Weather Forecasting," Forsdyke (Grosset & Dunlap, 1970)

"How Weather Affects Us," Provis (Benefic Press, 1963)

"Weather Experiments," Feravolo (Garrard Publishing Co., 1963)

"Our American Weather," Kimble (McGraw-Hill, 1955)

"Poems for Weather Watching," Riswall (Holt, Rinehart & Winston, Inc., 1963)

"Tornadoes of the United States," Snowden (University of Oklahoma Press, 1964)

"Atlantic Hurricanes," Dunn and Miller (Louisiana State University Press, 1964)

Pamphlets and Magazines

Life Magazine files
National Geographic Magazine
U. S. Weather Bureau, *Collection of Weather Publications*
Weatherwise (American Meterological Society, Boston, Mass.)

Individualized
Reading

A Movement? A Method?
Classroom Organization?
A Philosophy of Instruction?

Organizing the classroom for instruction must make provision for dealing with students, materials, and instruction. The next format discussed in this chapter—individualized reading—meets this criterion. Granting that the term *individualized reading* has somewhat different meanings to different users, this approach has for many years enjoyed wide acceptance and use in our schools.

Paradoxically its greatest potential strengths and weaknesses stem from the same factor. There is no concise definition of "what it is" and no blueprint for "how to do it." It forces freedom of choice upon teachers and its success depends upon creative responses. Teachers are freed from all externally imposed rituals. However, vulnerability lies in the fact that no protection can be offered to prevent teachers from developing their own nonproductive rituals. The consensus seems to be that freedom and lack of structure cannot work equally well for all teachers.

Background
and History

During the 1950s, frustration with the status quo in reading instruction reached a new high, and the climate for change seemed particularly good. A new emphasis on gearing reading instruction to individual pupil's needs and interests evolved through a movement which came to be called *individualized reading*.

Proponents of this reform movement had enthusiasm and fervor, both of which were essential if change were to be achieved. Two educational practices in particular, the use of basal readers and grouping by ability, came under fire.

There is little question that certain indefensible practices were to be found in the use of basals and grouping. Some teachers overrelied on basal texts to the exclusion of other materials. When this occurred, reading and learning to read could easily be reduced to deadly routines. Some pupils who had the ability to move through basals fairly rapidly were kept with the group with the result that their reading was severely rationed. These students were asked to complete tasks, such as workbook exercises, which added nothing to their growth in reading because they could already do these things.

Children at the other end of the achievement continuum were kept reading the same primer and first reader for two or more years even though their progress was not improved by this repetition. Over-reliance on basals (or any other material) implies less than optimum use of other instructional techniques and materials.

The other area of concern, that of dividing a class into three groups, took on the characteristics of a mechanical ritual unrelated to caring for individual differences and meeting individual needs. In some classrooms, children did read "round-robin," poorer readers were not only embarrassed, but provided unacceptable models of oral reading for the remainder of the group. It was probably impossible to enjoy a story read under such adverse conditions. These practices were not inherent in the use of basals or grouping, but rather had grown as a result of teachers and school systems failing to be creative in teaching. In an effort to bring about reform, some proponents of change made sweeping indictments against basal materials and grouping practices. It is generally agreed that it would have been more logical to focus on the actual *abuses* of basals and achievement grouping which were found in classrooms, rather than to attempt to proscribe them altogether (36). Although extreme positions have been abandoned by most advocates of individualized reading, a few examples are cited here for historical perspective.

> Individualized reading requires the complete abandonment of the basal reader and the basal reader system.
>
> One source of bias in many critics (of individualized reading), it should be recognized in advance, is the intellectual and emotional involvement in authorship of basal series.
>
> . . . it is everywhere reported that children who have disliked reading change their minds. It is reported that maladjusted children change their attitudes and fit in with the group in other activities. Everywhere it is reported that the children do quantities of reading, not only the good readers but all of them.
>
> Seldom are two children ready to be taught reading from the same materials at the same time.

Such generalizations raised more questions than they settled. Fortunately these prescriptive-proscriptive stances gradually diminished in the discussion of individualized reading. Feuds which focused on organizational mechanics separating the true believers from the suspect lost partisans. As Larrick (18) pointed out, much of what had been written about individualized reading tended to deal with, "how many minutes per child, (in conferences), how to keep records, how to sign up for books, how to manage the class." These problems, she believed, could be solved by teachers once they viewed reading as a personal involvement of pupils and once teaching ceased to be dominated by the demand to cover a stipulated content.

Philosophy of Instruction

The philosophy of individualized reading rejects the lockstep instruction which tended to become standardized within the framework of the graded system and traditional graded materials. The success or failure of an individualized program rests almost exclusively with the teacher, which is one of the reasons why individualized reading is so difficult to define.

As Jacobs (16) states, "In the first place, 'individualized reading' is not a single method, with predetermined steps in procedure to be followed." Brogan and Fox (3) concur, adding, ". . . the term refers to the variety of practices through which resourceful, sensitive teachers, working with and taking their clues from individual children, are helping each of them appropriately to move ahead in reading." In one sense, individualized reading focuses on the child-as-a-reader more than the teacher-as-a-teacher. Reading is seen as an act of personal involvement which is synchronized with the child's growth and development. The emphasis on child growth is commendable, but many teachers who favor this approach find the literature vague as to how one achieves reading goals.

Practices Associated with Individualized Reading

Over the years a number of practices have become associated with individualized reading (28). These include self-selection of materials by pupils, self-pacing in reading, individual pupil conferences with the teacher, and emphasis on record keeping by teacher, pupil, or both. One other notable characteristic is the absolute need for a wide variety of reading material in each classroom. This becomes mandatory if each pupil is to select books in which she is interested and which she can read.

Self-selection and Self-pacing

Self-pacing of reading and self-selection of reading materials are basic to the philosophy of individualized reading. Olson's (21, 22) writing is frequently cited as the basis for the emphasis on seeking, self-selection, and self-pacing. While these concepts are not new to education, the individualized reading movement has given them a new emphasis focused on reading instruction.

The principle underlying the advocacy of self-selection is psychologically sound. Since there are tremendous individual differences among pupils in a given classroom, there is little justification for assuming that different pupils' needs and interests will be met equally well by one basal series or a single text.

The efficacy of the practice of self-selection of reading materials is influenced by several factors. First, the child must have some interests she wishes to explore further. This ties the ego to the reading situation. Second, there must be materials available which fit her interests and which she can read independently.

The theory is that when these conditions are met, the child will seek out the materials which fit her needs, interests, and present reading level. If she selects wisely, she grows. Much depends on pupil success, and some proponents of seeking, self-selection, and self-pacing appear to have assumed that success is assured by this formula.

Carried to extremes, this idea of individualized reading can minimize the role of the teacher in guiding pupils to materials to the degree that self-selection almost becomes a fetish. There is some danger in attempting to close debate by re-asserting that "pupils, when permitted to do so, will select materials they can read." This may be true in a number of cases, but it is not an inevitable law of child behavior. As Spache (32) points out, many pupils have no felt need for reading, do not seek reading, have not ascribed any personally relevant values to reading, and are not "sufficiently insightful into their personal or social needs either to recognize their needs or to find solutions through the medium of reading."

Self-selection on the part of pupils is to a degree often limited by the fact that the teacher or some authority has previously chosen the one or two hundred books found in the classroom from among thousands which are available. This infringement on the principle of self-selection is not decried simply because we accept the gathering of materials as part of the teacher's role. Individualized reading and self-selection do not preclude the teacher from recommending books or guiding pupils toward certain materials, but this type of guidance does call for a high level of teacher competency. He must know the child's interest, her reading ability, and the difficulty level of materials if his suggestions are to help his pupils grow.

The factor of economy in the teacher-learning situation must also be considered. If after a period of "seeking" a child has not made a selection and settled down to reading, her behavior may indicate that she is not yet ready for self-selection. There is no evidence that a teacher praising a book or offering suggestions to pupils will result in undesirable psychological side effects. On the contrary, there is evidence that pupils respect teacher judgments and tend to be favorably disposed toward materials recommended by understanding teachers. With many pupils, self-selection can safely be tempered with guidance.

Teacher-Pupil Conference

The teacher-pupil conference is one of the major identifying features of individualized reading and is potentially one of its great strengths. This potential is realized only when the teacher is skillful in achieving desirable goals. The conference is a brief session in which the teacher gives his whole attention to one pupil so that she may express herself on a story which she has selected and read prior to the conference. The primary goal of the conference is to assure the child she has an appreciative audience.

The chief value of the conference is that it ties ego-satisfaction to the reading process. For a student to share her feelings about a book with her teacher is an excellent ego-building experience. If the conference is to yield maximum pupil growth, however, the teacher must be more than a listener. If he is only a passive listener, the pupil will tend to standardize her role in the conference. The type of responses she makes the first time will tend to set the pattern for subsequent conferences. In addition to being an appreciative audience, the teacher must also assume some responsibility for helping the child develop a higher level of values and self-understanding, goals often best achieved through judicious questioning.

The structure and prevalent practices of most of today's schools are not conducive to close personal relations between teacher and pupils. Large classes, too many classes per day, and administrative and instructional busy work often stand as barriers between teacher and pupil. We extol creativity and yet teach to the "golden mean." We establish professional philosophy which stresses the importance of teaching to children's needs and interests, yet it is possible for a student to complete her formal education without ever having had ten minutes of a teacher's undivided attention.

The teacher-pupil conference is worthy of further consideration because it also has possible therapeutic value. The conference serves as a catalyst which helps to produce teacher-pupil rapport, a factor which is highly underrated in its influence on learning. For some pupils, the teacher's positive response to their reading is a stronger motivation than the actual act of reading itself. The skillful sympathetic teacher can provide this extrinsic reward while slowly moving the child toward accepting reading as its own reward (39).

The conference provides the means by which the teacher can learn important facts about a child's psychological needs and the means she has adopted for fulfilling these needs. With this knowledge, the alert teacher is in a position to become a party to sound bibliotherapeutic practices. Discussing her reading with a respectful adult will help a child gain insights into her own problems and afford her examples of how others have met such difficulties (25).

Preparing for the conference is essential, but one should avoid a "standardized format." Veatch has listed the factors which teachers may wish to consider in setting up conferences (39).

1. As a general rule, the pupils inform the teacher when they feel ready to participate in a conference.
2. The teacher should be familiar with the book or story which a child plans to discuss.
3. Pupils are informed when and in what order they will be scheduled for the conference.
4. Provision must be made for all other pupils in the class to be engaged in some other meaningful activity. One suggestion is to have them selecting and reading books independently.
5. The teacher must be prepared to stimulate pupils through the use of questions. These should be questions that stimulate thought instead of asking only for factual information.
6. The class and teacher will have worked out some system for pupils to receive help pronouncing unknown words during their independent reading.

Frequency, length, and format of conferences were the basis for many questions from teachers in the early days of the individualized reading movement. Today, it is understood that practices in these areas must vary from classroom to classroom. No single proposal relative to format, frequency, or length of conferences would be equally good for all situations. A schedule which is logical for a classroom of twenty-four pupils will become unworkable with a class of thirty-five pupils. Furthermore, the length and frequency of the conference will also vary with different grade levels and different ability levels within the grade. A still further complicating factor is the difference found among readers themselves. The child who has read a story consisting of only several hundred words will probably not take as much sharing time with his teacher as the pupil who read *Charlotte's Web*. In no sense is it necessary to think of all conferences as embracing the same procedures or lasting for the same duration.

In the case of a facile reader who needs little encouragement to read, a brief exchange between the teacher and pupil would suffice on some occasions. A word of praise, a question about whether there are still a number of books in the classroom that she wishes to read, and an offer of help when needed could be considered adequate. Since the sharing-type conference is primarily an ego-building experience, it is obvious that some children will need more attention than others. Some pupils continually avoid a conference because reading is a threat rather than a pleasure. Unlike the good reader who fulfills her ego-needs through the success and enjoyment derived from reading, these pupils need constant encouragement.

Record Keeping

Record keeping received considerable attention in the early descriptions of and writing about individualized reading. For the most part, this activity had little or nothing to do with actual diagnosis of reading needs. The purpose seemed to be to emphasize the number of books read and to offer proof that the system was working. Over the years the emphasis on this activity has diminished. While it was true that there was some ego-building potential in seeing one's list of books grow, there were also certain potential negative effects. In some cases this extrinsic motivator became dominant as children read primarily to add titles to their lists. Also, it tended to introduce the element of "comparison of achievement" which individualized reading opposes philosophically.

Problems Encountered in Individualized Reading

Children reading independently, selecting what they wish to read, and reading at their own pace strikes some critics as being quite idealistic. To keep this philosophy from becoming unrealistic, a great deal of effort must be expended in classroom management. Over the years teachers have voiced a number of concerns, some of which are listed here in question form and then briefly discussed.

1. What type of materials are needed?
2. How does one initiate an individualized program?
3. When and how is on-going diagnosis achieved?
4. How is provision made for teaching the necessary reading skills?
5. When the teacher is involved in teacher-pupil conferences:
   a. what are the other students doing?
   b. how do these students get "instant help" on their reading problems?

How these and other issues are handled, determines the success or failure of an individualized program.

Needed Materials

A reading program embracing self-selection and self-pacing and designed to meet individual pupil interests cannot function in a learning environment which does not include a wide array of reading materials. This should not be thought of as a special problem related only to the individualized reading. There is no justification for any classroom or school not meeting this criterion regardless of methodological approach or program. Therefore, the need for materials is not a unique feature of individualized reading, but rather a factor which has been justifiably emphasized in this approach.

While there is little point in attempting to settle upon a fixed number of books which would be considered adequate, a minimum figure frequently mentioned is approximately one hundred different trade-book titles per classroom. Assuming that the same hundred books should suffice throughout the year, a hundred books in a third grade would be totally inadequate.

Factors which must be considered include: grade level; range of interests and abilities of pupils; class size; whether books can be rotated with other classrooms; whether the school supports a central library; and whether the same materials are used extensively in other subject areas, such as social studies and science, in the preparation of units.

Materials should not be tightly equated with trade books alone, although these would likely be the major source. Classrooms should contain magazines, newspapers, various reading kits, *My Weekly Reader, Reader's Digest* (skill-builder materials), and most other reading materials children might choose to work with. Reading material would of necessity cover many areas such as biography, science, sports, exploration, hobbies, fairytales, medicine, space, poetry, humor, adventure, myths, and travel.

Starting a Program

All elementary teachers are likely to be doing some things which fit logically under the heading "individualization." Any of the formal aspects of individualized reading such as self-selection or individual conferences can be started with one pupil, a small group, or the entire class. Obviously, the latter approach would present the most problems; therefore, perhaps one should start with one of the other alternatives.

The first prerequisite is, of course, the availability of materials; and to this must be added the prerequisite that the child be able to read some of these materials. A reading vocabulary of twenty words is needed to handle a preprimer, and with a few more words, a reader could make the transition to similar materials in different basal series. A sight vocabulary of fifty words and some ability at sounding out words would permit a reader to start her first trade book.

Within this ability range, a portion of the child's reading material might well be individual stories dictated by the pupil and printed by the teacher. This practice may be identified with the language-experience approach, but its practice is not precluded in individualized reading. Commercial picture dictionaries and teacher-pupil-prepared dictionaries would also be appropriate at this level.

Starting an individualized program by involving a small group of the more proficient readers in the class is another logical way to begin. This approach will present fewer organizational problems than involvement of the entire class. The teacher begins by calling together the students he has selected and explaining that he would like them to select their own books to read at their desks during the reading period.

Prior to this group conference, the teacher has gathered a number of books and placed them on the reading table. He has been careful to see that a number of "new books" are included and has deliberately included books which he thinks will appeal to the five or six students in the group. There would be nothing wrong with calling the children's attention to certain books.

He concludes the group conference with, "When you have selected the book you wish to read, go to your desk and read it silently; you may keep the book at your desk until you finish it." Within a day or two the teacher will again briefly assemble the pupils in the individualized group and explain that he would like to have each student tell him something about the book just completed and also to read a part of the book that was particularly interesting. In order to do this, he will schedule an individual conference with each pupil. Pupils are to tell him when they are ready for their conference, and he will schedule the time.

These directions and explanations have taken only a minute or two. The teacher now turns his attention to the remainder of the class, explains a seatwork assignment to a portion of the class, and conducts a planned session on word-analysis techniques with a selected group of students. He will observe how the pupils function in the newly organized individualized group. Do they find a book in a reasonable length of time? Is it at a level they can handle?

Providing for Diagnosis

Individualized reading is an organizational-instructional approach which by its very nature calls for considerable diagnosis if children are to progress smoothly in reading growth. Achievement of individualization may soon be thwarted for some pupils in the absence of on-going diagnosis. It is doubtful that such potentially excellent procedures as self-selection and self-pacing were ever envisioned to operate independently of diagnosis and teacher guidance.

In the absence of teaching built on diagnosis, pupils tend to reinforce whatever poor reading habits they have at present. The same mistakes will be made time after time, and it may be weeks before "self-correction" is worked out. One example is the case of a child who consistently miscalled a word throughout the entire length of a story. "In one class a child read a story about an old man and a 'termite' for four days. On the fifth day during his conference he discovered the word was 'turnip.' No wonder he had missed comprehension and the humor (23)."

There are no diagnostic techniques which are associated exclusively with individualized reading, nor are there any which need be thought to be foreign to it. The individual teacher-pupil conference may in some instances be a major source of diagnostic information, but the conference cannot be the only time and place where diagnosis takes place. Diagnosis must be on-going, and every reading activity in the classroom should be viewed as serving some diagnostic purpose (8).

All seatwork, whether teacher-prepared or conventional workbook exercises, has diagnostic value. A student's spelling performance, both on formal weekly tests and in her creative writing, will give clues to her ability to associate letter sounds with letters and letter combinations. Brief informal tests may be developed for testing any facet of reading from recognition of words to understanding figurative language.

Teaching Reading Skills

The early individualized movement was in part a reaction against reading instruction which often stressed individual skills at the expense of the "total reading process." In some classrooms, all pupils received the same instruction, worked on the same skill-building exercises, and read the same materials. When these practices were prevalent, there was room for suspicion that instruction was predetermined rather than based on pupil needs and abilities. Such uniform practices inevitably resulted in some children becoming bored with reading instruction, and thus there existed a need for reform.

Unfortunately, the attack on uniform skills instruction for everyone tended to spread to the teaching of skills per se. Actually, skills teaching was not explicitly rejected, but this facet of individualized reading instruction was neglected. In recent years the importance of skills teaching has been accepted by practically all proponents of individualized reading. But the vagueness as to how and when the teaching is incorporated into the program still lingers. Questions relative to teaching skills elicited two frequently repeated responses: (1) "Teach some skills in the teacher-pupil conference;" and (2)"Teach other skills as they are needed by the pupils."

The first answer suggests what is, on the whole, an uneconomical procedure, unless the child participating in the conference is the only one in the class who can profit from the instruction that is given. Any reading skill that can justifiably be taught to the entire class should be taught to the whole group. Those students who learn with the first presentation should be doing something else when subsequent presentations are made to pupils who did not learn. Assume that eventually only one child in the class has need for further instruction; provision is now made for her to receive it individually. This may be done by the teacher; a classmate may function for a few minutes as a "helper;" the materials may be on a filmstrip and the learner may operate the projector herself; or the child may work on a teacher-prepared worksheet or with a commercially prepared programmed lesson. Where reading instruction is integrated school-wide, the child may join five or six pupils from other classes, regardless of grade level, who have the same instructional need. This latter solution may fit under any one of a number of administrative titles such as, "remedial reading," "modified Joplin Plan," "ungraded primary," etc. The actual instruction may be provided by a full-time remedial teacher, a one-day-a-week teacher, a teacher aide, or a student teacher working under supervision.

The basic validity of the second response, "teach skills when they are needed," cannot be faulted, but it can be argued that it is both vague and difficult to implement when each child in the class is reading a different book. Concern for providing differentiation of skills instruction need not start from the premise that no two pupils, or larger groups in a class, cannot profit from the same instruction or drill. This extreme position is simply the antithesis of the practice which implies that all children in a class *could* profit from the same amount of time spent with the same book. Reliance on diagnosis, not slogans, is the only safe way to resolve what is appropriate instruction.

There are dozens of abilities and habits which may be listed under the heading *basic skills*. The three major areas with which the elementary teacher must be constantly concerned are *word recognition, ability to sound out or pronounce unknown words, and the knowledge of word meanings*. This is true regardless of the materials used, organization pattern followed, or one's philosophy of teaching.

Meaningful Class Activities during the Teacher-Pupil Conference

Individualized reading calls for a high degree of planning by the teacher, much of which will likely include pupil participation in outlining independent activities. Such activities are unlimited. The following brief listing is only illustrative. The tasks are not identified by grade level since many may be adapted to various levels. The listing includes class, group, and individual activities, covering skill develop-

While working with a group, a teacher may answer a question from a pupil outside the group.

ment, recreational reading, reading in curricular areas, and creative activities.

1. Children select books or other reading materials. This will likely include browsing and sampling. Selection is followed by independent reading of materials.

2. Conducting library research for an individual or group report. Such activity may relate to a unit in some other subject.

3. Creative writing experiences might include writing original stories; poems; letters to a classmate in the hospital or one who has moved away; invitations to parents to visit school; a riddle composition to be read to the class during a period set aside for such activities.

4. Preparing art work such as:
   a. Drawing or pasting pictures in a picture dictionary.
   b. Drawing a picture to accompany a pupil-dictated, teacher-written story.
   c. Preparing posters or book covers to illustrate the high point in a book or story which the pupil has read.

5. Using workbook pages or teacher-prepared seatwork guides for the development of particular skills such as:
   a. A dictionary exercise which follows an introduction of a skill such as alphabetizing by initial letter, or by two or more letters, use of guide words, pronunciation guides, or syllabication.
   b. Word analysis skills (associating sounds with graphic symbols, noting compound words, abbreviations, and the like).
   c. Study skills involving effective use of parts of a book such as the index, table of contents, glossary, appendix, library card catalog, reference materials.

6. Using an appropriate filmstrip with the entire class, a smaller group, or a pair of pupils. In each case, one pupil is appointed to move the frames.

7. Teaching and testing word meanings.
   a. Workbook pages or teacher-prepared seatwork may be provided.
   b. Children may work on "vocabulary building" cards or notebooks in which they write one or more common meanings for new or unknown words met in their reading.
   c. The teacher may place a list of words on the board. Pupils write as many sentences as possible, using a different connotation for the word in each sentence. Example: *Light*—light in weight; light as to color; light the fire; light on his feet; her eyes lighted up; light-hearted; etc.

8. Making a tape recording of a story. A group of four to six pupils may each read the part of one character. Practice reading and the actual recording may be done in the rear of the classroom or in any available space in the building.
9. Testing or diagnostic activities may be arranged. The entire class or any size group may take a standardized test (or reading subtest); tests which accompany basal series; *My Weekly Reader* tests; or informal, teacher-made tests. These will be scored and studied for the diagnostic information they yield.
10. Preparing interest corners, bulletin boards; devising choral reading activities for later presentation to the class.

These represent only a few of the reading-related activities which can be used. Teachers are limited only by their experience, creative ability, and the degree to which the pupils in their class have learned to function in independent activities.

Providing help for students doing independent reading. A problem that frequently arises when the teacher is involved in teacher-pupil conferences is how to help students who encounter difficulty in their reading. In most instances pupils need help on the pronunciation of unknown words. Some teachers permit the child to come to him and point out the troublesome word, and he whispers its pronunciation. If pupils do not abuse this privilege, it need not disrupt the teacher-pupil conference in progress. Other teachers feel that such interruptions detract from the intimate nature of the conference, and they appoint "helpers." These are the more proficient readers in the class who can usually help the other pupils.

One teacher solved the problem by appointing a "helper for the day" and making an extra provision in case this student could not provide the needed help. "For the rest of this week I am appointing Bill as a special helper. If you come to a word you cannot sound out, you may ask Bill; if he does not know the word, you should print it on one of these cards along with the number of the page on which it is found. Sometime during the morning I will come to your desks and help you read the sentences which have the hard words." In this situation the teacher must have the answer to questions such as, "How well does the 'helper' manage?" and, "Do the other pupils bother him for help so often that it interferes with his own reading?" This information may call for adjustments in procedure.

Sperber (33) suggests that a seating arrangement be worked out so that the class falls into three groups, each containing one or more good readers. These better readers serve as resources for helping other pupils in the group with words they may not know as sight words.

On occasion an entire class may be involved in a writing assignment while the teacher is engaged in conferences. In one first-grade classroom, the children were observed while writing a letter to a classmate in the hospital. The teacher printed a dozen words on the board, explaining that these might be words the pupils would be using and that they could look at the board for help on spelling. The words were: *dear, Susan, hope, soon, well, sorry, you, love, sick, missed, get, school, from.* This selection of words anticipated a large percentage of the "spelling interruptions" which might have ordinarily occurred.

Another approach is to encourage pupils to "spell the words the way you think they are spelled." Such free writing exercises can have a diagnostic value for the teaching of spelling and the analysis of *phonetic* skills.

SUMMARY

Both school-wide administrative practices and classroom organization have had important effects on instruction. In American schools, the tendency toward standardized teaching practices has been accentuated by two factors: the grade level system and the overreliance on graded instructional materials. Individualized reading represents a new emphasis on evoking classroom practices which fit individual pupil needs.

Seeking to find means of individualizing instruction is evidence of the awareness of pupil differences. Such awareness is absolutely essential to a sound reading program. However, what one does in actual practice as a result of this perception may or may not be sound.

An effective individual reading program of necessity must rest on a rather broad base. It may include, but cannot be limited to, children selecting books, reading these at their own rate, and occasionally reporting to the teacher on their reading. Individualized reading does not exclude practices which may be thought of as integral parts of other instructional approaches.

Any instructional program must include the teaching of all facets of reading. A few examples are study skills, word-recognition techniques, library research techniques, integration of reading instruction with other subject matter, expansion of meaning vocabulary and concepts, and appreciation of poetry and literature. These are essential skills, and they should be taught. This position is not rejected by those who advocate individualized reading, but the details of how and when such essentials are to be taught have not been carefully delineated.

It also must be remembered that both the virtues and defects ascribed to individualized reading are potential and not inherent in the approach. The achieving of potentials and the avoidance of pitfalls is exclusively a function of individual teachers in specific classroom situations. This is not unique to individualized reading. Precisely the same conditions hold for *any* method or instructional framework.

YOUR POINT OF VIEW?

Would you defend or attack the following premises? Why?

1. "In-class grouping" has not helped teachers in dealing effectively with individual differences.
2. The ungraded primary is, in essence, an attempt to break away from grade-level standards of achievement.
3. The unit approach relies too much on incidental learning and slights systematic instruction in reading.
4. Any practice which leads to children reading appropriate material would fit under the label *individualized reading instruction.*
5. Most of the individualized reading programs which have been described have more efficacy for better readers in a class than for poorer readers in the group.
6. Chronological age is the most practical and most justifiable criterion determining when children should enter school.

Respond to the following problems:

A. A certain school has been using an Individualized Reading Approach for a number of years. A study of children's reading performance led to the conclusion that "children seem to be reinforcing a number of poor reading habits." What sound principles of instruction would you hypothesize are being neglected in this program?
B. Assume that you are assigned the task of materially reducing the number of remedial readers normally found in a given school system. Would your recommendations deal primarily with teaching methods, school practices other than methodology, or both? Would you also have to deal with parents' attitudes?
C. *Premise:* "There are certain reading skills which can be taught as effectively by a computer as by the classroom teacher." Discuss and identify these skills.

BIBLIOGRAPHY

1. Ashley, L. F., "Children's Reading Interests and Individualized Reading," *Elementary English* (December 1970): 1088–96.

2. Austin, Kent C., "The Ungraded Primary School," *Childhood Education* (February 1957): 260–63.

3. Brogan, Peggy and Fox, Loren K., *Helping Children Read*. New York: Holt, Rinehart & Winston, Inc., 1961, p. 5.

4. Burns, Paul C. and Roe, Betty D., *Teaching Reading in Today's Elementary Schools*. Chicago: Rand McNally College Publishing Co., 1976. Chapter 10.

5. Burns, Paul C. and Schell, Leo M., eds., *Elementary School Language Arts*, second ed. Chicago: Rand McNally College Publishing Co., 1973. Part six.

6. Coody, Betty and Harris, Ben M., "Individualization of Instruction Inventory," *Elementary English 50* (March 1973): 431–35.

7. Eisenhardt, Catheryn T., "Individualization of Instruction," *Elementary English* (March 1971): 341–45.

8. Evans, Robert, "Teacher Evaluations of Reading Skills and Individualized Reading," *Elementary English* (March 1965): 258–60.

9. Garry, V. V., "Competencies That Count among Reading Specialists," *Journal of Reading 17* (May 1974): 608–13.

10. Gilliland, Hap, *A Practical Guide to Remedial Reading*. Columbus, O.: Charles E. Merrill Publishing Co., 1974. Chapter 7.

11. Gomberg, Adeline Wishengrad, "Freeing Children to Take a Chance," *Reading Teacher 29* (February 1976): 455–57.

12. Goodlad, John I., "Ungrading the Elementary Grades," *NEA Journal* (March 1955): 170–71.

13. ———— and Anderson, Robert H., *The Nongraded Elementary School*. New York: Harcourt, Brace & World, 1959.

14. Harris, Albert J. and Sipay, Edward R., *How to Increase Reading Ability*, sixth ed. New York: David McKay Co., Inc., 1975. Chapters 5–6.

15. Harris, Larry A. and Smith, Carl B., *Reading Instruction through Diagnostic Teaching*. New York: Holt, Rinehart & Winston, Inc., 1972.

16. Jacobs, Leland B., "Individualized Reading Is Not a Thing," in *Individualizing Reading Practices*, Alice Miel, ed. Bureau of Publications, Teachers College, Columbia University, 1958.

17. Karlin, Robert, *Teaching Elementary Reading*, second ed. New York: Harcourt Brace Jovanovich, Inc., 1975.

18. Larrick, Nancy, "Individualizing the Teaching of Reading," in *Reading, Learning and the Curriculum*. Proceedings of the Twelfth Annual Reading Conference, Lehigh University, Bethlehem, Pa., 1963, pp. 35–38.

19. Marksberry, Mary Lee, "Organizing Learning Experiences," *Elementary English* 52 (May 1975): 653–59.

20. Olson, Joanne P. and Dillner, Martha H., *Learning to Teach Reading in the Elementary School.* New York: Macmillan, 1976. Part 3.

21. Olson, Willard C., *Child Development.* Boston: D. C. Heath and Company, 1949.

22. ———, "Seeking Self-Selection and Pacing in the Use of Books by Children," in *Individualizing Your Reading Program,* Jeannette Veatch. New York: G. P. Putnam's Sons, 1959.

23. Putnam, Lillian R., "Controversial Aspects of Individualized Reading," *Improvement of Reading through Classroom Practice.* International Reading Association Proceedings 9, 1964, pp. 99–100.

24. Quandt, Ivan, "Investing in Word Banks—A Practice for Any Approach," *Reading Teacher* 27 (November 1973): 171–73.

25. Reeves, Harriet Ramsey, "Individual Conferences—Diagnostic Tools," *The Reading Teacher* (February 1971): 411–15.

26. Robeck, Mildred C. and Wilson, John A. R., *Psychology of Reading: Foundations of Instruction.* New York: John Wiley and Sons, Inc., 1974. Chapter 12.

27. Roeder, Harold H. and Lee, Nancy, "Twenty-five Teacher-Tested Ways to Encourage Voluntary Reading," *Reading Teacher* 27 (October 1973): 48–50.

28. Sipay, Edward R., "Individualized Reading: Theory and Practice," *Children Can Learn to Read—But How?* Rhode Island College Reading Conference Proceedings, Providence, 1964, pp. 82–93.

29. Slater, Mallie, "Individualized Language Arts in the Middle Grades," *Reading Teacher* 27 (December 1973): 253–56.

30. Smith, Nila Banton, *American Reading Instruction.* Newark, Del.: International Reading Association, 1965.

31. Smith, Richard J. and Johnson, Dale D., *Teaching Children to Read.* Reading, Mass.: Addison-Wesley Publishing Co., 1976. Chapters 2, 6.

32. Spache, George D. and Spache, Evelyn B., *Reading in the Elementary School,* third ed. Boston: Allyn and Bacon, Inc., 1973. Chapters 4 and 11.

33. Sperber, Robert, "An Individualized Reading Program in a Third Grade," *Individualizing Reading Practices.* Bureau of Publications, Teachers College, Columbia University, 1958, pp. 44–54.

34. Strain, Lucille B., *Accountability in Reading Instruction.* Columbus, O.: Charles E. Merrill Publishing Co., 1976. Chapter 4.

35. Stroud, J. B., *Psychology in Education,* rev. ed. New York: Longmans, Green and Co., 1956, pp. 375–77.

36. Sucher, Floyd, "Use of Basal Readers in Individualizing Reading Instruction," in *Reading and Realism,* J. Allen Figurel, ed. Proceedings, International Reading Association 13, Part 1, 1969, pp. 136–43.

324 Foundations for Teaching Reading

37. Wilson, Richard C., "Criteria for Effective Grouping," in *Forging Ahead in Reading*, J. Allen Figurel, ed. Proceedings, International Reading Association, pp. 275–77.

38. Wilson, Robert M. and Gambrell, Linda B., "Contracting—One Way to Individualize," *Elementary English 50* (March 1973): 427–29.

39. Veatch, Jeannette, "Self-Selection and the Individual Conference in Reading Instruction," *Improving Reading Instruction.* Joint Proceedings of Reading Conference and Summer Workshop, Vol. 1, The Pennsylvania State University, 1963, pp. 19–25.

40. Worth, Walter H. and Shores, Harlan, "Does Nonpromotion Improve Achievement in the Language Arts?" *Elementary English* (January 1960): 49–52.

v. West, Roland. *Individualized Reading Instruction.* Port Washington, N.Y.: Kennikat Press, c. 1964.

Chapter **10**

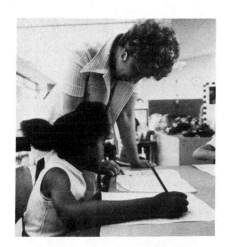

Diagnosing
Reading
Ability

It has been pointed out that children entering school show great differences in readiness to learn, and the differences in reading skills and ability increase in each succeeding grade. Since some children in second grade read at the primer level, their teacher must function at least part of the time as a first-grade teacher. In most third- and fourth-grade classrooms, there will be pupils who need instruction on skills *introduced* at earlier levels. Also, these same classrooms will contain children who are already fairly competent in the skills which are scheduled to be taught in these grades. For these children, more drill on mechanics which they have already mastered would be both wasteful and highly unmotivating. Figure 26 attempts to illustrate the overlap between grades and the range of reading abilities found at the primary level.

These facts, which apply to practically every classroom, emphasize the need for flexible or differentiated instruction. The one criterion that distinguishes excellent reading programs from others is the degree to which individual needs are ascertained and met. Teachers must be alert to differences among pupils in order to follow sound principles of teaching. Only through diagnosis will the teacher be able to assess needs and plan instruction for children whose needs vary considerably. Diagnosis should be thought of as continuous since children change rapidly. A diagnosis in September may be followed by a breakthrough on the part of the child in some vital skill or by a child's failure

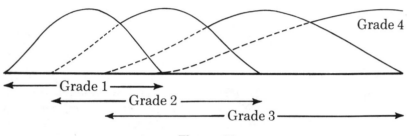

Figure 26

Graphic representation of reading
abilities in the primary grades. (Note
that the range of abilities increases
at each succeeding grade level.)

to master some new step in the reading process. In either case, the earlier diagnosis is obsolete.

Reading weaknesses and reading achievement can be assessed by either standardized or informal teacher-made tests. Although tests are designed for use at every grade level, no purpose would be served in a reading textbook by a separate discussion of tests each time a different instructional level is under consideration. The following discussion of tests and testing applies to the various levels of the elementary school with the exception that reading readiness tests are dealt with in Chapter 2.

Standardized
Tests

There are commercially printed tests which fall into two classes: those designed for group administration, and those designed to be administered individually. In both, credits are given for acceptable responses, and the child's score is determined by his correct responses, lack of errors, and rate of reading. Norms are usually provided, and any child's score can be translated into a grade-level equivalent. Usually subtests are scored separately, permitting the plotting of a profile which will indicate the areas of pupil strengths and weaknesses. Stan-

Establishing the ground rules for learning may be the key to learning.

dardized tests are widely used in our schools, and a larger number of them are becoming available each year. Most of these have real merit, yet it is doubtful that reading instruction is improving as a direct result of these tests. This is paradoxical. If tests have real merit, how could their widespread use not result in appreciable improvement in reading instruction?

The answer to this question is to be found in the way the tests are used (22). As pointed out in Chapter 1, the only justifiable purpose for the use of reading tests is to secure data about a child's reading ability so that a reading program for him can be built from the data secured. In actual practice, some schools and some teachers gain comfort from the use of tests because they are convinced that testing programs per se have educational value. Testing becomes an end in itself rather than a basis for instruction. In some communities a metal filing cabinet "with a folder for each pupil" is interpreted as prima facie evidence of good teaching practices. This reaction suggests that the school has lost sight of the principle that diagnosis alone has no salutary effect on the pupil diagnosed.

Group Tests

Tests designed for groups have some very obvious weaknesses. A second-grade teacher testing a large number of children at one time cannot hope to find out much about any individual child's reading needs or weaknesses. Such a test will differentiate between poor and good readers, but a formal test may not be the most economical method of securing these data. A considerable amount of teacher time must be spent in learning the precise procedure for administering and scoring the test and in analyzing the results. The skilled teacher who uses equal time and effort in informal reading situations will certainly arrive at an equally reliable division of pupils. In addition, she will also have a better idea of what specific weaknesses certain children have developed. From the standpoint of instruction, this is more important than simply knowing which children are impaired readers.

Another drawback to the use of group tests is that pupils' scores can be influenced by such factors as the misunderstanding of directions, the guessing of answers, and confusion in marking responses. If these go undetected in the group-administered test, the analysis of test scores will result in a distorted picture of the child's reading ability (18).

All achievement batteries designed to test pupils in the elementary school contain reading tests. Often these reading subtests are available in individual booklets which can be secured and administered independently of the rest of the battery. (The *California, SRA* and *Metropolitan* achievement batteries and the *Coordinated Scales of Attainment* are examples.) Since there are so many different reading tests, it is to be expected that many of them will measure virtually the same aspects of reading. Nevertheless, there are major differences among tests as to what they measure, the level of difficulty for which they are designed, the care which went into their construction, and the ease with which they are administered. Each of these factors affects two important attributes of reading tests—the consistency with which they measure reading skills, and the degree to which they actually measure the skills that they allegedly measure.

No full-time elementary teacher would have the time or the need to become thoroughly conversant with all standardized reading tests. However, it might be well to know where one can go for information about tests when that information is needed. Probably the most authoritative source for such information is *The Mental Measurements Year-book*, edited by Buros.* Information regarding tests can also be se-cured from publishers of tests and sample sets of tests can be pur-chased. In addition, many universities and colleges maintain testing bureaus which are equipped to advise teachers and administrators concerning tests and testing programs.

Individual Tests

Individual tests can minimize some of the shortcomings attributed to group tests. Teachers can observe one child quite closely during the administration of the test. This permits much more precise knowledge of reading errors made and whether or not the child understands the test directions. Individual standardized tests range in content from a single paragraph of oral reading at each grade level to a number of subtests including silent reading, oral reading with comprehension questions, spelling, letter recognition, sounding of blends, word mean-ings, and rapid recognition of sight words in isolation. The most sig-nificant subtests are the oral reading passages at each grade level. These are usually relatively short reading passages upon which the grade norms are based and, as a result, tend to rate pupils higher than their actual reading level on sustained reading material. Table 4 pre-

Table 4

Number of running words found on representative reading tests, grades 1–6.

	Running Words Found on:		
Grade Level	Durrell Analysis of Reading Difficulty**	Gray Oral Reading Paragraphs Test†	Gilmore Oral Reading Tests**
1	21	49	26
2	51	49	50
3	55	49	51
4	72	62	67
5	78	62	107
6	97	62	107

** World Book Co., New York
† Public School Publishing Co., Bloomington, Indiana

* Oscar Krisen Buros, ed., *The Sixth Mental Measurements Yearbook* (Highland Park, N.J.: The Gryphon Press, 1965). Also see Oscar Krisen Buros, *Reading Tests and Reviews* (Highland Park, N.J.: The Gryphon Press, 1968).

sents data on the number of running words (total number of words in the reading passage at each grade level) found in several reading tests designed for use in the elementary grades.

Representative Tests

A brief description of a limited number of both group and individual tests follows. These tests are selected because they illustrate different types of reading tests and because, in most cases, they are recent publications or recent revisions.

Group Tests

Gates-MacGinitie Reading Tests (1965). Publisher: Teachers College Press, Columbia University. Six separate tests are available for testing grades one through nine.

	Grade	Subtests	Forms
Primary A	1	Vocabulary, Comprehension	1–2
Primary B	2	Vocabulary, Comprehension	1–2
Primary C	3	Vocabulary, Comprehension	1–2
Primary CS	2.5–3	Speed, Accuracy	1–2–3
Survey D*	4–5–6	Speed, Vocabulary, Comprehension	1–2–3
Survey E*	7–8–9	Speed, Vocabulary, Comprehension	1–2–3

Nelson-Lohmann Reading Test (Grades 4–8). Publisher: Educational Test Bureau, Educational Publishers, Inc. This is a paragraph test using multiple-choice questions to measure the pupil's grasp of central ideas; word meanings derived from context, and details; and the pupil's ability to integrate ideas. There are separate tests for each grade level 4–8. Two comparable forms are available.

These tests are also part of the battery: *Coordinated Scales of Attainment*.

S.R.A. Achievement Series (1964). Publisher: Science Research Associates, Inc. These materials consist of three separate batteries for use at

---

* Available in both hand-scored and machine-scored editions.

grade levels 1–2; 2–4; 4–9. There are subtests for each area of the curriculum. The following data refer only to the reading subtests.

Grades 1–2. The reading test contains 4 subtests: verbal-picture association, language perception, comprehension, and vocabulary. Forms C-D.

Grades 2–4. The reading test consists of two subtests: vocabulary and comprehension. Forms C-D.

Grades 4–9. Three separate batteries are published in a single booklet. Batteries are for grade levels as follows:

4.5 to 5.5
6.5 to 8.0
8 to 9

Subtests: Comprehension, Vocabulary. Forms C-D.

California Achievement Test Batteries (1957 edition with 1963 norms). Publisher: California Test Bureau.

a. Lower Primary, Grades 1–2
b. Upper Primary, Grades 3–4
c. Elementary, Grades 4–6
d. Junior High, Grades 7–9
e. Advanced, Grades 9–14

Reading skills measured: Reading vocabulary and reading comprehension are tested. Each is covered by several subtests which yield part scores. The reading tests, which are part of the achievement battery, are available as separate tests under the title *California Reading Test*.

Four forms: W, X, Y, Z.

Stanford Achievement Tests (1966). Publisher: Harcourt, Brace Jovanovich, Inc. Five separate batteries cover grades 1–9. Each battery contains a number of subtests on reading.

Primary Battery I. Grades 1–2.5 (Word Reading, Paragraph Meaning, Vocabulary, Spelling, Word Study Skills).
Primary Battery II. Grades 2–3 (Word Meaning, Paragraph Meaning, Spelling, Word Study Skills, Language).
Intermediate Battery I. Grades 4–5 (same subtests as above).
Intermediate Battery II. Grades 5–6 (Word Meaning, Paragraph Meaning, Spelling, Language).
Advanced Battery. Grades 7–9 (Paragraph Meaning, Spelling, Language).

Each of the above batteries is available in forms: W, X, Y, Z.

Iowa Tests of Basic Skills (Grades 3–9). Publisher: Houghton Mifflin Company (3 alternate forms). This achievement battery yields eleven separate scores in the following major areas: vocabulary, reading comprehension, language skills, work-study skills, and arithmetic skills.

All of the subtests for each grade, three through nine, are included in one spiral booklet of ninety-six pages. These booklets are reusable since responses are made on separate answer sheets.

The reading comprehension test requires approximately one hour for administration at *each* grade level. It consists of a number of stories of graduated length and difficulty. Comprehension is tested by means of multiple choice items, the reader selecting the one best answer from among the four available. As noted above, the reading comprehension test is available only as part of the entire Basic Skills Battery.

American School Achievement Tests (Part I, Test of Reading). Publisher: The Bobbs-Merrill Co., Inc.

    a. Primary Battery, Grades 2–3
    b. Intermediate Battery, Grades 4–6
    c. Advanced Battery, Grades 7–9

Reading skills measured (all levels): Sentence and word meaning, paragraph meaning, and total reading score.
Four forms: D, E, F, G.

Individual Tests

Durrell Analysis of Reading Difficulty (Grades 1–6). Major subtests include a separate series of paragraphs for oral reading and recall, silent reading and recall, and listening comprehension. Other subtests measure visual recognition of letters and words, ability to give sounds of letters and blends, and spelling. Each individual test folder contains an extensive checklist of potential reading difficulties. This test has several limitations: only one form is available; grade level norms are based on rate but not on comprehension; and comprehension questions rely heavily on recall of detail, thus slighting other facets of comprehension.

Gates-McKillop Reading Diagnostic Tests. (Grades 2–6, a 1962 Revision of the *Gates Reading Diagnostic Tests*). Publisher: Teachers Press, Teachers College, Columbia University. This test consists of subtests measuring oral reading, rapid recognition of whole words, untimed sight-word recognition, auditory blending, spelling, recognizing word parts, and oral vocabulary (meaning). The total test yields twenty-eight scores, is somewhat complicated to administer, and is time-consuming.

Gilmore Oral Reading Test (Grades 1–8). Publisher: World Book Company. This test consists of ten paragraphs, arranged in order of difficulty, which form a continuous story. Each paragraph, representing a grade level, is followed by five comprehension questions. There are two forms of the test, both of which are included in the same spiral-bound booklet. The test yields separate scores on rate of reading, comprehension, and accuracy (pronunciation of vocabulary). The individual record blank permits a detailed record of reading errors.

Gray Oral Reading Test (1963). Publisher: The Bobbs-Merrill Co., Inc. This test consists of a series of thirteen paragraphs of increasing difficulty. As the subject reads orally, the examiner marks on an identical passage the errors noted such as mispronunciation, words not attempted, omission, substitution, repetitions, and the like. Comprehension of each paragraph is checked by a series of four questions. Each paragraph is timed. Scoring involves recording the number of errors, type of errors, time elapsed in reading each paragraph, and a comprehension score. Total score can be converted into a grade-equivalent score. There are four alternate forms of the test: A, B, C, D.

Informal
Teacher-made
Tests

Teachers can devise informal tests for any classroom purpose (25). The simplest screening test might consist of having a child read a paragraph or two from a book to determine whether he can successfully read that particular book (15). More thorough informal tests will yield important data about children's reading, and these tests have certain advantages for classroom use. First, they are simple to construct since the teacher has available graded reading materials from the preprimer level through the upper grades. Second, the child can be tested over longer passages of sustained reading than are characteristically found on standardized tests. Third, the use of teacher-made tests avoids the formality of the usual test situation. Informal testing is not likely to arouse the pupil tensions which sometimes accompany testing and which occasionally influence pupil performance. In this respect, the informal test more closely parallels the actual reading situations which the child encounters in the classroom (16). Finally, the teacher-made test is inexpensive and demands no more teacher time for administration and analysis than do other tests. At the same time, it yields very specific data on each child's weaknesses and needs, as do the individual standardized tests. The following steps might serve as a guide in the construction of an informal test.

Devise a checklist of reading behaviors. This is usually one page upon which the teacher can rapidly record reading errors and observations of related behavior. Figure 27 is an example which could be duplicated and filled out for each child in the class. The checklist can be used with any graded reading materials.

Testing
Mechanical Skills

In the final analysis, the act of reading is a type of global behavior that is made possible by the simultaneous application of a great number of skills (3). The terms *mechanical skills* and *comprehension skills*, as used in this chapter should not lead the reader to visualize a dichotomy. The simple fact is that critical reading or *comprehending* depends on the mastery of a myriad of related skills. It is true that when we give children assignments in reading we imply that the reader is to use the global skill labeled critical reading. However, actual instruction in reading almost always focuses on one or a limited number of skills.

The following pages provide illustrative materials which can be used or adapted for determining a child's present level of functioning in regard to a number of skills such as

1. Letter recognition.
2. Associating printed letters with sounds they represent.
3. Auditory discrimination of speech sounds in words.
4. Structural analysis (involving root words to which affixes have been added).

Figure 27

Reading Behavior Record.

Name_____ Age_____ Grade_____ Date_____
School_____ Teacher_____
Examiner_____

I. *Word Analysis*
  A. Knows names of letters?   Yes   No
     Needs work with:_____
  B. Attacks initial sound of words?   Yes   No
     Deficiencies noted:_____
  C. Can substitute initial letter-sounds?   Yes   No
     Further drill needed:_____
  D. Can sound out initial blends and digraphs?   Yes   No
     Deficiencies noted:_____
  E. If root word is known, can solve words
     formed by adding prefixes and suffixes.   Yes   No

II. *Sight Words* (Check if applicable)
  _____ Knows a word one time, misses it later.
  _____ Guesses at unknown words.
     _____ Errors frequently do not change intended meaning.
     _____ Errors indicate not reading for meaning.
  _____ Frequently adds words.
  _____ Omits unknown words.
     _____ Reads on.
     _____ Fills in omitted word.
  _____ Omits or skips words he knows or can solve.

III. *Reading Habits Noted*
  _____ Reads word by word   _____ Loses place frequently
  _____ Phrasing inadequate   _____ Does not utilize punctuation
  _____ Poor intonation   _____ Lacks persistence
  _____ Dialect interference: Explain_____

IV. *Sustained Reading* (Basal, textbook, trade book)

Book	Grade Level	Approx. Number of Running Words	Number of Errors
1.			
2.			

Figure 27 (cont.)

Errors noted (example): Said *lied* for *lying; banged* for *bumped; stuck* for *start* (corrected)

Needed help with: *clown, stomach, curious, squeal.*

Read with some hesitation, not smoothly, etc.

	Excellent	Average	Below Average
V. *Comprehension*	___	___	___
Recall of facts	___	___	___
Recognizes main ideas	___	___	___
Draws inferences	___	___	___
Maintains sequence of events	___	___	___
Understands humor	___	___	___
Interprets figurative expressions	___	___	___
VI. *Oral Reading Skills*	___	___	___
Relates with audience	___	___	___
Enunciation	___	___	___
Adequate volume	___	___	___
Reads with intonation	___	___	___
Phrases for meaning	___	___	___
VII. *Behaviors Related to Reading*	___	___	___
Attitude toward reading	___	___	___
Self confidence	___	___	___
Background knowledge	___	___	___
Language facility	___	___	___
Originality of expression	___	___	___
Range of vocabulary	___	___	___
Stock of concepts	___	___	___
Variety of sentence patterns	___	___	___

VIII. *Other Comments:* _____

_____

_____

_____

_____

_____

_____

_____

5. Syllabication.
6. Sight recognition of high frequency words.

**Letter
Recognition**

To determine if a child recognizes capital and lower case letter forms, prepare a set of alphabet cards each of which shows a capital letter on one side and its lower case form on the other side.

1. Present cards in mixed order and record errors made.

Alternate approaches:

2. Present letter forms in mixed order on page or large cardboard. Child points to and names each letter.

B	L	M	G	P
K	S	D	F	H

a	c	d	l	m
g	s	t	n	e

3. Matching capital and lower case forms: Duplicate a page of boxes similar to below. Child draws line to, or circles, matching lower case form.

	b		e		d		h
M	c	A	a	D	p	G	r
	m		h		b		g

**Letter-sound Relationships
(Initial and Final Consonants,
Medial Vowels)**

Prepare a page of pictures. Below each picture is a line on which the child is to do *one* of the following tasks.

Write the letter that represents

1. the first sound heard in the picture naming word.
2. the last sound heard in the picture naming word.
3. the vowel sound heard in the picture naming word.

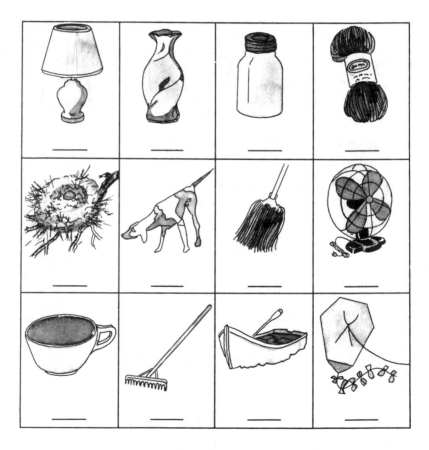

More difficult task: Child writes letter for initial, medial, and final sounds. (Picture naming words limited to three phonemes)

Initial consonants in sentence format

Each sentence emphasizes one initial letter-sound and can provide clues as to whether a child is experiencing trouble with any particular initial letter-sound.

1. Bobby brought back bunches of bananas.
2. Candy, the cat, can't come to class.
3. Dad didn't drop the dozen doughnuts on Dave's desk.
4. Father feels fine after falling four feet from the fir tree.
5. Go get a gun and a good guide if you hunt geese.
6. Henry hurt his hand with the heavy hammer.
7. Jean joined Joe in playing a joke on Jack.
8. Kate keeps the key in the kitchen.
9. The lucky lady located the lovely locket that she had lost at lunch.
10. My mother made Mike move the muddy mess.
11. Nick noticed a number of new nails in the workshop.
12. Polly put the pitcher in the pantry.
13. The rabbit ate the raw radishes, then ran rapidly down the ranch road.
14. Six surprised sailors saw Sam sneeze suddenly.
15. Ted tried to teach the tiny tot to talk.
16. On Wednesday, Wendy was washing the windows.
17. Yes, your younger brother yelled in the yard yesterday.
18. Zelda saw a zebra at the zoo.

Blends and digraphs

These words test the ability to sound most two-letter blends and digraphs in initial and final positions.

blank	church	slump	smart	skunk	speech
trump	brisk	plant	cloth	grand	champ
present	slant	which	drink	frost	chest
charm	fresh	crash	stand	crisp	swing

Auditory Discrimination

1. The teacher pronounces the four words in each series. The child repeats the one word that differs from the first word in the phoneme being tested.

Testing for auditory discrimination
is wise. A problem in this area can
trigger many other problems.

a. *Initial Consonants*

*t*oy	*p*at	*d*id	*w*ind	*d*ark	*f*arm
tall	pet	kid	went	drink	warm
hall	cot	doll	bend	dash	find
tack	put	dull	well	bark	full

*b*all	*h*ard	*l*ack	*k*ick	*m*arch	*r*ode
pull	yard	lock	pick	much	load
back	hunt	lamp	kill	met	right
burn	hurt	damp	kind	net	race

b. *Endings of Words*
   Child repeats the one word which does not rhyme.

pig	bake	ball	wet	bug	bag
dig	make	full	bet	hug	rug
big	bark	tall	pet	did	rag
bag	wake	wall	sat	mug	sag
pot	lick	leg	cut	fell	then
not	stuck	peg	hit	fill	hen
got	stick	lap	hut	sell	thin
God	kick	keg	but	bell	pen

c. *Initial Blends*
   Child repeats the word which does not begin with the blend sound.

dress	sled	blue	step	tree	plan
drop	sack	blow	sack	truck	place
draw	slip	bank	stop	train	pain
down	slap	black	steep	turn	play

d. *Vowel Sounds*
   Child repeats word having short vowel sound.

mate	fame	fight	joke	cute	team
mail	fan	mile	lock	dull	tell
mad	table	fine	note	true	see
take	flame	skim	snow	tube	feed

2. Testing child's ability to associate letter forms with sounds they represent using nonsense syllables which follow the CVC, CVVC, CVCV, and CVCC patterns. (Explain that the following are not words. Invite the child to pronounce each letter-pattern as if it were a word.)

baf	nem	gog	lut
kep	pab	med	bol
foz	ras	jum	pib
dut	hos	sug	taf
lig	tuv	vax	lod

(CVVC and CVCV)

beel	pcan	taid	doat
heam	reet	gode	lume
kine	saim	feaf	daik
fote	mave	cabe	heef

(*CVCC*)

banf	polt	mulk	deng
hent	resk	saft	milt
dist	fland	hamp	goft
juld	tilp	lonk	zold

**Structural
Analysis**

The sight-word tests on pages 345–46 contain only common root words. The words below test the child's ability to deal with inflectional endings, affixes, compounds and contractions.

a. *Easy root words plus endings* s, ed, ing

running	seated	playing	comes	played
asks	talking	lived	wanted	going
looked	wants	jumps	talks	sees
helps	coming	lives	walking	helping
wanting	likes	pleased	talked	looks
sits	helped	finding	runs	sitting
living	stops	plays	seeing	jumped

b. *Contractions, compound words, and derived forms usually learned at second-grade level*

happily	belong	I'll	slowly	behind	hadn't
bakery	didn't	friendly	report	surely	himself
princess	outside	loudest	I'd	everybody	believe
quickly	afternoon	return	herself	you'll	politely
I've	it's	really	suddenly	everyone	shouted
isn't	warmer	everything	doesn't	couldn't	yourself
beside	anything	can't	between	into	wasn't

c. *Contractions, compound words, and derived forms usually learned at third-grade level*

expect	explain	disappear	comfortable	rapidly
afternoon	ourselves	happiness	halfway	sawmill
you've	discover	invite	safety	invisible
family	they'll	include	upward	Thanksgiving
enjoy	unless	gentleman	peaceful	eyebrow
funniest	experiment	foolish	enchanted	firecrackers
finally	we've	contentment	bathroom	telescope

Syllabication

Words taken from spelling books at 3rd, 4th, and 5th grade level to test child's ability to break words into syllables. Pupil writes words in Column B. First word serves as sample.

	Primer level		*Intermediate level*
A	*B*	*A*	*B*
yesterday	yes ter day	beautiful	beau ti ful
grandfather	_____	geography	_____
birthday	_____	studying	_____
money	_____	history	_____
yellow	_____	interesting	_____
Easter	_____	difference	_____
stockings	_____	medium	_____
only	_____	electric	_____
afternoon	_____	average	_____
lessons	_____	citizen	_____

Word Recognition

Children who are progressing satisfactorily in mastering the developmental skills of reading are constantly expanding their sight vocabulary. To test sight vocabulary one could use the *Dolch Basic Sight Word Test** of 220 words. The material below consists of one hundred high frequency words taken from first grade basal materials. Any list of high frequency words, including the one below, will show considerable overlap with the Dolch List (7). While reading words in isolation is not reading, tests can reveal whether or not the child has mastered a number of high frequency "service words." If these words are not recognized instantly, the child will find reading, even at the primary level, a most frustrating task.

we	horse	they	boat
with	a	jump	to
yes	an	big	walk
stop	look	come	want
like	was	go	on

---

* Garrard Press, Champaign, Illinois.

help	find	think	house
very	little	and	my
all	best	could	can
this	old	boy	talk
some	try	may	girl
the	see	again	said
ball	mother	pretty	will
friend	any	which	father
went	over	then	small
did	wagon	live	blue
good	not	run	had
in	play	arm	she
me	what	up	your
hat	do	each	after
man	ran	his.	clean
that	new	got	many
saw	wish	red	most
you	dog	there	around
here	under	please	open
sure	ride	name	every

High frequency words (Irregular spellings)

a	I	any	are	all	too	the
been	come	do	get	head	they	his
put	good	would	have	two	very	you
give	is	use	put	done	their	what
once	of	gone	there	who	sure	does
look	some	know	said	many	was	your
one	here	only	to	could	walk	were

Testing
for Reversals

Each of the following words is also a word when spelled backwards. In exercise A, children read the words in isolation. In exercise B, each sentence contains a number of reversible words.

A

was	pin	no	pal	rats
step	tub	spot	on	nip

saw	trap	net	tip	lap
tap	rat	part	pot	star
pan	ten	tops	nap	pits
top	but	pat	tar	pets

B

1. Pam will pat the dog named Spot.
2. There was no top to put on the pot.
3. The words *star* and *tar* rhyme; but *pin* and *pan* do not.
4. Who was it that I saw pin the star on the net?
5. His pets Nip and Pal took a nap in the tub.

Measuring Comprehension

Any situation in which a child reads can provide clues to his reading strengths and instructional needs. Even the responses that children make on workbook pages can provide important diagnostic clues. Undoubtedly one of the best ways to evaluate reading is to listen to the child read a paragraph or two from a basal reader, social studies, or science text, or from a trade book.

Comprehension tasks for silent reading can also focus on important facets of critical reading (12). Some illustrations of exercises that might be used for this purpose are included in the following pages. Examples are

1. Tests of ability to use context clues.
   a. Sentence meaning
   b. Cloze procedures, paragraph length
   c. Sentences that do not "fit"
2. Drawing inferences.
3. Following directions.
   a. Sentence tasks
   b. Problem solving
4. Test of word meanings (malapropisms).
5. Determining *fact* or opinion.

Obviously, any idea that is incorporated into informal testing will have to be adapted to fit the difficulty level of the pupils involved.

Comprehension in Oral Reading

Material for a test over sustained reading can consist of passages read from textbooks (basals, social studies, science, etc.) or trade books. An alternative is to assemble pages or copies of pages in order of difficulty in a teacher-made folder. Comprehension questions are carefully developed for each passage. Some teachers prefer to have extra copies of the passages so that they can mark each error and weakness observed. A checklist such as shown on pages 337-38 can be used to record inadequacies such as letter-sound relationships, sight vocabulary word meaning problems, punctuation, intonation, and the like.

**Use of Context
Clues in Sentences**

In each of the following sentences two words are omitted. Read each sentence and fill in the words that complete the meaning of the sentence.

1. It is warmer in _____ than in _____ .
2. The bird built a _____ in the _____ .
3. A week has seven _____ ; a year has _____ months.
4. Apples, _____ , and _____ are fruit.
5. When you _____ five and three the _____ is eight.
6. Leaves fall from the _____ in the _____ .
7. Put a _____ on the letter and mail _____ .
8. John runs very _____ but Bill runs even _____ .
9. A decade is _____ years and a century is _____ years.
10. A baby cow is a _____ and a baby bear is a _____ .

**Use of Context Clues
in Sustained Reading
(Cloze Procedure)**

In the following passage, every sixth word is missing. The reader writes a word in each blank space and in doing so reveals an accurate picture of his comprehension of the passage. For further discussion of the cloze technique see Taylor (29) and Bormuth (1).

A helicopter is an aircraft _____ whirling wings. Pilots call it _____ whirlybird or a chopper. The _____ blades, called rotors, go round _____ round like a propeller on _____ back, but they really lift _____ copter just the way a _____ wing does.

The wonderful thing _____ rotors is that they can _____ the copter almost straight up _____ the ground and bring it _____ almost straight down. They can _____ it fly backward as well _____ forward. Or they can keep _____ hovering above one spot. This _____ that a helicopter needs no _____ runway for landing or taking _____ . A space just a little _____ than its rotors is usually _____ .*

Sentences that Do Not Belong

In each of the following paragraphs there is one sentence that "does not fit." Underline that sentence and tell why it does not fit in the paragraph.

1. John visited grandfather's farm. He saw some ducks and cows. John never liked lions. He helped grandfather feed the chickens.
2. Mary loves sports. She plays tennis and basketball. This summer she earned ten dollars. Mary enjoys watching sports on television.
3. Mark Twain wrote the book *Tom Sawyer*. It is about a boy who lives on the Mississippi River. One of Tom's friends is called Huckleberry Finn. The Colorado River formed the Grand Canyon.
4. The beaver is intelligent and works very hard. He has sharp teeth and can cut down small trees. The beaver can build dams in streams. He can blow water out of his trunk. Beavers do not eat fish.
5. One of the problems troubling our country today is pollution of our air and water. Automobiles, factories, and careless individuals all

---

* Mary Elting, *Aircraft at Work*, Irvington-on-Hudson (New York: Harvey House, Inc., 1964), p. 50 (Words in original 1. with, 2. a, 3. long, 4. and 5. its, 6. the, 7. fixed, 8. about, 9. take, 10. from, 11. back, 12. make, 13. as, 14. it, 15. means, 16. long, 17. off, 18. wider, 19. enough.

contribute to the problem. Everywhere, people are pleased with the environment. It will take years and great sums of money to clean up the air and water.

Comprehension through
Drawing Inferences

Read each numbered sentence and the statements a, b, c beneath it. Circle the statement you think is most logical.

Sample: The children went outside to build a snowman.
  a. It was May.
  b. It was August.
  c. It was January.
1. As we were riding along, father slammed on the brakes.
  a. It had started to rain.
  b. We were out of gas.
  c. A dog ran in front of the car.
2. The rooster crowed in the dim light.
  a. He was hungry.
  b. The sun was about to rise.
  c. He was saying "Good night."
3. The class went to the zoo and saw:
  a. A herd of cows.
  b. Two elephants.
  c. Donald Duck.
4. When the window broke the boy ran.
  a. He had broken the window.
  b. He was late for school.
  c. The noise frightened him.
5. There were an elephant and a giraffe in the barn.
  a. They had run away from the zoo.
  b. The farmer was a big game hunter.
  c. The farmer was taking care of the animals for a circus.
6. The woman ran into the store holding a newspaper over her head.
  a. It was raining.
  b. She was going to buy the paper.
  c. She was telling everyone the news.
7. The ambulance roared down the street sounding its siren.
  a. The ambulance was part of a parade.

b. Traffic was very light.
c. There has been an accident.
8. The family climbed into the car which was crowded with suitcases.
  a. They were going to a suitcase sale.
  b. It was vacation time.
  c. Father was going to the bank.

Following Written Directions (Sentence Tasks)

1. Put the letter *l* in front of each word if it will form a new word.
_and   _end   _make   _ate   _old   _ice   _ink

2. Write the plural form of each of the following words.
house_____   bird_____   glass_____
brush_____   box_____   bench_____

3. Add the ending *ed* if this will make another word.
know____   light____   men____   park____   wish____
talk____   ring____   visit____   jerk____   shoot____

4. Underline all compound words.
somewhere swimming upon   waterproof overnight movement
wonderful   newspaper important broadcast   careless   silverware

5. Rewrite the following words to make a sentence.
the station train of rolled out the

6. Circle each word to which we could add *s* to form another word.
fun   city   hurt   rub   came   run   seed   tell

7. Circle each word that can mean a person or persons.
going   he   Mary   pretty   they   someone   upon

8. Put the letter *s* in front of each word if this will form a new word.
_and   _car   _hot   _make   _lip   _kill
_pray   _ate   _mile   _nail   _ask   _win

9. Write the following words in alphabetical order.
elephant   elm   eel   envelope   easy

10. Place the correct number in the blank space.
1   2   4   8   16   ____

Problem Solving:
Following Written Directions

Each of the directions below asks you to study *Box A* and *Box B*. Then carry out the directions found in each of the numbered sentences.

1. If the sum of two odd numbers is always an even number, place a small *x* in the middle figure in line one, Box B.
2. If the sum of the third and fourth numbers in Box A is equal to the seventh number, circle A in Box A.
3. If this is an odd numbered sentence, circle the digit 6 in Box A.
4. If both lines 1 and 2 in Box B contain a square, put an *x* in the square on line 2.

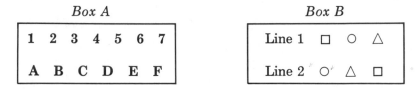

	Box A					

	Box B

1   2   3   4   5   6   7

A   B   C   D   E   F

Line 1   □   ○   △

Line 2   ○   △   □

5. If the sum of the digits in Box A is greater than 28, underline D in Box A.
6. If there are the same number of digits in Box A as there are letters, place a dot (·) in the circle on Line 2 of Box B.
7. If there are more odd numbers than there are even numbers in Box A, circle the E in Box A.
8. If the sum of the first two digits in Box A equals the third digit, circle the sixth letter in Box A.
9. If there are three vowels in Box A, circle one of the triangles in Box B.

Word Recognition
and Meaning

People often use one word when they mean to use a different one. In each of the following sentences there is one word that "does not fit." a. Underline this word. b. On the blank space following each sentence, write the word you think was intended.

1. She was selling magazine prescriptions. _____
2. Lincoln was a grate president. _____
3. The picture for the baseball team was hurt. _____
4. The waiter said, "I hope your stake is delicious." _____
5. The word *big* is a cinnamon for *large*. _____
6. Desert land must be irritated to grow crops. _____
7. The doctor said, "This child has an inflection." _____
8. After a rain, the humility is quite high. _____
9. The cliffs had become withered from the wind and rain. _____
10. "Aisle be seeing you" he said. _____

Diagnosis revealed the problem —
teaching is aimed at resolving it.

SUMMARY

The reading ability of children in any given classroom will cover a wide range of achievement. Diagnosis is a prerequisite for differentiation of instruction which, in turn, is an essential for a sound reading program. One of the principles stressed in Chapter 1 is that diagnosis provides the blueprint for instruction.

Formal testing involving the use of standardized tests is one type of diagnosis. Unfortunately, in some schools the administration of these tests is dictated by the calendar rather than by sound instructional philosophy. If the chief aim of testing is to arrive at grade-level scores for individuals and mean scores for classes, diagnosis is reduced to an educational ritual. Test results must be carefully analyzed for clues to each child's strengths and weaknesses.

Meaningful diagnosis must be ongoing. It should be remembered that anytime a child reads, he provides clues to his instructional needs. Listening to a child's oral reading of a paragraph or two from any textbook will provide as much information per time unit invested as will any testing situation. The alert teacher will note whether the material is too difficult, what types of errors are made, and whether the child's sight vocabulary, word attack skills, and phrasing are adequate. The child's responses in this reading situation will suggest what other informal diagnostic approaches are now appropriate. Examples of brief testing materials have been provided throughout this chapter.

YOUR POINT OF VIEW?

What is the basis for your agreement or disagreement with each of the following propositions?

1. In most classroom situations, critical reading is equated with supplying responses which arbitrarily have been decided upon as being correct. Creative reading which might lead to divergent interpretations is not encouraged.

2. In many schools the potential values which might be achieved from the use of standardized tests are lost because the school is more concerned with the ritual of administering tests than in "mining the test data."

3. The cloze procedure is a valid measure of reading comprehension.

4. Informal teacher-made tests can yield as much data about an individual child's reading as can standardized tests.

5. If capacity is held constant and equal amounts of expert instruction is given to all children in a class or group, those children who are lowest in reading achievement will make the smallest gain per unit of instructional time.

6. There is little basis for assuming that the school can prevent a substantial number of reading failures among pupils.

Respond to the following problems:

A. During the first week of school you suspect that Johnny cannot read the social studies text that has been adopted for class use. You have five minutes to work with him and you wish to verify or refute the above hypothesis. How would you use this time?
B. *Premise:* The "grade level" score achieved on reading tests is more representative of the child's ability to deal with basal reading materials than it is of his ability to deal with textbooks in the content areas. Can you provide evidence that supports this assumption?
C. Assume that the use of standardized reading tests in the elementary grades was prohibited for the next five years. Suggest logical hypotheses as to what would happen in reading instruction if this unlikely event occurred.

BIBLIOGRAPHY

1. Bormuth, John R., "Factor Validity of Cloze Tests as Measures of Reading Comprehension Ability," *Reading Research Quarterly* (Spring 1969): 358–65.
2. Buros, Oscar Krisen, ed., *Reading Tests and Reviews II*. Highland Park, N.J.: The Gryphon Press, 1975.
3. Farr, Roger, *Reading: What Can Be Measured*. Newark, Del.: International Reading Association, 1969.
4. ——— and Brown, Virginia L., "Evaluation and Decision Making," *The Reading Teacher* (January 1971): 341–46.
5. ——— and Roser, Nancy L., "Reading Assessment: A Look at Problems and Issues," *Journal of Reading 17* (May 1974): 592–99.
6. Hood, Joyce, "Qualitative Analysis of Oral Reading Errors: The Inter-Judge Reliability of Scores," *Reading Research Quarterly 11*, no. 4, 1975–76, pp. 577–98.
7. Johnson, Dale D., "The Dolch List Reexamined," *The Reading Teacher* (February 1971): 449–57.
8. Karlin, Robert and Jolly, Hayden, "The Use of Alternate Forms of Standardized Reading Tests," *Reading Teacher* (December 1966): 187–91.
9. Karlin, Robert, *Teaching Elementary Reading*, second ed. New York: Harcourt Brace Jovanovich, Inc., 1975. Chapter 2.
10. Kastner, Marie A., "Instructing and Motivating Pupils in the Light of Test Results," *Catholic Educational Review* (February 1969): 106–10.
11. Kaufman, Maurice, "The Oral Reading Sample in Reading Diagnosis," *Reading World 16* (October 1976): 39–47.

12. King, Martha L., "New Developments in the Evaluation of Critical Reading," *Forging Ahead in Reading*, J. Allen Figurel, ed. Proceedings, International Reading Association 12, Part 1, pp. 179–85.

13. Knafle, June D., "Word Perception: Cues Aiding Structure Detection," *Reading Research Quarterly 8*, no. 4, 1973, pp. 502–23.

14. Ladd, Eleanor M., "More Than Test Scores," *The Reading Teacher* (January 1971): 305–11.

15. McCracken, Robert A., "Using Reading as a Basis for Grouping," *Education* (February 1964): 357–59.

16. ————, "The Informal Reading Inventory as a Means of Improving Instruction," in Thomas C. Barrett, ed., *The Evaluation of Children's Reading Achievement*. Newark, Del.: International Reading Association, 1967, pp. 79–96.

17. Miller, Harry B. and Hering, Steve, "Teacher Ratings—Which Reading Group is Number One?" *Reading Teacher 28* (January 1975): 389–91.

18. Mitchell, Addie S., "Values and Limitations of Standardized Reading Tests," in *Forging Ahead in Reading*, J. Allen Figurel, ed. Proceedings, International Reading Association 12, Part 1, pp. 163–67.

19. Page, William D., "Pseudocues, Supercues and Comprehension," *Reading World 15* (May 1976): 232–38.

20. Pikulski, John, "A Critical Review: Informal Reading Inventories," *Reading Teacher 28* (November 1974): 141–51.

21. Prescott, George A., "Criterion-Referenced Test Interpretation in Reading," *The Reading Teacher* (January 1971): 347–54.

22. Putt, Robert C. and Ray, Darrell D., "Putting Test Results to Work," *Elementary School Journal* (May 1965): 439–44.

23. Ramsey, Wallace, "The Value and Limitations of Diagnostic Reading Tests for Evaluation in the Classroom," *The Evaluation of Children's Reading Achievement*, Thomas C. Barrett, ed. Newark, Del.: International Reading Association, 1967, pp. 65–77.

24. Ransom, Peggy E., "Determining Reading Levels of Elementary School Children by Cloze Testing," *Forging Ahead in Reading*, J. Allen Figurel, ed. Proceedings, International Reading Association 12, Part 1, pp. 477–82.

25. *Reading Teacher* (January 1971). Entire issue devoted to Testing.

26. Robinson, H. Alan and Hanson, Earl, "Reliability of Measures of Reading Achievement," *The Reading Teacher* (January 1968): 307–13.

27. Rodenborn, Leo V., "Determining, Using Expectancy Formulas," *Reading Teacher 28* (December 1974): 286–91.

28. Strain, Lucille B., *Accountability in Reading Instruction*. Columbus, O.: Charles E. Merrill Publishing Co., 1976. Chapter 6.

29. Taylor, Wilson L., "Cloze-Procedure: A New Tool for Measuring Readability," *Journalism Quarterly* (Fall 1953): 415–33.

30. Trela, Thaddeus M., "What Do Diagnostic Reading Tests Diagnose?" *Elementary English* (April 1966): 370–72.

Chapter 11

The Culturally Different Child as a Learner*

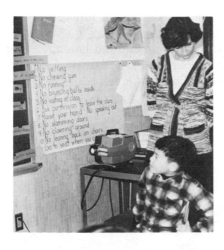

The learners discussed in this chapter have been identified by several different labels: socially handicapped, economically deprived, culturally disadvantaged, linguistically different, dialect speakers, children without, the leftouts, the newcomers, the educationally handicapped, the socially deprived, the alienated ones, the underachievers, children from depressed areas, and the children of the poor. The list is exhaustive and yet no one term fully and adequately describes these children. The term *culturally different* will be used throughout this discussion.

The term *culturally different* refers to the economically deprived child who is not profiting from the established curriculum and who is not learning to read. The term includes speakers of dialects from all racial groups—

* This chapter contributed by Dr. Ruby Thompson, The Reading Center, Atlanta University.

black, white, Indian-American, Mexican-American, and Puerto Rican, and others.

Not all dialect speakers are included. Many blacks, Mexican-Americans, and others who are "bidialectal" do not have reading problems. The major distinguishing factor between the reading achievement of learners from the same ethnic or racial group appears to be socio-economic level. Blacks from middle- and upper-class socio-economic strata do not experience the difficulties which their lower-class counterparts experience; middle-class whites fare better than their counterparts from low socio-economic backgrounds. This is to say that the cultural difference alone does not render a child a poor reader; linguistic differences coupled with economic deprivation are perhaps better discriminators. The bilingual child may be viewed from the same perspective.

Failure in reading has been the major educational problem of the children from these groups. Although these learners may differ in race, ethnic background, geographic placement, and cultural heritage, they share the common problem of reading failure. Since part of the problem is that the school is alien to these children, it is felt that if teachers know and understand them, the first objective of a good reading program has been met.

The life-style of the culturally different learner changes little. He lives in a culture of poverty.

1. Housing is usually substandard, crowded, and in unattractive surroundings. (The ghetto, dusty rural areas, tenement shacks, pitched tents, dilapidated trailers.)

2. Food and clothing are often inadequate according to nutritional and health standards.

3. Family ties are often unstable because of the restrictions imposed by the environment, poor economic conditions, and the psychological factors that these conditions manifest.

4. Groups are socially alienated from all middle-class society and therefore are not exposed to the factors that determine the criteria by which they are ultimately judged.

5. Jobs are usually those on the lower end of the continuum in terms of pay, prestige, and security—if jobs are held at all.

6. Educational levels of parents seldom exceed junior high school.

7. Exposure to the crime, violence, and prevalence of immorality that are bred and nurtured in their environments is early and continuous.

Although teachers can do little as individuals to change these conditions, they must be more sensitive to the deficits that such an environment may have imposed on the children. These include the tendency to have a poor self-concept, low aspirational levels, to be tardy and absent frequently, to be poorly oriented to school and school tasks, to display hostility toward school and school authorities, to resist or reject values which are foreign to them and which are forced on them by teachers whom they tend to distrust.

As a potential reader, the culturally different learner will come to school speaking his natural language which is not the language upon which the curriculum was constructed. He may not have auditory discrimination for some "standard" English speech phonemes, and he will be much more limited than most middle-class children in his development of readiness skills for reading.

Several other characteristics that have been associated with the culturally different learner are either erroneous or misleading. Examples include the ideas that the parents do not care about their children's academic achievement, that the children do not want to learn, that the children are naturally prone to violence inside and outside the classroom, and that they are genetically inferior in regard to school learning tasks. Sociological studies and surveys have refuted the first three. Respect for individuals, coupled with understanding of the limitations of testing situations and lack of validity of testing instruments, have hopefully stemmed a rush to judgment on the latter issue.

Suggestions for teachers of the disadvantaged have taken on a new and more humanistic perspective. Several authorities contributing to an International Reading Association project emphasized the importance of teachers as impact factors. Martin and Castaneda (35) noted that a realistic reading program for culturally different learners requires teachers who understand the linguistic and cultural needs of their pupils. Teachers must view reading as a part of language development and provide children with experiences which lead to concept development. They further attested to the importance of the teacher as a "significant other." One of the most significant indicators of a child's worth is shown through behaviors that reveal teachers as adults who care. Such behaviors include showing evidence that one values children's thoughts, and taking the time to encourage them in their use of language.

York and Ebert (51) pointed out that the key words for teachers of disadvantaged children are *respect* and *expectation*. If teachers treat their children with respect and also indicate genuine and realistic expectations for their performances in learning tasks, a positive learning environment will have been established. Effective teachers of culturally different learners make sure that each day, each child experiences success in the classroom.

Harmer (23) contended that there is no cookbook recipe for teaching reading to culturally different learners. Teachers should be well prepared for teaching skills, sensitive to pupils, and capable of creating an appropriate learning environment for children.

Suggestions for teaching at the junior-senior high school levels have emphasized that teachers capitalize on the informational needs of the students and encourage and accept oral expression of these adolescents. In addition, the ego needs of these young people must be met through their reading. A major task of the reading teacher is to provide a comfortable, nonthreatening atmosphere that facilitates behavior change. Learners should be allowed freedom in selection of materials and in expressing their reactions to the materials. They should be encouraged to work together and to be mutually helpful in their peer contacts (27).

Myths and Facts
about Language:
Former Theories Revisited

In the late 1960s and early 70s a number of theories were advanced which posited various types of *linguistic deprivation* among speakers of nonstandard English. These myths included: (1) the theory that culturally different learners had very limited language facility, (2) that the language they did use was haphazard and lacking a logical systematic structure, (3) that speakers of nonstandard English could not understand spoken standard English.

These three myths have long since been viewed as inadequate and unfounded generalizations based on insufficient research data. Later research, such as that conducted by Nolen (39), reported that there are no significant differences between black and white children's comprehension of spoken standard English. The children in the study were all of low socio-economic status.

Labov (30) substantiates the fact that spoken standard English is understandable to culturally different learners. His subjects were able to make accurate translation from standard English into their divergent modes. That is, they could comprehend the standard model even though they did not always imitate it.

Gantt (18), investigating the relationship between syntactical divergency and the listening comprehension of black children, concluded that the effect of dialect divergency upon listening comprehension of standard English seems to be limited. Black children from two school populations (Title I and non-Title I) were tested for syntactical characteristics and listening comprehension. Children from the non-Title I population did not differ significantly in syntactical characteristics from their Title I counterparts. The non-Title I learners did perform significantly better in mean listening performance. These findings lend themselves to the theory that socio-economic factors, not dialect divergencies, affect listening and, most possibly, reading.

Labov states that linguists have long demonstrated the fallacies of the verbal deprivation theory. All linguists agree that nonstandard dialects are highly structured systems, not accumulations of errors caused by the failure of their speakers to master standard English.

Abrahams points out in "The Advantages of Black English" that not only is black English [and other nonstandard dialects by implication] a series of linguistic forms, it is [they are] also "entire systems of speaking behavior" which contain nonverbal cues as well (1).

Should Children Speak Standard English before Reading It?

The previous edition of this book stated. "An unanswered question that faces the reading teacher is whether or not the child who speaks

Children with different speech patterns can communicate because they have not talked themselves into problems that otherwise would not exist.

a dialect should learn to speak standard English *before* he can learn to read it. Experimental data relative to this issue are, at the moment, inconclusive." New data lend themselves to answering the question with an unequivocal "no." All children who speak dialects do not have to learn to speak standard English *before* being taught to read.

Zintz concluded that "In itself, speaking nonstandard English is not detrimental to learning to read. A child with a nonstandard dialect has the same capacity to learn to read as a user of a middle-class standard dialect" (52). Gantt (18) suggests that if the oral production of standard English is an advantage for success in school, then children from better socio-economic neighborhoods profit most from this advantage. As Brooks (10) contends, "If we are honest with our students, we will set the record straight at the beginning: correct (standard) English is important to know for reasons of economic gain, social comfort, and mobility."

Teachers of children from any minority group should assume some responsibility for studying the learning patterns of these children. Further, their findings should be shared with other professionals in the field. Teachers on the "firing line" have opportunities to observe practices which are successful and to make concrete suggestions relative to techniques and procedures that hold the promise of success. Classroom data which focus on teaching strategies can be a source of great help to others who are working in similar situations or who are facing similar problems. Practices that work are of more value to teachers than are theories which still need to be tested.

Dialect Divergencies

A young black college student was working with a large corporation during the summer break. At an orientation meeting, in which some simple technological processes were being discussed, the student was taking notes:

The *floor* chart is basic to . . .
A good *floor* chart must be constructed . . .
Floor charts are keys to . . .

The notes were accurate except for one word; what the speaker was actually saying was:

The *flow* chart is basic to . . .
A good *flow* chart must be constructed . . .
Flow charts are keys to . . .

There are highly qualitative differences in the meanings of "floor charts" and "flow charts" and this student heard and recorded a slightly different auditory signal than the speaker had intended. She transcribed what she heard and, in the process, misinterpreted much of the lecture. But she had written this key word the way she perceived it in her dialect.

This incident points up two of the major problems in teaching the culturally different learner to read—lack of experience with words and concepts and the masking of critical phonemes which cause semantic differences (the latter being a dialect factor).

Dialect, broadly conceived, is the way people speak in different parts of the country or in their specific social classes. The components of dialect are pronunciation, grammar, and vocabulary. McDavid (33) adds that a dialect is a variety of a given language that is mutually intelligible with other dialects of that language. Since many culturally different children speak a dialect, the question that has been raised by linguists and pondered by reading teachers is: Do dialect divergencies cause difficulties in learning to read standard English?

Most hypotheses relative to the question of dialect interference in learning to read have been stated in general terms. Martin and Castaneda (35) hold to the position that children who come to school speaking a dialect other than standard American English encounter noticeable difficulty in learning to read; they experience a higher failure rate than do children who speak standard American English. This is true. But do the children fail in reading because of their dialect or because of factors such as lack of experiences that relate to reading, the quality of instruction they receive, and teacher expectations of failure? These and other factors could work together to produce a high failure rate.

Skinner (44) implies that the dialect of Appalachia is the cause of children's reading problems in that geographical area, and that the critical need for Appalachian schools, or any group in an analogous position, is a preschool oral language program which teaches standard English. This, he feels, will give the Appalachian child a better chance of success when he encounters the printed word in the first grade.

York and Ebert (51) believe that a reasonable degree of speaking and understanding standard American English is necessary if children are to read the academic texts. Moore (38) sees the "language of the book" as tantamount to a foreign language in the case of the child who speaks a nonstandard dialect. The problem is compounded when the child has a limited school vocabulary used in school books. Johnson (25) hypothesized that nonstandard dialects may give rise to difficulties in the many communicative efforts of other subject areas as well as in reading. The following discussion provides a brief overview of dialect divergencies.

Sound or Phonological Divergencies

Generally speaking, phonological divergencies refer to differences in speech sounds within words. A grapheme (written letter symbol) may represent different phonemes (speech sounds) in different dialects. For example, the standard English "poor" may be heard as "po" in some black dialects, while the standard English "head" may be pronounced as "haid" in nonstandard dialect used by some white speakers. The standard English "something" may be heard as "sumpin" in nonstandard English, and the word "oil" pronounced as "aul" in nonstandard.

Standard *English*	Black *Nonstandard*	Standard *English*	Spanish *Dialect*
that	dat	pool	pull
get	git	judge	chudge
earned	earnt	she	se
other	udder	vote	bote
touch	taut, tech	hat	hot
poem	purm	leave	liv
right	rat	dug	duck
help	hep	ship	sheep

The phonological differences between the speech patterns of dialect speakers and standard English usage have been rather thoroughly researched (5, 6, 21). However, research has not established the degree to which these phonological variations influence learning to read standard English. Thus, a number of hypotheses have been advanced which focus on the issues of dialect interference and how beginning reading should be taught to dialect speakers.

Some possible interference effects of sound divergencies in reading achievement and reading instruction and instructional materials have been noted by Goodman (21) and Saville (42). They believe that phonics programs which attempt to teach the relationship between letters and sounds cannot be universally applicable to all nonstandard dialects. The question is raised as to whether the use of materials such as i/t/a and others that are based on invariant pronunciation are appropriate for many of these learners. Furthermore, they point out that because a child learns at home to ignore certain speech sounds, meaning may be distorted for him when these phonemes are the critical distinguishable elements in a word.

Another foreseeable problem is the teacher's misinterpretation of the significance of "errors" they detect in children's oral reading. Some errors which are unrelated to the child's dialect can, and possibly should, be corrected on the spot. In other instances it may be unproductive at the moment to overemphasize errors which are perfectly logical in the child's dialect. When a child is compelled to insert phonemes that are ignored in his phonological system, he may end up with pronunciations that are unfamiliar and meaningless to him. These pronunciations may prove to be barriers to his progress in getting meaning from the printed page. Other phonological differences may involve variations in intonation (pitch, stress, and rhythm of the dialect). If the teacher insists on intonation patterns in oral reading or speaking which are unfamiliar to the reader, frustration and loss of meaning may be the result.

In studies of black English dialect, it has been noted that a number of nonstandard phonological patterns occur with considerable frequency. A few examples are dropping of certain final consonant sounds, omitting the sounds represented by r and l, substituting sounds ($th = d$), omitting some inflectional endings, and the like. These and other phonological variations result in generating hundreds of homonyms for the black dialect speaker which do not exist in standard English (told – toe – toll; road – row; past – pass; find – fine; seed – seat – see; hold – whole; call – called; etc.).

While some dialect divergencies are not crucial problems in children's learning to read, teachers of reading still need to be familiar with these dialects. This knowledge is essential since they must understand the language used by the students. This understanding indicates a degree of respect for the learner's language efforts. In addition, there are valuable teaching strategies which would not be available to teachers who do not understand the student's dialect.

**Grammatical and
Syntactical Differences**

Grammatical and syntactical divergencies refer to those differences in inflectional changes, verb forms, and verb auxiliaries, and to the ways in which words are put together in phrases and sentences. The following is an example that cuts across phonological, grammatical-syntactical differences and lack of a necessary concept. Assume a teacher read the sentence, "Edgar Allen Poe was a rich man." The students, drawing from the phonology, grammar, and syntax of their dialect may interpret the sentence to mean, "Edgar Allen (is) poor, was a rich man." The students have no concept of Edgar Allen Poe, writer; they assume that he is poor because of the phonological differences (poor = po) and because of the assumed syntactical link (Allen [is] poor).

The following are illustrative of grammatical divergencies found between standard English and standard dialects.

Standard	*Nonstandard*
	Omission of "s" in plurals and possessives
He gets to work early.	He get to work early.
I saw four cows.	I saw four cow.
John's dog runs home.	John dog run home.
	Omission of "ed" ending
He walked home.	He walk home.
I knocked three times.	I knock three times.
	Changes and omissions of verb forms
They were here.	They *was* here.
He is here.	He *be* here.
I am here.	I *be* here.
He is going.	He going.
We are always happy.	We *be* happy. (always)
Now we are happy.	We happy. (now)

Saville (42) suggests that because the children have perfected the syntax of their dialect, which is not the syntax of the classroom English, they will have difficulty reading the conventional basal reading materials. Goodman (21) points out that these grammatical divergencies will be reflected in the child's reading of standard texts and in his conversation. That is, he will substitute his dialect for what is written. This substitution process must be understood by the teacher if frustration is to be kept at a minimum. The intended meaning in listening activities may be misconstrued by both teacher and the pupil. This is especially true if the teacher does not realize the difference between school talk and the children's dialect, or if she is unable to accept the child's speech patterns.

Vocabulary Divergencies refer to word meanings and connotations of words that are peculiar to a dialect. Some examples are

Standard	Nonstandard
Carry that ball.	*Tote* that ball.
We're going to a *party*.	We're going to a *gig*.
I heard a loud *rap* (knock) last night.	I heard a loud *rap* (discussion) last night.
He is *bad*. (naughty)	He is *bad*. (superlative for good)
I want to *dig* it. (lift dirt)	I want to *dig* it. (understand)
He is *bright*. (smart)	He is *bright*. (light complexioned)
This stove is *hot*. (burning)	This stove is *hot*. (stolen)
The class is *on fire*. (particularly responsive)	This class is *on fire*. (poor in performance achievement)

These and numerous other variations in meaning are thought to cause difficulty in reading from texts that use words that have peculiar meanings in a learner's dialect. If the word has a negative meaning in nonstandard English, the teacher may find that she is guilty of unintentional insults and she may be placed in an embarrassing situation. Here are some points of view relative to when and how dialect differences should be dealt with.

1. *Teach standard English prior to reading instruction.* The proponents of this position recommend that language training in standard English be given to the dialect speaker so that he will be familiar with the grammatical and syntactical patterns he will find in his textbook and hear in his teacher's speech. Formal reading instruction is delayed until the language training program is completed. Training in language is achieved mainly by drill in which standard English is treated as a

Dialect divergencies a challenge?
Yes. An insurmountable problem?
No.

second language. Children repeat sentence patterns until they can generalize the grammar and syntax to other similar situations.

2. *Teach standard English in conjunction with the reading of dialect materials in planned units.* This alternative is based on the use of stories written in both the learner's dialect and standard English. The child is taught to see the differences between these dialect patterns, and he learns that the latter pattern is "school talk." Instruction centers chiefly on differences in grammar and syntax.

3. *Teach standard English through the "exemplar" method before and concomitant with formal reading instruction.* This approach seeks to teach the child patterns of standard English at opportune times. Conscious efforts are made to equip the child with skill in using standard English, but they are made with little regimentation. The teacher speaks using standard English patterns and exposes her learners to such patterns whenever possible.

4. *Teach children to read ignoring dialect differences in beginning reading stages. Then teach standard English as a tool of mobility in the upper grades and high school.* This position is posited on the idea that getting the child to talk and teaching him to read are the important emphases in beginning reading. Once the child has developed in word analysis skills and comprehension abilities, make him aware of variations in language usage and teach him alternate forms.

It seems unlikely that programs will be developed which utilize only one of these alternatives exclusively. It must be kept in mind that a child cannot instantly suspend the use of a dialect that he has used for years. Nor can he adapt completely to a different speech pattern. The learning of a new pattern must take place in a meaningful setting. If children do not understand why they are to speak in another way, they may resist language training in the classroom.

If language training in dialect differences is delayed until the upper grades, the self-concept of the learner must be reckoned with. Care must be taken to make him aware at this stage of the realistic values and rewards that will accrue from mastery of mainstream English.

The following principles for working with dialect speakers should be useful to teachers regardless of the methodology used.

1. Learning must be gradual and constantly reinforced for stability of gains.
2. Children must understand why they are being introduced to a different language pattern.
3. Care must be taken to remove "value" labels from the dialect of the learner and the dialect to be learned.
4. The learner's dialect must be respected by himself and by the teacher as a complete and usable linguistic system—not a "stepchild" of standard English.
5. Different learners will learn more readily from different techniques.

The teacher of beginning reading must know the different features of the learners' dialect and must be skilled in approaches for language training. With her also lies the task of determining which learners will benefit from language training for reading purposes and which will not.

Dialect Differences Not the Major Problem?

Prior to the 1970s, most theories and writings supported the position that dialect differences posed a major barrier to learning to read. More recently this support has eroded quite dramatically. Gantt (18) concluded that since the effect of dialect divergency upon listening comprehension of standard English seems to be limited, the effect of dialect divergency upon reading comprehension would also be limited.

Melmed conducted a study using children in third grade as subjects. One of the experimental groups consisted of children whose oral language usage qualified them as black dialect speakers. The purpose of the study was to discover what effect the existence of these phonological pairs of words had on both auditory comprehension of standard English sentences and the effect on reading comprehension when the printed material included one of a pair of black dialect homonyms. Data revealed that "the black youngster did significantly poorer in auditory discriminating of word pairs which are homonyms in black English but different words in standard English." However, the black group ". . . showed no inability to comprehend these words while reading orally or silently." One conclusion advanced was that confusion of the word pairs in the reading situation was minimal because the subjects utilized syntactical and contextual clues (36).

Zintz (52) makes the following observation relative to the effect of Spanish dialect: "It is apparent that linguistic interference for Chicanos is primarily phonological and morphological." Yet, he finds little evidence to support the idea that this interference is detrimental in learning to read English. The assumption that the Chicano's bilingualism, *per se*, causes language interference and is detrimental in learning to read English must continue to be tested. Perhaps more emphasis needs to be placed on semantic components in the reading situation.

Garcia studied the oral English syntactic patterns utilized by bilingual Spanish speaking adolescents. The subjects were from lower- and middle-class socio-economic backgrounds. The results indicated that these individuals utilized all of the syntactic patterns basic to standard English. The author states, "Reasons for the Chicano's reading and language difficulties must be sought among other factors perhaps within a cultural or motivational context" (19).

Goodman, who wrote persuasively about the negative impact of dialect divergencies on learning to read, has since modified his position. In *Dialect Barriers to Reading Comprehension Revisited* (22), he asserts that urban children develop an ability to understand the dialects of others in the community. Based on his miscue research, Goodman concluded that dialect involving miscues are not a major interference in the reading process. Meaning is not sacrificed since the miscues of the dialect user occur within the framework of his own language.

Importance of Socio-Economic Factors

It has been noted that children from racial minorities (blacks, American Indians, Spanish surnamed, etc.) achieve poorly in reading. An easy assumption, once widely held, was that race was the crucial variable. Next it was noted that many children from these groups used nonstandard dialects. Since the race variable did bare overtones of racism, one could switch to the dialect explanation. However, if one looked for other variables, some could be formed. An undeniable characteristic of third and fourth generation ethnic groups who spoke nonstandard language was *poverty*. Ethnic backgrounds, coupled with nonstandard language patterns, assured nonassimilation in mainstream America. Nonassimilation assured poverty!

An unfortunate tendency in America has been to ask the schools to solve problems that can be solved only by the total society. The schools have not been vehement enough in pointing out that they cannot solve social ills which date back to the founding of the nation. Both educators and taxpayers are now accepting the fact that throwing money at problems will not solve them. Over night, school funding did not overcome lifetime educational deprivations. There are many other deficits that accrue outside the school but which impinge on school learning.

It would be difficult to catalogue all of the attitudes and experiences stemming from poverty that also influence school learning. One would have to include parental attitudes toward education and the academic achievement of parents. These in turn would determine how much academic help is available to students in the home. Poverty breeds value systems which may be at odds with school goals and mores. It can inhibit experiences with books and the accumulation of knowledge that is school, rather than street, oriented. Student attitudes toward self, learning, authority, and survival are quite different in poverty and middle-class cultures. All of the above "stamp the student" in a myriad of ways.

Unfortunately, both what the prospective student has learned and what he has not learned influences teachers. Many reactions are negative such as, the students "can't learn," "are not interested," or "don't care." Once labeled, many students seem to cooperate in fulfilling the schools assessment of them.

Alternative Approaches for Working with the Culturally Different Learner

Most of the programs that have been suggested for dealing with the culturally different child appear to be modifications of existing programs. These may be new in the sense that they are deliberately planned for the economically deprived or culturally different child. But there are few innovations other than suggestions that attempts at developing "readiness" and language facility be intensified. However, this emphasis on preparing the child to become a good risk for the learning environment found in the school may hopefully provide teachers with important insights relative to these learners.

Current approaches which focus on preparing and teaching the culturally different child to read fall under two broad headings. One can be labeled *preschool intervention,* the other, *beginning reading strategies.*

Limitations of space preclude an intensive discussion of all the theory and teaching strategies suggested or used with the culturally different learner. Therefore, certain studies and points of view which illustrate major trends and philosophies will be examined.

Preschool Approaches for
the Culturally Different Learner

When the culturally different learner enters first grade, his major school problem will be lack of preparatory experiences. The school is structured to provide learning experiences which, to a large degree,

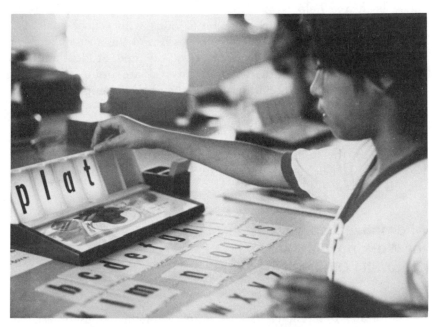

Establishing a climate for learning
may be the key to learning.

are foreign to these children. There are two obvious potential solutions: We may provide the child with the experiences he needs in order to cope with the tasks he must do in school, or we may alter the curriculum to fit the learner. The practice of providing readiness activities cuts across both of these alternatives. As readiness activities are varied to fit the learners' needs, the curriculum itself is altered.

In theory, readiness has for a long time been a part of most school programs. In one sense, these readiness programs represent a concession to children's nonreadiness for the schools' curricula. However, in actual practice the implementation of programs for readiness has always been more apparent than real. Shortly after children entered school, they received the formal reading instruction that had been planned for them. This occurred whether or not they were ready for these particular activities. Fortunately, many children had the background which enabled them to fit into the planned program. Many did not. For members of the latter group, had readiness training been realistically incorporated in their programs, many reading failures and frustrations might have been avoided.

While the culturally different child is on the same readiness continuum as other children, he has experience deficits that are significant to the school. He may be so different in terms of school preparation that readiness programs, as traditionally carried out, are simply not adequate for making him a good risk for beginning reading instruction. Sometimes, even a well-structured program of readiness activities may fail with this child. This failure may be attributed to the culturally different child's need for more of, or for a different type of, activities than those offered by the schools. For this type of learner, there must be a rethinking of readiness that will use his strengths and concentrate on eliminating his weaknesses.

The preschool approaches discussed in this section have attempted to redefine readiness in terms of the needs of the culturally different learner. They differ somewhat in philosophy and technique but share the common goal of making the culturally different child ready for first-grade reading instruction. The approaches included here are: intensified readiness, academic-preschool intervention, enrichment programs, and the Montessori approach.

Intensification of the
Traditional Readiness Program

This approach to preschool training is based on the philosophy that the traditional readiness program has the major components needed to prepare the culturally different child for reading instruction, but that there will be a need for reinforcement that extends for a greater duration of time.

The intensified approach is advocated by Cohen (12) who selected seven areas for emphasis with the culturally different learner: letter knowledge, visual discrimination of letters and words, auditory discrimination of sounds in words, developing a love of books, and interest in printed symbols, story sense, and memory for sequence. These areas were stressed by Cohen because they were found to have high correlations with reading success in grade one, they are the kinds of specific activities that can be handled by the school, and finally because they are most directly related to beginning reading instruction.

The enrichment activities of the traditional preschool programs in the form of field trips, drama, and other creative activities are also included in this program. Together, these activities comprise a cluster that has been advocated for many years in the literature on readiness. This program eliminates those activities that have been alleged to have little bearing on reading success, such as identifying the sounds of animals, types of transportation, and musical instruments; matching geometric shapes; and drill in eye-hand-motor coordination.

Children Not Ready for Reading Readiness Activities. If, after a period of time, the learner does not respond, Cohen suggests that intensification alone may not be the answer. Many children from depressed areas have not had the experiences that prepare them for a reading readiness program. The problem that must then be dealt with is "readiness for learning." Cohen lists four major goals for a "readiness for learning" program:

One: Self-Control. Teach the child self-control in working with others in the formal classroom. This goal may be achieved by the teacher ignoring misbehavior and rewarding good behavior.

Two: Class Decorum. School-break the child by teaching him the daily routines of the classroom, such as housekeeping, completing activities, conforming to rules, handling of books and other school materials, and developing attention span. The direct teaching approach is seen as perhaps the most effective procedure for teaching the daily routine. That is, the teacher openly modifies the child's behaviors with directions and stipulations. In some instances, the teacher must physically direct the pupils.

Three: Perceptual Training. Visual-motor-auditory skill development is, in essence, preparing the child in certain physiological areas and specifically includes:

1. eye-hand coordination   4. visual memory
2. general coordination   5. form perception
3. eye movements   6. visual imagery

Selected parts of such programs as Frostig's Program for the Development of Visual Perception, the Getman-Kane Program for Accelerated School Success, the Balance Board, the Walking Rail, and the Montessori Program (discussed later in this chapter) offer possible techniques for aiding the teacher. The teacher may wish to review such programs prior to developing her own activities.

Four: Language and Concepts. Teaching language and concepts necessary for beginning reading is thought by Cohen to be best met through the delineation of specific skills. The teacher provides stimuli that are designed and ordered sequentially to move the child from gross perceptions of objects to classifying objects according to their functions. The movement from simple discrimination to classifying is illustrated:

Have the children *identify* an object from a large group of pictures.

Have the children *match* related pictures (pictures of different houses, etc.).

Have children *group* objects according to functions (bicycle, car, etc.).

Have children *construct wholes from parts* (2–4 piece jig-saw puzzle).

Have children *group* then *classify* objects according to functions (e.g., those useful to man: foods, clothing, tools).

For language development, Cohen suggests the sequence of stages developed by Pasamanick (12) as a guide for teaching the culturally different child to cope with the language of the school.

STAGE I is based upon experiences familiar to the children and attempts to make the known more concrete. The naming of simple nouns and a few basic verbs are the focal points.

EXAMPLE: Children would name objects such as *chair, table, hat, dress;* and verbs such as *running, walking, peeping, laughing.*

STAGE II attempts to expand the child's noun and verb storehouse by having him combine two known words into a compound.

EXAMPLE: hat + box = hatbox
          shoe + shine = shoeshine
          sing + along = singalong

STAGE III concentrates on expanding the use of language as an expressive and descriptive tool through such activities as storytelling, show and tell, role playing, and relating experiences. These activities foster the development and use of sequencing skills, descriptive language, and word connectors.

STAGE IV encourages the child to use past language learning to categorize, catalogue, and perform other reasoning tasks.

The Academic Preschool

Perhaps the most radical procedures for making culturally different children ready for formal reading instruction are found in academic preschool programs. These programs concentrate on the direct teaching of specific language and reading skills. This is a teaching strategy in which the teacher presents stimuli designed to elicit specific language responses from the learner.

The Bereiter-Engelmann program (2, 9) is representative of the academic preschool approach and also serves as a model for the direct-instruction technique. Examples of this method and some of the specific language goals are provided below:

GOAL 1: To move from one word responses to complete affirmative and negative statements in reply to questions.

Teacher		*Pupils*
"What is this?"		"Dog."
"Say it all."		"This is a dog."
"Is this a dog?"		"Yes."
"Say it all."		"Yes, this is a dog."
"Is this a dog?"		"No."
"Say it all."		"No, this is not a dog."

GOAL 2: To respond with both affirmative and negative statements when told to "tell about something."

Teacher	*Pupil*
"Tell me about this ball."	"It is round."
	"It is black."
	"It is not big."
	"It is not square."

GOAL 3: To develop the ability to handle polar opposites for at least four concept pairs.

Teacher

Pupil

"If this is not up, what is it?" — "Down."

"Say it all." — "It is down."

"If this is not big, what is it?" — "It is little."

GOAL 4: To use the prepositions *on, in, under, over* and *between* in statements describing arrangements.

Teacher	*Pupil*
"Where is the turkey?"	"The turkey is *on* the table."

"Where is the long line?" — "The long line is *under* the short line."

"Where is the number 2?" — "The number 2 is *between* the numbers 1 and 3."

1 2 3

GOAL 5: To name positives and negatives for at least four classes.

Teacher	*Pupil*
"Tell me something that is clothing."	"A hat is clothing." "A chair is not clothing."
"Tell me something that is food."	"An apple is food." "A pencil is not food."

GOAL 6: To perform simple "if-then" deductions.

Teacher	*Pupil*
"If the circle is big, what else do you know about it?"	"It is white."

| "If the circle is little, what else do you know about it?" | "It is black." |

GOAL 7: To use *not* in deductions.

Teacher	*Pupil*
"If the circle is white, what else do you know about it?"	"It is not little."
"If the circle is black, what else do you know about it?"	"It is not big."

The Beginning Reading Program

The reading program is the extension of the language development program and is designed to familiarize children with letter names, to associate pictures visually with their naming words, to recognize and produce rhyming words, and to learn and use a limited number of sight words.

In the alphabet learning phase of the program, children familiarize themselves with the letter names of the alphabet through identity and position statements:

This is the letter A.

This is a big A.

This is a little A.

This A is standing up.

This A is lying down.

The child is taught first to spell words by letter sounds (CAT = kuh–ah–tuh) and is then presented clusters of words that follow the same spelling pattern (cat, fat, hat, bat). Word meanings are reinforced by yes-no questions of lexical terms.

Word recognition begins with the production of isolated words. A word is printed on the chalkboard and the rule "This is a word" is taught and followed by the identity statement, "This is the word MAN." The children then are encouraged to produce complete identity statements in answering questions such as, "Is this the word DOG?". "No that is not the word *dog*." "That is the word MAN." Action words are illustrated with gestures. Children are invited to suggest other words which they wish to learn. If there are no volunteers the teacher supplies another word.

Word placement exercises are used to teach visual discrimination of word forms and word meanings. Objects are labeled with 5″ × 8″ cards and identified by the teacher. "This card has a word on it. This is the word │TOY│." Five or more words are identified in this way and one word is placed on the proper object by the teacher. The children are asked: "This is the word what?" (Desk.) "So where does it belong?" (On the desk.) Each child has a turn at naming and placing a word. These words are then identified on the chalkboard. The rule "If all the letters are the same, the words are the same" is taught. The converse rule is also presented.

Word identity exercises help the children develop a small sight vocabulary which is used in developing simple sentences. First, the children are taught to recognize their own names and then receive drill on recognition of other children's names. Names of the parts of the body are also taught in this way. New sets of words (*is not, big*) are added for sentence making: "Joe is not big." Meaning is stressed in sentence reading by having children answer questions about their reading. "Is Joe big?" "No, Joe is not big." "Is Joe little?" "Yes, Joe is little." After children master the basic tasks, they are taught to read from teacher-prepared booklets.

This academic preschool program has been criticized on the basis that is a mechanistic conditioned-response approach and that it deals only with beginning reading. This latter criticism could also be leveled against other beginning programs (i/t/a, Words in Color, Programmed Reading, Computer Assisted Instruction). Jongsma (26) raises the "question of stability of gains" but feels that the specific and detailed objectives of the program will be helpful to teachers.

Results of the use of this type program are impressive. Bereiter and Engelmann (8) indicated that children from the first group using this approach scored from one-half to one and one-half years below average on pretests of language. By the end of the second year, their scores were approximately average for their age group. Mental age rose from about six months below average to about four months above average. Terminal achievement averaged at the 1.5 grade level in reading.

A second experimental group (2) with whom the same techniques were used over a two year period showed a mean reading achievement of 2.6. Although experimental data are still somewhat limited, these studies have reported statistical data to support claims of the program's effectiveness.

Enrichment Programs

The view that enrichment experiences are fundamental to offsetting the effects of economic deprivation is held by many educators. Several programs which place major emphasis on the development of readiness skills through enrichment activities have been proposed for use with the culturally different learner. The programs under Project Head Start may be looked at as prototypes of the enrichment-intervention model. The assumptions underlying these programs are

> That from birth through six years of age are important years in human development; that children of the poor generally have not had the experiences and opportunities that support maximum development during this period; that effective programs for these

The Culturally Different Child 383

children must be comprehensive, including health, nutrition, social services, and education; that for their own and their children's benefit, parents should be deeply involved in the design and implementation of local programs; and that a national child development program can focus attention on the needs of preschool and elementary school children from low-income families, and, though continued review of program effectiveness, stimulate local institutions to do a better job of meeting these needs (15).

Because of the diversity found in the numerous Head Start programs that were conducted, it is impossible to present a valid sketch of *the* program. Surveys of the curriculum emphasis found in the various programs indicated that a common feature was an attempt to influence sensory-motor development and language development. Only 50 percent of the directors responding indicated the development of pre-academic or academic skills as an important goal (15).

More specifically, it was found that few classes spent more than 5 percent of the time on auditory discrimination training and that visual-perception training varied from 5 to 40 percent of class activities. Amounts of language training in the formal sense varied from 5 to 30 percent. Activities which occurred with the highest frequency were motor training, informal language stimulation, and social interaction.

Although the Head Start programs have enjoyed a fairly high degree of support, there is little data to indicate that they had a significant influence on later school achievement. In some instances it has been suggested that this influence was minimal because of the lack of emphasis on developing specific cognitive skills. Another factor that might also account for lack of success on some counts is the brief duration of training. It could hardly be expected that intervention programs that consisted of a few hours per day for a few weeks could compensate for several years of living in the ghetto or in depressed rural environments.

Enrichment through Cognitive Emphasis

Deutsch (16) developed a program for working with culturally different children which he describes as "enrichment intervention." Children are provided specific readiness training in auditory and visual discrimination, language and concept formation development, learning letter names and forms, sounding and blending of letters into words, and left-right orientation. Although labeled *enrichment*, the program is based on systematic instruction aimed at cognitive development. Several other less extensive programs involving enrichment as the key to cognitive development had reported significant gains in reading readiness.

**The Montessori
Method**

The Montessori method and philosophy cut across many of the preschool programs previously discussed. Since it does not fit under any of the labels used thus far, and since it represents a long-established program for the culturally different child, some of the major features of this program will be reviewed.

Kohlberg (29) cites data from his pilot research studies to support the view that there is much promise in the Montessori method for stimulating the cognitive functioning that culturally different learners need for success in school.

One rationale given by Stevens (46) for using the Montessori method with culturally different children is that this approach concentrates on the development of those skills and abilities in which these children are most lacking: language facility, vocabulary expansion, an environment conducive to learning, and structured experiences for developing attention and concentration. "It has demonstrated in many cultures that it can introduce language and related reading-readiness skills to children from disadvantaged backgrounds" and "can be greatly expanded and elaborated within our current understanding of learning theory" (46).

The Montessori Language Program (37) is somewhat analogous to a word recognition program and includes (1) exercises of silence (i.e., paying attention); (2) stress on pronunciation of words; (3) recognition of printed symbols by shape; and (4) speech production through adequate manipulation of the vocal mechanisms. The language program does not deal with the language training that is felt necessary for the expression of concepts or for oral language usage.

The Montessori Reading Program (37) utilizes the "trace and say" task sequences which were designed to teach the child to recognize and pronounce letter sounds and to use these in word recognition. This writing-reading program stresses the sounds of the letters which is, in essence, a phonics approach. It is suggested that the time for beginning reading instruction will vary with different children, as will the pace at which they proceed. The child does not compete with the calendar or with other children. He competes only with himself.

Materials for the reading exercises consist of slips of paper or cards upon which familiar words and phrases are written. Both materials and tasks are simple: (1) the child reads (sounds out) the word and places it under the object it names; (2) phrase reading follows once the idea that "words represent thoughts" is grasped by the child. The phrase reading exercises are usually in the form of simple commands or directions which must be comprehended by the reader if they are to be carried out. The true reading in this program is thought of as "mental" rather than vocal. Oral reading is utilized for pronunciation, silent reading for meaning.

The total program encompasses not only major reading readiness skills, but also provides for "learning readiness." It lacks completeness in the area of language training. And this is the area where modifications may need to be made if it is to fully meet the needs of culturally different, dialect-speaking children.

Summary Statement about Preschools

These programs for the culturally different child demonstrate various approaches to compensatory education. Some programs, such as Head Start, stress enrichment experiences with incidental training in cognitive areas. Others, such as the academic preschools, stress cognitive development with less emphasis on enrichment experiences. Possibly an aim of future programs will be to establish experimentally the proper balance between these two.

In varying degrees, these programs have attempted to incorporate experiences and activities for developing

positive self-concepts	visual discrimination of letter
visual and auditory perception	shapes
knowledge of letter names	sight vocabulary
and sounds	left-to-right orientation
auditory discrimination of	language facility
letter sounds	concept formation

In many instances, the content of the traditional readiness program has been altered only slightly. In other programs, the actual teaching techniques appear to have been modified to fit the learner. Reports on the success of these programs suggest that, in many instances, gains may be short lived. This might be traceable to the fact that the program is terminated too soon or that the schools' follow-up program does not reinforce or build on the child's previous learnings. The descriptions of some programs have been too vague to invite replication.

Exceptions to this criticism might be the academic preschool and the intensified traditional readiness programs. One of the major needs in this area is specific suggestions for the transition from the preschool program to a beginning reading program.

Beginning Reading Programs for the Culturally Different Learner

Some of the suggestions relative to beginning reading instruction for the culturally different child are approaches that have been used for years in the regular classroom. Examples are the "language experience approach" and "individualized reading." Other theorists hold that these traditional approaches are inadequate unless they take into account the dialect differences which culturally different children bring to school. Still others propose that the materials for beginning reading be written in the child's dialect. This suggestion, which calls for development of vernacular texts, breaks new ground and is the center of some controversy.

The Language Experience Approach

The major premise of the language experience approach is that the child should learn to read materials based on his personal experiences and written in his natural language patterns. Usually the pupil dictates a story which the teacher writes down. When a child provides a story from his own experiences, it is hypothesized that he will have little trouble expressing himself for he will use concepts he understands.

School-structured experiences that are to be the basis for later dictations must be something the child can relate to and understand or he will not talk about them. To take a group of Puerto Rican or black children from a ghetto environment to visit a museum or a group of Mexican-American children to a printing company may result in meager verbal concepts for use in an experience story. Appalachian youngsters may not be able to talk fluently about a visit to a large industrial development.

These kinds of experiences may be vivid but they may not be the kind about which the children can express ideas. Experiences of this type might well be delayed until children have had many chances at dictating experiences from familiar surroundings that will stimulate them to learn and use new words and concepts.

Arnold (4) and Stemmler (45) report success in using a modified language experience approach with culturally different learners. The modifications consisted of pretraining in standard English and the use of science materials as the experience sources. Children were coached to respond in standard English to questions about the science material. These answers were then read by the children. Other teacher-prepared charts written in standard English were also used.

Such modification represents a popular trend; however, the use of subject matter and standard English for experience stories should not cause teachers to minimize the use of children's personal experiences, nor should the stress on using standard English patterns be so rigorous as to stifle children's expression.

Transcribing children's stories. In transcribing the experience stories of culturally different learners, certain problems are likely to be encountered by the teacher. The following are prerequisites for teachers who would use this approach:

1. Urge the children to express themselves in oral language.
2. Refrain from placing value judgments on the content of the stories, or on the child's nonstandard English.
3. Be able to discriminate the phonology of the child's speech and translate this to standard spellings.
4. Understand the syntactical system used by the child and be able to transcribe it.

A review of the literature revealed no authority suggesting that nonstandard spellings be used. It is quite obvious that were they used, confusion in learning sight words and word attack skills would result. Stewart (47) points out that dialect spellings would have to be replaced by standard spelling patterns before the child was taught letter-sound relationships. Also, teachers would have to be trained in the transcription of nonstandard pronunciations.

When common sense principles are carefully observed, the language experience approach offers the culturally different learner the same benefits that accrue to other groups of learners.

**Individualized
Reading**

Although individualized reading is widely discussed and practiced, there is so much variation in programs that no specific instructional guide is available. There are two major assets of this approach: one is flexibility and the other is openendedness. These same factors are also limitations in that they have inhibited meaningful research which could be replicated.

The discussion of individualized reading in Chapter 9 presents the philosophy and major practices associated with this approach.

There is some difficulty in fitting the individualized approach to beginning reading instruction, however, because there is no systematic methodology for using it at this level. The special advantages traceable to its use are more noticeable in the case of the independent reader than with the child who still needs to learn mechanics. Once the culturally different learner has gained independence in reading, he may profit from self-selection, self-pacing, ego-centered conferences, and the like to the same degree as do other groups. Since this approach has been strongly recommended as a follow up to any beginning approach with culturally different children, the following suggestions may help teachers maximize its potential benefits.

Self-selection of reading materials can be an important asset in harnessing the culturally different child's ego to the reading task. To achieve this goal one needs not only a wide variety of books on topics of universal appeal, but also materials that are of specific interest to these children. Books which portray their ethnic background and ethnic heroes must be available in the classroom collection. Teachers must remember to place on the reading shelves not only the "acceptable" stories, but also stories that focus on all aspects of the children's lives. The following lists contain titles that have been found by teachers to be popular with different ethnic groups:

Mexican Americans	*Black Americans*
Benito	Let My People Go
Citizen Pablo	The Riot Report
Manuela's Birthday	The Negro in America
A Mexican Boy's Adventure	Afro-Americans: Then and Now
Two Pesos for Catalina	Worth Fighting For
Juanita	The Autobiography of Malcolm X
Popo's Miracle	City Rhythms
And Now Miguel	What Harry Found When He Lost Archie
Out from Under	Tom B. and the Joyful Noise
First Book of Mexico	Mary Jane
Blue Willow	Roosevelt Grady
No, No, Rosina	Martin Luther King, Jr.: Peaceful Warrior
Awk!	
Garbage Can Cat	

Puerto Rican Americans	American Indians
Getting to Know Puerto Rico	Walk in My Moccasins
Young Puerto Rico	Tall as Great Standing Rock
The Three Wishes	In My Mother's House
Juan Bobo and the Queen's Necklace	Nika Illahee
Perez and Martina	The American Indian
Barto Takes the Subway	From Ungskah 1 to Oyaylee 10
Rosa-Too-Little	Benny's Flag
City High Five	Indian Two Feet and His Horse
Moncho and the Dukes	Apache Boy
Sleep in Thunder	Snowbound in Hidden Valley
That Bad Carlos	Indian Hill
Feast on Sullivan Street	Chief Seattle: Great Statesman

It is not suggested that books of this type constitute the entire reading fare for culturally different children. All good literature for children is appropriate, but the disadvantaged child, particularly, needs books and stories that deal with his culture and heroes from his ethnic group.

Criteria for selection of books and materials for the culturally different are similar to those which apply in any classroom.

1. The teacher must observe very closely the socio-cultural principles. Not only must the title be appealing, but the content of the books must not be beyond the child's experiences or conflict heavily with his cultural values.
2. The teacher must be aware of the linguistic principles of book selection. The child's language and the language of the book must not be far apart.

Teacher-pupil conferences must be highly stimulating if the culturally different learner is to respond. The use of questions by the teacher must again reflect an understanding of the child's culture, his attitudes, and the mores and values peculiar to that culture. A teacher's unfamiliarity with or insensitivity to these factors may impose a communication barrier and defeat the total purpose of the conference. A question that might conflict with the experiences of the economically deprived child might be the one asked in relation to the following story during a conference.

> The story is about a little boy whose life is in danger after he has shot himself in the brain. The boy is in another city visiting relatives and the hospital there has no surgeon. The only recourse is to call the surgeon in the boy's hometown. The hometown sur-

geon agrees to come right away, even after finding out that the boy's family is too poor to pay for his services. The call reaches the doctor at around nine o'clock and he promises to try to be at the hospital before midnight.

On his way out of town, the surgeon stops his car for a red light and a man in an old black coat with a gun gets in. The doctor is ordered to drive on. The doctor tries to explain where he is going but is not given the chance by the man in the old black coat. Soon, the doctor is ordered out of his car and is left standing on the road in the snow. The doctor calls a cab and arrives at the railway station only to find that the next train to his destination would not leave until midnight.

The doctor finally arrives at the hospital, but it is after two o'clock. He finds that he is too late; the boy died just an hour earlier. As the two doctors walk by the door of the hospital waiting room, the surgeon is introduced to the boy's father—the same man in the old black coat who took his car.*

Insensitive questioning: "Why do you think the boy's father would do such a bad thing as steal another man's car?"

Attaching the labels *steal* and *bad* to the man's actions might be insulting to the economically deprived child's values. For so long, the only way for him and for many whom he knew to survive was by taking. From this question he may be made to feel that all his deeds for survival have been "bad."

Perhaps a better question would be: "Why do you think the man in the black coat took the doctor's car instead of asking him for a ride?"

This question implies no judgments and allows the child to label the action and tell why he did so. From answers to questions such as this one, insights may be gained into the learner and his culture.

Diagnostic conferences with the culturally different child call for the teacher to be aware of the learner's syntactical and phonological system. Without this knowledge, the teacher will likely suggest corrections which are meaningless to the reader. For example:

Text	*Child's Reading*
We three boys were running.	We three boy be runnin'.
We passed a store.	We pass a sto.
Sam asked if we wanted to go in.	Sam, he ask do we wanna go in.
Joe did.	Joe, he do.
I did too.	I do too.
Sam went first.	Sam, he go firs.

---

* Story retold from Billy Rose, "Why the Doctor Was Late." Courtesy of the Bell-McClure Syndicate as condensed in *Reader's Digest Readings*—English as a second language, copyright, 1964.

Joe and I followed.	Joe and me follow.
The candy was good.	De candy good.

The teacher will be overevaluating if she lists the absence of final phonemes (boy*s*, runnin*g*, pass*ed*, ask*ed*, fir*st*) or the word (*was*) as "errors of omission." The adding of the italicized words (Sam *he*, Joe *he*) is not making "insertions" in the usual sense of the term, and using *do* for is and *be* for were do not meet the criteria for substitutions. The omission of certain phonemes, addition of certain pronouns, patterns of intonation, all reflect the characteristics of his dialect.

If the teacher is familiar with the language, vocabulary, and experiences of her children, she can, with minimum difficulty, plan for teaching skills. Chances are that the majority of the children will have similar pronunciations and attach similar meanings to most words. Informal diagnosis during the conferences can be the key to skills teaching for these groups.

Not only must individualized reading for the culturally different learner be built on the premise that "each child is a reader," it must also recognize the culturally different learner as a member of a specific group whose members have characteristics in common. There will be skills teaching that this group membership may make necessary, but the child's interests and needs as an individual must be considered.

The Vernacular Text Approach

For a brief period of time in the late 1960s, a number of authorities advocated that beginning reading materials should be written in the language of the dialect-speaking children. These materials were referred to as dialect readers, vernacular texts, or the bidialectal approach. The only difference between these and other materials was that they used the grammatical and syntactical patterns of the dialect speaker. No words were respelled to match the dialect speaker's phonology.

There were numerous proponents of vernacular texts. Baratz, writing in their support, states

> The overwhelming evidence of the role that language interference can play in reading failure indicates that perhaps one of the most effective ways to deal with the literary problems of Negro ghetto youth is to teach them using vernacular texts that systematically move from the syntactic structure of the ghetto community to those of the standard English speaking community (5).

Stewart (47) advocated the use of dialect-based texts because such materials cut the double learning load otherwise faced by this child. He reasoned that standard English must be acquired by these children, but that while they are trying to develop effective word-recognition skills, they should not be burdened with deciphering unfamiliar syntactic structures. Having the child begin reading in sentence patterns from his dialect will facilitate his mastery of the necessary word-reading skills. Then, he may move to what is, for him, the unfamiliar patterns from standard English.

One hypothesis was given by Goodman (21) who contended that since it *is* true that learning to read a foreign language is a more difficult task than learning to read a native language, it must follow that it is harder for a child to read a dialect which is not his own than to learn to read his own dialect.

Although various vernacular materials were developed and used for brief periods of time, their use did not become widespread. Many individuals within the ethnic groups for whom the materials were prepared viewed the materials as demeaning. It was also pointed out that these materials reinforced the language patterns that were alleged to interfere with success in beginning reading.

Leaverton et al. (31) developed a series of eight books for beginning readers. Each book contains two versions of the same material. One version utilized black English (everyday talk), the other standard English (school talk). Each book places emphasis on only one verb pattern. The progression from Book 1 through Book 7 is seen in the following examples:

Contrasting Verb Usage	*EVERYDAY TALK*	SCHOOL TALK
Book 1. *got* vs *have*	I got a mama.	I have a mama.
Book 2. omitting *is*, are use of is *are*	My mama she pretty.	My mamma she is pretty.
Book 3. Omitting "s" use of "s" (3rd person singular)	My mama work.	My mama works.
Book 4. omitting *ed* ending use of *ed* ending	Yesterday my daddy work hard.	Yesterday my daddy worked hard.

On The Playground (A Vernacular Story)

On the playground in my neighborhood, there be a big merry-go-round. It be in the middle of the playground. In the evening after school, my mama, she take us there. We ride a long time. My baby brother, he cry when it be time to go. I don't cry 'cause I can stay late. My daddy, he come and get me when it be time for me to go. My grandmama say she know I like the playground. She be right. If I tell 'bout the time I try to jump on and fall off, mama won't let me stay by myself. I got me a secret. You got a secret too?

Contrasting Verb Usage	EVERYDAY TALK	SCHOOL TALK
Book 5. *do* vs *does*	My baby sister do her ABC's at home.	My baby sister does her ABC's at home.
Book 6. use of *be* vs *are* and 7. use of *am, is,*	When we be good, he be happy.	When we are good, he is happy.

Book 8 has only one set of stories. These stories serve as a review of standard verb forms introduced in the series. Space is provided in several of the books for children to write their own stories. The stories are about the child's life-style, with illustrations that feature the child's drawings and photographs of children in home and classroom settings. The book becomes the property of the child as he completes each unit.

After the child has completed the vernacular readers, he can move into basal readers or programs using individualized reading or the language experience approach. The use of picture dictionaries, phrase reading exercises, and silent reading for meaning are suggested to reinforce what has been taught. Phonics is introduced by using the names of the children to associate initial sounds with letters and then having children apply this learning to other words.

SUMMARY

Beginning reading programs for the culturally different learner fall into two categories: they are either modifications of already existing approaches, or they are specifically centered around the learner's dialect.

The language experience approach is widely recommended for these children because the child reads and speaks in his natural language. Two innovations for this approach that are geared to the culturally different learner are the use of subject area content for dictation materials and stimulation of language usage before and during the reading.

Although the individualized approach is not feasible until independence in reading is gained, it has been cited in this chapter because it offers possibilities for use of dialect materials and ethnic content materials which create a reading environment which does not contradict, conflict with, or demean the reader's background.

The phonological differences between various dialects and standard English pose a real problem in regard to teaching letter-sound relationships. Neither linguists nor reading authorities have evolved programs for teaching these skills. However, the Bereiter-Engelmann approach resolves the problem to some degree since children are drilled on standard English before they move into reading.

The use of dialect or vernacular text materials for teaching reading to dialect speakers has been recommended by some authorities. While a number of the materials developed thus far are based on black dialect, the rationale for use of such materials has been generalized to other major dialects. Several factors have limited the use for dialect materials. These include the negative attitudes of parents and teachers; the absence of unequivocal experimental data as to the efficacy of these materials; and the fact that a great number of different materials would be needed in order to accommodate all dialect speakers.

In dealing with the culturally different child one important educational link is missing. In essence, this is the school's failure to provide continuity from the various preschool programs into the primary grades. As Orem (40) has pointed out, any researcher who attempts to evaluate the values of a preschool approach designed for culturally different learners is faced at the outset with a major problem, for the schools do not offer the continuity needed to maximize the benefits of the preschool and hence may cancel out the benefits which might accrue from the earlier experiences.

YOUR POINT OF VIEW?

Defend or attack the following statements:

1. Of all the factors that influence academic achievement in the school, the dialect or language habits of the culturally different child is the most important.
2. Systematic instruction in standard English should precede reading instruction for children using a nonstandard dialect.
3. a. In regard to the culturally different child, the major educational issue is that the school has ignored the needs and experiential backgrounds of these children.
   b. Agreement with statement *a* is tantamount to charging the school with racism.
4. The potential efficacy of vernacular texts has been overrated by most proponents of this approach.

5. a. The school (and society) has tended to operate from the premise that nonstandard dialects are inferior to standard English.
   b. The attitude expressed in *a* relative to nonstandard dialects is still prevalent.

6. *Premise:* "Language facility is the best single indicator of a child's mental ability."

   Statement: In the past, the school has made little effort to measure or evaluate the "language" of the culturally different, dialect.speaking child.

7. *Discuss:* What change(s) in society (i.e. outside the school) would tend to minimize the "nonstandard dialect problem" of blacks, Chicanos, and other minority groups?

BIBLIOGRAPHY

1. Abrahams, Roger D., "The Advantages of Black English," Jacksonville, Fla.: Southern Conference of Language Learning, 1970.

2. *Academic Preschool, Champaign, Illinois.* Washington, D. C.: U.S. Government Printing Office, 1970.

3. Allen, Virginia F., "Teaching Standard English as a Second Dialect," *Teacher's College Record* (February 1967): 355–70.

4. Arnold, Richard D., "English as a Second Language," *The Reading Teacher* (April 1968): 634–39.

5. Baratz, Joan C., "Teaching Reading in an Urban Negro School System," in *Teaching Black Children to Read,* Joan C. Baratz and Roger W. Shuy, eds. Washington, D. C.: Center for Applied Linguistics, 1969, pp. 92–114.

6. Baratz, Joan C. and Shuy, Roger W., eds., *Teaching Black Children to Read.* Washington, D. C.: Center for Applied Linguistics, 1969.

7. Bauer, Evelyn, "Teaching English to North American Indians in BIA Schools," *The Linguistic Reporter* (August 1968): 1–2.

8. Bereiter, Carl and Engelmann, Siegfried, "An Academically Oriented Preschool for Disadvantaged Children; Results from the Initial Experimental Group," *Psychology and Early Childhood Education,* Daniel Brinson and Jane Hill, eds. Toronto: Ontario Institute for Studies in Education, 1968, pp. 17–36.

9. Bereiter, Carl and Engelmann, Siegfried, *Teaching Disadvantaged Children in the Preschool.* Englewood Cliffs, N. J.: Prentice-Hall, Inc., 1966.

10. Brooks, Charlotte, *They Can Learn English.* Belmont, Calif.: Wadsworth Publishing, 1972.

11. Burg, Leslie A., "Affective Teaching-Neglected Practice in Innercity Schools," *Reading Teacher* 28 (January 1975): 360–63.

12. Cohen, S. Alan, *Teach Them All to Read.* New York: Random House, 1969.

13. ———, "Implications for Teachers: Senior High School Level," in Thomas D. Horn, ed., *Reading for the Disadvantaged.* New York: Harcourt, Brace and World, Inc. 1970.

14. Crittenden, Brian S., "A Critique of the Bereiter-Engelmann Preschool Program," *School Review* (February 1970): 145–67.

15. Datta, Lois-ellin, *A Report on Evaluation Studies of Project Head Start.* Washington, D. C.: Department of Health, Education, and Welfare, 1969.

16. Deutsch, Martin, "Facilitating Development in the Preschool Child: Social and Psychological Perspectives," *The Merrill Palmer Quarterly* (Spring 1964): 249–63.

17. Foerster, Leona M., "Language Experiences for Dialectically Different Black Learners," *Elementary English* 51 (February 1974): 193–97.

18. Gantt, Walter N.; Wilson, Robert M.; and Dayton, C. Mitchell, "An Initial Investigation of the Relationship between Syntactical Divergencies and the Listening Comprehension of Black Children," *Reading Research Quarterly* 10, no. 2, 1974–75, pp. 193–211.

19. Garcia, Ricardo L., "Mexican American Bilingualism and English Language Development," *Journal of Reading* 17 (March 1974): 467–73.

20. ———, "Mexican Americans Learn through Language Experience," *Reading Teacher* 28 (December 1974): 301–05.

21. Goodman, Kenneth, "Dialect Barriers to Reading Comprehension," *Elementary English* (December 1965): 853–60.

22. Goodman, Kenneth S. and Buck, Catheline, "Dialect Barriers to Reading Comprehension Revisited," *Reading Teacher* 27 (October 1973): 6–12.

23. Harmer, William R., "Implications for Teachers: Intermediate Level," in Thomas D. Horn, ed., *Reading for the Disadvantaged.* New York: Harcourt, Brace and World, Inc., 1970, pp. 191–198.

24. Horn, Thomas D., ed., *Reading for the Disadvantaged: Problems of Linguistically Different Learners.* New York: Harcourt Brace Jovanovich, 1970.

25. Johnson, Kenneth R., "Pedagogical Problems of Using Second Language Techniques for Teaching Standard English to Speakers of Non-Standard Negro Dialect," *The Florida FL Reporter,* Alfred C. Aarons, Barbara Y. Gordon, and William A. Stewart, eds. (Spring/Summer 1969): 78–80, 154.

26. Jongsma, Eugene A., "Preschool Education and the Culturally Disadvantaged," *Viewpoints* (May 1970): 95–116.

27. Kinneavy, James L. and Rutherford, William L., "Implications for Teachers: Junior High School Level," in Thomas D. Horn, ed., *Reading*

for the Disadvantaged. New York: Harcourt, Brace and World, Inc., 1970.

28. Knapp, Margaret O., "Black Dialect and Reading: What Teachers Need to Know," *Journal of Reading* 19 (December 1975): 231–36.

29. Kohlberg, L., "Montessori with the Culturally Disadvantaged," in *Early Education: Current Theory Research and Action*, Robert Hess and Roberta Meyer Bear, eds. Chicago: Aldine Publishing Co., 1966.

30. Labov, William, "Language Characteristics of Specific Groups: Blacks," in *Reading for the Disadvantaged: Problems of Linguistically Different Learners*, Thomas D. Horn, ed. New York: Harcourt Brace Jovanovich, 1970, pp. 155–56.

31. Leaverton, Lloyd; Davis, Olga; and Gladney, Mildred, *The Psycholinguistics Reading Series—A Bi-Dialectal Approach* (Teachers' Manual). Chicago: Board of Education, City of Chicago, 1969.

32. Loban, Walter, "Teaching Children Who Speak Social Class Dialects," *Elementary English* (May 1968): 592–99.

33. McDavid, Raven I., Jr., "Dialectology and the Teaching of Reading," *The Reading Teacher* (December 1964): 206–13.

34. McDonell, Gloria M., "Relating Language to Early Reading Experiences," *Reading Teacher* 28 (February 1975): 438–44.

35. Martin, Clyde and Castaneda, Alberta M., "Nursery School and Kindergarten," in *Reading for the Disadvantaged: Problems of Linguistically Different Learners*, Thomas D. Horn, ed. New York: Harcourt Brace Jovanovich, 1970.

36. Melmed, Paul Jay, *Black English Phonology: The Question of Reading Interference*, "Monographs of the Language-Behavior Research Laboratory." University of California, Berkeley (February 1971).

37. Montessori, Maria, *The Montessori Method*. New York: Schocken Books, 1964.

38. Moore, Walter, "Teaching Reading to Children from Culturally Disadvantaged and Non-English Speaking Homes," in *The Teaching of Reading*, John J. DeBoer and Martha Dallmann, eds. New York: Holt, Rinehart, and Winston, Inc., 1970, pp. 529–31.

39. Nolen, Patricia A., "Reading Nonstandard Dialect Materials; A Study at Grades Two and Four," *Child Development* 43 (September 1972): 1092–97.

40. Orem, R. C., ed., *Montessori for the Disadvantaged*. New York: G. P. Putnam's Sons, 1967.

41. Rystrom, Richard, "Dialect Training and Reading: A Further Look," *Reading Research Quarterly* (Summer 1970): 581–99.

42. Saville, Muriel R., "Language and the Disadvantaged," in *Reading for the Disadvantaged: Problems of Linguistically Different Learners*, Thomas D. Horn, ed. New York: Harcourt Brace Jovanovich, 1970, pp. 115–30.

43. Shuy, Roger W., "Some Considerations for Developing Beginning Reading Materials for Ghetto Children," in *Language and Reading: An Interdisciplinary Approach*, Doris V. Gunderson, ed. Washington, D. C.: Center for Applied Linguistics, 1970, pp. 88–97.

44. Skinner, Vincent P., "Why Many Appalachian Children Are Problem Readers—We Create the Problems," *Journal of Reading* (November 1967): 130–31.

45. Stemmler, Anne O., "An Experimental Approach to the Teaching of Oral Language and Reading," *Harvard Educational Review* (Winter 1966): 42–59.

46. Stevens, George L., "Implications of Montessori for the War on Poverty," in *Montessori for the Disadvantaged*, R. C. Orem, ed. New York: G. P. Putnam's Sons, 1967, pp. 32–48.

47. Stewart, William, "Negro Dialect in the Teaching of Reading," in *Teaching Black Children to Read*, Joan C. Baratz and Roger W. Shuy, eds. Washington, D. C.: Center for Applied Linguistics, 1969, pp. 182–201.

48. Stoodt, Barbra D. and Ignizo, Sandra, "The American Indian in Children's Literature," *Language Arts* 53 (January 1976): 17–21.

49. Vukelich, Carol and Watthias, Margaret, "A Language Process for Use with Disadvantaged Children," *Elementary English* 51 (January 1974): 119–24.

50. Wheat, Thomas E., "Reading and the Culturally Diverse," *Elementary English* 51 (February 1974): 251–56.

51. York, L. Jean and Ebert, Dorothy, "Implications for Teachers, Primary Level: Grades 1–3," in *Reading for the Disadvantaged: Problems of Linguistically Different Learners*, Thomas D. Horn, ed. New York: Harcourt Brace Jovanovich, 1970.

52. Zintz, Miles, *The Reading Process, the Teachers, and the Learner*, second ed. Dubuque, Ia.: William C. Brown Co., Publishers, 1975. Chapter 17.

PART 2

Beyond Beginning Reading

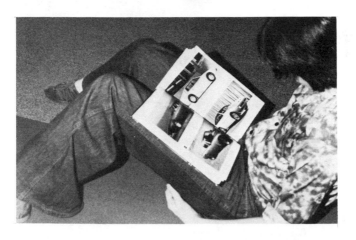

Chapter 12

Teaching Reading in the Primary Grades

In the primary grades children meet a number of concepts in reading which are strange or unknown to them. They encounter an increasing number of words not in their sight vocabulary, a fact which calls for a higher level of word recognition skill. The accelerated pace at which new tasks are introduced makes it essential that sound principles of teaching reading be followed. Growth in reading must be treated as developmental. Practically all skills previously taught must now be reinforced and extended. Mechanical and comprehension skills must be developed simultaneously and at a rate of growth which is considerably beyond that found in beginning reading. To prevent both gaps in learning and overemphasis of particular skills, instruction must be systematic and planned.

The primary grades are a period in which children's experience with reading will mold their later attitudes and reading habits.

Great damage can be done to some children by expecting them to read materials which at the moment they are incapable of handling. Other children may form malattitudes if they are forced to perform mechanical activities when they are capable of wide and extensive reading for pleasure and profit. Thus, a successful program in the primary grades, probably as much as at any instructional level, depends on the right combination of instruction in all facets of reading.

In the past, the concept of grade level has occasionally caused instruction to lose sight of the learner. Therefore, in this chapter few if any references will be made to specific grade levels. It is easy to accept the idea that the second-grade teacher teaches second graders and that third grades are populated by third graders. Experience in the classroom indicates that this idea is not very useful for instructional purposes since the classification of second or third grader does not define pupil achievement, but merely identifies the room that certain pupils are currently occupying.

Objectives of the Primary Period

The primary grades find the majority of pupils making rather rapid progress in reading. Significant changes which have an impact on reading are taking place among children. They develop abilities which are prerequisites for improving reading and interests which enhance the value of reading ability. Pupils in the primary years acquire a large store of general information, a wider interest in events not directly involving their own lives, and an increasing ability to deal with the abstract. They are now mature enough to concentrate for relatively long periods, developing capabilities for both independent work and teamwork.

An almost unlimited number of objectives for primary reading instruction could be advanced. Many of those listed here cannot be thought of as belonging exclusively to the primary period. Some were important in beginning reading and others will continue to be important throughout the intermediate, junior high, and secondary school levels. These objectives are to help the child

1. Develop a large sight vocabulary.
2. Expand her stock of concepts and word meanings.

3. Learn and apply phonic principles for sounding out unknown words.

4. Review and extend knowledge of language sounds associated with vowel and consonant combinations.

5. Use punctuation for smooth, meaningful reading.

6. Develop the skill of reading several words together as thought units, either phrases or sentences.

7. Reduce the number of occurrences of reading errors such as hesitations, regression, repetition, substitutions, or omissions.

8. Develop the ability to recognize known root words in new word forms which include prefixes or inflectional endings.

9. Further develop the attitude that reading is always purposeful and that she must clarify her purpose in specific reading tasks.

10. Use the context as an aid in attacking unknown words.

11. Enjoy and appreciate the vicarious experiences which are open to her in reading.

In addition to a systematic effort to extend skills previously introduced, many new developmental tasks are undertaken. Particular emphasis is placed on phonic and structural analysis. A number of prefixes and suffixes are taught with an emphasis on both structural and meaning changes involved. Silent consonants (knife, comb, island, light) and other spelling irregularities will receive attention along with syllabication and simple alphabetizing.

Comprehension skills are developmental also and should be developed systematically in the primary grades. Context clues become more important as unknown sight words are met more frequently. It is essential to learn new connotations for many words, and literal meanings cannot be insisted on for figurative expressions. The reader must follow the sequence of ideas and see their relationship to each other. The ability to analyze the meaning of sentences must be extended to paragraphs and larger units so that the main ideas of these larger units of material can be grasped.

The pace at which reading skills are taught in the primary grades is increased and the progress expected of pupils in a given period of time, such as a semester or year, is practically doubled when compared with the goals of beginning reading. The program necessarily includes simultaneous emphasis on the development of the mechanics of reading and the development of those comprehension skills which make reading rewarding and satisfying.

**Materials and
Teaching Schedule**

Use of
Basal Materials

The relation of the basal reader series to the total reading program
is much the same in grades two and three as in beginning reading.
Growth in reading is developmental, and basal reader materials are
designed with this fact in mind. Most facets of instruction are provided for in a logical sequence and each receives proper emphasis.
The essence of primary-level instruction is continuity and a systematic
building of skills. When a child's growth does not parallel the materials
found at her grade level, it is the pupil's achievement and rate of
growth, not the materials, that must determine the instructional program. The basal reader materials at this level not only stress the
mechanical skills of reading, but also emphasize comprehension, culti-
vating in the reader an attitude that demands comprehension from
reading. While vocabulary is still controlled, the expansion of the reading vocabulary at this level permits practice in reading for information,
organization of data, and interpretation and appreciation of literature
(3). These skills, systematically taught in reading instruction, should
easily transfer to all reading situations involving subject area materials
and textbooks. Instructional procedures for developing the mechanics
of reading and comprehension skills are discussed later in this chapter.
        In the transition from beginning reading to independent reading,
changes take place in the materials which children read. Pictures will
still be found in basal readers, but there will be fewer of them, and
the decline of the importance of pictures in providing context clues
will be quite obvious. Stories will be much longer, more interesting,
and include more concepts. These will not be built around the "one
family" theme. There will be fairy tales and tales of animals who think
and talk and have feelings. There will be stories of children who live
in different lands and do unusual things. The lives and contributions
of great men and women will be studied. Materials at this level call for
the reader to make interpretations. She must detect clues as to the
mood of characters, see the relationship between events, and grasp the
intended meaning of figurative or idiomatic expressions (25). Humor
may not always be overt, and inferences may have to be drawn in the
absence of absolute statements. The ability to read each word in a
passage is not the only criterion of reading. The child must also be able
to tell "if grandfather was serious or just playing a joke on the boys"
or "if Jerry was frightened by what he overheard" or "how the storm
affected the plans for a vacation."

Supplementary Materials

While basal reader series can provide the foundation for systematic instruction at this level, these materials should not be thought of as *the* reading program. Certainly the continued use of experience charts is justifiable in grades two and three. Experience stories written by individual pupils, as well as charts produced by the class as a whole, can be used extensively at the primary level. Since the sight vocabulary of pupils has been enlarged, this particular problem in the use of experience charts is minimized in the upper primary grades.

Bulletin boards also have many potential uses since children can now engage in independent reading and find materials which bear on topics under discussion. Pictures and newspaper and magazine articles offer interesting sources of material. When children know that there is a certain space in the room reserved for the use of such materials, they are motivated to do outside reading to find appropriate display materials. The bulletin board can be particularly effective when the teacher is working with units.

Another type of supplementary material that represents considerable potential is the graded news magazines. Examples are *News Pilot, News Ranger,* and *News Trails* for grades one, two, and three respectively.* These are weekly magazines containing news-related articles, puzzles, cartoons, humor, and illustrated stories of children from many lands. *My Weekly Reader†* is a graded magazine with different editions for each grade from kindergarten through advanced levels. These weeklies have certain advantages over texts in that they deal with timely topics which permit children to read and discuss controversial issues. Enjoying this flexibility, these children's magazines might score higher than certain other instructional materials when measured on the criteria of relevancy and interest.

Trade Books

In addition to materials designed specifically for teaching children how to read, there are a number of "trade" or story books published

---

* Scholastic Book Services, Englewood Cliffs, New Jersey and Pleasanton, California.
† American Educational Publications, Columbus, Ohio 43216.

every year. These materials are often referred to as "library books," but in any sound reading program such books will be present in abundance in every classroom. Until recently the number of such books which children with first-grade reading ability might read were quite limited. Today, hundreds of titles are available. Representative series include: *Beginner Books, Easy to Read Books, Early I Can Read Books, I Can Read Books.* Both the number of books and publishers producing such books are constantly being augmented (8, 10).

Trade or story books for beginning readers follow the principle of controlled vocabulary. The easier books contain as few as seventy-five different words. At a somewhat higher difficulty level, children may participate vicariously in a space flight while reading a book containing no more than 300 different words. This vocabulary, abetted by excellent illustrations, manages to deal with some fairly high-level concepts. Thus, in addition to story-type materials, there are also many books available in such areas as science, travel, biography, and exploration.

The extensive use of self-selected trade books as an integral part of the reading program is one of the basic trends of the individualized teaching movement. Today there are beginning books on a wide variety of topics ranging through fairy tales, joke books, space travel, poetry, ecology, and sports. This development has permitted creative primary teachers to provide their classes with a literary mix that formerly was available only at much higher grade levels.

Other educational advantages may accrue from the almost unlimited number of trade books now available. Indications are that the learning environment for blacks is now a little more meaningful. Black children now have a much better chance of reading *in school* about black heroes and blacks who have made substantial contributions to American culture. Undoubtedly of equal importance is the fact that non-blacks now also have this opportunity. One can only speculate as to what human tragedies might have been avoided and what benefits might have accrued to our society if this particular "right-to-read" had been realized much earlier.

Teaching Schedule

Teachers in the primary grades should have definite daily time periods scheduled for reading instruction. This should not suggest that reading be thought of as a subject analogous to mathematics, science, social studies, and the like, but that in addition to emphasizing reading in these areas, there must be time for teaching needed skills. Having a definite time period for reading instruction need not result in lockstep activities. Teacher-pupil contact need not be the same for all pupils every day. For instance, a number of poor readers may be given extra practice in word-attack skills while those pupils fairly proficient in this skill read independently in a subject area text or for recreation. At other times, the teacher may participate in the discussion of a story with a group of advanced readers while other pupils do seatwork on skill-oriented, teacher-prepared lesson sheets.

There is no one specific amount of time per day which can be said to be ideal for systematic reading instruction. Factors such as class size, pupils' achievement, the teacher's skill, and classroom organization would have to be considered in arriving at a schedule (31). In grade two, for example, an hour each morning and possibly a slightly shorter period in the afternoon would certainly be considered a minimum amount of time for scheduled instruction. Other short periods throughout the week should be devoted to particular reading problems as they arise in other instructional activities. Problems in word meaning, word attack, punctuation, and exploration of concepts all involve reading instruction and should be dealt with whether or not the curricular task is in the area of reading or language arts.

The Instructional Program

The instructional program in the primary grades must be based on the belief that reading growth is developmental in nature. Those children who learned the skills taught in beginning reading are now equipped to make more rapid growth in the reading process. Having mastered a number of letter-sound relationships, they can continue to build systematically on these insights. Children who can recognize several hundred words without recourse to analysis will continue to enlarge their sight vocabulary as a result of repeated experience with other as yet unknown words. If children developed the *set* to demand *meaning* from their reading, they will become more proficient at profiting from context clues and their meaning vocabularies will be expanded as a result of wider reading. The remainder of this chapter presents discussion and illustrations of teaching procedures that focus on a number of the goals of primary reading instruction.

When you've got their attention,
be sure it's worth their attention.

**Expanding
Sight Word
Vocabulary**

In other contexts throughout this book, the point is stressed that all mechanical skills and reading habits are closely related to comprehension of printed material. This relationship is reaffirmed here because in the following materials particular skills are of necessity discussed separately. In the actual reading process, no skill is applied in isolation. One does not read simply to profit from punctuation, phrase material properly, or apply analysis skills.

Developing sight vocabulary is one of the most important goals in the primary reading program. The pupil who fails to do so is in trouble as a reader. The child in the first grade will meet several hundred words on experience charts, on bulletin boards, and in basal readers. If she masters as sight words all the words that she meets in the preprimer, primer, and first reader of a given basal series, she will know between three and four hundred words, although this figure is

1st grade = 300-400
2nd grade = 800-1,000 wds
3rd grade = 1,600-2,000 wds

too high to be used as an estimated average for all pupils beginning their second year of school. If at the end of the second grade, a child knew only the words met thus far in any one basal reader series, she would know between 800 and 1,000 sight words. In the third year, she would again double her stock of sight words. Throughout the primary period, pupils read from a variety of sources, a practice which helps to expand sight vocabulary (14).

A number of procedures and exercises for helping children extend sight vocabulary are found in basal reader workbooks. In many instances, teachers can devise additional seatwork lessons for pupils who need added experience. A few typical techniques follow.

✓1. Chalkboard work on new words which are introduced in the day's reading assignment. It is considered desirable to study these new words prior to having children read the story silently. The new words are pronounced as they are printed on the board (*stump, footprints, suddenly, ocean*). Similarities to other words previously learned are pointed out, i.e., the *st* in *stump,* the word *foot* in the compound word *footprints,* the root word *sudden* in *suddenly.* Learning *ocean* as a sight word is stressed because of the difficulty of sounding it.

✓2. Using experience charts and personal experience records, labeling objects in the room, and matching captions with pictures. A series of pictures can be displayed and appropriate titles consisting of words, phrases, or sentences can be prepared on oak tag or cardboard. Children then match the proper written caption with each picture:

"The box is empty"   "A jet plane"
"Evergreens"   "Children in a school bus"
"A brown cow"   "Two boys"
"The tree has no leaves"   "A boy and a dog"

3. Using picture-word cards to teach "naming words." A picture of an object is pasted on one side of the card and the word for the picture printed on the other side:

house, car, tractor, bridge, shirt, television, giraffe, piano, dress, swing, police officer, cowboy, hammer, etc.

✓4. Introducing exercises which call for pupils to select the proper word to fill in a space left blank in a sentence. These exercises stress both meaning and differentiation between similar appearing words.

The kittens were asleep on the _____.
                                (stay/straw)

The bird built its nest in the _____.
                                (tree/tray)

They made a _____ for the puppy.
                    (bad/bed)
Mr. Brown sells _____ in his store.
                    (hats/hates)

A more difficult task is illustrated below where two similar appearing words are to be placed in two blanks in a sentence.

It was their _____ to go by _____. (plane/plan)
The _____ is about a _____ from here. (mile/mill)
The dog took the _____ to the _____. (bone/barn)
The train whistle went _____ _____. (toot/toot, two/too)
We must _____ to write on the _____. (line/learn)

5. Using word-drill periods and work sheets for seatwork which stress seeing the difference between similar appearing words.

    a. The easiest drill usually involves "family" words in which the initial letter or initial blend is the important visual cue:

> *l*ake, *t*ake, *m*ake, *c*ake, *r*ake
> *h*at, *c*at, *m*at, *f*at, *p*at, *r*at
> *f*all, *c*all, *t*all, *b*all, *h*all, *w*all

    b. A child is to supply a word containing the same ending as a pair of cue words.

>   make   take
> They used a boat to cross the l_____.
>   told   mold
> The teacher showed them how to f_____ the paper.

    c. Practice may be provided in discriminating between common service words which have marked similarities.

> *their, there; where, when, which; stay, stop;*
> *must, much; many, may; than, then, thin;*
> *horse, house; every, very; think, thank.*

    d. Practice may be given in rapid recognition of vowels in medial position (to be read orally):

> pin, pen, pan, pun
> men, tan, fun, fin, son
> sack, sick, sock, suck
> duck, kick, back, lock, neck
> fell, fall, full, fill
> bat, fit, hut, got, let

6. Combining phrases to form meaningful sentences. This exercise forces attention on both the configuration of words and their meanings.

In a *finish the sentence* exercise, children draw a line from the phrase in Column A to the phrase in Column B which completes the meaning:

A	B
The car	is on his head.
Around the house	give us milk.
The horse	is a beautiful lawn.
A straw hat	moves down the road.
Cows	drink milk.
Cats	has a beautiful saddle.

7. Identifying root words in inflected forms. The child writes the root in the space provided.

taken	_____	using	_____
carried	_____	goes	_____
earlier	_____	laziest	_____
parties	_____	angrily	_____
reaching	_____	wagged	_____

Developing Word Analysis Skills

Word analysis includes all methods of arriving at the pronunciation of unknown words. Gaining independence in reading implies a mastery of those techniques which will permit a child to read a passage containing words which she does not recognize instantly as sight words. Instruction in the primary grades will continue to focus on most of the word analysis skills taught in beginning reading, specifically phonics, structural analysis, and context and methods in combination. These skills become increasingly important because they are prerequisites for independent reading.

Phonic Analysis

Letter-sound relationship is one of the most important of the mechanical skills taught in the primary grades. The child must gain insight into a large number of these relationships and be able to apply them if she is to become an independent reader. In some instances, pupils in the primary grades are not systematically taught skills they need because these were included in the curriculum of previous grades. In an effort to mitigate against teachers associating particular phonics teachings with a particular grade level, an overview of the entire program is presented in Chapter 8, *Phonics Instruction*. Much of the material in Chapter 8 is germane to the primary grades; however, some teaching illustrations not included in that discussion will be presented here.

It should be kept in mind that children cannot profit from phonics instruction unless they are able (1) to discriminate visually between letter forms; and (2) discriminate auditorially between speech sounds that printed letters represent. Any child who has not mastered these skills should be provided further instruction regardless of her grade level (16).

Review of initial consonant sounds. Certain children will not have mastered this skill, others will need some review, while some pupils will need little if any further work. The following exercises for teaching mental substitution of initial consonants and blends illustrate the type of activities which may be used.

1. Add a letter to the front of each word to make a different word. Write the new word on the line provided.

it	(hit)	is	_____	and	_____
in	_____	ox	_____	ink	_____
at	_____	up	_____	am	_____
us	_____	ice	_____	ear	_____
an	_____	any	_____	all	_____

2. Change the first letter to make a naming word for an animal. Write the animal name on the line provided.

mat	(cat)	wig	_____	loose	_____
dish	_____	hole	_____	pen	_____
now	_____	box	_____	love	_____
boat	_____	house	_____	tub	_____
cup	_____	wear	_____	mitten	_____

3. Change the first letter to make a child's name.

back	_____	fancy	_____	due	_____
like	_____	hoe	_____	pail	_____
pane	_____	hose	_____	jam	_____
day	_____	sob	_____	hilly	_____
him	_____	drank	_____	loan	_____
late	_____	mill	_____	hat	_____

4. Initial Blends: Form a new word by adding one of these blends to the front of each word.

st	sp	sk
_____ate	_____ill	_____out
_____in	_____and	_____age
_____all	_____ring	_____ink
_____end	_____air	_____ice

5. Take away the first letter and then add an initial blend to form a new word.

lake _____	nap _____	tape _____
dog _____	late _____	now _____
mad _____	sand _____	sail _____
door _____	bee _____	may _____
bag _____	rider _____	mice _____

6. Initial Digraphs: Take away the first letter and add *wh, ch, sh, th* to form a new word.

lick _____	mile _____	rake _____
sale _____	but _____	kite _____
tower _____	fin _____	sick _____
hen _____	bank _____	bird _____
boot _____	deer _____	feel _____

Irregular consonant sounds. The following material focuses on the two sounds of g and c, the unsounded letters in *kn* and *wr* words, and the digraph *ph*.

7. On each blank space write g or j to show the sound that g represents.

_____giant	_____giraffe	_____gold	_____general
_____got	_____gang	_____gem	_____Gypsy
_____gate	_____George	_____gas	_____gym

8. On each blank space write k or s to show the sound that c represents.

_____cake	_____cent	_____cuff	_____cycle
_____cider	_____coat	_____city	_____cut
_____color	_____catch	_____cold	_____certain
_____cypress	_____circle	_____cellar	_____course

9. On the blank space write the letter which represents the *first* sound heard in each word.

_____knee	_____wrap	_____phone	_____wrote
_____know	_____write	_____photo	_____knight
_____knob	_____wring	_____phonics	_____Phillip

Working with vowel sounds. Children will have had considerable experience in discriminating between vowel sounds and the letter combinations representing these sounds. Some children will need further review of concepts covered in Chapter 8. The following exercises represent only a few of the teaching formats that might be used with primary-level pupils.

1. *Auditory discrimination:* "Draw a card" is a game that can be played by pairs of children, a small group, several teams, or by the entire class. Paste each of a number of pictures on a separate card. (These may be limited to pictures whose naming words contain either a short or long vowel sound.) Shuffle the cards and place them face down on the playing area. Children take turns drawing a card. Each child names her picture and tells the vowel sound heard in the naming word:

> "I drew a *fox*—I hear short *o* in *fox*."
> "I drew a *tree*—I hear long *e* in *tree*."
> "I drew a *vase*—I hear long *a* in *vase*."
> Etc.

2. *Auditory-visual discrimination:* Prepare and duplicate a page containing a number of word pairs. The words in each pair are identical except for vowel letters and vowel sounds. Pronounce one word in each pair. The children are to underline the word pronounced. In the examples below, the word to be pronounced is in italics.

a. *bed*	b. plan	c. *coat*	d. *pal*	e. met
bead	*plane*	cot	pale	*meet*

f. pan	g. *rod*	h. fed	i. *cute*	j. *rid*
pain	road	*feed*	cut	ride

3. *Long and short vowel words:* Each sentence shows two blank spaces and is followed by two words which, when placed in the proper blank spaces, will make "sentence sense." Children read the sentence and write the correct word in each blank space.

1. Our _____ won _____ games. (*ten/team*)
2. John and his _____ filled the _____. (*pail/pal*)
3. The children put their _____ on the _____. (*cot/coats*)
4. They used their scissors to _____ out _____ designs. (*cut/cute*)
5. The boys _____ down the _____. (*slide/slid*)

4. *Mental substitution of vowel letter-sounds:* Duplicate a work sheet similar to the following format. The top of the sheet contains a box containing the vowel letters. A stimulus word is shown at the left followed by three blank spaces. Children are to write three words in

which only the vowel letter is changed. Words must be sounded out since all vowel letters cannot be used in the series.

	a	e	i	o	u
hit		(hat)		(hot)	(hut)
pup		___		___	___
beg		___		___	___
pop		___		___	___
bid		___		___	___
hum		___		___	___
pet		___		___	___
ham		___		___	___

5. *Homonyms* (Two Vowel Patterns): Explain the concept that some words are pronounced the same but have different meanings and spellings. All the words in the following exercise follow regular spelling patterns and contain one of the vowel patterns *ee, ea, ai, a + e*. The purpose of the exercise is to have the child associate these visual patterns with the long vowel sound they represent.

Directions: *On each blank space write a word that sounds like the first word. The new word will have a different meaning and spelling.*

week	(weak)	main	(mane)
beet	___	sail	___
steal	___	made	___
heal	___	mail	___
meat	___	pale	___
creek	___	waste	___
seem	___	plain	___
real	___	tail	___
peel	___	pane	___

6. *Decode the mystery word:* This is an exercise that provides practice in associating letter-sounds in initial, medial, and final positions. In its simplest form it consists of three pictures whose naming words are made up of three letter-sounds. The pictures are arranged so that when the child uses the first letter-sound from the naming word of the first picture, the second from the second picture, and the final letter-sound from the third picture, she arrives at a CVC word.

Adding Context Clues

Prepare a series of sentences each of which contains one or more short-vowel words in which the vowel letter has been omitted. Children

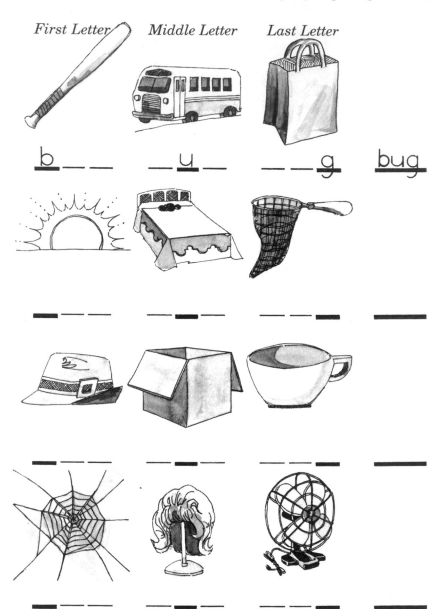

Figure 28

Decode the mystery word.

read the sentence using context clues to identify the word. They then write the vowel letter that represents the sound heard in that word.

1. The c__t drank milk from the c__p.
2. We had f__n on the b__s.
3. Two m__n wore r__d c__ps.
4. Did the p__p s__t on the r__g?
5. Billy's d__d read the m__p.

At practically all points on the reading continuum, the one ability that sets the good readers apart from poor readers is the degree to which the context helps the reader get unknown words. When children do not profit from context clues, this weakness is easy to detect by observing their reading behavior—either they do not "try" words or they insert words which do not belong. On the other hand, when a passage is read correctly, it is difficult for an observer to determine to what degree dependence on context clues contributed to the successful reading.

The good reader keeps in mind what has been read and how the sentence she is reading builds on this meaning. If context is not enough, she glances through the word to detect a prefix, the root word, or an inflectional ending. When no prefix is found, the first syllable is isolated. This may unlock the word. If not, she will work further through the word. These operations are performed so rapidly by a good reader that there may be no perceptible pause between the different modes of attack. If the word is not solved by this attack, the reader may go on past the word for additional context clues. This step may call for rereading the sentence, but if it is successful, meaning will have been reached.

When each method of attacking unknown words is discussed and examined separately, one might conclude that in a given situation a reader uses only one method. The exclusive use of one method in this way makes for slow and inefficient reading, although some children approach reading in this manner. The more ability a reader has in profiting from structural, phonic, and context clues, the less likely it is that she can tell which one was the key in helping her solve a particular word. The smooth, facile reader is one who attacks an unknown word simultaneously on every front on which it is vulnerable to analysis. Early in the first grade the child learns to sound the initial letters of words. This skill, plus pictures and context clues, makes it possible to eliminate many of the words that might otherwise have been plausible choices.

Mistakes in reading can be made even in situations where one has the ability to recognize all the words in a passage.

Mary had a little lamp
Its base was white as snow.

The child who knows the verse about Mary and her lamb may well be trapped into miscalling *lamb* for *lamp* and *face* for *base*, but as she reads further her mistake should become obvious.

Mary had a little lamp
Its base was white as snow,
She turned it on when she came in
And off, when out she'd go.

Since the reader has been taught to read for meaning, the mistakes on the first two lines do not permit a good fit with the concluding two lines. The reader would likely reason somewhat as follows: "Slow down —look again; that doesn't make sense; this is not about a lamb in school."

The more difficult the level of the material, the less likely it is that the immediate context alone will be an adequate tool for analyzing unknown words, but often with the smallest additional clue the word is easily solved. Assume that the pupil meets a sentence containing an unknown word: "Jack was sure his _____ would let him go." This is the opening line of a story and the author has yet to unfold the plot or background. There are many words which might complete an idea when this is all we know. Is Jack being held a prisoner? The word could be *captors*. Is he thinking of "getting permission?" The word might be *mother, father, friends, teacher*. If the reader notes something about the unknown word, she may get a valuable clue. For instance, "Jack was sure his p_____ would let him go." *Mother, father, teacher, friends* are eliminated if the reader can use initial sounds. Several possibilities remain, such as *pal, playmates, principal, parents*. The word *play* is known as a sight word. It is not found in this unknown word, so playmates is not suggested. It is possible that word configuration (length of word) might help the reader decide between *pal* or *parents*. With enough skill at phonic analysis to work her way through the first syllable, the reader is almost assured of arriving at the correct response. If she should try PA rents or PAR ents, either pronunciation will be close enough to suggest the correct word.

"It's my _____," said Jimmy. Here a number of possibilities occur to the reader: my *idea, turn, guess, opinion* or any number of possessions. This sentence alone does not provide enough context, but rarely does such a sentence stand alone. As we take into consideration the context supplied by several previous sentences, the unknown word falls into place.

The boys searched everywhere but they did not find the little lost puppy. "I hope Blackie doesn't get hit by a car," said Billy. Jimmy was very sad. He had been thinking all afternoon about not closing the gate when he had gone to mail the letter. The puppy must have gotten out when he left the gate open. "It's my _____," said Jimmy. Then he told about the gate.

Structural Analysis

The teaching of structural cues should receive considerable emphasis in the primary grades. In their reading, children will meet every type of structural change in word form found in English writing. Also, the frequency with which they meet inflected forms and affixes will increase drastically. Instruction should include a review and extension of children's experience with compounds, common word endings including plurals and contractions, affixes, and the like.

Compound words will not be difficult for the child who forms the habit of examining unknown words. The compound words she meets will be composed of shorter words that she has already learned. Basal reader series introduce a few compound words at first-grade level and provide drill on recognition and analysis at each succeeding grade level.

1. Noticing the structure of compound words.

   a. *The two words in columns 1 and 2 can be placed together to form one word. Write the two words together under 3 and say the compound that is formed.*

1	2	3
after	noon	afternoon
with	out	_____
every	one	_____
club	house	_____
air	plane	_____
door	way	_____
some	time	_____

   b. *Each word under 1 can be placed with a word under 2 to make a compound word. The first one is done for you.*

1	2	3
*after	way	afternoon
with	time	_____
every	plane	_____
club	one	_____
air	*noon	_____
door	out	_____
	house	_____

c. *Building compound words from materials provided below. Combine one word from the box with a word from the list to form a compound word.*

type	tooth	snap	after
any	grand	bed	light

_____ ache   _____ one
_____ noon   _____ write
_____ father   _____ shot
_____ house   _____ room

d. Recognizing compound words in sentence context. *Underline each compound word. Draw a line between the two words in each compound word* [mail/box].

(1) Everyone went to the football game that afternoon.
(2) John is upstairs writing in his scrapbook with his ballpoint pen.
(3) We ran halfway to the clubhouse without stopping.
(4) Frank received a flashlight, a raincoat, and a sailboat for his birthday.
(5) He read the newspaper headline, "Big fire at sawmill."
(6) They saw the shipwreck from a hilltop near the lighthouse.

2. Forming plurals by adding *es.*

Many plurals are formed by simply adding s, *as in* boys, girls, trees, farms, cats. *In many words* es *is added to form plurals.*

fox	foxes	inch	inches
box	_____	dress	_____
dish	_____	lunch	_____
brush	_____	mix	_____
bus	_____	match	_____
class	_____	fish	_____

All of the above words end with *s, ss, sh, ch,* or *x.* Make a rule for adding *es* to form plurals.

3. Forming the plural of words ending in *y.*
Change the y *to* i, *then add* es.

funny	funnies	body	bodies
fly	_____	army	_____
baby	_____	party	_____
puppy	_____	cherry	_____
lady	_____	family	_____

✓ 4. Recognizing contractions.

The two words in column A are often combined to form a different word found in column B. The apostrophe (') in these words indicates that a letter or letters have been omitted in forming the new word.

A		B
I am	=	I'm
I will	=	I'll
he will	=	he'll
he is	=	he's
has not	=	hasn't
I have	=	I've
have not	=	haven't

(In follow-up work sheets only column A is presented and the child writes the contraction.)

do not	_____
was not	_____
they have	_____
you will	_____
it is	_____
does not	_____

5. Doubling final consonants. The rule covering doubling of consonants is quite lengthy and involved. Most children, however, learn to do it without being conscious of a rule. In essence, the final consonant is doubled in a *one vowel word* when the last two letters are a vowel and consonant. If the one vowel word ends with two consonants, there is no doubling. An exercise such as the following might help children master this spelling and structural phenomena.

One vowel
One consonant   Double the consonant before adding *ed, ing, er.*

can	*canned*	*canning*	*canner*
plan	_____	_____	_____
skip	_____	_____	_____
pop	_____	_____	_____
drag	_____	_____	_____
stop	_____	_____	_____

Two consonants   Just add the endings *ed, ing, er.*

help	*helped*	*helping*	*helper*
click	_____	_____	_____

dish ___ ___ ___
earn ___ ___ ___
march ___ ___ ___
climb ___ ___ ___

6. Possessives. An apostrophe and the letter *s* (*'s*) indicate possession.

John has a bike.   This is John's bike.
Many girls have new hats.   These are the girls' new hats.
The cat eats from this dish.   This is the cat's dish.

Write the correct word in each blank space:

a. Two _____ were eating from the _____ bowl.
          (*cat's/cats*)
b. This is the _____ time to watch T.V.
          (*children/children's*)

7. Comparative forms.

Write the word that makes the sentence correct.

a. John is _____ than Bill, but Ted is the _____ runner on the team.
      (*fast/faster/fastest*)
b. November is _____ than July.
      (*cold/colder/coldest*)
c. If they took the _____ trail they should arrive in a _____ time.
      (*short/shorter/shortest*)
d. Our town has many _____ buildings, but not the _____ one in the state.
      (*tall/taller/tallest*)
e. We crossed the _____ bridge I ever saw.
      (*long/longer/longest*)

The structure or visual stimulus pattern of words is changed by a syllable added either at the beginning or at the end of that word. A child may know the symbol *load* as a sight word, but the first few times she sees *unload, reload,* or *unloading,* she may not see what is familiar. Instead, she may see the whole new configuration as unfamiliar. Thus, recognizing common prefixes will be an aid in learning new words where the root word is known (23). Children use words which contain prefixes and suffixes in spoken language long before coming to school. These words are often learned as sight words before formal instruction deals with the meanings of these suffixes.

Instruction cannot deal exclusively with the structural changes resulting from the addition of prefixes or suffixes. Exercises should force attention both to the structural change and the modification of meaning. Workbooks of all basal series have lessons devoted to the study of prefixes, but the teacher does not have to wait for a particular time or page in a workbook. The curriculum of the modern school does not impose such rigidity. It is just as appropriate to show pupils that prefixes change the meanings of words in a science, arithmetic, hygiene, or geography class as it is to discuss this point during the period devoted to reading instruction.

8. *Make a sentence with each of the following words. What happens to the meaning of each word lettered* b? *What can you say about the prefix* un?

a. clean	a. load
b. *un*clean	b. *un*load
a. fair	a. kind
b. *un*fair	b. *un*kind

9. *Make a sentence with each of the following words. What happens to the meaning of each word lettered* b? *What can you say about the prefix* re?

a. fill	a. read	a. visit
b. *re*fill	b. *re*read	b. *re*visit

10. *Make a sentence with the following words. Each word lettered* b *has a prefix. Explain what each prefix does to the word meaning.*

a. view	a. ability	a. agree
b. *pre*view	b. *in*ability	b. *dis*agree

Suffixes are word endings which give root words different shades of meaning (*er, or, ist, an, al, ure, ty, ment, ism, age, is, en, el, ive, ish, ant, ful, ly, less*, etc.). Since there are a great number of suffixes and very few have an absolutely fixed meaning, an attempt to teach concrete meanings for the majority would probably produce more confusion than learning. If a child develops the habit of *seeing* the more common endings so that she is not prevented from recognizing known root words, the new word is not likely to cause trouble. Composing sentences using the different forms of a word is a better method of teaching than having the child attempt to tell the precise difference between words like joy*ful*, joy*fully*, joy*ous*; depend*ent*, depend*able*, depend*ency*.

The English language is rich in the number of prefabricated units that can be attached to any number of root words to form new words:

heat:	heated, preheated, reheat, preheating, heatedly
war:	postwar, warlike, warring, prewar, wartime

luck: lucky, unluckiest, luckily, unlucky
place: placing, displace, replaced, replaceable

Assume that the word *happy* is a known sight word. Identifying the word *unhappily* theoretically calls for these skills: recognizing the prefix *un* and the suffix *ly* as units, perceiving the root word *happy*, applying the rule than words ending in *y* change *y* to *i* before adding an ending, and understanding syllabication—i.e., prefixes and suffixes usually stand as syllables and two like consonants usually divide, thus giving the pronunciation *un hap pi ly.* It is doubtful, however, that any reader goes through all of these mental steps since the process would be most uneconomical. The reader also has the context to suggest the word, and after she has met a word on several occasions, she will probably have mastered it as a sight word and will not have to resort to analysis.

Developing
Critical
Reading Skills

Reading skills are frequently divided into two types: *mechanical* and *critical reading.* This dichotomy is misleading because all reading skills are related to *comprehension or "getting meaning."* For example, learning to use punctuation might appear to be totally within the framework of mechanics, yet nothing can more quickly distort meaning than the inability to profit from the clues that punctuation provides. Word-by-word reading has implications other than just in the skills area. In addition to slowing the reading rate, this habit tends to force attention on words rather than on larger units. Reading must be thought of as a unitary process that is more than the simple sum of its parts. When a child is asked to read a sentence or a larger unit, she must employ every skill that the situation requires regardless of how or what these skills have been labeled.

At a given moment, a reader can comprehend at a level commensurate with her academic background, experience, and intellectual level. In the final analysis, the catalyst between writer and reader is the manner in which the latter uses her past experiences in the reading situation. As the child progresses in reading ability, the materials she reads increase in difficulty. The teacher's task becomes that of keeping children's concepts abreast of the material they are reading.

The following teaching procedures focus on developing and expanding concepts and language facility. All can be adapted to different levels of difficulty and mode of presentation. In many schools, teachers combine their efforts and jointly develop language-reading exercises to be used in learning centers.

Expansion of Meanings

Children's development of concepts cannot be left to chance. The school deliberately seeks to provide an environment which will lead to the development and expansion of concepts in every area of the curriculum. The following procedures can be used in helping children develop meanings. They are not limited to a particular grade level. While many of these techniques are used in the formal reading program, they are appropriate for teaching terms and concepts in all subject areas.

Using pictures. The use of pictures is an excellent method of expanding concepts and clearing up misconceptions. The role of pictures in beginning reading has been discussed previously in relation to helping pupils master sight words by suggesting context. Here we deal with

Learning each printed word symbol as a sight word during beginning reading instruction facilitates learning dictionary skills in the intermediate grades.

the utility of pictures in developing and expanding concepts. A picture of an eroded hillside is much more effective in fixing the concept of *erosion* than is a word definition of the term. Early basal readers rely heavily on pictures, but it is actually in the context areas that pictures have greatest value. Pictures are more likely to fix accurate concepts of *colonial architecture*, the *iron-plated Monitor*, an *anteater*, a *Chinese junk*, *terrace farming* or the *human circulatory system* than is language alone.

The same picture can be used at different levels for teaching words and meanings. For example, let us imagine a picture which would be available to almost any teacher—a downtown scene in a small city. We see a bus, a boy on a bicycle, various store fronts and offices, a police officer directing traffic, a fire hydrant, the city hall across from a parking lot.* Without going into more detail, we might build a hierarchy of concepts.

> *"Where is the policeman?"*
> "In the *street*."
> "Yes, he is really standing in the middle of where two streets cross
> —what is that called?"
> "That's an *intersection*."
> (The class level will determine whether the teacher should explain
> the term intersection.)
> *"How many kinds of travel or transportation do we see?"*
> "Some people are *walking*."
> "A boy on a *bicycle*."
> "There's a *bus*. It's a city bus."
> "There are lots of *cars*."
> "I see an *airplane* above the city."
> *"What kinds of transportation are not seen in the picture?"*
> "*Trains*."
> "Don't see any *boats*."
> "There are no big *trucks*—big trailers."
> (Teacher points to the symbol which identifies the telephone com-
> pany office.)
> *"What is in this building?"*
> "That must be the telephone office."
> "What's this sign across the street?"
> "City Water Company, it says."
> *"What do we call these types of businesses?"*
> (no response)

---

* This is a description of the poster picture "The City" found in *Readiness Pictures* (New York: Macmillan Co.).

"Did you ever hear the term *utilities* or *public utilities?*"
(The teacher prints the word on the board.)
"What other *utilities* do you think this city has—what others be-sides telephone company and water company?"

> "Electricity."

"That's right—what other name might it have?"

> "Light Company"

> "Power Company"

"Do you think of any other *utility* companies? Would there be a gas company?"

Other meanings the teacher can lead into are

> "Four stories high"
> "This canvas over the sidewalk is an *awning* or a *canopy.*"
> "This is a parcel post truck. Its purpose is to serve the people. How is it like the power company? How it is different?"

The picture we have attempted to visualize is a simple one which could be used at various grade levels. Through its use the teacher can stress

1. Noticing details
2. Symbols standing for things (the telephone symbol on a window)
3. Many different *names* standing for the same things
   a. Power company, public service company, utility company, etc.
   b. Canopy, awning
4. The same word having different meanings according to usage (i.e., *meter:* parking meter, gas meter, electric meter; meters in cars: speedometers, gas meter, and mileage meter)

The value of pictures lies in their wealth of detail and the fact that they stay in focus or can be referred to after a discussion has led away to other things.

Synonyms

The pupils are reminded that words which have the same meaning are called *synonyms.* "Give me another word that means the same as *big, work, fast*" will as a rule elicit responses from everyone in the group. Exercises that permit group participation can be followed by individual work involving a series of three-by-five cards each contain-ing the directions "Go to the board and write the word _____ .

Under it write as many synonyms as you can." Another series of cards may include a number of words some of which are synonyms for the stimulus word. The pupil selects the synonyms and writes them under the stimulus word. This latter task is the easier of the two and permits pupils of differing ability to participate. The following exercises illustrate this type of activity.

1. Write the word *timid* on the board. Under it write as many synonyms as you can think of.

2. Write the word *rapid* on the board. Under it write any word from the following group which is similar in meaning:

quick	speedy
shave	light
fast	fleet
grasp	throw
inquire	reduce
hastily	swift

3. Another exercise might call for the child to underline two words in a series which are similar in meaning:

almost	together	certainly	nearly
thrilling	spinning	exciting	frightening
nonsense	terrible	scolding	awful
matches	money	penny	postcard

Work sheets of varying difficulty can be used with pupils of different ability levels in a class. Similar exercises are applicable to expanding word meanings by teaching words of *opposite meanings*. The objective should always be to work out lesson plans that will assure that the pupils

See the words
Hear them pronounced
Experience their use in sentences

Sentence comprehension exercises can be used in which the child reads to determine whether two sentences carry the same meaning.

Read the following two sentences marked a. Do they have the same meaning? If so, write S in the box to indicate they have the Same meaning. Write D if the sentences have a Different meaning. Do the same for sentences b, c, d, etc.

a. Bill took his dog for a ride. ☐
a. Bill took his dog in the house.

b. The park is not far from where Mary lives. ☐
b. Mary's house is near the park.

c. Tom has a cat and a pony at the farm. ☐
c. Tom has a pet goat at the farm.

Antonyms

Review the definition of antonyms (words having opposite meanings) and cite a few examples: *huge—tiny; hot—cold; legal—illegal; start—finish*. Children can then volunteer other antonyms. There are many formats for working with antonyms; only a few will be illustrated here.

1. Write the word *release* on the board. Supply children with a list of words similar to the following. They then write any word that has a meaning nearly opposite to that of *release*.

grasp	trap
relief	free
hold	captive
clutch	repeat
dismiss	catch
receive	keep
mistake	

2. Read each of the following. Then complete the sentences by writing an antonym for the underlined word.

a. <u>Open</u> the window and _____ the door.
b. Elephants are <u>huge</u>, lady bugs are _____.
c. The lake was <u>shallow</u> at one end and _____ at the other.
d. He wiped his <u>dirty</u> hands on the _____ towel.
e. Sandpaper is <u>rough</u>, but it can make wood _____.

3. Read each sentence. Then, changing only one word, write a sentence that has the opposite meaning.

a. He said, "the team lost the game."

_____

b. The children were very noisy.

_____

c. Did you fail the spelling test?

_____

d. Be sure and go in the front door.

_____

Homonyms

Homonyms are words which sound exactly alike and are spelled differently. They are potential sources of trouble to young readers since both sight recognition and meanings may be confusing. Many common homonyms look very much like (*their, there; see, sea; hear, here; beat, beet; dear, deer; course, coarse*). The reader in the primary grades gets meaning from hearing the following sounds in these combinations, but she may not recognize all of the written symbols.

1. *Their* coats are over *there*.
2. The *plane* landed safely on the *plain*.
3. *Would* you please carry in some *wood?*
4. He felt *weak* for a *week* after he was sick.
5. "*Oh*," he said, "how much do I *owe* you?"
6. The boy *ate eight* pieces of candy.
7. *See* the ship on the *sea*.
8. *No*, I do not *know* where it is.

One method of expanding both sight and usage vocabularies is to list homonyms in columns with the word the child is most likely to be familiar with on the left. An exercise calling for the use of each word in a sentence will provide a check on the mastery of meanings.

The words in columns A and B are pronounced the same.

A	B	A	B
do	dew	sail	sale
dear	deer	hair	hare
way	weigh	made	maid
hall	haul	one	won
pair	pare	poor	pour

Mixing Synonyms—Antonyms—Homonyms

Each stimulus word under A is followed by three test words. Each of these is either a synonym, antonym, or homonym. For the first word

on the line in front of each word write: S if it is a synonym.
A if it is an antonym.
H if it is a homonym.

A
Sample: idle: (A) busy (H) idol (S) inactive
plain: ____fancy ____common ____plane
aisle: ____passageway ____I'll ____isle
real: ____reel ____true ____fiction
vain: ____modest ____conceited ____vein
minor: ____child ____miner ____adult

Each box below contains one of the letters A, S, H. If the letter is:

A—write an antonym for the word shown.
S—write a synonym.
H—write a homonym.

(H) there	(S) small	(A) innocent
___	___	___
(S) evil	(A) hate	(H) wait
___	___	___
(A) rich	(H) no	(S) feeble
___	___	___

For children who have trouble with these words, simple card games can be devised for two or more players in which one word of each pair is included in a draw pile and the other words shuffled and dealt to the players. When a card in the draw pile is turned up, whoever has the homonym for it in her hand pronounces the word on the stack and gives its meaning, then gives the meaning for the word in her hand. If she does each without help, she "takes" both cards. There are many variations which can be used with such cards.

Following is a list of easier homonyms which the child usually meets in the primary grades.

beat	beet	red	read
know	no	ring	wring

do	dew	would	wood
dear	deer	whole	hole
to two	too	sail	sale
knew	new	hall	haul
mail	male	pair	pare
road	rode	tail	tale
wait	weight	steal	steel

there	their	birth	berth
sun	son	ate	eight
oh	owe	some	sum
waist	waste	pain	pane
rap	wrap	so	sew
bee	be	by	buy
one	won	not	knot
see	sea	hear	here
hair	hare	our	hour
week	weak	maid	made
fair	fare	piece	peace

✳ Developing Different Meanings for the Same Word

The child's early language development is characterized by mastery of the concrete first and then a gradual moving up the ladder of abstraction. She may know such words as *air, blue, mine, broadcast, fence,* and she may know several meanings for each word; yet she will not be familiar with all the meanings of these words. The child will probably have mastered a number of meanings for the word *air.*

1. My daddy put *air* in the tires.
2. We hang clothes outside to *air* them.
3. We breathe *air*.

The same child may be confused by the following:

1. If asked to "*air* her views."
2. To hear that "her older brother gave his girlfriend the *air*."
3. That Mrs. Jones is disliked in the neighborhood because "she puts on *airs*."

The child may understand what is meant by *blue* in the sentence, "The boy had a *blue* boat." She may not be familiar with "The boy felt *blue* when his aunt left." She may understand "Grandfather rode the *horse*," but not have a concept of "The coach warned the boys not to *horse* around" or the expression "That's a *horse* of a different color" or "The mayor accused the council of beating a dead *horse*."

She may know one or two meanings of mine but some of the usages or concepts involving the word *mine* will undoubtedly be beyond her.

1. "The book is *mine*."
2. "Joe's father worked in the coal *mine*."
3. "That corner store is a gold *mine*."
4. "The tank was damaged by a land *mine*."
5. "Don't under*mine* the confidence of the people."
6. "Our break is over, let's get back to the salt *mine*."
7. "He was stationed aboard a *mine* sweeper."

The above examples point up how difficult it is to measure "size of vocabulary," for each child has several different kinds of vocabularies. The word *mine* would be in a child's meaning, speaking, and reading vocabularies if she could read sentence (1) above, even though that was the only usage which was familiar to her. And in some instances, if the child could "read"—that is, correctly say all the words in the sentence (4)—it would be concluded that *mine* was in her *reading vocabulary* whether or not she could explain the sentence. Inability to explain the usage would indicate only that the child did not understand this particular concept.

Adults' meaning vocabularies are larger than their speaking, writing, or reading vocabularies. The sounds "klee-shay" may conjure up meaning for an individual when she hears the word used in context, yet the written symbol cliché may be meaningless if she sounds "clish." The word *cache* may be mispronounced in reading but still produce meaning in the sentence "The bandits, under cover of darkness, returned to the mountain cache for their stolen loot." Meaning may escape the individual when the T.V. badman says, "Let's go, boys, we have to beat the posse to the kash."

Learning meanings is a fascinating and highly motivating experience for children. The teacher can point out that most words carry several different meanings according to how they are used. He might illustrate with simple words like *can, stick, run,* or *set.* As the teacher asks for different usages, he will write the children's responses on the board, at the same time attempting to fix the various meanings by using other known words.

"I *can* spell my name."—*can* means *able*
"I bought a *can* of beans."—*can* means a *container*
"Put the garbage in the *garbage can.*"—another type of *container*
"My mother said, 'Tomorrow I will *can* the peaches.'"—*can* means
to *preserve food.*

The last example may not be given by any child in an early elementary grade in an urban school, but this usage may be known to
almost every child in the same grade in a rural locality. Some other
usages of the word *can* may not be appropriate for an early grade level,
but would be at a higher grade level.

"*Can* it, Mack."—an order to stop talking
"If you leave now, the boss will *can* you."—dismiss from job
"Why don't you trade in that old tin *can* and get an automobile?"
—a battered old car

After several group exercises which stress that the objective is to
supply different meanings of a word, not simply different sentences,
the teacher can suggest a written game. Each child works independently, selecting her own words for illustrating different usages. In
order not to handicap the poorer spellers, the teacher may offer to spell
any words the children want to use in their sentences. "Just hold up
your hand and I'll come to your desk and write out the word you want
to use." This exercise has considerable diagnostic value in that it yields
data on spelling ability, language facility, legibility of handwriting,
ability to follow directions, and ability to work independently.

Some specific findings reported by one teacher include

1. Despite what appeared to be a thorough explanation of the objective, a number of pupils missed the point of the exercise and wrote
   different sentences using the same meaning of the word selected.
2. Several pupils misspelled words which they could spell correctly
   when the teacher pronounced or dictated these words. (The pupils
   slurred or omitted syllables when they said these words silently.)
3. The papers revealed many words misspelled *which the pupils
   thought they spelled correctly.* This data served as a basis for spelling review.
4. The handwriting was inferior to that which the child would do on a
   writing test.
5. This exercise disclosed great differences among pupils in their
   ability to use expressive language as well as exposing paucity of
   concepts among some pupils.

6. Misconceptions were found on many pages. These could be corrected individually with the pupil.

Selecting the
Appropriate Meaning

The ability to select the appropriate meaning of a particular word which has many meanings is essential for critical reading. The word *base* has many meanings: third base, the base of a triangle, the base line of a graph, a naval base, base motives, and a number of others. *Dividend* does not have the same meaning in mathematics that it does when used as an increment from investments in stocks and bonds. The literal definition of *island* as "a body of land entirely surrounded by water" is not the meaning implied by John Donne when he states, "no man is an island entire unto himself—each is a piece of the continent, a part of the whole." Nevertheless, this conventional meaning would have to be known in order to understand the author's intended meaning.

Cole (7) tells of a student in a chemistry class who asked his instructor for help in understanding the law: "The volume of a gas is inversely proportional to its density." The instructor tried without success to explain the concept embodied in the law. Finally, he asked the boy to define volume, volume of a gas, density, and inversely proportional. The boy had only one concept for *volume*—a book; *gas* was what is used in a stove; *density* meant thickness; he had no concept to go with *inversely proportional*. The boy had actually "memorized" the law, a fact which emphasizes the futility of such effort in the absence of understanding.

The child's need for learning new words and concepts never abates, but sometimes the great mass of material to be taught may interfere with the effective teaching of meanings. In other chapters a number of procedures have been suggested for helping children master unknown words. Some of these procedures have merit for use in the primary grades and should be used when appropriate. A technique used with success by some teachers is the *word meaning period*. Ten- to fifteen-minute periods are used in which pupils present and discuss words whose meanings they had not known when they met them in their reading. A number of variations can be introduced to keep the period interesting. A pupil reads the sentence containing the words she has just learned and tells its meaning in that context. Other pupils can volunteer to use the word in different contexts, supply synonyms, or give other words which have the same root.

Figurative Language and Idiomatic Expressions

Figurative language and idiomatic expressions are quite widely used both in basal readers and in subject texts (17). These expressions pose virtually no problem for some readers, but can be stumbling blocks for other children in getting the meaning. This occurs because some readers have developed the habit of expecting the words they read to have literal meanings. It has also been noted that some children can both use and understand such expressions in oral communication but are still confused or misled when they attempt to read them (19).

Although these expressions may increase the difficulty of a passage, they also add to its beauty or forcefulness. Cyrano de Bergerac, sword in hand but mortally wounded, describes the approach of death, "I stand—*clothed with marble, gloved with lead.*" Overstatements or gross exaggeration emphasize particular qualities—"He's as patient as Job," "strong as Hercules," "tall as a mountain." Likenesses are suggested through implied functions—"The ship *plowed* the waves," "The arrow *parted* his hair." Sometimes, in fact, words are used in such a way as to mean just their opposite. Obviously, understanding material containing such expressions depends on the reader's realization of the intended meanings.

Some examples of expressions that will be met in the primary or elementary grades follow. The mere fact that a child can read these correctly is not assurance that she interprets them correctly.

The old sailor *spun a yarn* for the boys.
Soon *night fell.*
Don't *throw your money away* at the circus.
Before long they were driving through *rolling hills.*
The *rich earth* spread for miles along the river.
He returned *heavy-hearted.*
The waves *pitched the boat* up and down.
Give me a *lift.*
They *picked themselves up.*
He *made his mark* as a successful coach early in his career.
The captain *barked* his orders.
A *finger* of light moved around the airport.

Workbooks have a limited number of exercises which attempt to give practice in interpretation of figurative language. The teacher must be alert when these exercises are used, however, for a pupil may check the correct response without clearly understanding the intended meaning. When a child makes an error in interpretation and her response is marked wrong by the teacher, all she has to do is erase her X and place it in the remaining choice, thus "correcting her error." Learning may not have taken place even though the exercise is corrected.

Although teachers understand that some pupils will need extra practice in developing skills, they often do not find the time to construct teacher-made work sheets. If exercises are duplicated, one preparation can be used with successive classes, and if several teachers at various grade levels cooperate, they will find work sheets designed for use at one grade level are appropriate for particular children in other grades. Pooling their effort will save time, add variety, and enhance the teaching in that school. The examples of exercises below were designed by teachers in grades three through five in one elementary school. These were then made available to all teachers.

1. What is the meaning of the words that are underlined? Write "same" before the sentence which explains the underlined words.
   a. Father said: "I was walking through the park and Mr. Brown gave me a lift."
   _____ picked father up in his arms.
   _____ lifted father off the ground.
   _____ gave father a ride home.
2. Finish the sentence with the one group of words (phrases) that makes the best meaning.
   a. The stones in the showcase were _____ .
   as big as watermelons.
   as high as a mountain.
   as shiny as diamonds.
3. Can you tell in your own words what each of the following expressions means? If any puzzle you, ask the teacher for help.
   a. A wolf in sheep's clothing.
   b. Keep the wolf from the door.
   c. Flew into a rage.
   d. The ship was watertight.

The following passage is filled with expressions which probably would pose no problem for adults but which might mystify a child who reads slowly or literally.

Joe, *flying down the stairs, rested his eye* on the hawk. Grandfather *buried his nose in a book* and acted as if he were *completely in the dark*. Grandmother and Sue *put their heads together* and tried to figure out *which way the wind was blowing*. Joe *tipped his hand* by carrying the gun. On the *spur of the moment* Grand-

mother *hit the nail on the head. Cool as a cucumber,* she called to
Joe, *"Freeze in your tracks* and put that gun back upstairs!" Joe's
spirits fell as his grandmother's words *took the wind out of his sail.*
He *flew off the handle* and told about the hawk. *"That's a horse
of a different color,"* said Grandmother, satisfied that she had *dug
up the facts.* "Let the boy alone," said Grandfather. "He will *keep
the wolf from the door."* Outside, Joe thought, "I'd better *make
hay while the sun shines,"* as he *drew a bead* on the hawk.

Although these expressions may not bother most children, more
difficult figures of speech will constantly confront them. The children
who are baffled by such expression need more experience with them.
For these pupils, the teacher should devise exercises over and above
those which are found in workbooks at their grade level. If the reader
is *thinking while reading,* she will probably develop the flexibility necessary to deal with this type of language.

Intonation as an Aid to Comprehension

Since intonation is discussed in detail in Chapter 6, we will focus
here on techniques for helping children to develop acceptable intonation patterns in reading. Much has been written about the necessity for children who are learning to read to recreate the melody of
spoken language. This melody is determined by the reader's use of
pitch, stress, and juncture (terminating the flow of speech). Teachers
of reading have always posited a relationship between reading with
"expression" and getting meaning. This concept is on the same continuum as Lloyd's statement *"The ability to relate the melody of speech
to the written page is the key to good reading.* Good readers do it;
poor readers don't do it."*

Profiting from punctuation. In oral language, intonation is provided
by the speaker. In decoding printed material, arriving at the proper
intonation is primarily the responsibility of the reader. However,
punctuation is a set of conventions by which the writer provides
important cues to help the reader arrive at a proper interpretation. If
these cues are not heeded by the reader, meaning is distorted or de-
stroyed. The lack of ability to use punctuation in making reading a
smooth and meaningful process appears with surprising frequency
among impaired readers. Experience in working with poor readers in-

---

* Donald J. Lloyd, *Reading American English Sound Patterns.* Row, Peterson and
Company, Monograph 104, 1962, p. 2.

dicates that this habit is not exceptionally difficult to eradicate. The ignoring of punctuation is one of the easiest defects to detect on any oral reading analysis, a fact which suggests that the importance of learning to use punctuation is underrated in reading instruction. The following techniques can help children understand the importance of punctuation.

Expert readers make good models.
The punctuation goes in before the
language comes out.

1. One of the most effective methods of dramatizing the utility of punctuation is through the use of a tape recorder. The reader records a passage. On the playback, she follows the printed passage as she listens to her recorded version. Errors are easily detected and insight comes a little easier when the child acts as her own critic.

2. *Punctuating sentences:* Duplicate a series of sentences which are ambiguous or whose meaning can be altered by use of punctuation. After several illustrations on the chalkboard, children can work independently.

> *Examples:*
> Father called Bill a touchdown.
> "Father," called Bill, "a touchdown!"
> A. That little girl said her mother is hungry.
> (*Punctuate B so that the little girl is hungry.*)

    B. That little girl said her mother is hungry.

    A. The policeman said his brother should get the reward.

        (Punctuate B so that the "brother" is talking. Who should get the reward now?)

    B. The policeman said his brother should get the reward.

    A. The newspaper said the mayor is a bit confused.

        (Punctuate B so that the mayor is critical of the newspaper.)

    B. The newspaper said the mayor is a bit confused.

    A. The doctor said his friend is ill.

        (Punctuate B to show the doctor is ill.)

    B. The doctor said his friend is ill.

    A. The dog said John is barking again.

        (Punctuate B so that John stops barking.)

    B. The dog said John is barking again.

3. Another procedure is to deliberately displace punctuation in a passage and thus illustrate how the meaning becomes lost. The same passage can be reproduced several times with varying degrees of distortion. The pupil sees how difficult it is to get meaning from a passage so treated. In the following three paragraphs, the first version completely obscures the meaning, the second version is frustrating but not impossible, and the third is reproduced correctly.

How Punctuation Helps the Reader

a. Billy listened, carefully as the teacher. Explained how punctuation helps. The reader commas periods exclamation marks and question marks? All help a reader get meaning. From the printed page. Billy wondered what would happen. If the printer got the punctuation marks mixed. Up it was hard for him to imagine. What this would do to a story.

b. Billy listened carefully as the teacher explained. How punctuation helps the reader. Commas periods, exclamation marks and question marks all help. A reader get meaning from the printed page. Billy wondered. What would happen if the printer got the punctuation marks mixed up. It was hard for him to imagine what this would do. To a story.

c. Billy listened carefully as the teacher explained how punctuation helps the reader. Commas, periods, exclamation marks, and question marks all help a reader get meaning from the printed page. Billy wondered what would happen if the printer got the punctuation marks mixed up. It was hard for him to imagine what this would do to a story.

The following material is written without punctuation marks or capital letters. Put in punctuation marks so that it is easy to get the meaning.

   a. What do you like to eat some boys and girls like hamburgers milk and ice cream.
   b. The farmer tried to hurry his horse was tired both sat down later the farmer got up to go on his horse wouldn't move.
   c. Father said jack come and play we will play ball watch mother.

Note: exercises similar to the above may be presented via the chalkboard, overhead projector, or duplicated for seat work.

Word Stress and Meaning

1. Write the same sentence several times and have children read the sentence stressing a different word each time. Explain that they are to stress the word(s) that are italicized.
   a. *I* said no. I *said*, no. I said *no!*
      Read this sentence as a question: I said no?
   b. a. *This* is your lunch.
      b. This *is* your lunch.
      c. This is *your* lunch!
      d. This is your lunch?
   c. a. *John* said, "Who lost a quarter?"
      b. John *said*, "Who lost a quarter?"
      c. John said, "*Who* lost a quarter?"
      d. John said, "Who *lost* a quarter?"
   d. Alternate approach: A volunteer reads one of the numbered sentences. The group or another volunteer gives the number of the sentence based on the intonation pattern heard.
      a. *That* plane will never fly again.
      b. That *plane* will never fly again.
      c. That plane *will never* fly again.
      d. That plane will never *fly* again.
   e. *Provide a clue* as to how the sentence is to be read (see column A), and have volunteers read statement B with the appropriate intonation.

A	B
(Clerk informing a customer)➤	This hat costs ten dollars.
(Customer shocked	
at high price)➤	This hat costs ten dollars.
(Customer surprised	

at low price)➤   This hat costs ten dollars.
(Speaker happy
with a gift)➤   This is my birthday present.
(Speaker thinks the gift was meant
for his baby sister)➤   This is my birthday present.
(Speaker is terribly
disappointed)➤   This is my birthday present.

2. Showing emotions through use of intonation patterns.
   Provide a number of mood-descriptive words followed by several sentences. A volunteer reads a sentence using intonation that conveys one of the moods. Individuals or the class identifies the emotion the speaker depicted.

sadness	disbelief	anger	surprise	disappointment	fear	etc.

   a. Which one of you wrote this?
   b. Put that thing down, John.
   c. Who is responsible for this mess?
   d. I don't believe he said it.
   e. Of course he didn't say it; how could he?
   f. Guess who won first prize?

3. Use intonation to express the opposite meaning.
   a. Oh, that's just lovely.
   b. Man, I'm really going to like school this year.
   c. Did you see that brilliant play?
   d. That's the number one team in the country.
   e. Oh no, it can't be raining again.

4. Devise *who, what, when, where* and *how* sentences. Have different children read each sentence so as to stress—
   who (said or did something)
   what (was said or done)
   where (it happened)
   when (it happened)
   etc.
   a. The announcer said it rained very hard yesterday in Chicago.
   b. The players practiced very hard the week after they lost the game.
   c. John said the bridge was washed away by the flood.
   d. Two men boarded the plane at 3:00 P.M. through Gate 10.

e. A police officer put a ticket on the brown car parked in the driveway.

Developing Appreciation through Critical Reading

Developing an appreciation for poetry and literature is not a function of chronological age, grade placement, or mere contact with good literature. One does not develop taste in literature as a result of one experience; taste evolves as a result of crossing numerous literary thresholds. Every teacher at every grade level should assume some responsibility for introducing his pupils to the world of good literature (33).

The purpose of teaching is to provide experiences which facilitate personal growth. The ability to appreciate good literature assures us of a lifetime source of pleasure. In addition, the reading and understanding of literature will inevitably lead to insights about self and the world about us. Literature is also a form of potential therapy for the alienated and those in flight from involvement. There are few human problems, fears, or aspirations which are not treated in literature.

Basic to helping children develop appreciation for literature is the recognition that appreciation comes only from actual participation. Reading is, in essence, a dialogue between reader and writer. Appreciation is personal; it cannot be standardized. Thus, appreciation may not result from such tactics as

1. Urging students to read good literature.
2. Providing a list of acceptable authors or established literary classics.
3. Prescribing an inflexible agenda of reading materials for groups of students.
4. Assigning the same reading to all students in a given class.
5. Assuming that all students in a given class or school year have the readiness, and the skills needed, to "mine" a traditional reading list.
6. Relying on evaluation methods which imply that all students should arrive at the same interpretation of a story, analysis of a particular character, or insight into an author's purpose.

Unfortunately the above procedures, in modified and sometimes disguised form, are often followed in actual teaching situations. These practices, of course, negate what we know about reading, readers, the learning process, and the development of taste in reading. There is a consensus that the schools' approach to teaching literature fails a great number of students who undertake the study of literature (29).

**Enjoying
Poetry**

In most instances the reading of poetry calls for a different reader-set than does narrative prose. While it is true that the poem is susceptible to more than one interpretation, the language of a poem must take precedence in determining the reading cadence. The poet's chief concern is not with facts but with feelings. To enjoy poetry one must have or develop an ear for language. The reader, like the poet, must be receptive to the language as it comes to her (30).

The poem is designed to be heard. While one may of course hear the words and the language rhythms as she reads silently, there is no better introduction to poetry than to hear it read orally. The teacher who is skilled in reading poetry should read to students. If a teacher prefers, he may turn for help to expert readers who have recorded a wide array of great literature and poetry. A number of modern poets such as Robert Frost, Langston Hughes, Mary McLeod Bethune, Carl Sandburg, e. e. Cummings, Arna Bontemps have recorded portions of their own works. Dozens of highly competent artists including Julie Harris, Richard Burton, Jose Ferrar, Basil Rathbone, Sir Cedric Hardwicke and others have recorded a number of great classics.*

The poet is by definition and practice a word and concept craftsman. He uses imagery, allusion, analogy, and symbolism; words are selected not for meaning alone but also for sound and rhythm. Emily Dickinson explains the process.

"Shall I take thee?" the poet said
To the propounded word
Be stationed with the candidates
Till I have further tried†

---

* A wide variety of recordings may be secured from the *National Council of Teachers of English*. These are completely catalogued in *Resources for the Teaching of English*, NCTE, 508 South Sixth Street, Champaign, Ill.

† Mabel Loomis Todd and Millicent Todd Bingham, ed., *Bolts of Melody—New Poems of Emily Dickinson* (New York: Harper & Row, Publishers, 1945), p. 228.

Thus, to paraphrase a poem is to destroy it. This does not imply that meaning is sacrificed in order to get other effects; nor does it preclude analysis or even group discussion for arriving at meaning.

The chief cause of the failure of the school to inculcate students with an appreciation for poetry lies in the language barrier. An inadequate language background stalls the communicative process between poet and reader.

> Who goes to dine must take his feast
> or find the banquet mean;
> The table is not laid without
> till it is laid within*

While the reader must come to poetry prepared, she need not, as part of a planned curriculum, be continually exposed to that for which she is not prepared. Good poetry is distributed over a wide range of difficulty. The school's responsibility is to match the student's present ability with reading tasks of commensurate difficulty.

Children should be encouraged to go with Frost to the meadow when he invites "you come too." They must also be encouraged to *feel* with Langston Hughes the institutionalized injustice involved, and the frustration of a people that are revealed in *Merry-Go-Round*. The poem opens with the words

> Colored child
> at carnival . . .

and pursues the dilemma of both the victims and the designers of racism when neither can figure out which is front and back (i.e., Jim Crow section) on the Merry-Go-Round. The child finally inquires "Where's the horse for a kid that's black?"† Since concepts are built on experience, we produce cultural and educational deprivation when children have no opportunity to interact with these and similar stimuli. The school must become a party to the child's *Right to Read*.

Analyzing and Dramatizing Stories

Some stories need to be analyzed and discussed. The discussion should not be conducted from the standpoint of "who remembers some-

---

* *Bolts of Melody—New Poems of Emily Dickinson,* op. cit., p. 229.
† Langston Hughes, *The Panther and the Lash,* New York: Alfred A. Knopf 1967, p. 92.

thing from the story," but by skillfully leading the children to see how the author is able to picture each character and show the type of person she is, how she conveys the characters' attitudes toward each other and toward themselves, how the reader is led to see the difference between unkindness and thoughtlessness, to see how people feel after making mistakes, what they do about them, and why it is not always possible to do exactly what one wants. Analysis of stories is not a testing period or a time for the recitation of facts. Analysis should lay the foundation for the type of insight Emily Dickinson developed before she could write, "There is no frigate like a book to bear us lands away."

Dramatizing stories or incidents from stories helps children develop understanding, imagination, and appreciation. To dramatize a story or scene, children must read the material critically and understand the author's purpose and the feelings she wishes to convey. In the dramatization these would find expression through tone of voice, emphasis, gesture, facial expression, and the like. In selecting material to be acted out, children will have to make correct judgments on the dramatic potential of various stories or situations. A story about a man lost on a mountain might be extremely interesting reading, but it is not well-suited to a third-grade dramatic production. One drawback is that only one character is involved.

Choral Reading

Choral reading offers many potential virtues, one of which is helping children develop good intonation in oral reading. Obviously, it is hoped that as they hear and use good models of intonation, this skill will transfer to silent reading and enhance their ability to read for meaning.

Choral reading should not be thought of as an activity reserved for expert readers. It can and should be used at various instructional levels and for a variety of goals. The reading ability of the participants simply determines the materials which might be used successfully. For example, a teacher discovered quite by accident that choral reading had extremely high motivational value for her third-grade class. She was showing a text-film of a story that the class had not read before. Each frame consisted of an attractive picture in color and two or three lines of text. She normally would call on individual children to read this material, but would occasionally say, "Let's all read." The response was so enthusiastic that she printed on chart paper poems such as "The

Wind," "Watching Clouds," "Railroad Reverie," "The Owl and the Pussy Cat," "Hold Hands," or any number of limericks. Later, she prepared duplicated sheets which contained several pieces of material appropriate for choral reading. She observed that choral reading was always the motivational peak of the day's activity.

In addition to the fact that it is an enjoyable activity, other values of choral reading are it

1. is a good technique for getting all children to participate.
2. can be a means of motivating children to want to read. The shy child or the poor reader is not likely to experience failure or frustration in this type of group reading experience.
3. provides an opportunity to teach good pronunciation and reading with expression.
4. permits the use of different materials for emphasizing different objectives such as phonic analysis, profiting from punctuation, and proper phrasing.
5. can be a creative experience since children can suggest different ways a poem or passage can be interpreted.
6. helps develop an appreciation for fine literature or poetry.

Oral Reading

Instruction in oral reading must be considered in light of the purposes for which it is used, the materials used, and how it is incorporated into the total reading program.

Opinions as to the relative value of teaching oral reading have changed considerably during the present century. At one time oral reading was widely practiced without much attention to the justification of the classroom procedures that were followed. Oral reading was equated with the school's reading program. The term *oral reading* may call to mind children in a circle reading round robin from the same book with each child in the group reading silently along with, behind, or ahead of the child performing orally. The poorer reader took her turn along with the rest and sighed, mumbled, and coughed her embarrassed way through the allotted paragraph.

The evils that result from a particular educational practice may be remembered long after the practice has either been discontinued or substantially modified. In some cases oral reading was overemphasized and children spent most of their time reading aloud. As a result, they read slowly, putting all the emphasis on the mechanics of reading and little emphasis on meaning. Gray (15) tells of a boy reading a long passage orally. He read with expression and good interpretation. The teacher asked him a question about the content of what he had just read. His reply was that he could not answer because he "wasn't listening."

Another abuse was that oral reading was often advanced as an end in itself rather than a means to several desirable ends. Oral reading was practiced in artificial situations with little thought given to creating a true audience situation. As these abuses were pointed out in the literature on teaching reading, a reaction against oral reading took place. The disadvantages and potential weaknesses were stressed to the point where many teachers may have thought that the issue was oral reading versus silent reading, rather than the *intelligent use* of oral reading. At the moment, the most popular position is the middle ground, which embraces the idea that a proper balance should be maintained between silent and oral reading. It is difficult to argue with the logic of this latter position; nevertheless, it is almost impossible to find what constitutes a proper balance. What is adequate and desirable for one teacher with a particular class may be an improper diet in another situation.

Teachers of beginning reading will use oral reading for a number of purposes, and its values can be found in many natural classroom situations. The most common situation is one in which a child reads aloud in order to convey information or pleasure to an audience of her classmates. Regardless of the situation, oral reading can be justified only when the purposes are logical, the goals educationally sound, and the preparation adequate to the occasion. There is much written in teacher's manuals about the preparation of students for reading tasks, but there are no reading tasks which make more justified demands for adequate preparation than does oral reading.

Reading in an audience situation can be an ego-building experience for the reader. Personal and social growth as well as self-confidence can be achieved. But the child must be able to read satisfactorily in order to elicit approval from others, and she should not be expected to read to a group unless adequately prepared. Furthermore, having one child read aloud from a book while others follow the same passage in their book minimizes the audience situation. Oral reading should, insofar as possible, make use of materials other than basal series used for instructional purposes with the class.

Oral reading can be an excellent means of teaching reading skills such as good phrasing, use of punctuation, reading with expression, and fluent reading without hesitations or repetitions. Oral reading is a logical extension of the language usage characteristic of children as they enter school. Practice in oral reading can help the child associate printed words with their speech equivalents.

It is often stated that oral reading provides an excellent opportunity for the diagnosis of reading skills and the discovery of pupils' reading weaknesses. This diagnostic function is a pupil-teacher situation centered around a teacher purpose and probably would not involve the child's reading to a group. It could be argued that this is not a true oral-reading situation since pupil purpose, informing an audience, is not paramount. However, reading to the teacher is a highly motivating situation for most children, providing the teacher is encouraging rather than critical.

It cannot be denied that oral reading provides many clues to the actual weakness in a child's reading. A child's response after reading silently may indicate that she is a poor reader, or that she is performing below a certain grade level. Such a diagnosis may not disclose *why* the child reads poorly. If the teacher can *hear* and *observe* the child's reading, he can discover important clues to her competence in sight vocabulary, attacking unknown words, use of context, use of punctuation, and whether she views reading as getting meaning. The teacher will not rely on only one sample of oral reading as an adequate diagnosis, but each instance of oral reading will be seen as a part of an ongoing diagnosis.

It is generally agreed that oral reading is a more difficult task than silent reading. Kovas (20) emphasizes this, pointing out that in oral reading the reader must know all the words and must get the author's point and mood so that she can convey it to the listeners. To do this she must use proper phrasing, paying heed to punctuation, while at the same time reading loud enough to reach all her listeners. Children will inevitably face situations which call for reading aloud. Since almost all purposeful oral reading takes place in a social setting, these instances will be important to the reader whose performance will place her in the position of being judged by others.

In summary, the following considerations should be observed when using oral reading:

1. The reader must have a purpose for the oral reading. She must have interesting data which she wishes to share with others.
2. The reader must be prepared. She must have mastered the mechanical skills required and have arrived at an acceptable interpretation of the author's intent.

3. Children are not always well-trained to *listen*. When children cannot listen critically, the primary justification for oral reading is missing.

4. Instruction during the oral reading itself will usually destroy the value of oral reading.

5. Too much oral reading can diminish its effectiveness. The stress should be on good oral reading, not on an endurance contest for either readers or listeners.

6. Oral reading must not become so artificial or mechanical for the reader that she forgets that she is reading for meaning.

7. The teacher should be ready to provide a good model of oral reading when such a model is needed by the group or an individual child.

8. It should be remembered that the larger the group involved, the more problems.

9. Oral reading may be a considerable threat to some pupils. These cases should be handled with sympathetic understanding.

SUMMARY

Reading instruction in the primary grades is a challenge to teachers because successful readers must utilize a great number of skills concomitantly. Any child who is deficient in one or more essential skills will be error-prone in her reading. Errors made while reading tend to produce other errors, the cumulative effect of which is to impair the child's self-confidence and influence her attitude toward reading. Undetected weaknesses result in a child reinforcing whatever bad habits she has at the moment. Since practically every reading skill is developmental, each must be extended at every level of instruction. The teacher will continue to stress the same fundamental skills introduced in beginning reading instruction; for example, instant recognition of words, phonic analysis, and using context clues are stressed in beginning reading. However, the need for these skills becomes more acute in the primary and intermediate grades because new words are introduced with increased frequency at these levels. Learning the reading process involves both increased mastery of skills previously introduced and adding new skills to the repertory.

The motivational challenge in "decoding words" deteriorates rapidly unless this activity is accompanied by decoding language.

Reading instruction should deal with teaching children how their language functions. They need to know how intonation influences meaning, that some words have many different meanings, that English abounds with figurative expressions which have special meanings. Children need to have some understanding of the sentence-pattern and word-order options that English can accommodate, and they need to interact with the language of feeling as well as that of facts.

YOUR POINT OF VIEW?

Would you defend or attack the following premises? Why?

1. A child made normal progress in beginning reading, but is now experiencing considerable difficulty in reading in grade two. The most tenable hypothesis as to her problem is that she has failed to master letter-sound relationships.

2. When a child in the primary grades is not making expected progress in reading, more instruction time should be devoted to reading even if this involves less time for other established areas of the curriculum.

3. Because of the nature of the teaching tasks in all elementary grades, teachers are inevitably remedial reading teachers if they teach all children in their respective classrooms.

4. The term *critical reading* implies the mastery and application of a great number of developmental skills. Therefore, a typical reader in third or fourth grade would not qualify as a critical reader.

5. Oral reading has little educational value in the primary grades.

6. One of the strengths of American schools is their success in arousing and maintaining pupil interest in recreational reading.

7. There is no particular group of skills needed for appreciation and understanding of literature that are not essential for critical reading in other situations such as the content areas.

Respond to the following problems:

A. Select the one variable below that you think is the most important factor in producing low achievement in the primary grades. Defend your choice.
   1. The child's inability to work effectively in a group situation.
   2. Negative self-concept and expectation of nonsuccess.
   3. Disparity between school tasks and home-neighborhood experiences.
B. Assume it is established that third-grade social studies textbooks are more difficult to read than are third-grade basal readers. What factors might account for this?

Beyond Beginning Reading

BIBLIOGRAPHY

1. Artley A. Sterl, "Words, Words, Words," *Language Arts* 52 (December 1975): 1067–72.

2. Buckley, Marilyn Hanf, "A Guide for Developing an Oral Language Curriculum," *Language Arts* 30 (September 1976): 621–27.

3. Buelke, Eleanor, "The Drama of Teaching Reading through Creative Writing," *Reading Teacher* (January 1966): 267–72.

4. Burron, Arnold and Claybaugh, Amos L., *Basic Concepts in Reading Instruction: A Programmed Approach.* Columbus, O.: Charles E. Merrill Publishing Co., 1972.

5. Bushman, John H., "Discussion Skills: Let Them Work for You," *Language Arts* 3 (September 1976): 628–31.

6. Chance, Larry L., "Using a Learning Stations Approach to Vocabulary Practice," *Journal of Reading* 18 (December 1974): 244–46.

7. Cole, Louella, *The Improvement of Reading.* New York: Farrar and Rinehart, Inc., 1938.

8. Cox, Donald R., "Criteria for Evaluation of Reading Materials," *The Reading Teacher* (November 1970): 140–45.

9. Cushenbery, Donald C., "Two Methods of Grouping for Reading Instruction," *Elementary School Journal* (February 1966): 267–72.

10. Ekwall, Eldon E. and Henry, Ida Bell, "How to Find Books Children Can Read," *The Reading Teacher* (December 1968): 230–32.

11. Fitzgerald, Sheila, "Teaching Discussion Skills and Attitudes," *Language Arts* 52 (December 1975): 1094–96,

12. Frame, Norman, "The Availability of Reading Materials for Teachers and Pupils at the Primary Level," *Elementary English* (March 1964): 224–30.

13. Froese, Victor, "Word Recognition Tests: Are They Useful Beyond Grade Three," *The Reading Teacher* (February 1971): 432–38.

14. Gates, Arthur I., "The Word Recognition Ability and the Reading Vocabulary of Second- and Third-Grade Children," *Reading Teacher* (May 1962): 443–48.

15. Gray, Lillian, *Teaching Children to Read,* 3rd ed. New York: The Ronald Press, 1963, p. 276.

16. Gray, William S., *On Their Own in Reading,* rev. ed. Chicago: Scott, Foresman & Company, 1960.

17. Groesbeck, Hulda, *The Comprehension of Figurative Language by Elementary Pupils: A Study of Transfer.* Unpublished Doctoral Thesis, Oklahoma University, 1961.

18. Harris, Mary McDonnell, "The Limerick Center," *Language Arts* 53 (September 1976): 663–65.

19. Holmes, Elizabeth Ann, *Children's Knowledge of Figurative Language.* Unpublished Masters Thesis, Oklahoma University, 1959.

20. Kovas, Helen, "The Place of Oral Reading," *Elementary English* (November 1957): 462–66.

21. Lamb, Pose and Arnold, Richard, eds., *Reading: Foundations and Instructional Strategies.* Belmont, Calif.: Wadsworth Publishing Co., Inc., 1976.

22. Martin, John E., "Guidelines for Planning Special Reading Facilities," *The Reading Teacher* (December 1970): 203–08.

23. Otterman, Lois M., "The Value of Teaching Prefixes and Word Roots," *Journal of Educational Research* (April 1955): 611–16.

24. Page, William D., "Are We Beginning to Understand Oral Reading?", *Reading World* 13 (March 1974): 161–70.

25. Painter, Helen W., "Critical Reading in the Primary Grades," *Reading Teacher* (October 1965): 35–39.

26. Personke, Carl R., "The Listening Post in Beginning Reading," *Reading Teacher* (November 1968): 130–35.

27. Raven, Ronald J. and Salzer, Richard T., "Piaget and Reading Instruction," *The Reading Teacher* (April 1971): 630–39.

28. Robinett, Ralph F., "An Interdisciplinary Approach to Oral Language and Conceptual Development: A Progress Report," *Elementary English* (April 1971): 203–08.

29. Russell, David H., in Robert B. Ruddell, ed., *The Dynamics of Reading.* Waltham, Mass.: Ginn and Co., 1970.

30. Sister M. Baptist, R. S. M., "The Promise That Is Poetry," *Catholic School Journal* (May 1965): 45.

31. Smith, James A., *Adventures in Communication.* Boston: Allyn and Bacon, Inc., 1972.

32. Thompson, Richard A. and Merritt, King, Jr., "Turn On to a Reading Center," *Reading Teacher* 28 (January 1975): 384–88.

33. Tinker, Miles A. and McCullough, Constance M., *Teaching Elementary Reading*, 3rd ed. New York: Appleton-Century Crofts, 1968. Chapter 9.

34. Wallen, Carl J., "Independent Activities: A Necessity, Not a Frill," *Reading Teacher* 27 (December 1973): 257–62.

Chapter **13**

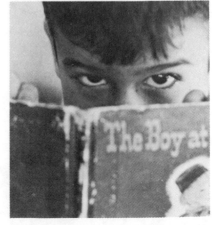

Teaching Reading-Study Skills

Formal education has many goals, one of which is to help the child become increasingly independent within the framework of the school setting. To achieve such independence the learner must master a number of related language tools or skills. One important cluster of skills has been designated reading-study skills or work-type reading skills. In our reading-dominated schools, these skills are of primary importance. Yet, in actual classroom practice, they are not always treated with this same importance. Obviously, the need for these skills becomes more pronounced as students move upward through the grades. A review of the literature on reading reveals general agreement about the major areas of reading-study skills; these include

1. Locating Information
2. Evaluating Material
3. Organizing and Summarizing Data

4. Retaining Essentials of What Is Read
5. Flexibility, or Adjusting Rate to Purpose

Any one of these major topics would probably include numerous specific skills; for instance, locating information would cover

1. Effective Use of Books
   a. Table of Contents
   b. Index
      (1) knowledge of alphabetical order
      (2) use of key words
      (3) cross-listings
      (4) following subtopics
      (5) significance of abbreviations and signals commonly used, e.g., "see also . . .," or commas and hyphens in page listings
2. Use of Special References
   a. Encyclopedia
   b. Atlas
   c. Dictionary
      (1) extended knowledge of alphabetical order
      (2) selection of proper connotation of word
      (3) recognition of inflected and derived forms of words
      (4) use of diacritical marks
   d. Use of Library Aids
      (1) card catalogue
      (2) *Reader's Guide*
      (3) bound periodicals

The study skills are an excellent illustration of what is meant by the term developmental. It can be seen that any given skill is not taught exclusively, or once for all time, at a given grade level. Each skill can be thought of as being a continuum which represents both increasing difficulty of learning tasks and increasing potential usefulness to the learner. For instance, skill in using a table of contents is first taught systematically in grade one when the teacher calls attention to the list of stories found in a preprimer. With this experience, no child will have mastered this skill to a degree required for effective use of the table of contents in a sixth-grade geography book. However, since the use of a table of contents, index, or appendix is not seen as part of the content of either geography, health, or arithmetic, these and other related study skills may be neglected in all courses of study (14, 29).

Brewer (2) states that if students are to be able to work effectively in content areas, ". . . the school must accept greater responsibility for initial teaching and provide guided practice in using the reading study skills. It is essential that these be interpreted as fundamental, and treated as such in order to progress in all curriculum subjects." While it is true that some children will learn study skills incidentally, the importance of these skills suggests that they should not be left to incidental learning.

Locating Information

As children become independent readers and attempt to find answers through wide and varied reading, they must understand and use all the hints and helps available in order to determine rapidly and accurately whether a particular book contains information in which they are interested. In other words, knowing how to use the book is a prerequisite for intelligent use of supplementary reading in the subject areas and in any unit work. In the intermediate grades, the increased need for study skills stems from the nature of the materials used, the need for wide reading, and the fact that supervision is not always readily available. While reading ability is a prerequisite for the development of study skills, this ability in itself does not assure that a pupil has mastered the study skills. When a pupil fails to develop adequate study skills, the educational process may become dull and unpleasant, and guidance and specific instruction must be provided to help children develop these skills (1).

During the past few years, we have witnessed a tremendous expansion of the availability of books, professional journals, and other printed matter of practically every area in human's experience. This advance in knowledge in the past two decades, even when compared with previous centuries, has been so dramatic that it has been labeled the era of the *knowledge explosion*. Competency in any given field has taken on a new meaning and educational methods, of necessity, will have to change radically to adapt to this new challenge.

The contents of any subject area cannot be encompassed within a single textbook or even a series of texts. The time lag between research, publication, and the adoption of textbooks causes even the most recent texts to be somewhat inadequate. Good teachers have always attempted to provide supplementary reading materials, but achieving this goal has not been easy. Today, providing a wide array of supplementary materials is not only desirable, it is an absolute necessity. Thus, study skills have rather abruptly increased in value to the learner while the school's respect for these skills and its ability to teach them effectively has lagged. The following discussion deals with facets of instruction that relate to locating information.

**Effective Use
of Books**

In teaching any of the study skills, the teacher at each grade level starts from, and builds on, what the student presently knows. To do this, the present ability level of each student must be determined. A good place to begin is with the textbook adopted for a given course. Teachers have learned from experience that many students are not particularly adept at "mining" a book, but meaningful learning situations can lead to the development of this facility (7).

It is easy to develop exercises that foster such growth. Some teachers do not particularly like the exercise approach, but we should keep in mind that any learning situation is, in essence, an exercise. The issue is how exercise materials and specific teachings are used in relation to the goals to be achieved. Some very important learnings deal with the mechanics of learning—*how* to use a card catalogue, *where* to look in an encyclopedia, *when* an appendix or glossary might be useful, *what* is likely to be found in an appendix or glossary, and the like.

Workbook exercises are often provided to help pupils understand the function of an index, table of contents, or appendix. It is common to find pupils who can work out correct solutions to workbook problems consisting of sample lines from an index but who still do not know how to get help from a real index. One of the best ways to teach children how to use a book effectively is to design a learning situation around a textbook which they will be using throughout the year. A social science, health, or other text would provide ample opportunities for teaching the functions of the table of contents, charts, indexes, or appendixes. The use of the text the child is using will give him something concrete to return to when he is in doubt. Skills learned in using one text should transfer to books in other areas.

Student deficiences in using a table of contents, index, glossary, and appendix are frequently not detected by teachers and often provisions may not be made for teaching these skills. Too often it is assumed these basic skills have been taught or are being taught elsewhere. For example, as an outcome of an in-service program, one group of teachers agreed to build a one-page testing-teaching exercise consisting of fifteen to twenty questions which would measure students' skill

How to Use a Book

1. The region in which we live is discussed under the heading
   _____ .

2. The last 16 pages in the book are called an Atlas. Looking at these
   pages can you define "atlas"?_____

   _____

3. On what page can you find a listing of all maps, graphs and dia-
   grams found in the book?_____

4. Does the book contain a picture of Wonder Lake?_____
   How did you go about answering this question? _____

5. Is there a picture of the Grand Coulee Dam in the text?
   _____

6. Under what heading must you look to find it?_____
   _____

7. In the index there is a main heading *Exploration*. What six sub-
   headings are found under it?_____

   _____

8. The book contains a double page map called Main Air Routes in
   the U.S. There is no heading "Main Air Routes" in the index. How
   can you find this map?_____

   _____

   _____

9. There are two sections of the book which provide the pronunciation of difficult words, these are _____
   and _____ .

10. The pronunciation of the following words is provided in the
    _____ . In the blank spaces show the pro-
    nunciation and page number where found:
    SHOSHONE _____ Page_____
    COMANCHE _____ Page_____
    FORT DUQUESNE _____ Page_____

11. A particular page contains the *definition* of difficult words used
    throughout the book. That page is called the _____
    _____ and is page number _____ .

in using parts of a book. The exercise was to be specifically applicable to the textbook students were using in one of their courses. Although the books had been in use for nearly three months, few students were able to complete the exercise without error. Teachers discovered glaring deficiencies and tremendous individual differences in students' ability to use these reader aids. In one class, the time students took to do the "book mining" exercise was noted. The range was from six to twenty-two minutes (a range of 400 percent), with some students unable to complete the task. An exercise similar to that under discussion is shown on page 461.

Such an exercise might be used initially with an entire class. For the proficient student, it will be a justifiable review, and for others it will serve as a diagnostic instrument. The observant teacher will note which students have difficulty and what their problems are. Teaching small groups and individual students the skills they need should be an outgrowth of the teacher's findings. General concepts will also be taught in the process. This particular experience was constructed for use with a sixth grade social studies text.

The exercise teaches a number of facts about the book. Question one takes the reader to the table of contents and requires that he be able to associate his home state with part of a larger geographical region of the United States. Question two calls attention to a sixteen-page atlas; and question three focuses on a second highly specialized table of contents which deals exclusively with maps.

Questions 4–8 deal with ways in which the index may be helpful. The reader must locate pictures through the use of key words and be prepared to look under different headings. (Grand Coulee Dam is found under Grand Coulee *Project*.) Topics may be listed as subheads under a more general heading. Thus, Dutch, English, Spanish and other explorations are all listed under *Exploration*. Questions 9–11 deal with information about pronunciation and meanings of more difficult words, and call attention to the fact that these aids are divided between the index and glossary.

Profiting from Reader Aids

Students sometimes fail to realize that a number of reader aids are included in most reference books and textbooks. Unfamiliarity with or disinclination to use these aids will inhibit students from "mining" books with maximum efficiency. Although the student has a need for this skill, he does not always recognize this need since he is not aware of the value of these aids or how they might improve his learning.

It will be noted that, for one purpose, the table of contents might be skimmed. With other goals in mind, it must be read critically. A comparison of different books would disclose that a table of contents may consist exclusively of chapter titles. This is similar to an outline composed of nothing but major topics. In some books, chapter titles are followed by a number of topics in the order in which they are discussed. Students may note that this, in essence, is a modified index containing only major headings in *chronological* order. The index, on the other hand, is in *alphabetical* order, dealing with smaller topics, and cutting across chapters.

The major learnings are (1) that parts of the book are deliberately designed as aids for the reader; (2) these are valuable aids and are used with profit by the efficient reader; (3) each of the different parts of a book has a definite purpose. The efficient reader must make instant decisions as to where to go for specific types of help; he learns what type of information is contained in each section, where the various aids are located, and how each may be used effectively. Once learned, this knowledge can be transferred and applied to any book. The following is an abbreviated treatment of what the reader might expect to gain from the helps found in most books:

As "Aids" for the Reader	Information the Reader Might Expect to Find
Title Page	Main title and subtitle. (The latter may set forth the limitations and narrow the topic.) Name of author, date published.
Table of Contents	Chapter titles followed by major topics discussed in each chapter. Is book divided into major parts (I, II, III)? What are these? Length of chapters give hint as to thoroughness of treatment.
Preface	To whom or to what group does the author address the book? What is his stated purpose? What new features does he stress? What unique features does he believe are found in the book?
Illustrations	Title, item and page where found.
Index	Major topics in alphabetical order; minor topics under each heading; key phrases, cross references, photographs, drawings, charts, tables.
Glossary	Difficult or specialized terms presented in alphabetical order, with a definition.

Appendix   Organized body of facts related to subject
                              under consideration. For example, in a
                              geography book the appendix may give the
                              areas of states or nations, populations, state
                              and national capitals, extent of manufactur-
                              ing, exports, imports, mineral deposits, etc.

Use of the Library

   Effective use of library resources may well be one of the most
underrated and undertaught skills in the entire school program. The
library is *basic* to the school's reading program (8). It is a place where
children read and receive guidance in both the use of books and in
research techniques. Children at all grade levels need the experience
of frequent contacts with a good school library.

Paperbacks are frigates that bear
us lands away. (Thank you, Emily.)

   Some teachers use the library effectively themselves but do not
assume responsibility for teaching students to do so. On the other
hand, there are a number of teachers who would score low on any
evaluation of their personal use of library facilities. To illustrate, one
school librarian and principal were convinced that a substantial number of the teaching staff were somewhat derelict in their personal use
of the library. Further, student use of the library for these teachers'

courses seemed to be less than optimum. A one-hour library unit was incorporated into the total in-service program. Each teacher was relieved of her regularly scheduled duties for a one-hour period, and this time was spent in conference with the librarian. The librarian assumed responsibility for discussing and pointing out resources which related directly to the various subjects taught by each teacher. Pamphlets, bound volumes, pertinent books, government documents, current magazines, and the like were located, and suggestions were made as to how the librarian might help the faculty member and the students in her classes.

Records disclosed that the attitude of a number of the teaching staff changed markedly after this experience. Some teachers visited the library more frequently, spent more time in the library, and checked out more materials. In addition, the students in these teachers' courses began to use the library much more effectively.

It is generally conceded that it is difficult to teach library usage in a classroom setting removed from the library materials themselves. However, certain facts related to the library can be discussed prior to a visit to the library.

Several teachers in one school built a model card catalogue drawer using a three-by-five index card box and constructing approximately one hundred author cards ranging from *A* through *G*. This model was used in the various classrooms and was particularly useful in working with individual students who were not yet competent in the use of the card catalogue.

Another useful teaching device consisted of a library checklist devised by teachers and the librarian. The list consisted of eight or ten specific tasks which the student was to perform in the library such as:

1. Find the book *King of the Wind* by Marguerite Henry.
2. a. Who is the author of the book *A Child's History of Art?* _____

   _____ .

   b. What is the call number of this book? _____

   c. Fill out a library card for this book _____ .
3. Where are the bound volumes of *My Weekly Reader* located?

   _____ .

These items provide guided practice in the use of title and author cards, location of books and journals on the shelves, and the proper filling out of library cards. Other tasks cover specific learnings related to the library.

To use this technique effectively, small groups or individual students go to the library at specific times. The librarian may give a brief explanation of how to use certain facilities in the library. Then each child may be handed a checklist of tasks. The problems may vary according to grade level and individual student needs. In some cases a student monitor may work one hour a week in the library helping other students with the checklist and other problems.

There are numerous ways in which teachers and the librarian may work together in teaching study skills. One account of such a cooperative endeavor describes a joint teaching venture in which one teacher and the librarians conducted a weekly library usage period. Topics included search techniques, organizing a paper, constructing a bibliography, outlining, and notetaking (16).

Reference Materials

Using reference materials is an important study skill which, as a general rule, is not thoroughly taught in our schools. Many students reach high school or even college with only a hazy idea of how to make a systematic search of available materials. The child, both in and out of school, is constantly faced with the problem of locating material and deciding whether it is relevant to his purpose (16). Although a few children in the upper primary level are ready for limited use of reference materials, it is in the intermediate grades that teachers have a major responsibility to teach these skills.

The Encyclopedia

The use of encyclopedias and other reference books should be deliberately taught. If such materials are located in the room, different children or groups can be taught their use at various times. Instruction here will parallel points already covered above, i.e., topics are arranged in alphabetical order, books are numbered in series, the alphabetical range covered is indicated on the cover, and cross listings and key words will have to be used. The teacher can make a set of card exercises, each card containing a question: "What book and what page tell about coal?" "About the Suez Canal?" "About Iron Deposits?"

Teaching any given unit in any content area can provide the framework for teaching efficient use of the encyclopedia to those students who need this instruction. Assume a health class is developing the topic *The Advance of Medicine*. Students might be asked to list all of the possible headings under which they might list data which relate to the topic. The responses might range from one suggestion to "look under medicine" to a half page of suggestions which might include medicine, surgery, disease, medical research, drugs, germ theory, space medicine, and public health. Other headings might include particular diseases such as cancer, tuberculosis, yellow fever, diabetes, poliomyelitis; or the names of individuals who made significant medical discoveries such as Walter Reed, Jonas Salk, Louis Pasteur.

Using the Encyclopedia

An encyclopedia is a book or series of books which tell you a little bit about a great number of topics. One skill you need is to know what *heading* or topic to look under for particular information. Usually an encyclopedia contains hundreds of headings which tell the reader to "see . . ." which is another heading under which the topic is discussed. For instance, Baking Soda. *See* Soda; Old Faithful. *See* Wyoming, Yellowstone National Park; Lennon, John. *See* Beatles; Knee Jerk. *See* Reflex Action; Toadstool. *See* Mushroom.

Using the drawing below write the number of the volume or volumes which will likely contain the information called for.

In which volume will you find these data:

1. Is more money spent on newspaper or television advertising _____ ?
2. Hitches, knots, and splices _____ .
3. Timber wolves _____ .
4. Is there a bird called a kite? _____
5. What is a "spelling demon?" _____
6. Data on animals that sleep through the winter. _____
7. The previous names of the city of Leningrad? _____
8. The state tree of Illinois. _____
9. Where does the sparrow hawk live? _____
10. The habitat of the Eastern gray squirrel. _____

Vol. 1	Vol. 2	Vol. 3	Vol. 4	Vol. 5	Vol. 6	Vol. 7	Vol. 8	Vol. 9	Vol. 10	Vol. 11	Vol. 12	Vol. 13	Vol. 14	Vol. 15	Vol. 16
A	B	C	D-E	F	G	H	I-J	K-L	M	N	O-P	Q-R	S	T-U	V-Z

**Using the
Dictionary**

The use of the dictionary is another important study skill associated with reading instruction at the intermediate level. The three
major goals in dictionary instruction are learning to (1) find a particular word, (2) determine its pronunciation, and (3) select the correct
meaning of the word in the context in which it is used. Teaching dictionary skills is often neglected by teachers even when they acknowledge the value of these skills. This neglect might stem from a teacher's
feeling of inadequacy about certain relatively difficult facets of dictionary use such as mastering diacritical markings or pronunciation keys.
On the other hand, teaching may fall short of maximum efficiency when
dictionary skills are taught as something extra rather than as an in-
trinsic part of the regular reading instruction. The use of the dictionary
should always be seen by both teacher and pupil as a means of getting
meaning, not as a form of rote drill or a penalty for making certain
errors (15).

Certain prerequisites are essential for successful use of the dictionary. A few of these skills or understandings are

1. The knowledge of alphabetical order
2. The understanding that a word can have many different meanings
3. The knowledge of root words and the various inflected and derived
   forms of root words
4. The understanding that letters and combinations of letters have
   different sound values in different situations and that some letters
   are silent
5. The knowledge that *y* on the end of some words is changed to *i*
   before adding *es* for plurals

Facility in the use of the dictionary paves the way for a number
of potential breakthroughs in the struggle for independence in reading
because it

1. Unlocks the sound or pronunciation of words
2. Discloses new meanings of words which may be known in only one
   or a limited number of connotations
3. Confirms the spelling of a word when one can only approximate its
   correct spelling
4. Expands vocabulary through mastery of inflected and derived forms
   of known root words

If these two become inseparable
friends, the one on the right has got
it made.

These skills are developmental in nature and must be refined and
extended as the child moves upward through the grades. The alphabetizing ability which is adequate for successful fourth-grade work
will be inadequate for junior high or high school. The brunt of teaching dictionary skills falls on the intermediate grades simply because
most of those skills are introduced during these years of instruction.
The success the child feels and the utility he sees in dictionary usage
can be most important factors in how he reacts to the dictionary as a
tool for helping him in all facets of communication. He must be shown
that dictionary skills are permanently needed; failure to master these
skills can color his attitudes and learning development for many years
to come.

A number of developmental tasks are associated with dictionary
usage and there is general agreement among educators on what these
tasks are and the order in which they should be presented.

Developmental Tasks in Dictionary Mastery

1. Recognize and differentiate between letters
2. Associate letter names with letter symbols
3. Learn the letters of the alphabet in order

4. Arrange a number of words by alphabetical order of their initial letter
5. Extend above skill to second and third letters of words, eventually working through all letters of a word if necessary
6. Develop facility in rapid, effective use of dictionary, i.e., where do H, P, V come in the dictionary; open dictionary as near as possible to word being studied
7. Develop the ability to use accent marks in arriving at the pronunciation of words
8. Learn to interpret phonetic spelling used in dictionary
9. Use pronunciation key given somewhere on each double page of most dictionaries
10. Work out different pronunciations and meanings of words which are spelled alike
11. Determine which is the preferred pronunciation when several are given
12. Select the meaning which fits the context
13. Profit from guide words found at the top of each page to tell at a glance if the page contains the word being sought
14. Use intelligently special sections of a dictionary; geographical terms and names, biographical data, foreign words and phrases

Although particular skills are characteristically taught at a given grade level, what the individual child has learned or not learned should determine what is taught. Fortunately, dictionaries are available at all levels of difficulty from simple picture dictionaries to massive unabridged editions. The needs of the child and the goals of the teacher should determine how these differences in dictionaries will be utilized in the classroom. A child who is expected to use a dictionary which calls for skills far beyond what he has mastered will profit little from the experience. Any classroom practice which puts the child in such a position has little if any educational justification.

Using Maps

The ability to read maps is an important skill in our highly mobile society, and students should be provided opportunities to develop this skill in various content subject areas. Formats for teaching map reading can vary from involving the entire class, to individual pupils, pairs, or teams of pupils pursuing certain learning tasks at interest corners or learning stations. The following exercises are based on the use of a simple outline map of the continental United States, as illustrated in Figure 29.

1. Use a series of letters to represent the location of major cities. Students write the names of those cities to be identified.
2. Draw a line connecting two cities (San Francisco—St. Louis) and estimate the number of miles or kilometers from one to the other.
3. Use numbers to represent various states. Students identify and write the names of selected states.
4. Color or cross batch one state. Students write the names of all adjoining states.
5. Identify lakes, rivers, mountain ranges, national parks, time zones, etc.
6. Color or cross batch a state or region which is a major producer of oil, wheat, coal, iron ore, etc.

The same type of activities can be used in map study of foreign countries and regions such as Canada, Central and South America, Europe, Africa, and Asia. Through the use of actual road maps, a number of map reading activities can be developed. A few illustrations are

A. Plan a trip from Wilkes Barre, Pa. to Nashville, Tenn. Select the "fastest route," or the most scenic route.
B. List in order the routes on which you will travel.
C. Estimate the approximate distance to be traveled on each route.
D. Plan side trips to historical sites, state or national parks.
E. Map a trip from Syracuse, N.Y. to Salt Lake City, Utah using only interstate highways.

Figures 29 and 30 are illustrative exercises.

On the map which follows, numbers represent certain states. Letters represent major cities or state capitals.

1. Write the name which identifies city A. It is a state capital and the burial place of Abraham Lincoln. _____
2. The number 4 is found in the state of _____ .
3. The letter B locates a city identified with the "Birth of the Blues" and is the home of good Dixieland Jazz. _____

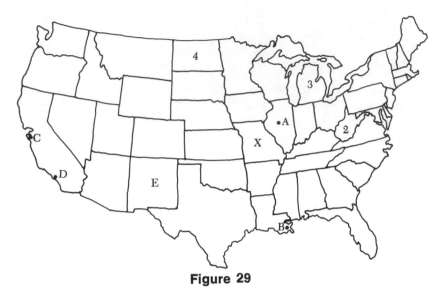

Figure 29

Can you locate the various states and
major cities on a map of the U.S.?

4. Number 2 indicates a state formed at the outbreak of the Civil
   War; it is _____ .
5. The state of Missouri is represented by an X. Starting at the north
   and moving clockwise, name the states which border on the state
   of Missouri. _____ _____ _____ _____

   _____ _____ _____
6. Does Idaho border on Canada? (Answer yes or no). _____
7. Write the name of the southwestern state marked E. _____
8. The inland state marked 3 has more water boundary than land
   boundary. It is the state of _____ .
9. The state directly west of the state marked 4 is the state of

   _____ .
10. Two cities in California are marked C and D. C represents
    _____ ; D represents _____ .

*Map Reading**

   Maps often contain guides for finding places or cities. The following, example *A*, tells us how to locate the city of Detroit. Example *B*
locates Austin, Texas.

* From: Arthur Heilman and Elizabeth Holmes, *Smuggling Language into the
Teaching of Reading* (Columbus, Ohio: Charles E. Merrill Publishing Co., 1972),
p. 102.

Example A: Detroit, Michigan, is found by drawing a line down from 17 and a line over from *F*. The place where the two lines meet is the location of Detroit.

Example B: Lines drawn from *10* and over from *L* locate the capital city of Texas which is _____ .

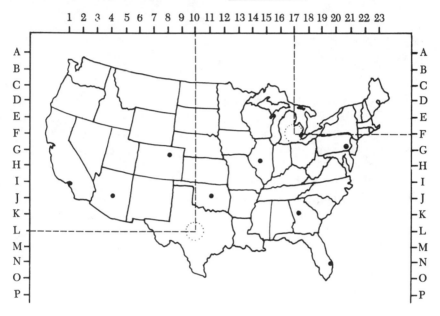

Figure 30

TEACHER: "The problems below provide clues which will guide you to the location of certain cities. You are to name these cities. Complete all the problems you can without using a map. Then use a map of the U.S. if needed. (You need not draw lines on the map; use imaginary lines.)"

1. H–15 Capital of midwestern state; Lincoln buried there.

_____

2. I–1 Not state capital, but the largest city in southern California.

_____

3. J–11 Capital of southwestern state (Will Rogers country).

_____

4. D–23 Capital of state located in northeast corner of U.S.

_____

5. K–17 Capital and largest industrial city of this southeastern state.

_____

6. C–7 Straight lines drawn from these points would intersect in the state of _____ .

7. G–21 Large city in eastern Pennsylvania (not capital).
_____

8. J–4 Capital of southwestern state. _____
9. N–20 Atlantic coastal city. _____
10. G–8 State capital of the "mile-high city."_____

Interpreting and
Evaluating Material

Locating information is an important part of the learning process, but this step is only a prelude to the ultimate goal of assimilation of material. The ability to locate information will have little impact on personal or academic growth if the student is unable to read the material he has located.

Teaching students how to read critically is undoubtedly the most difficult task attempted in our schools. In fact, if the matter is pressed beyond the usual textbook definitions, asking a group of teachers to *define* critical reading is more likely to result in chaos than in unanimity. Practically all of their definitions are abstractions, simply because critical reading involves so many variables.

Interpreting and evaluating material is probably as close a synonym for *critical reading* as can be found. Illustrations of the analytical abilities involved include

1. Knowing what the author has said
2. Grasping the validity of statements and knowing when and how to check validity with other sources
3. Differentiating between facts and opinion
4. Noting when inferences are being drawn and drawing them when they are not stated
5. Detecting author bias as well as inaccuracies which might not be traceable to bias
6. Understanding one's own biases as these relate to what is being read
7. Taking into consideration an author's use of allusions, satire, humor, irony, and the like
8. Developing some criteria for judging an author's competency in the area in which he writes

Undoubtedly this list could be extended. Each of the above abilities is developmental in nature and should be taught at all grade levels. The reading tasks found in the intermediate grades are characterized by an increasing difficulty that requires a high degree of competency if the reader is to grow increasingly perceptive. This point holds even as we move into the high school and beyond. How many adults are immune to propaganda, know both sides of controversial issues, and do not let their emotions color interpretations while reading? Parke (20) suggests that students read for much the same reasons as do adults; namely, to keep informed, secure answers to questions, solve problems, follow directions, and share with others. It is likely that students do more reading that calls for interpretation and evaluation than do adults simply because this is the nature of being a student.

The test of critical reading often applied in our schools is the students' demonstration of the ability to restate or write what an author has said. The inability to discern what the author is saying may well be evidence of inability to read the material critically, but paraphrasing, by itself, is not evidence of critical reading either. Restating the gist of a passage but failing to detect author bias will result in a transfer of author bias to the reader's own thought. Knowing what the author is saying without seeing that some statements are contrary to fact will inhibit critical reading, as will reciting strongly expressed opinions as if these were statements of verifiable facts.

Interpreting and evaluating calls for the application of a number of the mechanical reading skills and higher level abilities listed above. Students need both guidance and systematic practice in developing work habits and study techniques (25), a number of which are dealt with in the following discussion.

Need for Background Knowledge

All of the skills required for critical reading are developmental in nature. The readers' previous experiences, or lack of such experiences, impinge on each new reading situation (13). Thus, factors such as how extensively and how effectively various skills have been practiced will have a bearing on the present level of critical reading.

As Durrell (9) points out, "The efficiency of transferring ideas from one person to another is seldom high," and there is an unavoidable loss for the reader in this process. Eller (10) lists a number of obstacles to critical reading found in the school, in society, or in both. Some of them follow.

1. Pupils form the opinion that anything in print is true.
2. Children are conditioned to accept authority blindly.

3. Schools have relied on single texts in the various content areas, and the teacher stresses "what the book says." Thus, children do not learn to look for differences of opinion or for interpretations.
4. Schools avoid controversial topics and emphasize uniformity.

Each of these points is inevitably tied in with experience and is thus affected by a person's background and knowledge. It is likely that the greatest barrier to critical reading is the reader's lack of background and experience. The teacher has to deal with this problem regardless of the level or the curriculum area in which she teaches. In reality, we are dealing with two questions. First, what does the reader bring to the reading situation in the way of experience and understanding? And second, what does he need in order to understand the particular reading he is attempting? The higher one goes through the grades, the more need there is for this type of preparation because the reading materials deal with concepts which are often beyond the present stock of concepts held by some students in the room.

A third-grade class is reading a story about bees storing honey in a hollow tree. The facts that the bees "belonged to a farmer," worked for him in a hive he provided, and yet one day swarmed and left the hive, may call for a good deal of explanation by the teacher, or by bee experts in the class, before all aspects of this story are meaningful to every member of that third-grade class.

A high school or college student reading *John Brown's Plea to the Court* can hardly be expected to arrive at a sound critical analysis of this passage unless some background facts are also known: who was John Brown?; when did he live?; what political-social issue was involved?; what experiences did John Brown have in Kansas prior to the Harper's Ferry episode?; was John Brown's attitude shared by a large number of people living at that time?; how would one describe John Brown's emotional maturity?; is the real issue here the question of whether the end justifies the means?

Almost all the prerequisites for, and obstacles to, critical reading are related to the two skills of discerning a writer's purpose and of drawing inferences. The presence or absence of bias, a lack of background, the habit of accepting that which is in print or that which is allegedly backed by authority, and the lack of experience in dealing with controversial topics, all help to determine whether critical reading can take place. College students too have trouble discerning an author's purpose. Students in a reading improvement course, after reading and discussing several serious paragraphs, were given the following passage by Mark Twain. Each student was to read the passage silently and to write a sentence or two answering these questions: "What is the author's purpose? How does he achieve it? What is the author's mood?"

> It was a crisp and spicy morning in early October. The lilacs and laburnums, lit with the glory fires of autumn, hung burning and flashing in the upper air; a fairy bridge provided by kind Nature for the wingless wild things, that have their home in the tree-tops and would visit together; the larch and the pomegranate flung their purple and yellow flames in brilliant broad splashes along the slanting sweep of the woodland; the sensuous fragrance of innumerable deciduous flowers rose upon the swooning atmosphere; far in the empty sky a solitary oesophagus slept upon motionless wing; everywhere brooded stillness, serenity, and the peace of God.*

Hundreds of students, and a smaller number of teachers and adults, have responded in essence: "It is a beautiful fall day. He describes nature, the beautiful colors, and the peace and quiet one finds in nature." Despite the first line a number of readers move the day into spring. Occasionally a reader says, "I wondered about the oesophagus, but thought it might be a tropical bird." However, once adults are shown the ridiculous nature of the passage, they seriously doubt that others would be so easily taken in by it.

The abilities related to critical reading operate in all reading situations, not just in those that occur during the clock-hour devoted to formal instruction in reading. They operate whenever reading is used in the pursuit of knowledge, whether in history, geography, economics, health, mathematics, science, or literature (28). The reader must know the meaning of the words used and the different shades of meaning words have in different contexts. He must separate main thoughts or ideas from qualifications; he must detect the author's purpose, bias, and intent. From the first grade through college, the teacher has a major responsibility to structure reading situations so that these factors and many others are kept in proper focus.

Reading provides the needed background for clearing up vague and hazy concepts. It is difficult to determine the number of such concepts that children harbor. One teacher discovered that many students in her class had vague ideas as to the origin and meaning of the term *Freedom of the Press*. These came to light as a result of an assignment which called for students to write briefly on the meaning of this term. Several recurring ideas were that freedom of the press was strictly an

---

* Mark Twain, "A Detective Story," from *The Man That Corrupted Hadleyburg* (New York: Harper & Row), p. 304.

American invention, that what one printed had to be true, and that
freedom did not extend to criticism of the government. The following
are a few representative examples of students' comments.

> Freedom of the press originated in the United States which made
> it possible for a person or a newspaper to express opinion without
> being persecuted.
>
> The right to express our own ideas on any subject with the excep-
> tion of derogatory remarks about our country or government.
>
> This (freedom of the press) originated in the early 1800's as an
> outgrowth of the press being inhibited. It was brought about by a
> trial.
>
> Freedom of the press means all men have the right to express their
> inner feelings in written or oral language. But there is a law saying
> that one cannot yell "fire" when there is no fire.
>
> The right to report current happenings as factual information which
> is relatively free from personal or group bias.

Resisting propaganda depends to a large degree on the reader's
background or "data bank," or in his being wise to the techniques
people use when they use language that does not fit the facts. The critical reader assumes responsibility for questioning what he reads. While
he respects language, he knows that some people use it to control the
behavior of others. The purpose here is not to explain all of various
propaganda techniques that are used to obscure meaning or take the
reader on a detour. The teaching examples which follow might help
students detect these devices.

I. List a number of popular propaganda techniques. Discuss these
   with the class and then have each student or teams write examples.

   1. Beg the issue or throw up a smoke screen. Here one does not
      discuss the real issue, but switches the discussion to other topics.
      For example: Candidate A has charged that B has violated the
      law by not filing a statement of his campaign expenses. B replies,
      "A has accused me of not filing a statement of expenses. Why
      should he care? Is he a police officer. Have I ever lied to the
      voters? Who voted against raising taxes last year? I'll tell you
      who did—I did! And I'll tell you something else; A voted for the
      tax bill. I support every worthwhile charity in this community,
      I was born here, I went to school here! Can A make this
      statement?"
   2. Generalize from too few cases.
   3. Ignore the *idea* and attack the person suggesting it.

4. Use a false analogy.
5. Appeal to authority.
6. Rely on guilt by association.
7. Use a faulty cause-and-effect relationship.
8. Misuse figures or statistics.

II. *Step 1.* Prepare a number of propositions that might be an issue in any community.

   Step 2. Follow each proposition with an imaginary statement that someone included in a "Letter to the Editor." Students analyze and point out "what the writer was up to."

Proposition: "Should the city council pass an ordinance which would require fluoridation of the city water supply in an effort to decrease tooth decay among children of the community?"

Letter to the Editor: "Of course some people favor fluoridation, they spend so much time in the Roaring Twenties Bar that they probably don't drink enough water to care how it tastes."

Letter No. 2: "The real issue is that fluoride is a poison. We shouldn't poison our fine water supply." (Beware of jumping to a conclusion: Fluoride *is* a poison. What is the missing detail?)

Proposition: "Should the voters approve a proposed school bond issue?"

Letter to the Editor: "As Lincoln said, 'You can fool all of the people some of the time,' and this is one of those times! Our schools are as good as any in the country. The people pushing this school bond proposal want to raise your taxes. I say vote this bond issue down."

Proposition: "Should we adopt a city ordinance, proposed as a safety measure, which would prohibit the sale of fireworks?"

Letter to the Editor: "The Fourth of July is one of our great holidays. This proposal is unpatriotic. It is a direct slap at free enterprise. There are a lot of American firms which make fireworks. The next thing you know somebody will try to outlaw automobiles because people get hurt in accidents."

Proposition: "Should the city construct a swimming pool in city park?"

Letter to the Editor: "The people in this town do not want a municipal pool. It is obvious that if the people favored this harebrained idea we would have had a pool by now!"

Proposition: "Should we extend the runways at our municipal airport so that jet planes can land here?"

Letter to the Editor: "When we built the airport the planners said the present layout would be adequate for at least twenty years. That was just ten years ago. Those people are experts and we should listen to them."

Clues to Use
While Reading the News

Teachers use newspapers and other mass media for both the teaching of critical analysis and mechanical skills which relate to such analysis. The potential values in the use of such materials are numerous. There are also barriers to significant learning, two of which are inadequate planning and the tendency to avoid discussion of issues which might prove to be controversial. Children should be permitted and encouraged to interpret and analyze advertisements, political cartoons, editorials, and syndicated columns.

"Clues to use while reading the news" can be developed by noting and discussing details such as the following:

1. *Compare the editorials* found in four or five metropolitan papers which deal with a particular current issue. Assume there are apparent differences of opinion; what might account for these differences? (1) Political orientation of editor or publisher; or (2) does a particular newspaper have a standing policy on certain issues (labor-management, foreign aid).

2. *The political cartoon:* Gather cartoons, from different papers and drawn by different artists, which deal with the same topic. Ask students to analyze and put into words what the cartoon is attempting to say. Student interpretation of any given stimulus will vary considerably. This will facilitate discussion and help students to see the importance of "the reader's background" which includes bias, emotional attachments, and the like. Such factors always function in any interpretation of a cartoon, editorial, feature article, or news story.

3. *Detecting propaganda techniques:* The teacher or a committee of students might prepare and duplicate an editorial which by design contains biased statements, factual errors, and various propaganda techniques. Each student has a copy of the material and independently edits or rewrites the editorial. Next, have class discussion of the original material and substitutions, deletions, and corrections made by members of the group. Differences between student reactions will in many cases be marked, particularly if the topic is chosen wisely. In the discussion,

students will be exposed to points they missed and points of view different from their own.

4. *Study a current issue longitudinally:*
   a. Compare different newspaper and news magazine treatment of this problem.
   b. Attempt to account for differences in editorial points of view.
   c. Study several columnists' or news analysts' interpretations.
   d. Analyze the day-to-day statements of the decision makers or those spokespersons attempting to mold public opinion. Based on the issue being studied, these might be legislative leaders, State Department officials, labor leaders, candidates for high office, the President, White House staff, etc.

Determining "Fact or Opinion"

In reading materials in the various content areas, children are frequently faced with the task of deciding whether a statement is fact or opinion. Young readers (and older ones also) develop habits which are not always helpful in this type of problem solving. One such habit is the tendency to accept "what is written" as being factual. Second, when one strongly agrees with a statement, it is frequently accepted as a fact. Third, if a position is developed logically or if something is repeated often enough, it may be accepted as factual. Thus, the statement "finding a four leaf clover *always* brings good luck" may be doubted; while the statement "finding a four leaf clover *can* bring one good luck" may seem a bit more logical.

Probably the best way to help children develop skill in differentiating fact from opinion would be immediate discussion of statements as they are met in textual material. This is difficult to do because it would call for a particular and limited *set* in regard to the material. There are other goals which through practice have earned higher priorities. Another possibility is to collect statements of fact and opinion from various sources and devote a period to their discussion. Obviously all items could pertain to one subject area such as social science, health, geography, or literature. On the other hand, exercises might deal with general statements or cut across various content areas. The following examples illustrates the latter approach.

Read each statement carefully. If the sentence states a fact, write *F* on the line in front of the sentence. If the sentence states an opinion, write *O*.

_____ 1. Democracy is the best form of government for man.
_____ 2. Wild animals will not attack if you do not run.
_____ 3. Pollution is the most serious problem in the world today.
_____ 4. Rich people do not pay a fair share of taxes.
_____ 5. Football is the roughest of all sports.
_____ 6. Different brands of aspirin are essentially the same.
_____ 7. Compact cars are not as safe as larger cars.
_____ 8. The U.S. spends too much money on arms and weapons during peace time.
_____ 9. Man will never be able to settle on the moon.
_____ 10. In the U.S. women live longer than do men.

Following Written Directions

The ability to follow written directions is a prerequisite for success in many school activities as well as real life situations. However, in a recent survey of the literature, Galgoci found that emphasis on teaching related to written directions is seriously lacking in the schools. Over a five-year period, only one journal entry was found in the three major reading journals surveyed. Furthermore, in several consecutive *Yearly Summaries of Research in Reading,* no research dealing with written directions was cited. An in-depth study of a widely used basal series led Galgoci to conclude: "If scant attention is being paid in the professional journals concerning children's ability to follow written directions, the situation is no better as far as suggestions for developing this ability through the use of a basal reader series is concerned."*

Providing practice in following written directions can begin as early as first grade and continue through college. A few examples at different difficulty levels are provided next.

Read each statement and follow directions.

1. Write the plural of each of the following words.
   a) dog _____   d) woman _____
   b) goose _____   e) box _____
   c) leaf _____   f) church _____

---

* Lois J. Galgoci, "Following Directions: Neglected in Research and Teaching." (Masters' paper, Pennsylvania State University, 1972).

2. Cross out the word that does not belong.

coffee—tea—milk—cup—grapejuice

3. Write a sentence using the following words.

repairs—was—the—need—in—clock—of

4. Circle every number that can be divided evenly by 3.

13—33—63—15—25—45

5. Write a homonym (same pronunciation) for each of the following words.

a) red _____   d) cite _____

b) flour _____   e) wood _____

c) vane _____   f) paws _____

Following Written Directions: Each of the numbered tasks 1–7 relate to the boxes below. Read each item carefully and follow the directions.

1. If either row II or row III contain more odd-numbered boxes than even numbered boxes, write the word *YOU* in box eleven.

2. If the words in boxes 1 and 7 are synonyms, circle the word in box one.

3. If the sum of any two numbers in row I is equal to the number found in ANY box in row III, write the word YES in box three.

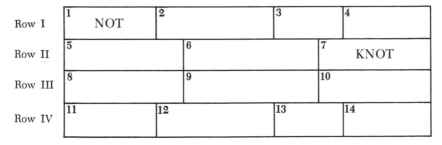

Row I	1 NOT	2	3	4
Row II	5	6	7 KNOT	
Row III	8	9	10	
Row IV	11	12	13	14

4. If the number in the boxes in any row total exactly 18, write the word VERY in box thirteen.

5. If there are two rows of boxes which contain more odd numbers than even numbers, write the word YES in box six.

6. If all of the boxes are numbered consecutively, write the word WELL in box fourteen.

7. If the sum of any two numbers in row II is equal to the number found in box 13, write the word READ in box 12.

When directions are carried out correctly the only responses called for are found in row IV.

Row IV   you   read   very   well

Following Written Directions: This exercise will test your ability to understand and follow written directions. Each of the items 1–10 relate to the circles below and/or to the material in Box One in the middle of the page. All responses are to be made in Box One.

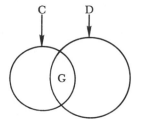 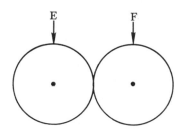

1. If the area G is common to both Circles C and D, circle the 2 in Box One.
2. If the radius of Circle E is equal to the radius of Circle F, underline the number 6.
3. If one straight line could be drawn to bisect both Circles E and F, circle the K in Box One.
4. If a vertical line could be drawn to represent the radius of Circle F, circle the M in Box One.

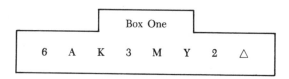

5. If the letters identifying the four circles are not in alphabetical order, circle the first digit in Box One.
6. If both a two letter and three letter word may be made using letters in Box One, underline the number 3.
7. If the sum of any two digits in Box One is equal to any other number in Box One, underline the letter A.
8. If the material in Box One begins with a letter and concludes with a triangle, place a dot in the triangle.
9. If Circle C could fit in Circle D, draw a line under the letter Y.

10. If every number in Box One is followed by a letter, draw a straight line connecting the letters A and K.

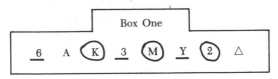

Paraphrasing

The ability to paraphrase, or restate in one's own words, the author's main ideas is usually the criterion by which the pupil's critical reading ability or comprehension is judged. The inability to paraphrase often implies one of two things: either the pupil did not fathom what the author was trying to tell him, or he lacks the language facility to restate what he read. Paraphrasing is one of the most effective and, at the same time, one of the least used techniques available to teachers at all levels. Walpole (27) states, "Paraphrasing provides a simple classroom technique which not only commits the pupil to a specific task of interpretation, but also enables him to study other versions and see how people interpret the same passage in widely varying ways." Paraphrasing exercises provide an almost ideal example of a means of integrating all of the language arts. First, the student gets experience in interpretive reading. Second, by writing he gains experience in all facets of composition, such as sentence and paragraph construction, organization of material, and grammatical usage. This technique can be highly motivating to students if care is exercised in the selection of reading passages.

In order to paraphrase accurately or restate the essence of what an author has written, one must be able to grasp the meaning as he reads. Paraphrasing demands that one see the relationships between various parts of a passage and how these parts are related to the total effect sought by an author. As a rule, good readers have developed the ability to read in "thought units." Thus, their reading habits lead them naturally into logical and meaningful phrasing. They have learned to see the relationships between words and how the author builds a pattern of thought units into a larger whole. The point under discussion cuts across several factors which have been listed as related to critical reading: main ideas, paraphrasing, adjusting to author's organization, and seeing the relationship between a part and the whole.

The following illustrations have been used with high school groups. In each case, passage A was read by the student who was then asked to write a sentence or two restating what the author said. Immediately following this, each pupil was given passage B which was the same passage divided into meaningful thought units. All of the students state that it was easier to get meaning from passage B. The point of the exercise was to help students see that in their reading for meaning they must do what was done for them in passage B, i.e., read in meaningful thought units. Such an exercise can be developed for use at practically any reading level.

Passage A

A man rises, sometimes, and stands not, because he doth not, or is not believed to fill his place; and sometimes he stands not, because he overfills his place: He may bring so much virtue, so much justice, so much integrity to the position, as to be a libel upon his predecessor, and cast infamy upon him, and a burden upon his successor.*

Passage B

A man rises, sometimes,
and stands not,
because he does not,
or is not believed to fill his place;
And sometimes he stands not,
because he overfills his place:
He may bring
so much virtue,
so much justice,
so much integrity to the position,
as to be a libel upon his predecessor,
and cast infamy upon him,
and burden upon his successor.

Passage A

Man, of whom David had said (as the lowest diminution that he could put upon him), 'I am a worm and no man'—he might have gone lower, and said, I am a man and no worm.

Passage B

Man,
of whom David had said,

---

* Paraphrased from John Donne, *Complete Poetry and Prose of John Donne* (New York: The Modern Library, 1946), p. 338.

(as the lowest diminution that he could put upon him)
'I am a worm and no man'—
He might have gone lower,
and said,
I am a man and no worm.

Retention of
Material Read

The organization of our schools and the curricular materials used make learning very dependent upon reading. Once the mechanical process of recognizing printed words is fairly well established, the most frequently cited weakness of students at *all* educational levels relates to inefficient retention of what is read. Remembering what is read is synonymous with "learning from reading." Of most reading that students are expected to do, this is the primary goal.

When we subject students to an examination of materials read, we are in essence sampling the knowledge they have gleaned and retained. We often find that reading is relatively ineffective when judged by what students retain. Approximately the same degree of efficiency (or inefficiency) in retention is found when the material is presented orally via lecture. Some loss in the communicative process is inevitable. Since the role of the teacher is to guide and direct learning activities, we should seek to examine every approach or technique that will further that purpose.

Retention of material read is influenced by many factors, one of which is the reader's *set*, a psychological term referring to perception. This is often discussed under the general heading of the "reader's purpose." It is probably true that, as teachers, we sometimes fail in helping students develop a meaningful purpose for reading. Sometimes more stress is placed on the ritual of covering material than on assimilation. This misemphasis is seen, for example, when a teacher gives a reading assignment just as a class period ends; or when there is no further elaboration than "your assignment for our next meeting is Chapter 8—read Chapter 8 for Friday."

Many students will follow these instructions with no appreciable learning taking place. It is also unlikely they will make contributions if the material is discussed in class. When the reader's only purpose is to fulfill an assignment, he will read Chapter 8, or any other chapter, without conscious interaction with the material. If, as he finishes the reading, his teacher were suddenly to appear and ask, "What have you just read?" the answer would be, "I don't know, I was just trying to finish the assignment."

Use of Questioning to
Inculcate a Learning Set

Studies indicate that questions that are considered prior to the actual reading have a salutary effect on both learning and retention (6). Questions provide a purpose for reading and alert the reader to important issues to be covered. In this sense, questions provide a preview of what will be met in the reading situation. This technique is one of the highly justifiable procedures of most "study programs" (4).

The use of questions should not be limited to preparing students for assignment. A greater value for questions results from helping the student formulate concepts. Yet, as Smith (24) points out, questions per se have no inherent value. In any teaching situation, questions can be used most unimaginatively. The efficacy of questioning lies in the interaction which may take place between teacher and student as together they explore the *meaning* of what is being taught and learned. "The artful teacher initiates and sustains the kind of thoughtful discourse that helps students ruminate and organize ideas."

Learning Strategies
Influence Retention

Retention is not a simple process of memorizing, which at best can have only a short-term influence. The learning strategies that children develop in their efforts to cope with the school's demands are a most important influence on retention. The school can and probably has overemphasized short-term memory of factual data as a learning strategy. If and when this occurs, readers fail to develop other important learning-to-learn strategies which are essential in retaining what is read.

Retention is related to what has gone on before as well as to what intervenes between learning and measurement of recall. Retention involves integrating or restructuring new data with those which are already stored. This involves the reader in answering the question, "What do I know that impinges on this reading experience?" Relationships must be perceived and concepts organized and extended. In many school situations it may be concluded that retention is inadequate, while the real issue may be that little learning actually occurred. When interest is lacking, reading is not a self-sustaining activity and reading assignments become educational rituals. Retention results when readers become intellectually or emotionally involved in which they are reading.

Rate of Reading

The rate at which one can assimilate meaning from printed symbols becomes a reading problem when students are expected to understand curricular materials for which their reading skills, habits, and abilities are inadequate (21). The intermediate grades are probably the first level at which a concern for rate of reading is justified since at this point emphasis begins to be placed on the various content areas. In recent years there has been considerable emphasis on the need for improving rate of reading. The impetus for this concern with rate undoubtedly came first at the college level, where, for the past several decades, considerable attention has been given to this problem. College reading improvement programs grew out of the conviction that many college students have the capacity to meet the demands of the college curriculum but that their reading habits make them poor academic risks. It is undoubtedly true that many teachers, ranging from high school to the intermediate levels, are convinced that this is also the case with many of their students.

Over the years the term *rate of reading* has been widely but not always wisely used. It has been a popular practice to speak of the rate of reading of the average high school senior, college freshman, or adult. The impression was often left that the figure quoted, such as 325 or 375 words per minute, had some real significance. The implication was that once an individual's rate for reading a given passage was established, this figure could be cited as though it were a constant for any reading situation. The emphasis on rate led some individuals to confuse the entire reading process with the number of words one could allegedly cover in a specified period of time. In an effort to lessen this tendency, it became popular to talk about "rate of comprehension," a term which emphasized that reading is getting meaning. But this term was also subject to semantic confusion since several factors are always at work in determining rate of comprehension (23). There are a number of variables which influence the rate at which different reading materials can be assimilated.

1. The reader's knowledge of the general subject matter
2. The vocabulary load, difficulty level of words and concepts

3. The reader's degree of motivation
4. The reader's purpose for reading the material
5. The physiological state of the reader, whether fatigued, etc.
6. The length of the reading period
7. Mechanical factors such as size of print and length of line
8. The readability of the material as determined by such factors as style of writing, sentence structure, and sentence length
9. The reader's mastery of the mechanical skills of reading, such as number of words known as sight words, ability to sound unknown words, ability to profit from punctuation, and freedom from the habit of inserting, omitting, or repeating words or phrases
10. The number of figures, illustrations, cross-references, and footnotes the material contains

Consideration of these factors reveals that no one sample of reading behavior can provide a valid basis for establishing a person's rate of comprehension. Any figure arrived at would be valid only for the particular material read under the precise conditions which prevailed while it was being read. Regardless of the fact that the term *rate of reading* is vague and may lead to confusion, there is little question that the rate at which pupils read curricular materials is an instructional problem which tends to become more acute as they move through the grades.

Varying Rate According to Material and Purpose for Reading

A facile reader must develop several different rates for reading different types of printed matter. This fact merits careful attention in the intermediate grades because here the pupil must read a great variety of materials in various content areas. The child should learn to adjust his reading behavior to the material and to the objectives he has for reading it. A magazine article may be read with good comprehension at several hundred words per minute while the same reader may have to spend several minutes in reading a mathematical problem stated in forty words. Or assume that a pupil, having read a particular passage, is attempting to recall the five largest cities of the United States. He has tentatively settled for New York, Chicago, and San Francisco, but the other two city names do not come to mind. As he rereads, it would be a slow and possibly wasteful effort to read carefully

A library is a reader's alma mater.

every word and sentence of the entire section which contains the desired information. If the pupil had mastered the technique of scanning material, he could quickly find the one or two sentences that contain the desired data; these could then be read carefully.

Developing Flexibility

The term *flexibility*, as applied to reading, refers to the ability to read different materials at different rates. An analogy might be made between reading and walking. Just as most individuals have settled into a particular characteristic gait in walking, they have also developed a favorite reading pace. However, all individuals can walk faster when circumstance demands it. Examples would include the threat of rain, being late for an appointment, or the likelihood of missing a bus. In the absence of such motivators, the individual settles back into his characteristic gait.

It should be obvious to anyone who reads widely that there is little justification for reading all material at the same rate. Such a habit would be wasteful in many situations. The flexible reader is one who has developed the ability to "adjust to the terrain." He has developed the ability to discern where more rapid reading is appropriate, and he has developed the ability to read more rapidly in such situations.

Initial training in learning to read concentrates heavily on word recognition. It is obvious that the individual who fails continually to increase his sight vocabulary can hardly be expected to learn to read more rapidly or more efficiently. The need for growth in rate of reading is an excellent example of the developmental nature of reading. Unfortunately, formal instruction in reading makes little provision for helping students develop this skill.

Improving Rate through
Improving Reading Skills

The problem of improving rate can be oversimplified unless we keep in mind that rate is influenced by the reader's skills, habits, and attitudes toward the material being read. It would be unrealistic to attempt to improve a slow rate of reading without dealing with those factors which are its basis. When slow reading is simply a habitual response stemming from a lack of basic reading skills, it can be dealt with by practice in those skills. Lack of skills, or the development of habits such as guessing, substituting or omitting words, adding words to salvage meaning, or ignoring punctuation, inevitably contribute to slow reading. Inadequate word-attack skills may prevent a child from arriving at correct pronunciation or cause him to arrive at the pronunciation very slowly. Word-by-word reading is usually related to these problems.

Reading in phrases is a skill which relates to rate of reading on two scores. Word-by-word reading is time-consuming and also tends to interfere with comprehension. A child who has been taught to read for meaning will have to repeat sentences and parts of sentences when he loses the thought because he has been so slow in piecing the various word units into a meaningful whole. When word-by-word reading is habitual—that is, when it has been reinforced by many thousands of reading experiences—it is sometimes advisable to give the reader practice in reading easy phrases. Gradually, more difficult reading material can be used. The teacher can make up drill exercises which use phrases in isolation, exercises which show logical phrases underlined, or short passages where the student underlines logical phrases. These three procedures are illustrated in Figure 31. Figures 32 and 33 on the following pages, present a sustained reading passage arranged in phrases.

Figure 31

1. The following phrases or short sentences are designed to give practice in reading a number of words as one thought unit. Some pupils read one word at a time—that is, they pause after each word: up, the, mountain. *Since this is a logical thought unit, it should be read:* up the mountain. *Read the phrases from left to right across the page.*

In the car   down the hill   at the farm   from the house
had to leave soon   in the big house   he will be   has gone away
the white horse   eat some cake   ran to the house   the show
can see it   the pretty dress   will look good   we can see
much too much   the tiny boat   on the paper   to the fair

2. In the following paragraph logical thought units have been separated. Be sure to read each phrase as a whole. There are many different ways we could read the same passage. The following is only one example.

Billy saw the car   coming down the road.   He said to himself,
I hope I can get a ride   to town.   He began to wonder
if he should   accept a ride   if he didn't know   the driver.
The car pulled up   and slowed down.   He saw a man
and two boys   about his age.   The boys shouted,   "Hi, Billy."
He recognized the twins.

3. Underline phrases which could be read as one unit. Remember that there may be several different ways to arrange words in thought units. Underline the way you think is best.

The twins, Roger and Sandy, had moved to town several weeks ago. "Hop in the car," said Sandy. "Have you met my dad?" asked Roger. Billy shook hands with Mr. Farrell. As they neared town, Mr. Farrell said, "Can you come and play with the boys at our house or must you go straight home?"

SUMMARY

Study skills, which include locating information, organizing and evaluating material, effective use of library resources, and adjusting reading rate to purpose and material, are a most important cluster of reading skills. Their importance to the learner is not always paralleled by the effectiveness with which they are taught. One of the reasons for this is that these particular skills cut across all subject areas, while responsibility for teaching them is left vague.

Ideally, helping children develop efficient study skills should be an integral part of the *teaching* in all content areas. Ironically, in many

Figure 32

The passage below tells something about the reading process. The material has been arranged in short phrases to provide practice in phrase reading. The ability to read in phrases is learned through practice. After reading this material several times, you should be reading it both faster and more smoothly. Try to apply this skill when you read other materials which have not been phrased.

(Read down the columns, reading each line as a unit.)

This exercise
is arranged
in columns
of phrases
to help you
in developing
the habit of
reading phrases.
Try to read
each line

"as one unit."
That is—
do not read
each/word/
as/a/unit/.
With practice,
you will find
you can read
several words
as units.

As you read
other materials
which have not
been phrased,
let your eyes
and your mind
cooperate
in selecting

several words
which are

"logical thoughts."
This will help you
to read
more rapidly,
more smoothly,
and with good
comprehension.
Your eyes
and your mind
are capable
of dealing
with several
smaller words
or with a
very large one.
For instance—
Mississippi
Rhode Island

cheerfulness
peppermint
in olden days
cold and rainy.
The examples
cited above
are relatively
long units.

They were easy
for you to read
because they are
familiar.
You have seen
each of them
many times
and you know
their meanings.
These phrases

were not related
to each other.
Other phrases
on this page
are related.
This is a bit
more difficult
to read smoothly.
First because
the thought units
vary in length.
Secondly,
some readers
might select
different
phrasing patterns
than shown here.

classrooms the "content" itself takes precedence over the process of developing effective skills in locating, evaluating, and organizing this material.

When study skills are neglected, teaching often becomes ritualistic. All pupils read the same material and are given no guidance or even opportunity to explore the world of books. An example is provided by

Figure 33

Read down the columns. Read the material several times and note how "phrasing" can help you get the meaning.

Delaration of Independence*

. . . —We hold
these truths
to be self-evident,
that all men
are created equal,
that they are endowed
by their Creator
with certain
unalienable Rights,
that among these
are Life,
Liberty
and the pursuit
of Happiness. —

That to secure
these rights,
Governments
are instituted
among Men,
deriving
their just powers
from the consent
of the governed,—

That whenever
any Form
of Government
becomes destructive
of these ends,
it is the Right
of the People
to alter
or to abolish it,
and to institute
new Government,
laying its foundation

on such principles
and organizing
its powers
in such form,
as to them
shall seem
most likely
to effect
their Safety
and Happiness.
Prudence, indeed,
will dictate
that Governments
long established
should not
be changed
for light
and transient causes;
and accordingly
all experience
hath shewn
that mankind
are more disposed
to suffer,
while evils are sufferable,
than to right themselves
by abolishing
the forms to which
they are accustomed.
But when
a long train
of abuses
and usurpations, . . .
evinces a design
to reduce them
under absolute

Depotism,
it is their right,
it is their duty,
to throw off
such Government,
and to provide
new Guards
for their future
security.— . . .
WE, THEREFORE,
the Representatives
of the UNITED STATES
OF AMERICA,
in General Congress,
Assembled, . . .
do, in the Name
and by Authority
of the good People
of these Colonies,
solemnly publish
and declare,
That these
United Colonies are,
and of Right
ought to be FREE
AND INDEPENDENT STATES, . . .
—And for the support
of this Declaration,
with a firm reliance
on the protection
of divine Providence,
we mutually pledge
to each other
our Lives,
our Fortunes
and our sacred Honor.

* Heilman and Holmes, op. cit., p. 108.

an observation of a study hall in which row after row of students were listlessly attempting to answer questions found at the end of a particular chapter in their history text. They had read the textbook and were now required to answer a number of factual questions.

Some important study skills do appear to deal primarily with mechanics. Examples include dictionary usage; profiting from reader aids such as a glossary, index, and appendix; use of the card catalogue and other library aids. However, these need not be taught mechanically. They are best learned as part of larger educational activities such as unit work which will call for ascertaining definitions and pronunciation of unusual terms, deciding upon the specific connotation of a word, and finding related materials in a wide variety of sources. These and other opportunities for learning are on-going—they occur daily. Thus, one need not resort to lengthy drill on dictionary or reference material skills. The study skills are developmental in nature and are best taught and learned as part of a total growth process.

Other types of study skills focus on critical reading and interpretation of a wide variety of written materials. In essence, these skills involve sorting out what is significant and germane to one's goal, making critical judgments relative to ideas and concepts, drawing inferences, and predicting outcomes. Study skills are important tools for problem solving in all areas of the curriculum.

YOUR POINT OF VIEW?

Would you defend or attack the following premises? Supply a rationale for each of your choices.

1. Rate of reading, or rate of comprehension, is determined by such factors as intellectual level, background experience, and concepts held. Therefore, working directly on "speeding reading" will be ineffective unless these factors are dealt with.

2. As a general rule, the questions found in intermediate and junior high school level textbooks deal with isolated facts and do not help the child to organize information and see relationships.

3. Due to automation and the knowledge explosion in recent years, reading ability is more important today than it was twenty-five or fifty years ago.

4. One of the strengths of American schools is their thoroughness and effectiveness in helping pupils develop study skills.

5. In regard to dictionary usage, there are few if any new skills introduced beyond fifth or sixth grade. Thus, learning dictionary skills is not developmental beyond this level.

6. A reader whose rate of reading does not vary appreciably as he reads different types of materials is probably an inefficient reader in some of these situations.

7. While study skills are important, pupils who progress through the grades will master these skills through incidental learning.

Respond to the following problems:

A. Group A consists of 100 sixth graders who consistently read material in a social studies text at 260 words per minute. Group B consists of 100 sixth graders who consistently read this material at 150 words per minute. Develop a hypothetical description which compares and contrasts the "skills and reading behaviors" of the pupils in these two groups.

B. Based on the study of a typical basal reader series, develop a definitive statement as to how thoroughly these materials deal with the teaching of the reading-study skills.

BIBLIOGRAPHY

1. Artley, A. Sterl, "Effective Study—Its Nature and Nurture" in *Forging Ahead in Reading*, J. Allen Figurel, ed. Proceedings, International Reading Association 12, Part 1, pp. 10–19.
2. Brewer, A. Madison, "The Reading Study Skills," *Improving Reading Instruction*. Joint Proceedings of the Twenty-fifth Reading Conference and First Intensive Summer Workshop, Vol. I. The Pennsylvania State University, University Park, Pa., 1964, pp. 25–30.
3. Calder, Clarence R. and Zalatimo, Suleiman D., "Improving Children's Ability to Follow Directions," *The Reading Teacher* 24 (December 1970): 227–31.
4. Carner, Richard L., "Levels of Questioning," *Education* (May 1963): 546–50.
5. Cook, Jimmie E., "Teacher Survival Kit: The Dictionary," *Language Arts* 53 (October 1976): 755–57.
6. Daniels, Hazel, "Questioning—A Most Important Tool in the Teaching of Reading," *Education for Tomorrow—Reading*. Joint Proceedings of the Twenty-sixth Reading Conference and the Second Intensive Summer Workshop, Vol. II, The Pennsylvania State University, University Park, Pa., 1965, pp. 61–65.
7. Dawson, Mildred A., "Learning to Use Books Effectively," *Education* (September 1962): 20–22.
8. Dechant, Emerald V., *Improving the Teaching of Reading*, 2nd ed. Englewood Cliffs, N.J.: Prentice-Hall, 1970. Chapter 13.
9. Durrell, Donald D., "Development of Comprehension and Interpretation," *Reading in the Elementary School*. Forty-eighth Yearbook, Part II,

National Society for the Study of Education. Chicago: University of Chicago Press, 1949.

10. Eller, William, "Fundamentals of Critical Reading," in *The Reading Teachers' Reader*, Oscar S. Causey, ed. New York: The Ronald Press Co., 1958, pp. 30–34.

11. Forgan, Harry W. and Mangrum II, Charles T., *Teaching Content Area Reading Skills*. Columbus, O.: Charles E. Merrill Publishing Co., 1976. Chapter 7.

12. Heilman, Arthur, "Teaching the Study-Reading Skills at the Elementary Level," *Reading, Learning, and the Curriculum*. Proceedings of the Twelfth Annual Reading Conference, Lehigh University, Vol. 3, Bethlehem, Pa., 1963, pp. 41–46.

13. Howards, Melvin, "The Conditions for Critical Reading," *Fusing Reading Skills and Content*. Newark, Del.: International Reading Association, 1969, pp. 171–74.

14. Huus, Helen, "Antidote for Apathy—Acquiring Reading Skills for Social Studies," *Challenge and Experiment in Reading*. Proceedings, International Reading Association 7, 1962, pp. 81–88.

15. Lake, Mary Louise, "Improve the Dictionary's Image," *Elementary English* (March 1971): 363–65.

16. Lauck, Mary Ruth, "Every Teacher a Reading Teacher," *Reading, Learning, and the Curriculum*. Proceedings Twelfth Annual Reading Conference, Vol. 3, Lehigh University, Bethlehem, Pa., 1963, pp. 18–21.

17. McKee, Paul, *Reading—A Program of Instruction for the Elementary School*. Boston: Houghton Mifflin Co., 1966. Chapters 9 and 11.

18. Newcastle, Helen, "Children's Problems with Written Directions," *Reading Teacher* 28 (December 1974): 292–94.

19. Olson, Joanne P. and Dillner, Martha H., *Learning to Teach Reading in the Elementary School*. New York: Macmillan, 1976. Chapter 14.

20. Parke, Margaret B., "Reading for Specific Purposes," *Elementary English* (March 1964): 242–45.

21. Robinson, Helen M. and Smith, Helen K., "Rate Problems in the Reading Clinic," *Reading Teacher* (May 1962): 421–26.

22. Scabo, Robert J., "The Study Skills Scene," *Reading World* 16 (October 1976): 56–57.

23. Shores, J. Harlan, "Dimensions of Reading Speed and Comprehension," *Elementary English* (January 1968): 23–28.

24. Smith, Nila Banton, *Reading Instruction for Today's Children*. Englewood Cliffs, N.J.: Prentice-Hall, 1963. Chapters 10, 11, 23, and 24.

25. Snoddy, James E. and Shores, J. Harlan, "Teaching the Research Study Skills," in *Reading and Realism*, J. Allen Figurel, ed. Proceedings, International Reading Association 13, Part 1, 1969, pp. 681–88.

26. Thomas, Ellen Lamar and Robinson, H. Alan, *Improving Reading in Every Class*. Boston: Allyn and Bacon, 1972.

27. Walpole, Hugh R., "Promoting Development in Interpreting What Is Read in the Middle and Upper Grades," Supplementary Educational Monographs, University of Chicago. Chicago: University of Chicago Press, No. 61, pp. 162–67.

28. Wardeberg, Helen L., "Do We Apply What We Know about Comprehension?" in (Con-Challenger) *Current Issues in Reading*, Nila Banton Smith, ed. Proceedings, International Reading Association 13, Part 2, 1969, pp. 85–96.

29. Whipple, Gertrude, "Essential Types of Reading in the Content Fields," *Improvement of Reading through Classroom Practice*. Proceedings, International Reading Association 9, 1964, pp. 31–33.

30. Zintz, Miles V., *The Reading Process, the Teacher and the Learner*, 2nd ed. Dubuque, Iowa: William C. Brown Co., 1975. Chapter 12.

The Intermediate Grades—Problems and Challenges

The intermediate grades constitute one of the crucial instructional periods in the child's education. The curriculum for this period has developed out of a series of adult concepts and theories as to what children *should* be learning. Theory, however, often does not take into account all aspects of the learning situation. As a result some goals and classroom practices of the school fit children as we wish them to be, rather than as they actually are.

The intermediate grades coincide with a period in child development during which learning should be a natural, pleasurable experience. Unfortunately this highly desirable outcome is not achieved by the large majority of pupils in these grades. It is true that children will have acquired enough reading ability and related language tools to permit them to read on many topics and to develop background in some areas of interest. It is reasonable to expect them to be able to move at a more accelerated pace than they did in the primary grades.

However, the school and the culture which supports it seem somewhat impatient with learners at this stage of their development. This is exemplified by two facts. First, the curricular materials are often beyond the present reading ability of many pupils. Second, there is a diminished emphasis upon teaching the language tools which are needed for "mining" all subjects, and an air of urgency about having pupils accumulate facts in various subject areas.

The school has become a party to the utilitarian delusion that you can move children along the road to becoming scientists and mathematicians before they have acquired mastery of the language tools which are essential in these and all other academic areas. It is paradoxical that *reading instruction* in the intermediate grades suffers because of our inordinate respect for knowledge. It will be alleged that reading skills are also respected, yet no provision is made for assuring that pupils will have developed reading ability commensurate with the demands of the various content curriculums (1, 6).

Goals of Intermediate-Level Instruction

In addition to working with the skills introduced in the primary grades, the intermediate-level teacher must provide guidance in a large number of even more complicated reading tasks. The application of skills previously taught also becomes more complex. For instance, visual discrimination taught in beginning reading involves perception of structural differences between whole word symbols. In grade four, the child must perceive minute differences within words in order to use a dictionary. Also, getting meaning from context was relatively simple in beginning reading since the connotation of an unknown sight word was undoubtedly in the child's meaning vocabulary. In addition, the unknown sight word was probably the only new word on the page. In the intermediate grades a paragraph in a social science text may contain a number of new and difficult concepts as well as several unknown sight words.

The following objectives, while perhaps not including every facet of instruction, do provide a fairly representative picture of the breadth of the reading program in the intermediate grades.

1. Individual evaluation should take place to determine the capacity of students and the present level of achievement in all facets of reading including
   a. sight-word vocabulary
   b. word-attack skills
   c. level of silent reading
   d. meaning vocabulary and concepts
   e. ability to profit from listening situations including oral directions
   f. oral reading skills
   g. facility in finding information, use of reference materials
   h. work habits and attitudes
   i. rate at which curricular materials can be read
2. Following diagnosis, the teacher should devise a flexible reading program to take care of individual differences and needs revealed in the initial diagnosis.
3. Reading instruction must be deliberate and systematic. Inestimable damage to children can result from the philosophy that "children learn to read in the primary grades and read to learn at the intermediate level." They must do both at each level.
4. In addition to specific reading instruction per se, instruction must also be incorporated with the teaching of all subject matter. Children must be *taught to read* science, mathematics, health, and social science materials. It is not intended that reading instruction be seen or treated as dichotomous, but rather that items 3 and 4 be complementary parts of a total program.
5. The child should be helped to expand her stock of concepts. This is essential in all content areas.
6. Practice should be provided in various types of functional reading —in newspapers, magazines, and books—to supplement basic texts in subject areas.
7. Guidance should be supplied in reading for recreation, pleasure, and personal growth.
8. The child's reading interest should be widened to build a sound foundation for life-long personal reading activities.
9. Appreciation should be developed for good literature, poetry, and drama.
10. A wide selection of materials should be made available in all fields —science, literature, biography, current events, social studies, and the like.

11. A program should be devised for guiding the growth of intellectually gifted children.

12. Children should be helped to increase the rate at which they can comprehend printed word symbols in combination. This skill becomes increasingly important at this instructional level since the curriculum materials in the various content areas make ever-widening demands on readers.

13. Steps should be taken to improve critical reading skills such as:
    a. coping with figurative or picturesque language
    b. drawing inferences
    c. classifying ideas and selecting those that are germane to the reader's purpose
    d. evaluating ideas and arriving at the author's purpose or intent
    e. detecting bias and differentiating between fact and opinion

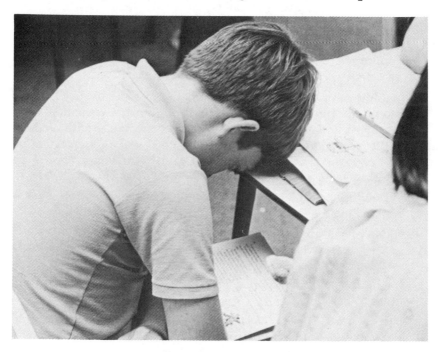

Be a national resource — become a
book addict.

14. The following reading-study skills should be developed and extended:
    a. using books effectively—making maximum use of the index, table of contents, and appendix

b. acquiring facility in the use of a dictionary
c. using reference books effectively
d. understanding graphs, maps, charts, and tables
e. using library resources, card catalogue, and periodical indexes
f. taking notes and outlining materials for a given purpose

15. Diagnosis should be continuous and on-going throughout each instructional year. An initial diagnosis serves only for initial procedures.

Instructional Problems at the Intermediate Level

The intermediate grades present a formidable challenge to the teacher of reading. The pitfalls are as numerous and as serious as those found at any instructional level. Academic failures and loss of interest in school occur because of certain instructional practices which actually inhibit rather than enhance pupil growth. The following major barriers to good instruction are discussed in this chapter.

1. A change of emphasis from *learning to read* to *reading to learn*.
2. Failure to deal with variability among pupils in regard to mastery of reading skills.
3. Diminished emphasis on systematic teaching of reading skills.
4. Inadequate integration of reading instruction with the teaching of content subjects.

A Transition Period

Teachers agree that ideally the process of learning to read progresses smoothly without perceptible breaks through a series of grade levels. There are certain factors in the total school framework, however, which cause many teachers to feel that an abrupt transition occurs between third and fourth grades. The end of the third grade and the beginning of the fourth is often designated as the period of "independent reading." There is evidence in classroom behaviors that some teachers do succumb to the philosophy that the intermediate grades should be characterized by a shift in emphasis from "learning to read" to "reading to learn" in the various subject-matter areas. The use of a number of nonintegrated textbooks in various content areas tends to substantiate the idea that this is a transitional period.

These factors form the basis for the generalization that reading skills are taught in the primary grades and applied in the intermediate and later grades. A further generalization is that since reading skills are taught in the primary grade, children who have been through these grades have mastered the skills. It is true that once pupils reach the intermediate level they are expected to do more reading, grade by grade, while less time is devoted to the actual process of learning to read. A study of the relationship between reading ability and a language-factor intelligence test at all grade levels indicated, however, that the correlation between these measures was lowest at grade four. The authors posited a "fourth grade hump in reading" which may be accounted for by the increased difficulty of concepts, style of writing, and specialized vocabulary found in reading materials at this level. A second hypothesis was that this finding might reflect a decline in the systematic teaching of reading at the fourth-grade level (17).

Every instructional level in the school presents its own unique challenges to teachers. Undoubtedly it is not intentional that the intermediate grades constitute a break in the continuity of instruction in the elementary school. Nevertheless, the emphasis on separate textbooks in the various subject areas is one of the chief sources of instructional problems. These books call for a fairly high level of independent reading ability and special facility in a number of reading-study skills such as the ability to use the dictionary, reference materials, graphs, charts, and tables.

These curricular materials confront the reader with an ever-increasing number of unknown and relatively difficult concepts (12). In addition, much more complex sentence structure and a variety of organizational patterns are found which frustrate many pupils. It is necessary to know many new and more difficult connotations for words met previously and to understand a large number of idiomatic and figurative expressions. The amount of reading which is required is suddenly increased, and pupils must develop the ability to read and comprehend at a more rapid rate. They must also develop flexibility in their reading to be able to adjust rate to both difficulty level and purpose. Instructional procedures for coping with these and other problems are discussed in the remainder of this chapter.

Coping with Variability among Pupils

Individual differences in reading ability tend to increase with reading instruction. A given group of pupils will show greater individual differences at the end of four years of schooling than they did at the end of the first year. Good teaching aims at moving every child along at her maximum rate. The gifted child will move further in a given period of time than will the average child. Thus, the better the teaching, the greater will be the differences between children's achievement. Although different facets of the reading program receive varying degrees of emphasis at different grade levels, in the intermediate grades the emphasis almost has to be on what the individual child needs regardless of what is found in the curriculum guide.

Basal materials continue to be used extensively at the intermediate level in many schools. Recent editions of these materials contain a much wider variety of content than did former editions. Nevertheless, the intelligent use of basals becomes more difficult at this level, primarily because of the wide range of pupils' needs and achievement levels. Faced with this diversity of reading ability, teachers cannot rely on a single grade-level text. Obviously, such material will be appropriate only for those children who are progressing at approximately the rate that matches the pace built into the material.

Importance of Diagnosis

Diagnosis is essential to a successful reading program at the intermediate level. Principles of teaching reading do not vary with grade level or with the materials being used. The variability of pupils in the intermediate grades makes a number of principles, discussed previously, particularly appropriate to this period: (1) no child should be expected to deal with materials she cannot read; (2) instruction must be at the learner's present level; (3) a thorough diagnosis will single out the pupils needing special instruction and indicate the skills in which the student is deficient; (4) once weaknesses are discovered, instruction must be fitted to individual needs.

An illustration of the importance of following sound principles of instruction is provided by the pupil who has failed to master phonic analysis skills. Experienced teachers know how unlikely it is that she will simply outgrow her inadequacy. The fact that the child has come this far without developing insights and techniques for overcoming her problem is in itself evidence that she is not likely to do so in the absence of skillful guidance and teaching. If a child has not developed the ability to hear the differences between the first syllables of words such as *dim*ple, *demo*nstrate, *dum*found, *domi*noes, *dam*sel; or *mar*ble, *mor*tal, *mur*mur, *mer*cy, *mira*cle, it is useless to attempt to teach her a number of rules regarding short vowels, long vowels, or vowels followed by varying numbers of consonants. The child must be taught to make auditory discriminations, and the fact that this is ordinarily taught in first grade does not alter the fact that in this case it will have to be done now. Until the inability to discriminate between speech sounds is overcome, the student can make little real progress in gaining independence in sounding. The principle of going back to where the child is applies to every learning step in phonic analysis, such as learning initial consonant sounds, learning substitution of initial sounds, recognizing blends, distinguishing between long and short vowel sounds, and understanding syllabication.

Standardized tests and teacher-made informal reading tests appropriate for all of the elementary grades have been discussed in detail in Chapter 10. The reader may wish to refer to this discussion found on pages 328–53. A commendable practice in the intermediate grades is the use of teacher-prepared comprehension questions over the various subject materials covered. Such tests can serve two purposes. They are diagnostic from the teacher's standpoint, and they can provide excellent guidance for the reader. To devise tests which serve both these purposes is difficult and time-consuming. As a result, many attempts at preparing such tests tend to isolate facts and details. In this connection, it should be remembered that the pupil at the intermediate level needs practice in evaluating ideas, seeing relationships, and drawing inferences.

Grouping of pupils for instructional purposes is essential in the intermediate grades. The great variety of reading materials available make possible a number of grouping practices which can be used effectively. Highly structured groups become less practical in the intermediate grades, yet all the virtues of grouping can be achieved if a variety of tasks at varying levels of difficulty are devised.

While the teacher works with a group of pupils who need review on word-attack skills, more advanced readers can be reading independently from supplementary sources. This reading can be influential in extending reading horizons and developing new reading interests. During some reading periods the teacher can work with the advanced group stressing appreciation or critical analysis of a poem or story while the skills group works independently on teacher-made or workbook skill-building exercises. At other times the teacher may not work with any particular group but will give individual help. There will be some situations where instruction can involve the entire class: for example, when giving instruction in the use of the dictionary, in group planning of a unit, in word–meaning sessions, when reading to the group, or when giving instruction in how to find materials. These instances of class-wide instruction would undoubtedly be followed by grouping techniques based on pupils' present achievement and individual needs.

While a majority of the pupils in a social science class may profitably use the assigned textbook, there are numerous other materials available at all levels of difficulty. Some of these lend themselves to use by the entire class; other materials and tasks will be more appropriate for either accelerated or impaired readers.

1. A film may be shown to the entire class.
2. Pictures which illustrate a particular concept appropriate to the topic can be gathered and placed on the bulletin board. Perhaps this project can be carried out by some of the less competent readers.
3. A special vocabulary lesson can be worked out using new terms children are likely to meet in their reading.
4. Each child can also make her own "new word list" which grows out of her reading on the topic.
5. Newspaper and magazine articles may be read by some pupils in the class.
6. Models, charts, or other illustrations which clarify some facet of the project may be prepared and displayed. With some guidance from the teacher, this task may be made quite appealing to poorer readers.
7. Better readers may report to the class on material found in reference or other books.

The Intellectually Capable

The problem of arousing and maintaining interest in reading is not confined to the below average reader. The excellent student also faces certain educational hazards in our schools. Since we teach great masses of children in large groups by textbook methods, it is almost inescapable that the more facile readers will not always be stimulated by our standardized methods and materials. The intermediate grades can become a very critical period for gifted students as far as maintaining interest in reading is concerned. The challenge of the intellectually able student is present at all grade levels but becomes more pronounced at the intermediate level because the child's abilities and interests are often beyond the standard curricular materials. When bright pupils are expected to "adjust" to this condition, they often become satisfied simply to get by or, worse, to become uncritical readers. They may plod through required reading which demands no mental exercise on their part.

It is true that there are marked differences in reading achievement and needs among pupils who are classed as intellectually capable. Some of this group will need instruction in the fundamental skills of reading. Their ability to deal with concepts may be far in advance of their reading level. A larger group of the extremely capable will be advanced both in the mechanical skills and in the ability to deal with concepts. For these pupils, graded materials at their grade placement level will be mastered without as much repetition and guidance as is characteristically given to the class. The problem will not be alleviated by having these children do more work at this level, i.e., simply reading other textbooks. This solution will not extend the talented, who will acquire little additional information by spending time with other texts.

While stating that every child should be educated to her maximum ability to profit from instruction, our schools have been relatively unsuccessful in achieving this goal with the intellectually capable. Regardless of high ideals, our mass educational structure has in many cases led us to gear instruction to the "golden" mean. This is not to be construed as an expression of disaffection for universal free education, but rather as a recognition of the need to effect a solution for one of its obvious shortcomings. If pupils are helped to develop study skills which lead to independence in reading and are provided easy access to interesting supplementary reading materials, the school has at least fulfilled its obvious obligations. However, there are many other instructional responsibilities that should be fulfilled for all children but which are particularly acute in the case of the intellectually capable.

The following procedures have been particularly successful in motivating the more able students.

1. If the school has a central library, pupils should be allowed to visit it whenever the need arises and not be restricted to specified library periods.

2. Pupils should be given systematic instruction in the use of library resources such as encyclopedias, *Readers Guide to Periodical Literature,* bulletins, newspapers, and current magazines.

3. Time should be provided for independent reading, and the reading done at such times should always be purposeful. The gifted child, or any child, should never be kept occupied with busy work.

A book in the hand is worth three
on the shelf.

4. As a child develops interest in a particular topic or field, she should be kept supplied with challenging materials which will extend her growth. She should be praised for all serious effort and accomplishment.

5. Children should be encouraged to make plans and carry them out independently after the initial planning with the teacher.

6. The teacher can afford to use more analysis of stories or literature with the more capable pupils. This might take place on an individual or small-group basis.

7. Those pupils capable of such work should be encouraged to participate in special creative activities such as:
   a. writing biographies of famous persons from material they have gathered from many sources.
   b. describing historical events based on wide reading about these happenings.
   c. writing plays or dialogue involving historical personages.
   d. making "resource maps" in social studies.
   e. giving oral reports based on outside reading which will be a contribution to the knowledge of the group (23).

8. Children should be encouraged to gather resource materials on a topic on which the class is working. These would include pictures, current magazines, bulletins, books which deal with any facet of

the topic, and films. Such materials could be used in developing an "interest corner."

9. Pupils should be given access to professional recordings of plays, poems, or prose. Such materials, as well as films and books, may be borrowed from libraries, curriculum centers, or the local state department of education depository.

10. Children should be encouraged to do research on topics which help them see the social forces which shape their society. This type of activity will make "learning for responsible leadership" more than an empty phrase.

The Impaired Reader

As noted earlier, the intermediate grades are characterized by an increased emphasis on various content areas. Those children with inadequate reading skills cannot function successfully in this educational environment. They are placed in the untenable position of being expected to read materials which they are incapable of reading. For these children, the systematic teaching of reading is an absolute necessity, yet their need is often ignored in the rush to "cover" textbooks in structured content areas.

It is an educational paradox that, as the number of impaired readers in our schools increased, the school tended to rely more and more on reading. Textbooks became more widely used, and the basic curricular materials became more rigid and inflexible. As a result of this trend, children who cannot read adequately now constitute the schools' greatest problem. This problem has been accentuated recently as the plight of the "culturally different" child is acknowledged by the society and the school. The real meaning behind the "Right to Read" slogan is a reaffirmation of the principle that children must be taught *how* to read if the school expects them *to* read.

There is also a tacit recognition of the fact that the time is past when mere tinkering with the educational system will be accepted as a satisfactory response. Children cannot be held indefinitely as hostages. Thus, the school is faced with an identity crisis. It must decide whether it is to be an educational or custodial institution.

The higher illiteracy. Chase (2) suggests that there are two kinds of illiteracy that threaten civilization. One is nonreading, or failure to crack the first code. The second he calls the "higher illiteracy," wherein people who can read are incapable of thinking and feeling while they read. The following discussion identifies some of the areas in which the school must provide guidance if children are to become critical readers.

Perhaps we can gain some insights into why children lose interest in reading if we study the answers that some fifth and sixth graders gave to the question *"What is reading?"* Daniels, in compiling the children's responses, noted that "many show signs of insight and creative thinking; others lack the real understanding of what the printed page is" (3). The examples cited here are illustrative of the latter:

> Children's Answers To: "What Is Reading?"
>
> "Reading is a subject that contains a group of words that you read such as math, social studies and English."
>
> "Putting letters together to make a word."
>
> "Reading is a subject that most people like. Reading is good for you if you don't read too long."
>
> "Reading is a lot of words that are all mixed up together to make neat letters and meaningful words. It is something that you pronounce with your tongue, lips, and teeth."
>
> Reading is looking at a book or paper and sounding out the letters and by doing that you are making words. Making those words as you go along is what is called reading."
>
> "Reading is a subject in which you have a Book which has stories which you read. You also have a workbook which has something about the story which you read in the textbook. Also in your workbook you learn the vowel sounds."

These definitions of reading suggest that one of the major issues in reading instruction is whether we should continue doing what we have been doing, or whether we should attempt some other approaches to harnessing the child's ego to the reading task.

Need for Systematic Reading Instruction

In order to assure that children continue to develop skills that are commensurate with the reading tasks they are asked to perform in the intermediate grades, systematic instruction must be continued. Hopefully, some reading instruction will be incorporated with the teaching of all subject matter courses; however, such teaching is not likely to meet the needs of those children who are weak in a number of reading skills.

Systematic instruction does not imply that all pupils will be receiving the same instruction. This would be justifiable only if all pupils in a given class were at the same developmental level. Since this is never the case, instruction must be differentiated if it is to be relevant. While meaningful differentiation of instruction is difficult to achieve it is not impossible.

The statement of *how* we might solve the reading problem in our schools makes the task seem deceivingly simple. The solution would be, "we must systematically teach reading more effectively and more extensively than is our present practice." Achieving this goal, up to the present at least, has escaped us. No teacher or educational administrator at any educational level argues against the importance of reading ability; however, many have not as yet become personally involved in helping to devise programs and guidance in the development of reading skills in all areas of the curriculum (20).

Learning to Read is a Long-Term Developmental Process

The structure of American education is embedded in, and influenced by, the grade-level system. The development of curricular materials for use in all grades is to some extent patterned on growth gradients in all subject areas. An underlying premise of the graded system is that students finishing a given grade have mastered the language skills and concepts that will prepare them for the developmental tasks of the next grade.

The theory is sound, but in actual practice a large number of students in the intermediate grades have not mastered reading skills *commensurate with the tasks they will be asked to perform in these grades.* Another group of students may be fairly close to the expected growth level, but as months and years go by, they fail to *advance* in reading ability at a pace equal to the reading demands placed upon them.

The recognition of a problem is the first step in arriving at a solution. Unfortunately, the problem under consideration is so large and so complex that little progress has been made in alleviating it. Since there are no easy solutions, educators at various levels (elementary, junior high, secondary, and teacher training institutions) all live in the hope that some group other than themselves will tackle the problem and evolve a solution.

Undoubtedly, one of the causes of the problem is the failure of the teacher to understand the nature of the reading process. The purpose here is to discuss the developmental nature of reading. In recent years the statement, "Reading is a developmental process," has been repeated so often that it now sounds almost like a cliché. This concept deserves more respect and attention than it has received "Reading ability is a developmental process" means that the very complicated process of learning to read is not mastered at any particular time such as age ten or twelve. Nor can it be assumed that the ultimate ability to read critically is achieved at any particular point on the educational continuum.

Thus, an adequate reader at grade three may be considerably less efficient at grade four and be in serious trouble by grade six. The statement implies recognition that the nature of human learning and the nature of the reading task precludes the possibility of mastering the reading process by a given chronological age or a designated number of years of formal schooling. The developmental aspect of various reading skills is discussed in the following section.

Illustrations of Developmental Skills

Reading is an integrated total response which is made up of a very large number of separate skills, abilities, memory patterns, and the like. Any of the dozens of reading skills could serve as an example of how growth must take place at higher levels of efficiency. Without attempting to determine how many separate skills go into reading, we can isolate a few and illustrate how each is developmental in nature.

Acquisition of sight vocabulary. The development of a sight-word vocabulary is probably one of the more obvious examples of what is implied by the term *developmental process.* Instant recognition of words is a basic skill which is a prerequisite for reading at any level. Although it is true that mere recognition of words is not reading, it must be remembered that the absence of this ability precludes reading. For example, the individual who has no sight-recognition vocabulary is not a reader. One who fails to recognize as few as 5 percent of the words in a passage is handicapped; one who is stopped on 10 percent is a seriously impaired reader. For these people, frustration is inevitable.

Along with expanding her sight vocabulary, the child will of course be using phonics and related word-attack skills. The point of the discussion is that the normal reader is constantly learning to instantly recognize new words. She may resort to letter-sound analysis the first few times she meets a new word. However, as she meets the same word time after time, she should rely less and less on analysis. When a reader fails to add words to her sight vocabulary, she is not maintaining a "normal learning pattern." The following lines of words represent visual patterns of increasing difficulty which must be mastered as children move upward through the grades:

> an and hand sand band land baker barber barker
> banker barter medal metal meddle mental medical
> elegant element elephant elegance eloquence general
> generous generally genesis generalize national natural
> nationally naturally nationality

As an increasing number of new words are met, certain irregular spellings occur more frequently (combinations: *que, ph, igh, wr, mb, ch = k or s, psy, kn,* etc.). Many words containing these patterns are learned as sight words. Children will also meet many sight words which have come to English from other languages: *debris, corps, reign, cache, rouge, yacht, sphinx, chassis, suave, chaos.*

Word-attack skills. Applying word-attack skills is developmental in nature, at least up to the point where they are utilized automatically. Experience indicates that lack of ability in phonic analysis is a major stumbling block for many pupils in the middle and upper grades. Word attack skills must be both reviewed and extended at this level. The child who has experienced little difficulty with simple compound words such as *sidewalk, anyhow, somewhere* and *barnyard* may need drill and guidance in dealing with words like *floodgate, homespun, praiseworthy, foreshadow,* and *supernatural.*

Children who have applied letter-sound relationships in solving shorter words often experience difficulty with multisyllabic words. Some children develop the habit of "giving up" on lengthy words because they lack skill in breaking these words into syllables. They need guided practice in order to gain the confidence needed to solve words such as *overproduction, reenforcement, unworthiness, misrepresentation,* and the like.

Children also need to develop an ear for accent within longer words. This is most logically taught along with dictionary usage. Exercises can be developed which stress accent-shift in longer words (examples: confírm—confirmátion; úniverse—univérsal; elígible—eligibílity).

Other developmental skills. The developmental nature of many other reading skills is self-evident. Examples would include locating information, use of library resources, improving rate of reading, expanding meaning vocabulary, and critical reading. A final illustration consists of six sentences each taken from a basal reader at successive grade levels. This material reflects the need for growth on the part of the reader in regard to <u>sight words</u>, <u>sentence patterns</u>, <u>profiting from punctuation</u>, <u>using proper intonation</u>, <u>drawing inferences</u>, as well as other skills.

Grade 1   "I will run and bring some water."
Grade 2   "I know where the field mouse lives down by the brook."
Grade 3   "The next night, when his father got home, Bob said, "I read that book about the other Bob.""
Grade 4   "Sir," said the duck, who was trying to recover his dignity while hopping around on one foot—not an easy thing to do, "Sir, I am minding my own business and I suggest that you do the same."
Grade 5   The missile range was known as Station One, and when the men talked over the radio from there they would say, "This is Station One," or just, "This is One."
Grade 6   "We can be sure that the Trojans, on hearing this, will not risk bringing her wrath down upon themselves by destroying our offering."*

An Unresolved Problem— Integrating Reading Instruction with Subject Matter

The idea that various facets of reading must be taught concurrently with subject matter is constantly verbalized by teachers and educators. Even in schools which are departmentalized with one teacher responsible for social science, another for science, and so forth, a respect for the integration of reading and the content subjects emerges in the slogan "every teacher a teacher of reading." The nature of the reading materials and the great difference between pupils' instructional needs make it logical and even mandatory that some reading instruction be related to the social sciences, science, literature, arithmetic, and other subject areas.

It is unfortunate when the school views the curriculum as a series of separate tasks only one of which involves reading instruction. It is occasionally suggested that the duty of the school is to teach children to read as quickly as possible so that they can cope with other areas of the curriculum. In one sense, no one can disagree with this position, but in this setting, reading can easily become thought of as an assortment of mechanical skills which the reader applies to subject matter. Here we have more than a hint of compartmentalization, and this atti-

* David H. Russell et al., *The Ginn Readers* (Boston: Ginn and Co., 1961).

tude is easily transferred to pupils who think they "read" reading one hour, "do" arithmetic another, and "study" social science, health, or science at other times.

Textbooks and Heavy Concept Load

Because of the rigid control of vocabulary in beginning reading materials, teachers frequently have the problem of arousing and maintaining interest in these materials. By the time the intermediate level is reached, the teacher's problem has traveled full circle. Difficult words and concepts are introduced in the content textbooks in such profusion that many pupils are frustrated and often lost.

Meaningful reading at the intermediate level depends on the acquisition and continual extension of concepts. Here, pupils are confronted with more difficulties per reading unit than they met in their primary reading. One of the major reading problems is coping with the gap which tends to develop between the child's store of meanings and the demands made by the curricular materials she is expected to read.

Hildreth (9) writes, "The middle-grade pupil can now expect to meet new words he has never seen before in the proportion of about 1 in 10, even in material prepared for his age group and a still larger proportion of strange words in difficult texts." The problem of meaningful reading is complicated by the fact that in the intermediate grades, as well as at higher levels, there are found a great number of idiomatic expressions, abstract terms, figurative terms, and new connotations for words met earlier. In the primary grades, even though the occurrence of these is less frequent, teachers are alerted to them through the teaching manuals accompanying the basal reader series used. Also, deliberate instruction is provided in the workbooks which supplement the reader series. With the shift to separate textbooks in the content areas, there tends to be less emphasis on helping pupils with meaning difficulties precisely at the point where help is most needed. Examples of difficult concepts from fourth- and fifth-grade geography, science, and arithmetic books are cited below. Teachers found that many pupils did not understand these concepts even after the material had been assigned and covered in class.

> Many years and great sums of money will be needed to *harness the river.*
> It (blood) is carried through other *branching tubes* called veins.
> When you are frightened, your *pupils get bigger.*
> *Check* by doing each example again.
> You bite and chew your food with the *crowns of your teeth.*
> *Ornithologists* have examined the crops of many birds to find out what kind of food they eat.

Most of the *infections* and *contagious* diseases are caused by bacteria.

Birds help to keep the *balance of nature.*

We can use a *ruler* to subtract fractions.

Cloud formations make what is called a *mackerel sky.*

The native city is *backward* and ugly.

The Mediterranean became a *melting pot* for surrounding civilization.

The people who lived in *fixed settlements* made far greater progress than the Nomads.

Now, as in ancient times, the Mediterranean is a great *connecting* highway.

There is plenty of *home-grown wool.*

Business and industry were *paralyzed.*

Science has *unlocked the greatest force in nature.*

China was not entirely *sealed off* from her neighbors.

A *belt of irrigated land* stretches almost all the way along the coast.

In time, *the front of Europe shifted* from the Mediterranean Coast to the Atlantic Coast.

As the *globe* shows, Europe and Asia really form one *land mass.*

The *shrinking world* and new inventions have made this possible.

If some day the river is controlled it will be a great *life-saver* instead of a *life-destroyer.*

Gradually the continent was opened up. Another "jewel" had *been added to the British crown.*

The top of the world will have a new meaning in the future.

Almost every farmer grows some *cash crop* besides food for his family.

Britain was busy for many years in getting *stepping stones* along the sea-ways.

It is a matter of record that many middle-school students do not read and assimilate subject-matter material with the ease and to the degree that the schools apparently expect. In seeking an explanation for this, certain logical answers are a threat to the school. To admit that these students do not have the language facility and reading ability that is required to handle this material could be an indictment of the school as much as it is of the students. The school must certify that sixth grades are populated by sixth graders and that the curricular materials selected by the schools are sixth-grade materials.

Another hypothesis which may have gained more acceptance than is warranted is that although students have been taught to read, each subject area demands special reading abilities. These are thought to be associated primarily with a given content area. Further, the materials in each subject area are saturated with special vocabulary, all of which is new to the student. A brief discussion of this point of view follows.

The examples of language, abstracted from textbooks cited above, do point out the difficulty of the materials. However, much of the difficulty stems from "general concept load" and language usage which cuts across all subject materials. With the exception of a few terms such as *ornithologists, cash crop, mackerel sky, contagious,* the material italicized in each sentence could have appeared in any number of reading situations.

Different Skills for Different Subjects?

Much of the literature on teaching reading in the content areas has emphasized that different content subjects (social studies, science, math, health, history) require a different set of reading skills. This is one of the most widely repeated bits of conventional wisdom to be found in literature on reading. In journal articles, textbooks, and curriculum guides, one reads that "The learning needs to utilize reading abilities unique to each of the content areas" . . . "Evidence indicates that certain specific skills are required for reading in different curriculum areas and for different purposes" (Evidence usually consists of

Cracking the library code gives you
access to the vault, where you can
pick your own treasure.

other statements to this effect). "It seems reasonable to expect that the reading skills required for science material will differ from those required for materials of history, mathematics, or other content areas, each of which requires its peculiar combination of abilities"(25).

This concept has been repeated until we have become conditioned to believe it. Perhaps it should be reexamined because it may be accurate to only a small degree. It is undoubtedly true that there are a few special skills such as interpreting maps, graphs, charts, formulas, mathematical symbols, and the like, that can be matched with a specific content area. However, these are quite minor when evaluated in light of the total reading expected in these areas.

It is, of course, possible to associate particular skills with a given content area, and such associations will appear to have surface validity. For example, each of the following skills have been identified with *one* of the content areas science, mathematics, social studies, or English.

adjust rate to purpose	read for main ideas
attitude of the reader	noting and weighing details
drawing conclusions	using contextual clues
word attack skills	organizing ideas
getting main ideas	discriminating between
locating information	relevant and irrelevant
specialized vocabulary	information

When this is done, it is sometimes not readily apparent that these same skills are equally applicable to ALL of the other areas also. The inability to apply these skills in any subject area would handicap the reader. While classification skills are needed in the reading of science material, they are also essential in reading social science and mathematics. Ability to cope with precise, compact writing may be associated with mathematics, but it cannot be disassociated from the reading of history or literature. This can be illustrated with hundreds of examples ranging from poetry to Lincoln's Second Inaugural Address or William Faulkner's acceptance speech upon receipt of the Nobel Prize for Literature. Drawing inferences cannot be thought of as belonging exclusively to one area of the curriculum. A pupil may in the course of a day be asked to draw inferences as to what happens when a decimal point is inserted between digits in two-digit numbers; what effect mountains located between the sea and the plains have on rainfall on the plains; and what happens to the circumference of a balloon placed in the freezer compartment of a refrigerator.

A factor which may lead to the hypothesis that certain essential skills of reading are more appropriate to one content area than another is that many pupils can read successfully from basal readers and yet do poorly in subject areas. The reasons for this have been discussed previously. The basal readers present a controlled vocabulary; teachers are alerted to new words and difficult concepts found in each lesson, and systematic instruction is provided to help the pupil over these potential difficulties. Since all reading skills are developmental, the real issue may well be the difficulty level of the material in subject-area textbooks. These materials call for a more extensive development of essential reading skills rather than a different configuration of skills for each content area. If students cannot read a given textbook, either the school selected material too difficult, or it failed to provide the students with the overall reading-language tool that they need for digging the content.

"Specialized Vocabulary" Emphasis

There is a second bit of conventional wisdom (which, again, has some basis in fact), but which is frequently overemphasized. This is the belief that the major problem in teaching any content area is the specialized vocabulary of that subject. While this vocabulary can be a problem, it is only a small part of a larger problem. There is no question that a number of words and concepts closely associated with each content area should be taught. However, our main shortcoming in the past has not been a failure to recognize this need, but rather that there was tendency to overemphasize it. This resulted in drawing attention away from the fact that students' deficiencies in overall language and concept development was the real problem.

The reading of all content material depends on the reader's ability to process the *total* language stimulus. Students do poorly in content areas because their ability to manipulate language is not commensurate with the difficulty level of the material the school assigns. Further evidence that the problem is lack of language facility is the difficulty students experience when they attempt to write. Again, the problem is not "specialized vocabulary," but lack of mastery of the language process, the student's inability to express what they know, what they have experienced, and what they feel.

Since the problem is a paucity of concepts, overemphasizing specialized vocabulary can provide an incomplete map that does not fit the reading territory. Very few words have only one fixed meaning. The narrow meaning of a word met in one content textbook may be inappropriate the next five times the word is met in other settings.

If one starts with the words provided in the glossary of any content textbook and then adds any other content-related words that come to mind, the issue is brought into focus. This expanded list of words will constitute an infinitesimally small portion of the words that the student must deal with in reading that text. We must not let specialized vocabulary become the tree that obscures the forest. Teaching a special meaning for a few dozen, or a hundred words, in the absence of adequate reading-language skills will not solve the problem of reading in the content areas.

For example, in a science text the word *catalyst* was defined as "a substance that increases or decreases the speed of a chemical reaction without undergoing a permanent change in itself." It should be apparent that the reader needs a very extensive command of language in order to cope with this definition (substance, chemical reaction, undergoing, permanent). In addition, the reader must store other meanings for the term *catalyst* so that she can understand that a person, a thing, a characteristic, or an event can serve as a catalyst in human affairs. In newspapers, magazines, and other textbooks, the reader will find reference to certain catalysts which bring on a recession, an economic recovery, a life of crime, or success or failure in many endeavors.

A social studies text explained the term *relief* exclusively in relation to maps. "The difference in elevation between the high and low levels of land surface." Students, in order to read with meaning, also needed to know that relief is a political issue in the U. S.; that relief is what is sent to flood, hurricane, or earthquake victims; that Custer died because no military relief columns came in time. Relief is what students feel when the test is over or when the teacher is absent. Relief is a term used in printing, art, and architecture. No baseball team can make it without a corps of *relief* hurlers.

An *anvil* is more than the glossary definition of "a bone in the ear." The *ANVIL CHORUS* can fill both ears, as well as the auditorium. The "bone in the ear" will not help students understand Sandburg when he writes

Lay me on an *anvil*, oh, God.
Beat me and hammer me into a crowbar.
Let me pry loose old walls—
   and loosen old foundations.

Teaching specialized vocabulary in each of the content areas is a necessary part of teaching. But equally important is the expansion of concepts and other language skills. The language facility that children need in mining the content areas goes far beyond the special vocabulary found in the glossary. This brings us to the major challenge in reading instruction at the intermediate level.

Developing
and Expanding
Concepts

Some of the major problems met at the middle-school level have been identified and discussed earlier in the chapter. The school has gradually been allotting less time and energy to the teaching of reading-language skills, while at the same time assigning more and more material that has to be language processed. From the standpoint of *learning*, this has proved to be self-defeating. The textbooks we adopt may demand more language skill than the school has taught, but children *cannot* apply more skill than they have developed.

Language is the tool of the school and mastery of language serves as the basis for future learning. Children in the middle grades need experiences with reading and language that will help them expand their stock of concepts and develop the ability to crack the meaning code. Language competencies which must be taught include

1. The ability to decode small units of language, (proverbs, quotes, etc.), which pack meaning into the sentence.
2. The ability to reduce the uncertainties caused by words having the same pronunciation but different spellings and meanings.
3. Mastery of words often confused. Since the English language contains over a half million words, look alike and sound alike words pose a problem.
4. An understanding of how "new words" move into the language at a very fast rate.
5. A gradual mastery of words which pose problems in pronunciation and meaning. The fact that English has borrowed thousands of words from other languages has accentuated this problem.
6. Acquiring the meanings of a number of root words from other languages, particularly those which are used dozens of times in different English words (graph, logy, pseudo, dem, etc.).
7. Learning different meanings for the same word, understanding figurative language, differentiating between fact and opinion, etc.

Procedures for Expanding
Reading-Language Skills

The balance of the chapter presents a number of teaching exercises that can be used to help middle-school students expand concepts and reading skills. These are illustrative and can be modified and adapted in many ways. Each can be presented as a class activity. Later, as more materials are introduced, these can become activities housed in learning centers and used by individuals, pairs of students, teams, or smaller groups.

Working with Homonyms

Through the study of homonyms, children expand their ability to work with language. They develop concepts and learn both the visual patterns and meanings of these word pairs. The following exercises illustrate different tasks and exercise formats. Each can be adapted to fit different difficulty levels. There are many other ways in which material could be presented, these are simply illustrative.

A. Word-meaning study: Provide definitions of words which may present meaning difficulties or whose meanings may be confused.

> raise: to elevate, cause to rise
> raze: to demolish, overthrow, completely remove
> principle: a fundamental or basic truth, law, or point
> principal: the chief officer, as head of a school
> reign: to exercise authority, to govern, "the king's reign was 10 years"
> rein: a bridle to guide or control a horse
> stationary: fixed in place, not moving
> stationery: paper, and other items for writing
> coarse: common, rough, inferior quality, unrefined
> course: a course of study; a path such as a racecourse, golf course, etc.

B. "Make a Pair"

On each blank space write a homonym for the word shown.

reel _____		pale _____	
plain _____		night _____	
ate _____		hear _____	
made _____		blew _____	

C. Same as A except provide a cluebox which contains (in mixed order) the words the child will need to make a pair.

knew	would	steal	whole
some	weak	wrap	wait

week _____	steel _____
hole _____	new _____
rap _____	weight _____
sum _____	wood _____

D. "Use A Pair"

Use a different pair of the above homonyms to complete each sentence below. Sample: after a (*week*) in the hospital he felt very (*weak*).

1. The _____ group worked very hard digging the huge
   _____ .

2. It is better to diet than to just _____ for your
   _____ to go down.

3. The _____ bars were so heavy that the thieves decided
   not to _____ them.

4. Jim said, "I sort of _____ I would get a _____
   football for my birthday."

5. He did have _____ trouble with addition, often arriving
   at the wrong _____ .

E. "One Plus Won"

Write a pair of homonyms in the blank spaces to complete each sentence. One word is provided at the left. Sample: (One) John _____ only _____ prize at the carnival.

(through)   1. The catcher _____ the ball _____
              the infield and a runner scored.

(new)   2. Mary _____ the _____ coat was too
              expensive.

(there)   3. The twins said that _____ house is over
              _____ by the park.

(red)   4. Bill _____ the title, "The _____
              Baron Flies Again."

(plain)   5. The pilot decided to land the _____ on the
              smooth _____ beyond the river.

(pain)   6. He felt a sudden _____ as his arm broke the
              window _____ .

F. Can you write the homonyms which fit the following definitions?

Strong, heavy metal   take another's property
   s _____ ;   _____

Large body of water	to observe visually
_____ ;	_____
Breakable part of window	when something hurts
_____ ;	_____
Just above the hips	to squander
_____ ;	_____
A story or account of	dogs wag this
_____ ;	_____
Opposite of female	delivered by postman
_____ ;	_____
Two of anything	a fruit (odd shaped)
_____ ;	_____

G. Devise sentences which "sound right" but which contain the wrong word from a pair of homonyms. The child underlines this word and then writes the word that belongs in the sentences.

1. We eight our lunch together. _____
2. The old flower mill is closed down. _____
3. I do not believe in whiches or goblins. _____
4. The injured dear was easy pray for the wolves. _____ _____
5. Please weight for me after school. _____

H. Make the sentence correct by writing the two words in front of each sentence in the proper blank spaces.

bare
bear
  1. The _____ was standing in a _____ spot in the woods.

not
knot
  2. He did _____ know how to tie the _____.

their
there
  3. Over _____ on the hill stands _____ new home.

herd
heard
  4. The cowboys _____ the thundering _____ coming closer.

I. Complete the following sentences by writing a pair of homonyms in the blank spaces. If you are baffled by a sentence, go to the *clue box*. It contains *one* word that will fit in each sentence. (One word in the box will not be used)

1. It is no fun to _____ stung by a _____.
2. Mother said," _____ this junk into the _____."
3. When _____ these bills come _____ he asked?
4. Dave said, "I would have _____ you a present, but I didn't have a _____!"

5. The king was _____ out of office after holding the
_____ for 14 years.

```
                    ┌──────────────┐
                    │   Clue Box   │
        ┌───────────┴──────────────┴───────────┐
        │  cent   where   throne   hall   do   ring  │
        └────────────────────────────────────────┘
```

J. "Homonyms with Helpers!"

Each sentence below contains two blank spaces; complete the
sentence by writing homonyms that begin with the letter shown.

1. The wild b_____ in the zoo would b_____ his
fangs.
2. S_____ numbers when added equal the s_____
of ten.
3. Going without food for a w_____ will make a person
w_____.
4. The injury to his h_____ took several days to
h_____.
5. The L_____ Ranger was in the bank getting a
l_____.
6. H_____ in the park you can h_____ all kinds of
birds.
7. The coach said,"Don't b_____ like a baby if you get hit
by a b_____."
8. W_____ you please bring in some w_____ for
the fireplace?
9. She seemed to be in a d_____ for at least three
d_____ after winning the contest.
10. He took a p_____ to determine how many fishermen
use a bamboo p_____.

Homographs

Homographs represent another interesting group of English word
pairs. These are words which have identical spellings but which are
different in pronunciation and meaning. The differences in pronunciation may be either in accent (*pro'duce, pro duce'*) or in both accent
and syllabication (*re bel', reb'el*). Pronunciation and meaning clues are
not found in the words themselves, but rather in the "sentence context"
in which they are found. Thus, the same spelling may represent a noun,

verb, adjective, etc., and the pronunciation is determined by the word's *function* in a sentence. Most common homographs are learned by ear; that is, the word must "sound right" in the sentence context. Exercises employing various sentence formats may be used in helping children master and understand these words.

1. *In each sentence there is one italicized word. Write this word on the line following the sentence, showing how the word is broken into syllables and which syllable is accented.*

   Sample: The dentist said, "I will *extract*
   the tooth."   *ex tract′*

   a. "I *object*," said the lawyer.   _____
   b. The judge did not *convict* the man.   _____
   c. She opened the bottle of vanilla *extract*.   _____
   d. The store sells groceries, meats and *produce*.   _____
   e. A rope will *contract* when it is wet.   _____

2. *Rewrite each italicized word on the space provided. Break the word into syllables and show which syllable is accented.*

   Sample: That *record* was quite difficult to *record*.
                 rec′ ord   *re cord′*

   a. One does not *desert* a friend in the middle of the *desert*.

     _____   _____

   b. The teacher will *record* all grades in her *record* book.

     _____   _____

   c. What caused the *rebels* to *rebel?*

     _____   _____

   d. Did the sanitation workers *refuse* to collect the *refuse?*

     _____   _____

   e. The coach was *present* to *present* the awards.

     _____   _____

3. *Use the accent and syllabication clues that are shown, and write a sentence using the stimulus word.*

   pro′ duce _____
   ob ject′   _____
   con′ tract _____
   per mit′   _____
   con tent′   _____

4. *Write sentences using one syllable homographs such as the following list. Mark the vowel sound heard (either – or ⌣) to indicate the pronunciation of the word.*

wĭnd – wīnd   līve – lĭve   bāss – bǎss
lēad – lĕad   rēad – rĕad

5. *Present a word that has two meanings and pronunciations followed by a definition of one of its meanings. The student writes the proper word indicating syllabication and accent.*

Sample: desert: "to leave or abandon"   de'sert
rebel: "one who fights against authority"   _____
invalid: "not well, sick or disabled"   _____
conduct: "to lead, carry or transmit"   _____
moderate: "not extreme"   _____
content: "satisfied, happy"   _____

Words of Recent Origin

English is a living language, and living things grow and change. The changes that take place in a language are determined by its users and not as a result of previously adopted rules. It is likely that more new words were added to English in the past thirty years than in any previous century. Children should be invited to think about this phenomenon and discuss possible causes for it. An excellent way to develop insight is to prepare a list of recently coined words and then place them in categories.

The following are some newly coined words that were suggested by one class. Children had worked in small teams, relying both on their knowledge and on any and all materials avaliable in the classroom and library.

Astronaut, transistor, groovy, soul, uptight, laser beam, flowchart, radar, talking typewriter, heat shield, computer, thermofax, keypunch, dune buggy, teflon, megaton, formica, rap, right on, panasonic, Medicare, orlon, dragstrip, smog, seat belt, skybus, astrodome, heart transplant, yippie, lunacart, cassette, antibiotics, aerospace, polyester, telestar, snowmobile, maxi-mini-midi, and dozens of other words.

As a next step they decided to group words into categories and some of the first that came to mind were *slang, medicine, transportation* and *space exploration.* In the process they found that headings such as "science" or "technology" were too broad since these terms cut across every other heading. There was quite a list of trade names for products: *Thermofax, Formica, polyester, teflon,* etc. Words such as *lunacart, Medicare,* and *telestar* were analyzed and provided insights into the logic of coining new words. The study of slang terms proved interesting, particularly when an older *Dictionary of Slang* was studied. It became obvious that this is one of the most prolific areas for new words, but also that the mortality rate is very high.

Working on a unit devoted to *New Words in English* leads to an understanding of how language works and how it develops. An increased respect for the power, precision, and flexibility of language is usually an outcome. Motivation is high during such study, particularly among students who have become satiated on "reading skills instruction." A great number of reading and writing experiences can grow out of the study of newly coined words.

Confusion of Word Meanings

Some words which look very much alike are often confused in meaning. Wide reading, which insures meeting such words in many different contexts, is probably the most desirable method of expanding meanings. However, teacher-made exercises can also be useful and highly motivational. As a rule, children enjoy working with word meanings, particularly if the difficulty of the exercise material is geared to their needs. Below is an example of a teaching-testing exercise.

1. Some words which look very much alike are often confused as to *meaning*. Study the following words and then, in the sentences below, fill in the blanks with the proper word.

alter:	to change or modify	council:	a governing group
altar:	place used in worship	counsel:	to advise
medal:	a decoration awarded	affect:	to influence
	for service	effect:	a result produced
meddle:	to interfere		by a cause
cite:	to quote, or use as	carton:	a box or container
	illustration	cartoon:	a drawing, a
sight:	to see, act of seeing		caricature
site:	location		

meddle – medal: 1. It might be a good idea to give a _____ to people who never _____ in others' affairs.

alter – altar: 2. In over 500 years, no attempt had been made to _____ the _____.

carton – cartoon: 3. You will find a humorous _____ on every _____ of breakfast food.

sight – site: 4. He hoped to catch _____ of the _____ where the new club was to be built.

2. The meanings of the pairs of words which follow are not given above. Place the proper word in the blanks in each sentence. Use a dictionary if you are doubtful about the meaning of any word.

miner – minor:
1. Most states have laws which prohibit a _____ from working as a _____.

course – coarse:
2. The fairways of the golf _____ were covered with _____ grass.

dairy – diary:
3. During the day Bill worked in a _____, but each night he would write in his _____.

descend – decent:
4. We should try to find a _____ trail if we hope to _____ the mountain before dark.

precede – proceed:
cannon – canyon:
5. When an army is to p_____ through a c_____ surrounded by the enemy, it is the usual custom to have a barrage by c_____ p_____ the march.

Working with Malapropisms

In speaking and writing, children often reveal misconceptions by their choice of words. They might be interested in the fact that there are approximately 600,000 words in English. Since no one can learn the meanings of all of these words, it is to be expected that sometimes we will use one word when we mean to use another. Perhaps the children can be introduced to Mrs. Malaprop, a character in a play* who continuously used words which had meanings different from what she intended. Once she hired a guide and said to him, "You lead the way and we will *preceed* you." When she meant to say that the guide would *escort* the party she said, "This gentleman will *exhort* us."

The author chose the name Mrs. Malaprop to emphasize this language characteristic. When someone makes a humorous mistake like the above examples, it is called a *malapropism:* The prefix *mal* = "bad"; the word *apropos* = "fitting, suitable, to the point." An exercise such as the following provides children with the opportunity to work on detecting and correcting inappropriate use of words.

Directions: Read each sentence and find a word that "does not fit." Underline this word. Then in the blank space following the sentence, write the word that you think was intended.

---

* *The Rivals* by Richard Sheridan (1775).

1. He look very extinguished in his new suit. _____
2. The cook prepared bacon and eggs on the girdle. _____
3. Don't play near the fire hydrogen. _____
4. The old prospector saw a marriage on the dessert. _____
5. The police arrested a restless driver. _____
6. A man was walking his dog on a lease. _____
7. She has an analogy to pollen. _____
8. I enjoyed my conservation with the pilot. _____
9. There were many futile farms along the river. _____
10. Is the whale the largest manual? _____

Misconceptions

During the intermediate grades many children will encounter a number of words and concepts which will puzzle them. Many such instances will occur in subject-matter texts as well as in basal readers. Whereas the child comes to school with the "meanings" which are adequate for dealing with beginning reading, she is by no means familiar with the various connotations of the words with which she must cope in the primary and intermediate grades. A lack of concepts and insufficient knowledge of various connotations of words is not the only problem with which the teacher must deal in expanding meaning. A related problem is that of misconceptions harbored by pupils. The school cannot be held responsible for misconceptions which children have picked up elsewhere. It may be impossible in overcrowded classrooms to prevent misconceptions from arising or going undetected. Nevertheless, the extent to which this problem exists should motivate teachers to seek ways of modifying instructional techniques, for the confusion of meanings is a barrier to reading and learning.

One of the axioms of teaching reading is that "new" words in a lesson should be mastered both as sight words and as meaning-bearing units before the child is expected to read that lesson. Often little attention is given to mastering shades of meaning, and too much is taken for granted when the child is able to "call the word." As a result, many teachers would be shocked at the misconceptions still harbored by some children in their classes. The following responses on vocabulary tests illustrate some rather striking misconceptions, even though it is not difficult to imagine how some of these arose. The responses are given verbatim.

regard-	a. like you were guarding something
	b. to think of someone as a cousin
	c. to re-do your work
priceless-	a. something that doesn't cost anything

	b. you want to buy something and you think it's not worth it
brunette-	a. a kind of permanent
	b. a girl that dances
	c. a prune
shrewd-	a. when you're not polite
	b. being kind of cruel
	c. guess it means rude
lecture-	a. 'lected for president

When asked to give the meaning of "conquer," one boy volunteered, "It means like to *konk her* on the head." Another, when meeting the written word *mosquitoes* for the first time, concluded it was the name of a fairy—"most quiet toes." A preschool child hearing an older sibling make a reference to a dinosaur immediately responded, "I like to go to the *dime store.*" An eight-year-old listening around Christmas time to a choir on television asked, "What does the *si door im* mean?" His parents were at a loss until he repeated the line, "Oh come let us si door im."

Some of these examples illustrate what takes place when a child is confronted with concepts beyond her present grasp. She usually changes them to a more concrete meaning which is known to her. Although illustrating how the child deals with unknown words which she *hears*, these examples can also provide us with insight into what happens when a child *reads* unknown words.

Pronunciation and Meaning Problems

Problems can be dealt with in the context in which they are met, but there is nothing educationally unsound in reviewing or teaching a series of such words by means of either the chalkboard or a lesson sheet. One value of the latter procedure is that a given exercise can be used with only those pupils who reveal a need for it, several times if needed. A list of words that are difficult to pronounce might include: *aisle, fatigue, coyote, exit, plague, sieve, cache, posse, gauge, corps, beau, feign, nephew, antique, bouquet, isthmus, agile, chaos, ache, plateau, quay, bivouac, czar, recipe, stature, reign, viaduct, suede.* A number of exercises can be devised to teach the pronunciation and meaning of such words. A few are listed below.

1. In the first column the difficult words are listed and adjoining columns contain the dictionary pronunciation and meaning:

cache	căsh	a hole in the ground, or a hiding place
feign	fān	to imagine; invent, hence, to form and relate as if true
quay	kē	a stretch of paved bank or a solid artificial landing place made beside navigable water, for convenience in loading and unloading vessels
bivouac	bĭv oo ăk	an encampment for a very short sojourn, under improvised shelter or none

2. Use the difficult word and a synonym in the same sentence: "As they reached the *plateau* the guide said, 'It will be easier walking on this *flat level* ground'."

"Climbing mountains is hard work," said the guide. "We will rest when you feel *fatigued* so tell me when you get *tired*."

3. Prepare a card for each word; one side of the card contains the difficult word and its pronunciation; the other side has a sentence using the word.

c h a o s
(kā ŏs)

When a tornado strikes a community, *chaos* results. Houses are blown down, fires break out, fallen trees block the streets, telephone poles and wires are down, and the fire department cannot get through the streets.

4. Prepare a short paragraph in which the difficult word is used in several contexts.

From the aerial photographs it was difficult for him to *gauge* whether the railroad was narrow or regular *gauge*. He recalled that the day the picture was made the fuel *gauge* registered very nearly empty. He remembered attempting to *gauge* the effect of a tail wind on his chances of returning safely.

Working with High Frequency Root Words

English has borrowed many roots and prefixes from other languages, particularly Latin and Greek. Learning the meaning of those that appear frequently in English words can be of great benefit to children in developing language facility. Middle-school children will have met and will continue to meet numerous examples, such as *auto*, *mobile, photo, graph, bio, zoo, geo, logy, dem, crat, trans, port, sphere,* etc. In addition, they have met many prefixes and other terms related to the metric system: *cent, milli, kilo, meter, micro, mega.*

In the past, the teaching of roots was usually delayed until high school. One approach, that of handing out three or four pages of Greek and Latin roots and asking students to learn them, usually resulted in very little learning. This mass of material was "presented" rather than taught. The task was overwhelming and not much fun. There are other ways to help children learn the meanings of root words.

Demonstrate how some common words are derived from borrowed roots and how roots are often combined.

> auto: (Greek for *self*)
> mobile: (French for *to move*)
> *automobile:* capable of moving under its own power
> graph: (Greek for *to write*)
> *autograph:* to write one's self, or one's name

The following illustrates how a number of other roots are combined with *graph.*

Root				*Root*
photo	(light)	+ graph	(to write):	photograph (to write with light)
tele	(far)	+ graph	(to write):	telegraph
phono	(sound)	+ graph	(to write):	phonograph
geo	(earth)	+ graphy	(to write):	geography
bio	(life)	+ graphy	(to write):	biography
cardio	(heart)	+ graph	(to write):	cardiograph
mono	(one)	+ graph	(to write):	monograph (a writing on one topic)

Combining the root *logy* (to study) with other roots:

Root
bio + *logy* = study of living things
geo + *logy* = study of the earth
theo (God) + *logy* = theology: study of God, religion
psyche (mind) + *logy* = psychology: study of the mind
zoo (animal) + *logy* = zoology: study of animals
anthrop (man) + *logy* = anthropology: study of man
Others: meteorology, pathology audiology, phonology

Another variation is a teacher-planned period devoted to learning important word roots and to demonstrating the possibilities of word building through the addition of prefixes, suffixes, and other roots. For example, *dict* is a root meaning "to say." To *predict* is to say in advance, and implies that an event is pre *dict* able. This same root permits one to say that if one is to *dict*ate, her *dict*ion in *dict*ating should be clear and that her pronunciation should not contra*dict* the *dict*ionary. The study of word meanings can be a fascinating and rewarding experience.

Prefix		Root		
con	(with, together)	*tract*	(to draw):	contract
re	(back)	*tract*	(to draw):	retract
ex	(out of)	*tract*	(to draw):	extract
im	(into)	*port*	(to carry):	import
trans	(across)	*port*	(to carry):	transport
re	(back)	*port*	(to carry):	report

Root		Suffix		
port	(to carry)	*able*	(capable of):	portable
dict	(to say)	*tion*	(act of):	diction
grat	(thanks)	*full*	(full of):	grateful

When pupils evince interest in word building (roots, prefixes, suffixes), the teacher can make available teacher-constructed exercises similar to the examples below. Knowledge of roots and prefixes will help a child work out the meaning of many words that at first glance may appear strange and difficult.

Build a word. Read the definition, then add a prefix, suffix, or both to the root word shown. Make the word you build fit the definition.

depend: to rely on (clues: un – able – in – ent)

	depend		trustworthy, reliable
_____	depend	_____	not trustworthy, not dependable
_____	depend	_____	self-reliant
	depend	_____	relies on someone else

agree: to consent, no conflict (clues: ment – dis – able)

_____	agree	_____	not agreeing
	agree	_____	pleasing, pleasant
_____	agree	_____	not pleasing, unpleasant
	agree	_____	a contract, or understanding

(clues: dis – ment – im – un – able)

_____	agree	_____	failure to agree
_____	favor	_____	not good, not helpful
_____	content	_____	unhappy
_____	employ	_____	out of work

Working with Smaller Units

Recalling the fifth and sixth graders' responses to "What Is Reading?" (discussed earlier in this chapter), one senses that the children quoted saw reading as a series of mechanical tasks. Their reading experiences had not introduced them to the power and beauty of language. The prospective teachers who found it difficult to recall any writing "that should be preserved" thought that their reading experiences in school put very little emphasis on savoring the beauty of language. (Discussed below.)

It is quite possible that in our haste to get into subject matter we assign chapters, books, and plays with the admonition that these be read critically. Obviously, no one can read a book or a chapter critically unless she can read paragraphs and sentences that way. This is often forgotten in actual practice. The school seems to have little time for analyzing the meaning of a sentence because it is so busy assigning larger units. Thus, much of our behavior is self-defeating.

The only way to teach critical reading is to take the necessary time. Students must develop their own interpretations of a passage and test them in open discussion with peers and teacher. Any passage that merits critical reading is in essence much of a projective technique as a multicolored inkblot. Whether one interprets the inkblot or the sentence "as face answereth face in water, so the heart of man speaketh to man," the interpretation draws upon her unique experiences.

Analyzing and discussing small units of printed matter permits children to become involved with language. They have dialogues with the author, and they are exposed to interpretations radically different from their own. They often note how imprecise their peers are in explaining a concept; then they see this in their own efforts. As a result, they begin to learn that language is raw material that must be shaped and molded, that using language is a *creative activity*.

The teachers' experiences as a barrier. Having noted above how some children view reading, we might wonder how prospective teachers have fared after years of exposure to reading. An experience with a college class of prospective teachers illustrates how educational experiences mold the reading behavior of young adults.

In a course devoted to the teaching of reading, the discussion one day focused on the issue of how a teacher gets across to children that reading enhances human growth in all important areas. How can you convince children that through reading one can become what she hopes to be; that all the great thoughts of poets, philosophers, and statespersons belong to one who reads?

It was generally agreed that teachers are the key to whether or not children will see reading as the door to many treasures or an attempted confidence job on the part of the establishment. Teachers, it was agreed, cannot convince children of the many virtues which reside in reading unless they themselves are experiencing this. Teachers of reading must be *reading* teachers!

This seemed to be an excellent time to illustrate how reading had affected the lives of these students soon to be teachers. An impromptu assignment was given which was phrased somewhat as follows: "Assume that everything that has been written will mysteriously disappear from print at the end of this hour. However, each of you can preserve any passage or quotation that has been of importance to you. Write those quotes or passages that you wish to have preserved for future generations." The students looked straight ahead, then at each other, then at their notebooks, then at each others' notebooks. Very few wrote anything. Something obviously was wrong and so the assignment was modified: "If you can't provide an exact quotation, paraphrase the idea, write it in your own words, give the essence of it." Not much happened even then. Gradually some participants did write something, but many of the class could conjure nothing to write. After a few minutes the activity was terminated.

The group was asked if they would like to discuss what had just occurred—or maybe it wasn't significant. The consensus was that it should be explored. The idea was rejected that the element of surprise

Asking readers to explain "Each snowflake in an avalanche pleads not guilty" will grab more minds than Chapter 6.

would account for their inability to write something of value. It was agreed that everyone could have summarized something from a textbook that they had read that week, the chapter on study skills, for instance, or its counterpart for Psychology 201, or History 312, etc. Somehow they felt that none of this needed to be preserved for posterity. They could also have written the titles of books or plays they had read in high school or college. Their problem had been to distill something specific from these experiences.

Someone suggested that their experience with this assignment was probably somehow related to the then-current, vague but recurrent demand for "Relevance in Education." Prior to this they had not realized they had this educational deficit, so they had never missed what their education had failed to provide.

Use of quotes. One excellent technique for developing discussion and understanding of language is to write a nonfactual sentence on the chalkboard. Children are then invited to vote as to whether the author is right or wrong. (The same result is achieved by having children indicate whether they *agree* or *disagree* with the statement.) An example which can be used at several different grade levels is "Good men are more miserable than other men." Most groups divide on the issue of agreement or disagreement with the statement. Individuals then state the reasons they feel as they do. Such discussion provides valuable insights into the critical reading process: "A good man shouldn't be miserable;" "He has no reason to be miserable;" "Good men are made miserable when they see suffering, injustice, poverty, war," etc.

Many college students and adults show some hostility toward the assignment, raising such questions as "the material is taken out of context." What does he mean by "miserable?" "What's the definition of a 'good man'?" etc. As these and other questions are discussed, insights into reading are developed. It is established that the author is dead; we cannot ask him what he meant by *miserable* and *good men.* Soon the readers see that in the final analysis these words (and all words one reads) take on the meaning that each reader gives them.

The following are a few examples of quotations that might be used as stimulus statements for discussion. When discussions begin to extend far beyond the time you think should be allotted to this activity, you can assume that children are learning much about critical reading.

It is the good reader that makes a good book.
Character is what you are when no one is watching.
Don't criticize a man until you have walked in his shoes for a day.
The longest journey begins with the first step.

All mankind is of one author.
You must have a good memory to be a successful liar.
As a man sows, so shall he also reap.
You can judge a man by his enemies as well as by his friends.
The riches that are in the heart cannot be stolen.
Error of opinion may be tolerated where reason is left free to combat it.
People are lonely because they build walls instead of bridges.
Man is the only animal who can talk himself into problems that otherwise would not have existed.

Interpretation and discussion of proverbs. Working with proverbs is an excellent way to focus on smaller units of language. Proverbs are brief statements that seem to reflect great wisdom. The fact that they are brief and pithy keeps them in circulation. Their brevity also permits different interpretations since the meaning is not spelled out in detail. People of all cultures develop and use proverbs. Since people everywhere seem to have problems, interests, and needs, the same "message" may occur frequently. It is interesting to compare the differences in how the idea is expressed. An example is the idea that

"If something has to be done, do it—and get started on it right away!"
"Don't put off 'till tomorrow what you can do today."
"A journey of a thousand miles begins with a single step."
"He who hesitates is lost."
"Procrastination is the thief of time."
"Without starting you will arrive nowhere."
"Nothing ventured, nothing gained."
"He who is not ready today, will be less so tomorrow."
"Make hay while the sun shines."

Another idea is that your choice of companions will reveal the type of person you are:

"A man is known by the company he keeps."
"Birds of a feather flock together."
"Better to be alone than in bad company."
"He who lies down with dogs gets up with fleas."
"If you live with the lame, you will soon learn to limp."

There are innumerable ways in which proverbs can be converted into reading-language experiences. A few illustrative examples follow.

1. *Prepare a number of "pairs of proverbs." Children are to read each pair and indicate if the two statements have much the same meaning or if they have opposite meanings.*

Directions: If statements A and B have the same meaning, write S in the box; if the meanings are opposite write O.

1. a) He who hesitates is lost.
   b) Always look before you leap.

2. a) The road to fame is paved with pain.
   b) The path to glory is not lined with flowers.

3. a) If at first you don't succeed, try again.
   b) Everything is difficult at first.

4. a) A stitch in time saves nine.
   b) Never put off 'till tomorrow what you can do today.

5. a) Beauty is in the eye of the beholder.
   b) Tis the good reader that makes a good book.

2. *Directions: Sometimes we repeat a proverb without thinking about what it really means. Read each of the following statements and write in your own words what it means.*

a) If the shoe fits wear it. _____

_____

b) Mighty oaks from tiny acorns grow. _____

_____

c) Too many cooks spoil the broth. _____

_____

d) The pen is mightier than the sword. _____

_____

e) Don't cross the bridge 'till you come to it. _____

_____

3. *Establish a learning center (or use a bulletin board to display proverbs or quotations). Encourage children to:*
   a) Read these materials
   b) Add other proverbs which they find.

c) Select one or more proverbs and write their interpretations of the meaning(s). These are left for other children to read and to add their interpretations.

✗ 4. *Write on a card a pair of proverbs which appear to be contradictory. Have a student explain or describe a situation in which the first of these statements is good advice. Then the same or a different student cites a situation in which the second proverb would be good advice.*

✗ 5. *Using library resources and children's previous experiences, make a list of proverbs from other lands or cultures. From this list, select any proverbs which deal with the same idea or topic (friendship, honesty, loyalty, courage, defeat, etc.).*

Arriving at sentence meaning. One of the most successful approaches for developing and expanding concepts is a language game called Sentence Meaning. This consists of a page of numbered sentences which are unrelated to each other. Each sentence contains one or more words whose meaning should be known or learned. As the student reads each sentence she marks it *T* if it is true, or *F* if it is false. Obviously, one can design exercises which deal with general concepts or have the material focus on any one of the content areas. A few illustrative items follow.

Social Studies
_____ 1. *Carnivorous* animals feed primarily on vegetation.
_____ 2. The term *amnesty* means a loss of memory.
_____ 3. A *glacier* is a huge mass of ice.
_____ 4. *Monsoon* is a type of monkey widely used in medical experiments.
_____ 5. It is not illegal to *paraphrase* a court decision.

Science
_____ 1. An unproved scientific theory is nothing more than a *hypothesis*.
_____ 2. Most metals *contract* when heated.
_____ 3. *Specific* directions are very brief, with some steps omitted.
_____ 4. Electrical current flows freely through *insulators*.
_____ 5. *Ornithology* is the scientific study of birds.

Mathematics
_____ 1. The radius of a circle is twice the length of its diameter.

2. The sum of the two smallest angles in a right triangle always
_____ total 90 degrees.

_____ 3. The perimeter of a circle is equal to its circumference.

_____ 4. An event that occurs biannually occurs twice a year.

5. If the top side of square A equals the bottom side of square B,
_____ the two squares are equal.

General Vocabulary

1. A highly skilled person with much experience is called an
_____ *apprentice.*

_____ 2. Shoes made entirely from *synthetics* cannot have leather soles.

_____ 3. The term *equivalent* means equal.

_____ 4. A *travesty* is a brief written account of ones travels.

_____ 5. The root *thermo* in thermometer means heat.

_____ 6. Etc.

In using sentence-meaning exercises, the teacher's role is to serve as a catalyst for student discussion and sharing of ideas. This end may be achieved by following guidelines such as the following:

1. Do not collect and score the exercises. Go over them in class so that students note their errors immediately. They also note that learning is taking place as a result of the discussion of each item.

2. One way to score the exercise and facilitate discussion is to ask for a volunteer to supply the answers for items 1–4. These responses are written on the classboard (1-F; 2-T; 3-T etc.). Next inquire, "who has an answer different from what we have on the board?" Have another volunteer provide answers for items 5–8, etc. Halfway through the page, this scoring-discussion format may be changed to, "does anyone want the answer to any other items on the page?" Naturally, the answer to every item on the page is called for which makes for excellent discussion.

3. Be sure to have dictionaries available. Encourage students to provide "dictionary definitions" for the crucial word(s) in the various sentences.

Fact—opinion and agree—disagree statements. After several years of school and heavy reliance on textbooks, children tend to accept without question what they find in print or what is stated with authority or by an authority. Fact-oriented school tasks tend to make readers vulnerable when they meet statements that have surface validity but which may be biased or untrue. Students are constantly bombarded by adver-

sauss what is a "fact"

tisements, news broadcasts, politician's statements, and conflicting scientific claims which present only one point of view. Thus, one may read that atomic energy plants are perfectly safe or definitely a hazard. Brand X aspirin is superior to all other brands. Product A contains *no* aspirin and is superior to *all* aspirin. High cholesterol foods are/are not a threat to health and survival.

As laws are passed that attempt to make language users more responsible to the consumer, those who use language to control behavior become more sophisticated in their use of language. Thus children, as consumers of print and products, must develop survival skills. Fact or opinion exercises help to develop such skills. The purpose of this type of language experience is to sharpen actual analysis of what one reads and to demonstrate how personal bias, previous experience, and background knowledge may color one's interpretation.

Directions: Read each sentence carefully. If the statement is a fact, write F in front of the sentence. If the statement is an opinion, write O.

_____ 1. Air travel is safer than any other method of transportation.

_____ 2. The American Revolution was caused by taxation without representation.

_____ 3. The love of money is the root of all evil.

_____ 4. It is very difficult to get a good job without a college education.

_____ 5. All brands of aspirin are essentially the same.

_____ 6. Before the end of this century, the U.S. will establish colonies on the moon.

_____ 7. Democracy is the best form of government that has been developed by mankind.

Agree—Disagree offers a change of pace from the above. Using this format, students write or discuss why they agree or disagree with a particular statement.

Directions: Read each statement and tell why you agree or disagree with it.

1. Large cities are not desirable places to live. _____

_____

2. The rich people in the U.S. do not pay a fair share of taxes. _____

_____

_____

3. The aim of advertising is to control the behavior of consumers. ___

_____

_____

4. Reading ability is a major factor in determining what occupations one can enter. _____

_____

_____

5. Violence on television is a major cause of crime. _____

_____

_____

SUMMARY

Learning to read is a long-term developmental process. The curricular tasks found in the intermediate grades call for wide and extensive reading. To meet these demands successfully, pupils will need guidance in reading *curricular materials*. This means that skill in reading geography, science, and mathematics must be developed in the actual study of these subjects as well as in a period devoted to "reading." In the intermediate grades there is danger of a too literal acceptance of the old dictum that "a pupil learns to read by reading" or "nothing improves one's reading like more and more reading." This is true for readers who have mastered the necessary reading skills, but there is a fallacy in these statements when applied to any child who is deficient in reading skills. The more reading a pupil with poor reading habits does, the more she reinforces her poor habits. Reading with instruction and guidance aimed at improvement is the key. Learning in all content areas, from this point on in the grades, depends primarily on reading skill. The facts taught in science, geography, history, and mathematics are important, but the school's basic task is to teach each child the reading skills which will enable her to read independently in any of these content areas. Since many children still need instruction in reading skills, any reduction of emphasis on this facet of reading is a serious omission.

The fact that the major portion of the reading required of middle-school students consists of assignments in various textbooks creates problems for both teacher and pupils. This prescribed reading often fails to arouse or sustain the reader's interest. Children develop the habit of reading without feeling and personal involvement. In addition to text material, they need to have experiences in reading that illustrate the power, beauty, and precision of language.

This can be achieved through working with smaller units of language that call for interpretation rather than memory of facts. These should be brief statements that pack meaning into a sentence and illustrate the use of powerful and incisive language. In addition, reading skills should be expanded through use of materials that help to develop insights into how language functions.

YOUR POINT OF VIEW?

What is the basis for your agreement or disagreement with each of the following statements?

1. Variability among pupils in the intermediate grades could be reduced by improved teaching in earlier grades.
2. Good teaching in the intermediate grades will increase the individual differences in reading ability of children found in these classrooms.
3. In recent years the curriculum reforms in content areas have been geared to the intellectually capable child without adequate concern for the average learner.
4. There is little evidence in either the curriculum materials or instructional objectives to indicate that there is an educationally significant transition between the primary and intermediate grades.
5. If we agree that we cannot talk in terms of *the meaning* of a passage, we must conclude that it is impossible either to evaluate or to teach critical reading.
6. A valid criticism of subject matter textbooks is that they present an unrealistically large number of concepts which are beyond the grasp of pupils in the grades for which the texts were designed.

Respond to the following problems:

A. Illustrate the concept that reading is a long-term developmental process by tracing the developmental nature of learning in one of the following areas: *meaning vocabulary; use of library resources; appreciation of poetry or literature.*
B. "Individual differences in achievement increase as we move upward through the grades." Which one of the following factors would you prefer to defend as being most important in effecting these differences in achievement? Why?
   1. Pupil ability
   2. School promotion policies
   3. Competency of instruction
   4. Factors outside the school

C. *Premise:* "Misconceptions are more likely to arise in the content areas than in the materials used for reading instruction." Based on a study of curriculum materials, provide data that would support this assumption.

BIBLIOGRAPHY

1. Burron, Arnold and Claybaugh, Amos L., *Using Reading to Teach Subject Matter.* Columbus, O.: Charles E. Merrill Publishing Co., 1974.

2. Chase, Francis S., "In the Next Decade," Supplemental Educational Monographs, no. 91, *Controversial Issues in Reading and Promising Solutions,* Helen M. Robinson, ed. Chicago: University of Chicago Press, 1961, pp. 7–18.

3. Daniels, H. Perk, Children's Answers to "What is Reading?" New York: Vantage Press, Inc., 1969. Used by permission of the author.

4. Dulin, Kenneth L., "Using Context Clues in Word Recognition and Comprehension," *The Reading Teacher* (February 1970): 440–45.

5. Fillmer, H. Thompson, "The Middle Schooler's Reading Program," *Language Arts* 52 (December 1975): 1123–26.

6. Forgan, Harry W. and Mangrum II, Charles T., *Teaching Content Area Reading Skills.* Columbus, O.: Charles E. Merrill Publishing Co., 1976.

7. Groff, Patrick, "How Do Children Read Biography about Adults?" *The Reading Teacher* (April 1971): 609–15.

8. Guszak, Frank J., "Questioning Strategies of Elementary Teachers in Relation to Comprehension," in *Reading and Realism,* J. Allen Figurel, ed. Proceedings, International Reading Association 13, Part 1, 1969, pp. 110–16.

9. Hildreth, Gertrude, *Teaching Reading.* New York: Holt, Rinehart, & Winston, Inc., 1958.

10. Johns, Jerry L., "Reading Preference of Intermediate-Grade Students in Urban Settings," *Reading World 14* (October 1974): 51–63.

11. ———, "Strategies for Oral Reading Behavior," *Language Arts 52* (December 1975): 1104–07.

12. Kennedy, Larry D., "Textbook Usage in the Intermediate-Upper Grades," *The Reading Teacher* (May 1971): 723–29.

13. Klosterman, Sister Rita, "The Effectiveness of a Diagnostically Structured Reading Program," *The Reading Teacher* (November 1970): 159–62.

14. Lamme, Linda Leonard, "Are Reading Habits and Abilities Related?" *Reading Teacher 30* (October 1976): 21–27.

15. Lundsteen, Sara W., "Levels of Meaning in Reading," *Reading Teacher 28* (December 1974): 268–72.

16. MacGinitie, Walter H., "Difficulty with Logical Operations," *Reading Teacher 29* (January 1976): 371–75.

17. Manolakes, George, and Sheldon, William D., "The Relation between Reading-Test Scores and Language-Factors Intelligence Quotients," *Elementary School Journal* (February 1955): 346–50.

18. Millsap, Lucille, "The Ubiquitous Book Report," *The Reading Teacher* (November 1970): 99–105.

19. Morrison, Virginia B., "Teacher-Pupil Interaction in Three Types of Elementary Classroom Reading Situations," *The Reading Teacher* (December 1968): 271–75.

20. Rauch, Sidney J., "Reading in the Total School Curriculum," in *Forging Ahead in Reading*, J. Allen Figurel, ed. Proceedings, International Reading Association 12, Part 1, pp. 212–17.

21. Sauer, Lois E., "Fourth Grade Children's Knowledge of Grammatical Structure," *Elementary English* (October 1970): 807–13.

22. Sawyer, Diane J., "Linguistic and Cognitive Competencies in the Middle Grades," *Language Arts 52* (December 1975): 1075–79.

23. Schulte, Emerita Schroer, "Independent Reading Interests of Children in Grades Four, Five and Six," *Reading and Realism*, J. Allen Figurel, ed. Proceedings, International Reading Association 13, Part 1, 1969, pp. 728–32.

24. Sheldon, William D.; Lashinger, Donald R.; Mahone, Patricia; and Dagastiono, Lorraine, "A Summary of Research Studies Relating to Language Arts in Elementary Education: 1975," *Language Arts 53* (December 1976): 932–64.

25. Shores, J. Harlan and Saupe, J. L., "Reading for Problem-Solving in Science," *Journal of Educational Psychology* (March 1953): 149–58.

26. Smith, Lewis B., "They Found a Golden Ladder, Stories by Children," *Reading Teacher 29* (March 1976): 541–45.

27. Sullivan, Joanna, "Receptive and Critical Reading Develops at All Levels," *Reading Teacher 27* (May 1974): 796–800.

28. Swick, Kevin J. and Ross, Colvin, "Affective Learning for the Real World," *Language Arts 53* (February 1976): 160–61.

29. Turner, Thomas N. and Terwilliger, Paul N., "Multi-Dimensional Creativity," *Language Arts 53* (February 1976): 155–59.

30. Vacca, Richard T. and Vacca, Joanne L., "Consider a Stations Approach to Middle School Reading Instruction," *Reading Teacher 28* (October 1974): 18–21.

Index

on